THE COMPREHENSIVE BIG HORN WOOD PELLET GRILL AND SMOKER COOKBOOK

BECOME A BBQ MASTER WITH 550 DELICIOUS RECIPES FOR SMOKING AND GRILLING: BEEF, PORK, LAMB, FISH, VEGGIES ETC

ANTHONY WALKER

Copyright © 2021 by Anthony Walker All rights reserved worldwide.

No part of this book may be reproduced or transmitted in any form or by any means, electronic or mechanical, including photo- copying, recording or by any information storage and retrieval system, without written permission from the publisher, except for the inclusion of brief quotations in a review.

Warning-Disclaimer: The purpose of this book is to educate and entertain. The author or publisher does not guarantee that anyone following the techniques, suggestions, tips, ideas, or strategies will become successful. The author and publisher shall have neither liability or responsibility to anyone with respect to any loss or damage caused, or alleged to be caused, directly or indirectly by the information contained in this book.

CONTENTS

INTRODUCTION 11
What the BIG HORN Wood Pellet Grill is 11
How Does the BIG HORN Wood Pellet Grill Work? 11
The Pros of the BIG HORN Wood Pellet Grill 11
Better to Use Your BIG HORN Wood Pellet Grill 13
Cleaning Approaches for Your BIG HORN Wood Pellet Grill 14

POULTRY RECIPES 15
Smoked Turkey Breast 15
Cajun Brined Maple Smoked Turkey Breast 15
Smoked Boneless Chicken Thighs 15
Fig Glazed Chicken Stuffed Cornbread 16
Italian Grilled Barbecue Chicken Wings 16
Grilled Honey Chicken Wings 17
Peanut Butter Chicken Wings 17
Easy Bbq Chicken Wings 17
Smoked Chicken Vermicelli Noodles 18
Chicken On A Throne 18
Thai Chicken Satays 19
Chile Cilantro Lime Chicken Wings 19
Spatchcocked Chicken With Toasted Fennel & Garlic 20
Bbq Turkey Drumsticks 20
Jalapeno Chicken Sliders 20
Smoked Chicken With Apricot Bbq Glaze 21
Whole Smoked Chicken 21
Spiced Smoked Chicken Quarters 21
Bbq Chicken Drumsticks 22
Chicken Lollipops 22
Smoked Chicken Leg & Thigh Quarters 23
Juicy Jerk Chicken Kebabs 23
Traeger Mandarin Wings 24
Baked Prosciutto-wrapped Chicken Breast With
Spinach And Boursin 24
Wild West Wings 24
Bacon Wrapped Chicken Wings 25
Bourbon Chicken Waffles 25
Smoked Wings 26
Chile Chicken Thighs 26
Chicken Parmesan Sliders With Pesto Mayonnaise 26
Green Chile Chicken Enchiladas 27
Smoked Turkey Wings 27
Grilled Chipotle Chicken Skewers 27
Roasted Whole Chicken 28
Bbq Spatchcocked Chicken 28
Savory Smoked Turkey Legs 28
Grilled Garlic Chicken Kabobs 29
Hot Turkey Sandwich With Gravy 29
Grilled Parmesan Chicken Wings 30
Turkey & Bacon Kebabs With Ranch-style Dressing .. 30
Roasted Prosciutto Stuffed Chicken 31
Lemon Parmesan Chicken Wings 31
Smoke Roasted Chicken With Herb Butter 31
Smoked Avocado Turkey Tamale Pie 32
Spiced Cornish Hens With Cilantro Chutney 33
Spatchcocked Turkey 33
Bbq Chicken Tostada 34
Delicious Sweet And Sour Chicken Drumsticks 34
The Grilled Chicken Challenge 34
Chicken Egg Rolls With Buffalo Sauce 35
Applewood-smoked Whole Turkey 35
Grilled Hand Pulled Chicken 36
Chicken Cordon Bleu Rollups 36
Asian Bbq Chicken 36
Cornish Game Hen 37
Smoked Whiskey Peach Pulled Chicken 37
Bacon Weaved Stuffed Turkey Breast 37
Cornish Game Hens 38
Grilled Honey Chicken Kabobs 38
Fried Chicken Sliders 39
Roasted Honey Bourbon Glazed Turkey 39

Roasted Stuffed Turkey Breast 40	Smoked Maple Syrup Thanksgiving Turkey 43
County Fair Turkey Legs 40	Bbq Chicken Thighs 43
Texas Style Black Pepper Turkey 40	Savory Grilled Chicken Burrito Bowls 44
Carrot Celery Chicken Drumsticks 41	Bacon Wrapped Turkey Legs 44
Savory Cajun Bbq Chicken 41	Bbq Chicken Legs 45
Whole Smoked Honey Chicken 41	Bacon-wrapped Chicken Breasts 45
Grilled Honey Garlic Wings 42	Nashville Spiced Smoked Chicken 46
Dry Brine Traeger Turkey 42	Grilled Chicken Wings 46
Sweet Cajun Wings 43	Beer Chicken 46
Smoked Whole Chicken 43	Tandoori Chicken Leg Quarters 47

BAKING RECIPES 48

Cornbread Chicken Stuffing 48	Vanilla Chocolate Chip Cookies 61
Crème Brûlée 48	Bacon Chocolate Chip Cookies 61
Blueberry Pancakes 49	Spiced Carrot Cake 62
Skillet Buttermilk Cornbread 49	Basil Margherita Pizza 62
Chili Cheese Fries 49	Baked Pear Tarte Tatin 63
Chocolate Peanut Cookies 50	Onion Cheese Nachos 63
Pumpkin Bread 50	Traeger Baked Protein Bars 63
Baked Irish Creme Cake 51	Green Bean Casserole Circa 1955 64
Baked Cast Iron Berry Cobbler 51	Smoked Lemon Tea 64
Quick Baked Dinner Rolls 51	Smoky Apple Crepes 64
Traeger Baked Focaccia 52	Donut Bread Pudding 65
Pretzel Rolls 52	Smoked Cheesy Alfredo Sauce 65
Baked Bourbon Maple Pumpkin Pie 53	Smoked, Salted Caramel Apple Pie 66
Crescent Rolls 54	Cake With Smoked Berry Sauce 66
Anzac Coconut Biscuits 54	Spiced Lemon Cherry Pie 67
Cherry Ice Cream Cobbler 54	Baked Parker House Rolls 67
S'mores Dip Skillet 55	Eyeball Cookies 68
Chicken Pot Pie 55	Maple Syrup Pancake Casserole 69
Strawberry Basil Daiquiri 55	Baked Chocolate Coconut Brownies 69
Cheese Mac 56	Garlic Cheese Pull Apart Bread 69
Sopapilla Cheesecake By Doug Scheiding 56	Rosemary Cranberry Apple Sage Stuffing 70
Baked Pumpkin Pie 57	Smokin' Lemon Bars 70
Savory Beaver Tails 57	Dark Chocolate Brownies With Bacon-salted Caramel 71
Sourdough Pizza 58	Mexican Black Bean Cornbread Casserole 71
Chicken Pizza On The Grill 58	Eggs Ham Benedict 72
Blueberry Bread Pudding 58	Pound Cake 72
Beer Bread 59	Mint Butter Chocolate Chip Cookies 72
Ultimate Baked Garlic Bread 59	Smoked Lemon Cheesecake 73
Grilled Beer Cheese Dip 60	Double Chocolate Chip Brownie Pie 73
Grilled Apple Pie 60	Pineapple Cake 74
The Dan Patrick Show Pull-apart Pesto Bread 60	Pizza Bites 74

Baked Peach Cobbler Cupcakes 75	Easy Smoked Cornbread 80
Irish Soda Bread 75	Cinnamon Pull-aparts 80
Pull-apart Dinner Rolls 76	Smoky Pimento Cheese Cornbread 80
Double Vanilla Chocolate Cake 76	Chocolate Lava Cake With Smoked Whipped
Smoked Vanilla Apple Pie 77	Cream 81
Savory Cheesecake With Bourbon Pecan Topping 77	Baked Cheesy Parmesan Grits 81
Bananas Rum Foster 78	Garlic Lemon Pepper Chicken Wings 82
Baked Chocolate Brownie Cookies With Egg Nog ..78	Cast Iron Pineapple Upside Down Cake 82
Lemon Chicken, Broccoli, String Beans Foil Packs 79	Smoker Wheat Bread 82
Baked Potatoes & Celery Root Au Gratin 79	Blueberry Sour Cream Muffins 83

SEAFOOD RECIPES 84

Roasted Halibut With Spring Vegetables 84	Smoked Sugar Halibut 96
Bacon Wrapped Shrimp 84	Kimi's Simple Grilled Fresh Fish 96
Spicy Crab Poppers 85	Lemon Lobster Rolls 96
Hot-smoked Salmon 85	Florentine Shrimp Al Cartoccio 96
Grilled Pepper Lobster Tails 85	Lemon Herb Grilled Salmon 97
Peper Fish Tacos 86	Smoked Lobster Scampi 97
Grilled Maple Syrup Salmon 86	Whole Vermillion Red Snapper 98
Lemon Shrimp Scampi 87	Sweet Smoked Salmon Jerky 98
Alder Smoked Scallops With Citrus & Garlic Butter	Baked Whole Fish In Sea Salt 98
Sauce 87	Spiced Smoked Swordfish 99
Traeger Jerk Shrimp 88	Grilled Salmon Steaks With Dill Sauce 99
Smoked Mango Shrimp 88	Spicy Lime Shrimp 100
Prosciutto-wrapped Scallops 88	Barbecued Shrimp 100
Grilled Lobster Tails With Smoked Paprika Butter 89	Grilled Artichoke Cheese Salmon 100
Barbecued Scallops 89	Garlic Blackened Salmon 101
Lobster Tail 89	Grilled Salmon Gravlax 101
Swordfish With Sicilian Olive Oil Sauce 90	Oysters Margarita 102
Citrus-smoked Trout 90	Traeger Baked Rainbow Trout 102
Cider Hot-smoked Salmon 90	Grilled Fresh Fish 103
Lime Mahi Mahi Fillets 91	Grilled Lemon Shrimp Scampi 103
Smoked Honey Salmon 91	Cedar Smoked Garlic Salmon 103
Grilled Garlic Lobster Tails 92	Thai-style Swordfish Steaks With Peanut Sauce 104
Traeger Smoked Salmon 92	Cajun Catfish 104
Smoky Crab Dip 93	Delicious Smoked Trout 104
Vodka Brined Smoked Wild Salmon 93	Shrimp Cabbage Tacos With Lime Cream 105
Grilled Shrimp Brochette 93	Smoked Salt Cured Lox 105
Cajun-blackened Shrimp 94	Teriyaki Smoked Honey Tilapia 106
Flavour Fire Spiced Shrimp 94	Oysters In The Shell 106
Smoked Crab Legs 94	Garlic Blackened Catfish 106
Simple Glazed Salmon Fillets 95	Wood-fired Halibut 106
Grilled Oysters With Mignonette 95	Garlic Pepper Shrimp Pesto Bruschetta 107

Grilled Blackened Saskatchewan Salmon 107
Grilled Mussels With Lemon Butter 107
Bbq Roasted Salmon 108
Bbq Oysters 108
Moules Marinières With Garlic Butter Sauce 108
Garlic Grilled Shrimp Skewers 109
Planked Trout With Fennel, Bacon & Orange 109
Lemon Scallops Wrapped In Bacon 110
Seared Ahi Tuna Steak With Soy Sauce 110
Grilled Whole Steelhead Fillet 111
Tequila & Lime Shrimp With Smoked Tomato
Sauce 111
Smoked Cedar Plank Salmon 112
Grilled Lemon Lobster Tails 112
Pacific Northwest Salmon 112
Smoked Salmon Candy 112
Traeger Crab Legs 113
Baked Steelhead 113
Smoked Fish Chowder 114
Salmon Cakes With Homemade Tartar Sauce 114

VEGETABLES RECIPES 115

Grilled Beer Cabbage 115
Braised Creamed Green Beans 115
Smoked Pickled Green Beans 115
Roasted Pickled Beets 116
Bacon Wrapped Corn On The Cob 116
Traeger Smoked Coleslaw 116
Cast Iron Potatoes 117
Roasted Potato Poutine 117
Mashed Red Potatoes 118
Grilled Chili-lime Corn 118
Carolina Baked Beans 118
Baked Garlic Duchess Potatoes 119
Roasted Pumpkin Seeds 119
Baked Sweet And Savory Yams By Bennie Kendrick . 119
Grilled Fingerling Potato Salad 120
Sweet Potato Marshmallow Casserole 120
Grilled Broccoli Rabe 120
Grilled Asparagus & Honey-glazed Carrots 121
Christmas Brussel Sprouts 121
Baked Bacon Green Bean Casserole 121
Roasted Tomatoes 122
Sicilian Stuffed Mushrooms 122
Smoked Mashed Potatoes 122
Baked Sweet Potato Casserole With Marshmallow
Fluff 123
Tater Tot Bake 123
Baked Breakfast Mini Quiches 124
Grilled Street Corn 124
Portobello Marinated Mushroom 124
Broccoli-cauliflower Salad 125
Smoked Jalapeño Poppers 125
Butternut Squash 125
Roasted Artichokes With Garlic Butter 125
Butter Braised Green Beans 126
Smoked Bbq Onion Brussels Sprout 126
Salt Crusted Baked Potatoes 127
Baked Kale Chips 127
Roasted Hasselback Potatoes By Doug Scheiding 127
Traeger Grilled Whole Corn 128
Baked Artichoke Parmesan Mushrooms 128
Whole Roasted Cauliflower With Garlic Parmesan
Butter 128
Roasted Fall Vegetables 129
Steak Fries With Horseradish Creme 129
Red Potato Grilled Lollipops 129
Roasted New Potatoes 130
Baked Heirloom Tomato Tart 130
Smoked & Loaded Baked Potato 130
Baked Stuffed Avocados 131
Roasted Garlic Herb Fries 131
Roasted Olives 132
Green Bean Casserole 132
Baked Sweet Potatoes 132
Chef Curtis' Famous Chimichurri Sauce 132
Roasted Jalapeño Poppers 133
Roasted Sweet Potato Steak Fries 133
Roasted Tomatoes With Hot Pepper Sauce 134
Smoked Asparagus Soup 134
Smoked Parmesan Herb Popcorn 134
Roasted Mashed Potatoes 135
Roasted Do-ahead Mashed Potatoes 135
Roasted Sheet Pan Vegetables 135

Smoked Pico De Gallo 136	Grilled Zucchini Squash Spears 140
Roasted New Potatoes With Compound Butter 136	Roasted Asparagus 140
Roasted Beet & Bacon Salad 137	Smoked Beet-pickled Eggs 140
Grilled Corn On The Cob With Parmesan And Garlic 137	Parmesan Roasted Cauliflower 141
Traeger Baked Potato Torte 137	Grilled Asparagus And Spinach Salad 141
Roasted Red Pepper White Bean Dip 138	Double-smoked Cheese Potatoes 141
Twice-smoked Potatoes 138	Spicy Asian Brussels Sprouts 142
Skillet Potato Cake 139	Potluck Salad With Smoked Cornbread 143
Baked Loaded Tater Tots 139	Stuffed Jalapenos 143
Roasted Vegetable Napoleon 139	Grilled Cabbage Steaks With Warm Bacon Vinaigrette 144
Grilled Asparagus And Hollandaise Sauce 140	

BEEF LAMB AND GAME RECIPES 145

Cheddar Bacon Beef Burgers 145	Irish Pasties 156
Roasted Duck 145	Flavour Smoked Tri Tip 157
Smoked Bacon Brisket Flat 145	Bison Tomahawk Steak 157
The Perfect T-bones 146	Smoked Beer Corned Beef 157
Burnt Beer Beef Brisket 146	Smoked Spiced Pulled Beef Chuck Roast 158
Baked Venison Tater Tot Casserole 147	Blackened Saskatchewan Tomahawk Steaks 158
Grilled Tomahawk Steak 147	Whiskey Bourbon Bbq Cheeseburger 159
Grilled Garlic Tri Tip 147	Rosemary-smoked Lamb Chops 159
Bbq Beef Ribs 148	Smoked Beef Ribs 159
Smoked Brisket With Traeger Coffee Rub 148	Savory Leftover Brisket Tostadas 160
Herb Chipotle Lamb 149	Smoked Corned Beef Brisket 160
Lemon Tomahawk Steak 149	Savory Cheese Steak Rolls With Puff Pastry 160
Garlic Beef Meatballs 150	Smoked Garlic Meatloaf 161
Spiced Cowboy Steak 150	Savory Teriyaki Smoked Steak Bites 161
Texas Hill Country Brisket With Mustard Barbecue Sauce 150	Cheese Onion Steak Sandwiches 162
Flavour Tri Tip Burnt Ends 151	Smoked Black Pepper Beef Cheeks 162
Grass-fed Beef Burgers 152	Smoked Teriyaki Jerky 162
Jalapeno Pepper Jack Cheese Bacon Burgers 152	Smoked Red Wine Beef Roast 163
Grilled Bacon-wrapped Hot Dogs 152	Bbq Beef Short Ribs 163
Slow Smoked Rib-eye Roast 153	Green Bell Pepper Cheese Steak Burger 164
Italian Meatballs 153	Garlic Cheese Bacon Burger 164
Grilled Double Burgers With Texas Spicy Bbq Sauce 153	Smoked Texas Bbq Brisket 164
Roasted Mustard Crusted Prime Rib 154	New York Strip Steaks With Blue Cheese Butter 165
Wagyu Corned Beef Hash 154	Flavour Bbq Brisket Burnt Ends 165
Beer Chili Bratwurst 155	Roasted Prime Rib With Mustard And Herbs De Provence 165
Standing Venison Rib Roast 155	Delicious Grilled Steak 166
Hot Coffee-rubbed Brisket 155	Texas Shoulder Clod 166
Spiced Smoked Kielbasa Dogs 156	Savory Smoked Brisket 166

Lime Carne Asada Tacos 167
Beef Caldereta Stew 167
Spicy Beer Beef Jerky 167
Grilled Balsamic & Blue Steak..168
Delicious Reverse Seared Picanha Steak 168
Flavour Texas Twinkies 169
Grilled Beef Shawarma 169
Flank Steak Breakfast Potato Burrito..........................170
Smoked New York Steaks 170
Sweetheart Steak With Lobster Ceviche 170
Garlic Pigs In A Blanket 171
Spicy Chopped Brisket Sandwich 171
Carrot Elk Burgers 172
Reuben Sandwich 172
Smoked Chuck Roast Tater Tot Casserole 172
Garlic Standing Rib Roast...173
Grilled Dill Pickle Tri Tip Steak...................................173
Mustard Garlic Crusted Prime Rib 174
Smoked Longhorn Brisket...174
Smoked Tri-tip 174
Grilled Rib Eyes With Hasselback Sweet Potatoes....175
Smoked Burgers 175
Flavour Texas Smoke Beef...175
Grilled Skirt Steak Quesadillas....................................176
Smoked Beer Brisket..176

COCKTAILS RECIPES...177
Smoked Berry Cocktail 177
Smoking Gun Cocktail 177
Traeger Smoked Daiquiri...177
In Traeger Fashion Cocktail 178
Smoked Apple Cider...178
Grilled Blood Orange Mimosa 178
Sunset Margarita 178
Ryes And Shine Cocktail 179
Grilled Peach Sour Cocktail..179
Zombie Cocktail Recipe...180
Smoked Hot Buttered Rum 180
Strawberry Mule Cocktail 180
Garden Gimlet Cocktail...181
Grilled Hawaiian Sour 181
Smoked Pomegranate Lemonade Cocktail.................181
Smoked Mulled Wine 182
Batter Up Cocktail 182
Smoked Ice Mojito Slurpee 182
Grilled Frozen Strawberry Lemonade.........................182
Smoked Sangria...183
Smoked Pumpkin Spice Latte 183
Fig Slider Cocktail 184
Bacon Old-fashioned Cocktail 184
Smoked Salted Caramel White Russian 184
Smoky Scotch & Ginger Cocktail.................................185
A Smoking Classic Cocktail 185
Cran-apple Tequila Punch With Smoked Oranges ...185
Smoked Cold Brew Coffee 186
Smoked Hibiscus Sparkler 186
Smoked Jacobsen Salt Margarita 187
Smoked Barnburner Cocktail 187
Smoked Pineapple Hotel Nacional Cocktail 187
Dublin Delight Cocktail 188
Grilled Peach Mint Julep 188
Smoked Irish Coffee 189
Smoked Texas Ranch Water 189
Traeger Old Fashioned...189
Traeger Boulevardier Cocktail 190
Grilled Rabbit Tail Cocktail 190
Traeger Paloma Cocktail 190
Smoked Grape Lime Rickey..191
Honey Glazed Grapefruit Shandy Cocktail 191
Smoked Plum And Thyme Fizz Cocktail 191
Grilled Peach Smash Cocktail 192
Smoked Eggnog...192
Traeger Gin & Tonic...193
Smoke And Bubz Cocktail 193
Smoked Raspberry Bubbler Cocktail..........................193
Smoky Mountain Bramble Cocktail............................194

PORK RECIPES...195
Southern Sugar-glazed Ham...195
Pulled Pork Sliders Hawaiian Rolls 195
Smoked Baby Back Ribs 195
Lynchburg Bacon..195

Bbq Baby Back Ribs With Bacon Pineapple Glaze By Scott Thomas 196	Spiced Grilled Pork Chops 212
Bbq Sweet & Smoky Ribs 196	Maple-smoked Pork Chops 212
Pork Belly Burnt Ends 197	Beer Pork Belly Chili Con Carne 212
Dry Rub Grilled Ribs 197	Competition Style Bbq Pulled Pork 213
Bbq Pork Shoulder Steaks 197	Roasted Ham With Apricot Sauce 214
Spiced Coffee-rubbed Ribs 198	Pulled Pork Corn Tortillas 214
Grilled Pork Loin 198	Texas Grilled Ribs 214
Grilled Pork Belly 199	Hot & Fast Smoked Baby Back Ribs 215
Grilled Bbq Pork Chops 199	Bourbon Chile Glazed Ham 215
3-2-1 Spare Ribs 199	Grilled Pork Tacos Al Pastor 215
Maple Syrup Bacon Wrapped Tenderloin 200	Egg Bacon French Toast Panini 216
Pulled Pork Taquitos With Sour Cream 200	Smoked Rendezvous Ribs 216
Asian-style Pork Tenderloin 201	Bbq 3-2-1 St. Louis Ribs 217
Baked Candied Bacon Cinnamon Rolls 201	Baked Pig Candy 217
Chinese Alcoholic Bbq Pork Tenderloin 201	Sweet Bacon 218
Bbq Bacon-wrapped Water Chestnuts 202	Roasted Bacon Weave Holiday Ham 218
Smoked Pork Loin With Sauerkraut And Apples 202	Raspberry Spiral Ham With Glaze 218
Bbq Breakfast Grits 203	Pork & Pepperoni Burgers 219
Whiskey- & Cider-brined Pork Shoulder 203	Bbq Brown Sugar Pork Belly 219
Pig On A Stick With Buffalo Glaze 204	Classic Pulled Pork 219
Traeger Roasted Easter Ham 204	Everything Pigs In A Blanket 220
Simple Smoked Ribs 205	St. Louis–style Pork Steaks 220
Grilled Mac And Cheese Quesadillas 205	Apple & Bourbon Glazed Ham 221
Grilled Prosciutto Wrapped Asparagus 206	Spicy Ribs 221
Smoked Sausage & Potatoes 206	Pineapple-pepper Pork Kebabs 221
Mini Sausage Rolls 206	Delicious Smoked Bone-in Pork Chops 222
Bbq Pork Shoulder Roast With Sugar Lips Glaze 207	3-2-1 Bbq Baby Back Ribs 222
Smoked Chorizo & Arugula Pesto 207	Old-fashioned Roasted Glazed Ham 223
Wet-rubbed St. Louis Ribs 208	Smoked Pork Spare Ribs 223
Savory Pork Belly Banh Mi 208	Baked Maple And Brown Sugar Bacon 224
Double-decker Pulled Pork Nachos With Smoked Cheese 209	Bbq Brown Sugar Bacon Bites 224
Bacon Stuffed Onion Rings 209	Apple-smoked Bacon 224
Baked German Pork Schnitzel With Grilled Lemons 209	Smoky Bratwurst 224
Smoked Bacon Roses 210	Holiday Smoked Cheese Log 225
Bbq Pork Short Ribs 210	Stuffed Pork Crown Roast 225
Pork Loin Porchetta 210	Smoked Sugar Pork Steaks 226
Prosciutto Wrapped Dates With Marcona Almonds .211	Competition Style Bbq Pork Ribs 226
Jamaican Jerk Pork Chops 211	Grilled Ham & Egg Cups 227
	Baked Beans 227

APPETIZERS AND SNACKS 228

Chicken Wings With Teriyaki Glaze 228	Bacon-wrapped Jalapeño Poppers 228

Bacon Pork Pinwheels (kansas Lollipops) 229
Bayou Wings With Cajun Rémoulade 229
Pulled Pork Loaded Nachos 230
Citrus-infused Marinated Olives 230
Chorizo Queso Fundido 230
Grilled Guacamole 231
Pigs In A Blanket 232
Simple Cream Cheese Sausage Balls 232
Deviled Eggs With Smoked Paprika 232
Smoked Cashews 233
Pig Pops (sweet-hot Bacon On A Stick) 233
Chuckwagon Beef Jerky 234
Smoked Cheese 234
Roasted Red Pepper Dip 235

RECIPE INDEX 236

INTRODUCTION

What the BIG HORN Wood Pellet Grill is

A wood pellet grill — also known as a wood pellet smoker — is a special type of grill that uses indirect, pellet-generated heat and smoke to cook food in several different ways. With a pellet grill, you can enjoy traditionally grilled favorites or leave the meat to cook slowly on low smoke throughout the day. You can also use a pellet grill like a type of outdoor oven.

Like other grills, a pellet smoker makes an excellent addition to a campout, tailgating party and your own backyard.

How Does the BIG HORN Wood Pellet Grill Work?

So now you know what they do, but how do pellet grills work?

Much of what a pellet grill does is automated, meaning there's a very small learning curve on figuring out how to operate it correctly. Wood pellets are loaded into a storage chamber called the hopper, where a motor and combustion fan ignite the pellets and circulate that smoky wood flavor throughout the main cooking chamber.

Once they're going, pellet grills work basically like a gas grill or kitchen oven, trapping heat under the hood to cook your food, all while the hopper continues to circulate the aroma and flavor of your choice of wood pellets. Air fans ensure that heat and smoke are evenly dispersed during the cook time, and temperature control dials give you the option to cook either low and slow or hard and fast, depending on the taste and texture that you're trying to achieve.

The Pros of the BIG HORN Wood Pellet Grill

1. Laid-Back Approach

If you're not the type of person to babysit your grill, opting for a pellet grill can be a far better option. Compared to gas, pellet grills cook slowly and thoroughly with minimal intervention and safety concerns. You'll even find that many have easy-to-use features that allow you to monitor the cooking process remotely.

For example, some pellet grills are equipped with digital controllers that allow you to set specific cook times. You can even use a smartphone app to adjust the grill settings. The only maintenance you'll have to consider with a wood pellet grill vs propane grill is making sure the hopper has enough pellets.

2. Minimal Maintenance

Because pellet grills typically cook for longer, most of the fats and grease will be burnt away, compared to gas grills. At most, you'll have to clean the firepot and any juices and drippings that are collected. You could also opt to season the smoker after cooking to burn away any traces of food.

3. Superior Flavor

The number one reason why people suggest pellet grills are better than gas grills is their flavor profiles. With pellet grills, you will have a diverse selection of different types of wood that you can cook with. Instead of using regular flavorless gas, these appliances allow you to inject different flavors into the meat. A few of the most popular flavored pellets on the market include pecan, mesquite, hickory, and apple. There are plenty of manufacturers that have an extensive product list of fabulously flavored wood pellets. If you buy them in bulk, you're likely to get better discounts than you would with gas canisters.

Another exciting aspect of the flavors from wood pellets is you can customize them to your liking. You could mix apple and mesquite pellets for a unique flavor for ribs and brisket.

4. Versatility

Interestingly enough, pellet grills are far more versatile than gas grills because they give you several different ways to cook. You can easily set the temperature low, close the lid for smoking, or use it as a traditional grill. Some of the higher-end models even allow you to sear and braise, as well.

5. Enhanced Moisture and Meat Quality

Most people who opt for gas grills search for a quick and efficient outdoor appliance for everyday meals. With a pellet smoker, you have more control over how your meat cooks, especially if you want juicier cuts.

Since this appliance cooks for longer times and at lower temperatures, you'll find the inside of meat will be more moist. You might also find that it's a preferable option for higher-quality cuts of meat that need more attention.

Better to Use Your BIG HORN Wood Pellet Grill

1. Use Lighter-Flavored Wood

Switching up your hardwood changes the flavor of what you're cooking.

You'll want to leave the big smoke flavors for meat and veggies and use a lighter-flavored wood for your baked goods.

You simply want the wood flavor to lightly touch your baked goods. Go ahead and experiment to see which flavors you like the best. Go ahead and combine them, too.

2. Prep Your Ingredients

Just like with baking in the house, you want to prep your ingredients ahead of time. Then, put it all together so it's ready to cook when you are.

For example, if you're having an evening party, put your dessert together in the morning, so you just have to slip it into your grill when you're ready to cook.

3. Keep It Simple

Whether you're a novice baker or a seasoned expert, let the flavor of your hardwood season your baked goods and give it a light smoky flavor.

So, keep your dessert simple and let the grill do the work. There's no reason to over complicate your dessert. After all, the fun of having a party is hanging out with friends and family.

Think cookies, cake, crumbles, and even fruit. Grilled fruit is delightful and refreshing when you put some cool whip on the side.

4. Use a Recipe You Know

A great tip is to use a recipe you know and are comfortable with. You can basically make anything you'd like on your pellet grill. So, pull out your favorite cookie, brownie, cake, pie, or cheesecake recipe. You don't really have to make any modification to cook on your grill.

Do note, though, that recipes may cook a bit faster, so you'll want to check often for doneness.

Cleaning Approaches for Your BIG HORN Wood Pellet Grill

To prove to you just how easy it can be let's review the common methods of cleaning.

1. The Obvious Approach: Brushing

This method works best if it is done immediately after grilling while the grate is still hot. Before the grates cool off, scrape each grate with a brush, both top and bottom sides. You can also dip the brush in water which will create a steam that loosens the grease. Not only will this make cleaning time shorter, but it will discourage insects from hanging around your grill. Depending on your grate you may need to wipe them down with a cloth after scrapping.

2. The Lazy Approach: Burning

The idea behind this method is simple, get the grate super hot (550° F) until all the caked on grease burns up. You can throw the grates in a self-cleaning oven or simply place some aluminum foil down on top of the grate, close the lid and light up the grill. After about 10-15 minutes all of the grease should be a white powder, simply brush it off and you're done.

3. The Neat Freak Approach: Soaking

Although, brushing and burning are the standard methods for cleaning, all grates should be soaked at least a couple times a year.

Just fill up the sink or a large bucket with water and a bunch of dish soap. Add a little baking soda and let the grates soak for an hour. Afterward, scrub and rinse.

4. The DIY Approach

You can easily make your own scrubber with a block of hardwood. Use the block to scrub the grates after grilling, eventually, you will carve grooves into the block that fit perfectly onto your grate.

Aluminum foil is another easy DIY scrubber and also a lifesaver if you have to use a lazy person's grill. Simply heat up the grates, then wad up some foil and scrub away. Let's jump into some do-it-yourself methods to cleaning up those nasty grates.

POULTRY RECIPES

Smoked Turkey Breast

Servings: 2-4
Cooking Time: 120 Minutes

Ingredients:
- 1 (3-pound) turkey breast
- Salt
- Freshly ground black pepper
- 1 teaspoon garlic powder

Directions:
1. Supply your smoker with wood pellets and follow the start-up procedure. Preheat the grill, with the lid closed, to 180°F.
2. Season the turkey breast all over with salt, pepper, and garlic powder.
3. Place the breast directly on the grill grate and smoke for 1 hour.
4. Increase the grill's temperature to 350°F and continue to cook until the turkey's internal temperature reaches 170°F. Remove the breast from the grill and serve immediately.

Cajun Brined Maple Smoked Turkey Breast

Servings: 4
Cooking Time: 180 Minutes

Ingredients:
- 1 Gallon water
- 3/4 Cup canning and pickling salt
- 3 Tablespoon minced garlic
- 3 Tablespoon dark brown sugar
- 2 Tablespoon Worcestershire sauce
- 2 Tablespoon Cajun seasoning
- 1 (5-6 lb) bone-in turkey breast
- 3 Tablespoon extra-virgin olive oil
- 2 Tablespoon Cajun seasoning

Directions:
1. In a large food safe container or bucket, combine all of the ingredients for the brine with 1 gallon water. Stir until the salt is dissolved.
2. Place the turkey breast in the brine and weigh it down to ensure it is fully submerged. Cover and brine in a refrigerator for 1 to 2 days.
3. Remove the turkey breast from the brine and pat dry. Drizzle with the olive oil using your hands to cover all areas of the bird. Season liberally with Cajun seasoning. Probe: 165 °F
4. Supply your smoker with wood pellets and follow the start-up procedure. Preheat the grill, with the lid closed, to 225° F.
5. Place the turkey breast directly on the grill grate, close the lid and cook for 3 hours. After 3 hours, increase the temperature to 425°F and continue to cook for another 30 minutes or until the internal temperature reads 165°F when a thermometer is inserted into the thickest part of the breast. Grill: 225 °F Probe: 165 °F
6. Remove the turkey breast from the grill and allow to rest for at least 15 minutes before slicing. Slice and serve. Enjoy!

Smoked Boneless Chicken Thighs

Servings: 8 - 10
Cooking Time: 55 Minutes

Ingredients:
- 2 Tbsp Ginger Root, Grated
- 5 Lbs. Boneless Skinless Chicken Thighs
- ⅔ Cup Brown Sugar
- 2 Cups Chicken Broth
- 1 Tsp Chinese Five-Spice Powder
- 5 Garlic Cloves, Minced
- ¼ Cup Honey
- 1 Tbsp Sweet Heat Rub
- ½ Cup Soy Sauce
- 1 Yellow Onion, Minced

Directions:
1. Supply your smoker with wood pellets and follow the start-up procedure. Preheat the grill, with the lid

closed, to 225° F. If using a gas or charcoal grill, set it up for low heat.

2. Remove chicken from marinade and place on a metal sheet tray. Using a mesh strainer, strain the marinade directly into a cast iron skillet.

3. Place skillet with marinade and chicken on the grill. Allow chicken to smoke for 10 minutes, then increase grill temperature to 400°F.

4. Grill an additional 15 minutes. Make sure to stir marinade periodically. The sauce will begin to reduce and thicken as it cooks.

5. After 15 minutes, baste chicken thighs with marinade, then flip and baste the other sides. Grill an additional 15 minutes, then baste again.

6. Cook until glaze has caramelized and thickened, then remove from grill and serve hot.

Fig Glazed Chicken Stuffed Cornbread

Servings: 10
Cooking Time: 120 Minutes

Ingredients:

- Black Pepper
- 6 Tablespoons (For The Chicken) Butter, Unsalted
- 3 Chicken, Whole
- 2 1/5 Cups (Replace With Craisins For A Different Flavor) Dried Figs, Chopped
- 1 Egg
- 2 Tablespoon Extra-Virgin Olive Oil
- 1/2 Cup Heavy Cream
- 1/2 Cup Honey
- Kosher Salt
- 4 Tablespoon Lemon, Juice
- 1/2 Onion, Chopped
- Champion Chicken Seasoning
- 1 1/2 Teaspoon Finely Chopped Rosemary, Fresh
- 1 Pound Sweet Italian Sausage
- 3 Cups Water, Warm

Directions:

1. Mix figs, honey, lemon juice, and warm water. Cover with plastic wrap and let figs soften for 30 minutes. Strain the figs and reserve the liquid for glaze.

2. Heat olive oil over medium heat and sauté the onions with rosemary. Add the sausage. Cook until browned. Place into a large bowl, add the cornbread and figs. Season with Champion Chicken Seasoning. Stir. In a separate bowl, Stir together egg, heavy whipping cream, and chicken stock. Pour over the cornbread/fig mix and stir together. Set aside.

3. Rinse chickens and pat dry. Season liberally with Champion Chicken Seasoning, kosher salt and black pepper. Don't forget the cavity! Stuff cavities with Stuffing. Top each Chicken with 2 tablespoons butter.

4. Supply your smoker with wood pellets and follow the start-up procedure. Preheat the grill, with the lid closed, to 300° F. Place in a roasting tray and cook until internal temp reads 165°F.

5. While chickens cook, place the fig liquid, balsamic vinegar and butter over. Reduce to thicken and baste chickens with about 160°F or 10 minutes before finished. Rest for 10 minutes. Carve and serve!

Italian Grilled Barbecue Chicken Wings

Servings: 4
Cooking Time: 18 Minutes

Ingredients:

- 1 cup KRAFT Zesty Italian Dressing
- 2 pounds chicken wings/drummettes
- 1/2 cup barbecue sauce

Directions:

1. Pour dressing over chicken in large bowl; toss to coat.
2. Refrigerate at least 30 minutes to marinate.
3. Supply your smoker with wood pellets and follow the start-up procedure. Preheat the grill, with the lid closed, to 400° F. Drain chicken; discard marinade.
4. Grill chicken 8 minutes on each side or until done.
5. Brush with barbecue sauce; grill for another 2 minutes.
6. Remove from grill and serve.

Grilled Honey Chicken Wings

Servings: 4 - 8
Cooking Time: 30 Minutes

Ingredients:
- 2 Chipotles Chopped In Adobo
- 1 Apple Cider Vinegar
- 2 Tablespoons Balsamic Vinegar
- ¼ Cup Brown Sugar
- 2 ½ Lbs Chicken Wings, Trimmed And Patted Dry
- ¼ Cup Honey
- ½ Cup Ketchup
- ¼ Cup Adobo Sauce
- 2 Tablespoons Sweet Rib Rub
- 2 Teaspoons Worcestershire Sauce

Directions:
1. Supply your smoker with wood pellets and follow the start-up procedure. Preheat the grill, with the lid open, to 350° F. If you're using a charcoal or gas grill, set up the grill for medium high heat.
2. In a large bowl, whisk together the apple cider vinegar, ketchup, brown sugar, honey, chopped chipotle peppers with adobo sauce, balsamic vinegar, Worcestershire sauce, and Sweet Rib Rub. Whisk the glaze until it's well combined.
3. Add the wings to the glaze and place the bowl in the refrigerator. Marinade the chicken wings for up to 12 hours. Once the wings have finished marinating, remove the chicken wings from the marinade and place the chicken wings onto the wing rack.
4. Once all the wings have been placed on the wing rack, place the wing rack on the grill. Insert a temperature probe into the thickest part into one of the wings and grill the wings for 5 minutes, and then rotate the rack 180° and grill for another 5 minutes. Remove the wings once they have an internal temperature of 165°F and the juice from the chicken runs clear.
5. Remove the wings from the grill and serve immediately.

Peanut Butter Chicken Wings

Servings: 4
Cooking Time: 35 Minutes

Ingredients:
- 1 Tsp Black Peppercorns, Ground
- 2 Tbsp Brown Sugar
- 4 Lbs Chicken Wings, Trimmed And Patted Dry
- 2 Tbsp Honey
- 1/4 Cup Peanut Butter
- 10 Oz Peanuts, Whole
- 2 Tsp Sweet Rib Rub
- 1/2 Red Onion, Minced
- 1/2 Cup Strawberry Preserves
- 1 Tbsp Thai Chili Sauce
- 1/4 Cup Worcestershire Sauce

Directions:
1. Place chicken wings in a 9 x13 glass baking dish. Pour mixture over chicken, cover with plastic wrap, and refrigerate for 2 hours.
2. Supply your smoker with wood pellets and follow the start-up procedure. Preheat the grill, with the lid open, to 400° F. Preheat griddle to medium-low flame. If using a gas or charcoal grill, set it to medium-high heat.
3. Place wings directly on grill grate, over indirect heat, and cook for 20 to 25 minutes, rotating wings every 5 minutes.
4. Meanwhile, place shelled peanuts on the griddle, turning occasionally with a metal spatula for 5 to 7 minutes, to lightly roast. Remove from the griddle and set aside to cool.
5. Remove wings from grill and allow to rest for 5 minutes. While wings are resting, shell the peanuts, and transfer to a resealable plastic bag. Use a rolling pin to crush the peanuts, then scatter peanuts on top of the chicken wings. Serve warm.

Easy Bbq Chicken Wings

Servings: 4
Cooking Time: 40 Minutes

Ingredients:
- 1 Pack Chicken Wings
- Extra Virgin Olive Oil
- Champion Chicken Seasoning

Directions:

1. Supply your smoker with wood pellets and follow the start-up procedure. Preheat the grill, with the lid closed, to 350° F.
2. Blot the defrosted chicken wings dry with paper towels.
3. Brush oil onto each side of the wings and sprinkle with seasoning.
4. Grill at 350° for 40 minutes or until wings are crispy. Flip halfway through. Serve hot.

Smoked Chicken Vermicelli Noodles

Servings: 4 – 6
Cooking Time: 120 Minutes

Ingredients:
- 2 Cup Broccoli
- ¼ Cup Chicken Stock
- 6 - 8 Chicken Thighs, Boneless, Skinless
- 1 Tbsp Chili Flakes
- 1 Tsp Cornstarch
- 4, Chopped Garlic Cloves
- 3 Tbsp Hoisin Sauce, Divided
- Knob Of Fresh Ginger, Grated
- 1, Thin Red Bell Peppers, Sliced
- 1 Tbsp Rice Wine Vinegar
- 8 Scallions, Sliced
- 1 ½ Tbsp Sesame Oil, Divided
- 1 Tbsp, Toasted Sesame Seeds
- 3.5 Oz Shitake Mushrooms, Sliced Thin
- 8 Oz Snow Peas
- 3 Tbsp Soy Sauce
- 2 Tbsp Sweet Chili Sauce
- 3 Tbsp Vegetable Oil
- 1 Lb Vermicelli Noodles, Or Linguini, Cooked And Drained

Directions:
1. In a large bowl, whisk together rice wine vinegar, 1 tablespoon of Hoisin sauce, and 1 tablespoon of sesame oil. Toss chicken to coat and allow to marinate for 1 hour.
2. Supply your smoker with wood pellets and follow the start-up procedure. Preheat the grill, with the lid open, to 225° F. If using a gas or charcoal grill, set it for low, indirect heat. Place chicken directly on the grill grate and smoke for 1 ½ to 2 hours, or until the internal temperature reaches 165° F. Remove it from the smoker, cover with foil, and rest for 10 minutes, then slice thin and set aside.
3. In a glass measuring cup whisk together 2 tablespoons of Hoisin sauce, soy sauce, sweet chili sauce, chicken stock, ½ tablespoon of sesame oil, and cornstarch. Set aside.
4. Preheat griddle to medium flame, then add oil. Working quickly, sauté ginger and garlic for 15 seconds, then add bell pepper and mushrooms and continue cooking for another minute, then add in snow peas and slaw. Toss in cooked pasta, chicken, scallions, and pour sauce over. Cook for one minute until sauce thickens and is well incorporated.
5. Transfer to platter and serve hot. Sprinkle with chili flakes and sesame seeds, if desired.

Chicken On A Throne

Servings: 6
Cooking Time: 75 Minutes

Ingredients:
- 1 can of low-carb beer or sugar-free dark-colored soda, about 12oz (350ml)
- 1 whole chicken, about 4lb (1.8kg)
- 3 tbsp barbecue rub, plus more

Directions:
1. Supply your smoker with wood pellets and follow the start-up procedure. Preheat the grill, with the lid closed, to 350° F.
2. Pour half the contents of the can into a glass for drinking. Set the half-full can aside.
3. Blot any juices off the chicken with paper towels. Sprinkle 2 teaspoons of the rub in the body and neck cavities. Sprinkle the remaining rub evenly on the outside. Tuck the wing tips behind the bird's back.
4. Carefully lower the chicken (body cavity side down) over the can. Place the chicken upright on its can on the grate. (For stability, pull the legs forward and rest them on the grate to essentially form a tripod.) Roast the chicken until the internal temperature in the thickest

part of a thigh reaches 165°F (74°C), about 1 hour. (Check on your bird periodically to make sure it hasn't tipped over.) If it hasn't yet reached that temperature, continue cooking for about 15 minutes more.

5. Use heavy-duty insulated rubber gloves and tongs to carefully transfer the chicken to the kitchen. Let rest 5 minutes and then carefully ease the chicken off the can. Discard the can and its steaming liquid, being careful not to burn yourself. Carve the chicken and serve.

Thai Chicken Satays

Servings: 4
Cooking Time: 10 Minutes

Ingredients:
- 1½lb (680g) boneless, skinless chicken breasts
- for the marinade
- ½ cup unsweetened canned light coconut milk
- 2 garlic cloves, peeled and coarsely chopped
- ¼ cup loosely packed fresh cilantro leaves
- 1-inch (2.5cm) piece of fresh ginger, peeled and coarsely chopped
- 2 tbsp light soy sauce
- 1 tbsp Asian fish sauce
- 1 tbsp light brown sugar or low-carb substitute
- 2 tsp sambal oelek (optional)
- 1 tsp Thai-style curry powder
- 1 tsp ground cumin
- 1 tsp ground turmeric
- 1 tsp coarse salt
- 2 tbsp vegetable oil
- for serving
- butter lettuce leaves, washed and dried
- cherry tomatoes
- Peanut Sauce

Directions:
1. Use a sharp knife to slice the chicken breasts lengthwise into strips, each about 1 inch (2.5cm) wide. (If the chicken breasts are unusually thick, butterfly them before cutting them into strips.) Place the breasts in a resealable plastic bag.
2. In a blender, make the marinade by combining the ingredients. Blend until fairly smooth. Pour the marinade over the chicken, turning and massaging the bag to thoroughly coat the chicken. Refrigerate for 2 hours.
3. Supply your smoker with wood pellets and follow the start-up procedure. Preheat the grill, with the lid closed, to 450° F.
4. Remove the chicken from the marinade and let any excess drip off. (Discard the marinade.) Thread each chicken strip on a bamboo skewer, pushing the point in one side of the chicken and out the other as if sewing. Leave very little of the tip exposed because it will burn easily.
5. Place the skewers on the grate perpendicular to the bars. Grill until the chicken has grill marks and is fully cooked, about 3 to 5 minutes per side.
6. Remove the skewers from the grill. Place the lettuce leaves on a platter. Place the satays atop the leaves. Scatter cherry tomatoes over the top. Serve with the peanut sauce.

Chile Cilantro Lime Chicken Wings

Servings: 4
Cooking Time: 20 Minutes

Ingredients:
- 1 Tsp Ancho Chili Powder
- 2 Tsp Blackened Sriracha Rub Seasoning
- 2 Lbs Chicken Wings, Split
- 2 Tbsp Cilantro, Chopped, Divided
- 1 Tsp Cumin
- 1 Lime, Zest & Juice
- 1 1/2 Tbsp Olive Oil

Directions:
1. In a medium bowl, combine 1 tablespoon of cilantro, lime juice and zest, olive oil, Blackened Sriracha, ancho chili powder, and cumin.
2. Place chicken wings in a resealable gallon bag and add cilantro mixture. Transfer to the refrigerator and marinate for 1 hour, turning occasionally.
3. Supply your smoker with wood pellets and follow the start-up procedure. Preheat the grill, with the lid closed, to 350° F. If using a gas or charcoal grill, set it up for medium heat.

4. Remove chicken wings from the marinade and place on the grill over indirect heat. Grill for 15 to 18 minutes, turning and rotating every 3 to 5 minutes.

5. Remove chicken wings from the grill, garnish with remaining cilantro, and serve warm.

Spatchcocked Chicken With Toasted Fennel & Garlic

Servings: 6
Cooking Time: 45 Minutes

Ingredients:
- 6 Pound whole chicken
- 1 Tablespoon toasted fennel seed
- 2 Clove garlic, minced
- 1 Tablespoon salt
- 1/2 Tablespoon pepper

Directions:
1. To Spatchcock the chicken, remove the backbone by cutting down both sides of the backbone.
2. Next turn the bird over and make a cut down the keel bone, which is right in the center. This will allow the chicken to lay flat.
3. Supply your smoker with wood pellets and follow the start-up procedure. Preheat the grill, with the lid closed, to 450° F.
4. While the grill is preheating, rub the chicken with the fennel, garlic, salt, and pepper, and let it come almost to room temperature (this will help it cook faster).
5. Place the chicken, skin-side down on the grill. Cook 8 to 10 minutes, or until there are good grill marks. Grill: 450 °F
6. Turn the chicken over and cook until the meat reaches an internal temperature of 160 degrees. Enjoy! Grill: 450 °F Probe: 160 °F

Bbq Turkey Drumsticks

Servings: 6
Cooking Time: 120 Minutes

Ingredients:
- 1/2 Tbsp Black Pepper
- 1 Tbsp Brown Sugar
- 1/2 Tsp Cayenne Pepper
- 1/2 Tbsp Coriander, Ground
- 1/2 Tbsp Granulated Garlic
- 1 Package, Approx 4 Lbs Honeysuckle White® Turkey Drumsticks
- 1 Tbsp Kosher Salt
- 2 Tbsp Olive Oil

Directions:
1. Supply your smoker with wood pellets and follow the start-up procedure. Preheat the grill, with the lid open, to 225° F. If using a gas or charcoal grill, set it up for low, indirect heat.
2. Place Honeysuckle White® Turkey Legs on a sheet tray, coat with olive oil, then season with a blend of salt pepper, cayenne, brown sugar, granulated garlic, and ground coriander.
3. Place turkey legs in the smoking cabinet and smoke for 1 ½ hours, checking the internal temperature after 1 hour.
4. Increase the temperature to 325°F, transfer the turkey legs to the bottom grill grate and cook for another 25 to 30 minutes, until the internal temperature reaches 170°F.
5. Remove turkey drumsticks from the grill, allow to rest for 10 minutes, then serve warm.

Jalapeno Chicken Sliders

Servings: 8-10
Cooking Time: 180 Minutes

Ingredients:
- 3 Pounds Boneless Skinless Chicken Breasts
- 8-10 Slices Cheese Of Choice
- 1/2 Cup Chicken Broth
- Pickled Jalapeños
- 1 Tsp Smoked Infused Sweet Mesquite Jalapeno Sea Salt
- 1/2 Cup Salsa Verde
- 1 Package Slider Buns
- 3 Tablespoons Sweet Heat Rub

Directions:
1. Add the chicken breasts, chicken broth, and salsa verde to a disposable aluminum foil pan. Season

everything generously with Sweet Heat and 1 tsp of Smoked Infused Sweet Mesquite Jalapeno Sea Salt. Cover tightly with aluminum foil.

2. Supply your smoker with wood pellets and follow the start-up procedure. Preheat the grill, with the lid open, to 275° F. Place the aluminum foil pan on the grill and cook for 3-4 hours, or until the chicken is completely cooked (165°F internal temperature), tender, and falling apart. Remove from the grill and let cool slightly.

3. Shred the chicken with the meat claws and toss with the Sweet Heat rub. Then, build the sliders: top the slider buns with a scoop of the pulled chicken, a slice cheese, and a few slices of pickled jalapeños. Serve immediately.

Smoked Chicken With Apricot Bbq Glaze

Servings: 4
Cooking Time: 60 Minutes

Ingredients:
- 2 Whole Chickens, halved
- 4 Tablespoon Chicken Rub
- 1 Cup Apricot BBQ Sauce

Directions:
1. Supply your smoker with wood pellets and follow the start-up procedure. Preheat the grill, with the lid closed, to 375° F.
2. Season chicken with Chicken Rub and place on grill meat side up. Cook 1 hour or until internal temperature has reached 160°F in the breast and 175°F in the leg. Grill: 375 °F Probe: 160 °F
3. Baste each chicken half with a bit of the Apricot BBQ glaze and return to grill for 10 minutes. Grill: 375 °F
4. Remove chicken from the grill and allow to rest 5-10 minutes. Portion each half by removing the leg and cutting each breast in half leaving you with four legs and 8 breast pieces. Serve with your favorite vegetables or sides. Enjoy!

Whole Smoked Chicken

Servings: 6
Cooking Time: 180 Minutes

Ingredients:
- 1/2 Cup kosher salt
- 1 Cup brown sugar
- 1 (3 to 3-1/2 lb) whole chicken
- 1 Teaspoon minced garlic
- Chicken Rub
- 1 lemon, halved
- 1 Medium yellow onion, quartered
- 3 Whole garlic cloves
- 5 thyme sprigs

Directions:
1. For the Brine: Dissolve the kosher salt and brown sugar in 1 gallon of water. Once dissolved, place the chicken in the brine and refrigerate overnight. Make sure chicken is fully submerged weighing it down if necessary.
2. Supply your smoker with wood pellets and follow the start-up procedure. Preheat the grill, with the lid closed, to 225° F.
3. While the grill preheats, remove the chicken from the brine and pat dry. Rub with the minced garlic and Traeger Chicken Rub. Next, stuff the cavity with the lemon, onion, garlic and thyme. Tie the legs together.
4. Place chicken directly on the grill grate and smoke for 2-1/2 to 3 hours or until an instant-read thermometer reads 160°F when inserted into the thickest part of the breast. The finished internal temperature will rise to 165°F in the breast as the chicken rests. Let rest for 15 minutes before carving. Enjoy! Probe: 160 °F

Spiced Smoked Chicken Quarters

Servings: 4
Cooking Time: 120 Minutes

Ingredients:
- 4 chicken leg quarters
- For the rub:
- 2 tbsp paprika
- 1 tbsp thyme
- 2 tbsp chili powder

- 2 tbsp cayenne pepper
- 1 tbsp garlic powder
- 1 tbsp onion powder
- 1 tbsp kosher/table salt
- 2 tbsp black pepper
- 1 tbsp olive oil

Directions:

1. Supply your smoker with wood pellets and follow the start-up procedure. Preheat the grill, with the lid closed, to 220° F.
2. Pat down chicken pieces with a paper towel to make them dry. Cut off any excess fat that's visible on the outside of the meat.
3. Apply a thin layer of oil to the chicken skin. In a small bowl, combine all the BBQ rub ingredients thoroughly. Apply BBQ rub generously to your chicken thighs, rubbing in firmly and thoroughly.
4. Transfer chicken quarters to your smoker rack. Close the lid.
5. Cook until the quarters reach an internal temperature of 165°F, about 2 hours.
6. Once cooked, increase the grill temperature to medium heat. Cook for just a few minutes, turning regularly, for a crispy skin.

Bbq Chicken Drumsticks

Servings: 4
Cooking Time: 120 Minutes

Ingredients:

- 8 chicken drumsticks
- 2 Tablespoon Chicken Rub
- 1/2 Cup 'Que BBQ Sauce

Directions:

1. Season each drumstick and let rest for 20 minutes.
2. Supply your smoker with wood pellets and follow the start-up procedure. Preheat the grill, with the lid closed, to 275° F.
3. Hang the drumsticks on the leg hanger (alternatively, place directly on the grill grate flipping halfway through) and cook for 1 hour. Grill: 275 °F
4. Remove the drumsticks from the hanger (or grate) and place in a pan. Grill: 275 °F Probe: 190 °F
5. Cover with foil and cook for 45 more minutes or until meat reaches an internal temperature of 190 degrees F. Grill: 275 °F Probe: 190 °F
6. Remove the foil and sauce all drumsticks in the pan.
7. Cook for an additional 15 minutes so sauce can set. Grill: 275 °F
8. Remove from Traeger and let rest for 15 minutes before serving. Enjoy!

Chicken Lollipops

Servings: 8
Cooking Time: 60 Minutes

Ingredients:

- 18 Pieces chicken drumsticks
- Cajun Shake
- 1 Stick butter
- 'Que BBQ Sauce
- Louisiana Brand Hot Sauce (Optional)

Directions:

1. To turn regular chicken legs into lollipops, you'll need a sharp knife and a pair of kitchen shears. Start by making a cut all of the way around the leg just below the knuckle, cutting through the skins and tendons using either a sharp knife or a pair of kitchen shears. Push the meat down to the large end and pull/cut the remaining skin and cartilage off the knuckle. You might want to also remove the tiny bone right against the leg. Remove this bone with your fingers or the shears, and trim away the tendons sticking out the top.
2. Season the chicken with the Cajun Shake. Wrap the bones of the drumsticks with a small piece of aluminum foil to keep them from turning too black. Let the chicken sit for an hour in the fridge to allow the flavor to permeate.
3. Supply your smoker with wood pellets and follow the start-up procedure. Preheat the grill, with the lid closed, to 180° F.
4. Place the chicken lollipops on the grill grate and let them smoke for 30 minutes.
5. After you remove the chicken, increase the grill temperature to 350°F and let it preheat, lid closed for 15 minutes. Place the stick of butter in a baking pan or

aluminum pan and put it on the grill to allow the butter to melt while the grill is coming to temperature. (The butter doesn't need to cover the chicken. It just keeps the drumstick moist and of course, gives it a little added buttery finish.)

6. Arrange the lollipops in the pan with the bones sticking up straight. Let the chicken cook for about 40 minutes or until the internal temperature registers 165F on an instant-read thermometer. Grill: 350 °F Probe: 165 °F

7. Meanwhile, warm up the barbecue sauce in a small saucepan on the stove over low heat. If you want it to have that Louisiana kick, add in a few squirts of the hot sauce, to your taste. Once it starts to thin, turn down the heat to just keep it warm. If the sauce needs to be thinned, pour in a little bit of the butter used in the pan until it reaches a thickness that is thick enough to adhere to the drumsticks but not gluey.

8. Dip the lollipops into the barbecue sauce so that it is completely covered. You can also brush the barbecue sauce on the bones if you want a uniform look and sheen on the lollipops.

9. Increase the temperature to 450F. Place the chicken directly on the grill grate and cook until the internal temperature registers 175F, about 10 more minutes. Keep an eye on the lollipops to make sure that the glaze doesn't burn. You're looking for that perfect caramelization of the barbecue sauce on the outside with a crisp skin to give a little texture. Grill: 450 °F Probe: 175 °F

Smoked Chicken Leg & Thigh Quarters

Servings: 6
Cooking Time: 120 Minutes

Ingredients:
- 8 chicken legs (thigh and drumstick)
- 3 Tablespoon olive oil
- Pork & Poultry Rub

Directions:
1. Place the chicken pieces in a large mixing bowl. Pour oil over the chicken to coat each piece, then season to taste with the Traeger Pork & Poultry Rub. Massage the chicken pieces to encourage the oil and seasonings get under the skin. Cover and refrigerate for at least 1 to 2 hours.

2. Supply your smoker with wood pellets and follow the start-up procedure. Preheat the grill, with the lid closed, to 180° F.

3. Remove the chicken from the refrigerator, letting any excess oil drip back into the bowl. Grill: 180 °F

4. Arrange the chicken on the grill grate and smoke for 1 hour. Increase Traeger temperature to 350°F and continue to roast the chicken until the internal temperature in the thickest part of a thigh is 165°F or the chicken is golden brown and the juices run clear, about 50 to 60 minutes. Grill: 350 °F Probe: 165 °F

5. Remove from the grill and allow the chicken to rest for 8 to 10 minutes and serve. Enjoy!

Juicy Jerk Chicken Kebabs

Servings: 4
Cooking Time: 12 Minutes

Ingredients:
- 1 Tablespoon All Spice, Ground
- 2 Lbs Chicken, Boneless/Skinless
- 1 Tablespoon Cinnamon, Ground
- 1/4 Cup Extra-Virgin Olive Oil
- 3 Garlic, Cloves
- 2 Inch Piece Ginger, Fresh
- 3 Green Onion
- 1 Lime, Juiced
- 1 Tablespoon Nutmeg, Ground
- 1 Cup Orange Juice, Fresh
- Pepper
- 1 Red Onion, Chopped
- Salt
- Skewers
- 1/4 Cup Soy Sauce
- 1/4 Cup Thyme, Fresh Sprigs

Directions:
1. Soak the bamboo skewers in water for about 30 minutes (the longer the better).

2. In a food processor, combine orange juice, oil, soy sauce, thyme, allspice, nutmeg, cinnamon, garlic, onions, ginger, lime juice, salt and pepper. Puree until smooth.
3. In a large resealable bag, pour all but 1/4 cup of the mixture in along with the sliced up chicken breasts. Seal the bag and marinate in the fridge for 2 - 3 hours.
4. Supply your smoker with wood pellets and follow the start-up procedure. Preheat the grill, with the lid open, to 450° F. Skewer the chicken and grill for about 7 minutes. Flip and continue grilling for about 5 minutes, or until the chicken is cooked through and grill marks appear. Serve with the remaining 1/4 cup of marinade.

Traeger Mandarin Wings

Servings: 2
Cooking Time: 30 Minutes

Ingredients:
- 1 Bottle (12 oz) mandarin orange sauce
- Beef Rub
- Chicken Rub
- 2 Pound chicken wings, flats and drumettes separated

Directions:
1. Coat chicken wings with mandarin sauce. Sprinkle Traeger Beef Rub and Traeger Chicken Rub onto wings. Marinate for at least 30 minutes.
2. Supply your smoker with wood pellets and follow the start-up procedure. Preheat the grill, with the lid closed, to 350° F.
3. Place wings directly on the grill grate and cook for 30 minutes. Enjoy! Grill: 350 °F Probe: 165 °F

Baked Prosciutto-wrapped Chicken Breast With Spinach And Boursin

Servings: 4
Cooking Time: 60 Minutes

Ingredients:
- 1 Tablespoon olive oil
- 10 Ounce baby spinach leaves, washed and dried
- 2 Whole packs (5.2 oz) Boursin Garlic & Fine Herbs Gournay Cheese
- 2 Pound boneless, skinless chicken breasts
- Pork & Poultry Rub
- 14 Slices prosciutto

Directions:
1. Heat olive oil in a medium sauté pan. Add spinach and sauté until wilted, about 3 to 5 minutes. Transfer to a strainer and squeeze out excess liquid. Place spinach and cheese in a medium bowl. Mix well and set aside.
2. Butterfly each chicken breast and open like a book. Cover with plastic wrap and using a meat mallet, pound out thinly. Season the chicken with Pork & Poultry Rub.
3. Lay a sheet of plastic wrap about 2 feet long down on a flat, clean surface. Lay down slices of prosciutto, slightly overlapping and double-wide. Place the chicken on top of the prosciutto leaving a 1- 1/2 inch border.
4. Spread the spinach mixture on top of the chicken. Roll it up tightly to create a log. Tie off the ends tightly and transfer to the refrigerator. Refrigerate 2 to 3 hours or overnight.
5. Supply your smoker with wood pellets and follow the start-up procedure. Preheat the grill, with the lid closed, to 300° F.
6. Carefully remove the plastic wrap and place directly on the grill grate. Bake for an hour and a half, or until the internal temperature reaches 162°F to 165°F. Remove from Traeger and let rest for 10 minutes before slicing. Enjoy! Grill: 300 °F Probe: 162 °F

Wild West Wings

Servings: 4
Cooking Time: 60 Minutes

Ingredients:
- 2 pounds chicken wings
- 2 tablespoons extra-virgin olive oil
- 2 packages ranch dressing mix (such as Hidden Valley brand)
- ¼ cup prepared ranch dressing (optional)

Directions:
1. Supply your smoker with wood pellets and follow the start-up procedure. Preheat, with the lid closed, to 350°F.

2. Place the chicken wings in a large bowl and toss with the olive oil and ranch dressing mix.
3. Arrange the wings directly on the grill, or line the grill with aluminum foil for easy cleanup, close the lid, and smoke for 25 minutes.
4. Flip and smoke for 20 to 35 minutes more, or until a meat thermometer inserted in the thickest part of the wings reads 165°F and the wings are crispy. (Note: The wings will likely be done after 45 minutes, but an extra 10 to 15 minutes makes them crispy without drying the meat.)
5. Serve warm with ranch dressing (if using).

Bacon Wrapped Chicken Wings

Servings: 6
Cooking Time: 60 Minutes

Ingredients:
- 2 Pound chicken wings
- 24 Ounce beer
- 2 Teaspoon red pepper flakes
- Cajun Seasoning
- 1 Pound bacon

Directions:
1. Plan ahead, this recipe requires 12 to 24 hours to brine the wings. Trim the tips off of the wings and discard or set them aside for homemade stock.
2. Cut the skin flap between the flat and the drummette so the wing stays a little more straight and is easier to wrap.
3. Place the wings in a large bowl and cover with the beer and red pepper flakes (if desired).
4. Refrigerate for 12-24 hours before grilling.
5. Remove the wings from the brine and pat dry. Season liberally with Traeger's Cajun Shake.
6. Wrap each wing with a piece of bacon. You can secure with toothpicks, if necessary.
7. Supply your smoker with wood pellets and follow the start-up procedure. Preheat the grill, with the lid closed, to 450° F.
8. Place the wings directly on the grill grate, close the lid, and cook for 30 minutes.
9. Flip the wings and cook for an additional 30 minutes or until the bacon is crisp and the chicken is fully cooked (at least 165 degrees F). Enjoy!

Bourbon Chicken Waffles

Servings: 8
Cooking Time: 30 Minutes

Ingredients:
- 1 Shot Of Bourbon
- 3 Cups Bread Crumbs
- 4 Horizontally Half Sliced Boneless, Skinless Chicken Breast
- Butter Flavored Cooking Spray
- 3 Eggs
- 1 Tsp Garlic Powder
- 1 Tsp Paprika, Powder
- Red Velvet Cake Mix
- 16 Oz. Reduced Fat Sour Cream
- Sweet Rib Rub
- ¼ Cup Vegetable Oil
- 1 ¼ Cup Water
- 1 Tbsp Worcestershire Sauce

Directions:
1. Supply your smoker with wood pellets and follow the start-up procedure. Preheat the grill, with the lid closed, to 350° F. If you're using a gas or charcoal grill, set up the grill for medium heat.
2. In a large bowl, combine the sour cream, bourbon, Worcestershire sauce, paprika, garlic powder, and Sweet Rib Rub seasoning. Add the chicken, turn the chicken breasts to coat, and cover the bowl. Refrigerate for 4-12 hrs.
3. Remove the chicken from the refrigerator and drain the marinade from the chicken. Mix together 3 cups bread crumbs and 2 tbsp Sweet Rib Rub. Mix the coating together and bread the chicken breasts.
4. Moisten a paper towel with cooking oil and using a pair of tongs, lightly grease the grill rack.
5. Grill or smoke until the internal temperature of the chicken reaches 170°F and the chicken is crispy and golden brown.

6. While the chicken is cooking, mix the eggs, vegetable oil, water, and red velvet cake mix in a bowl with the electric mixer.
7. Add the mix into the waffle iron and cook. Make as many waffles as the mix allows.
8. On a plate, place the cooked chicken on top of the waffles and top with maple syrup or honey.

Smoked Wings

Servings: 6
Cooking Time: 50 Minutes

Ingredients:
- 24 chicken wings, flats and drumettes separated
- 12 Ounce Italian dressing
- 3 Ounce Chicken Rub
- 5 Ounce 'Que BBQ Sauce
- 3 Ounce chili sauce

Directions:
1. Wash all wings and place into resealable bag. Add Italian dressing to the resealable bag containing the wings. Place in refrigerator and allow to marinate for 6 to 12 hours.
2. Supply your smoker with wood pellets and follow the start-up procedure. Preheat the grill, with the lid closed, to 225° F.
3. Remove wings from marinade and shake off excess marinade. Season all sides of the wings with Traeger Chicken Rub and let sit for 15 minutes before putting wings on the Traeger.
4. In a small bowl, combine the BBQ and chili sauces. Set aside.
5. Cook wings to an internal temperature of 160°F. Remove the wings and toss in chili barbecue sauce. Grill: 225 °F Probe: 160 °F
6. Increase the grill temperature to 375°F and preheat. Once at temperature, place the wings on the Traeger and sear both sides until the internal temperature reaches 165°F. Grill: 375 °F Probe: 165 °F
7. Remove the wings from grill and let rest for 5 minutes. Serve with your favorite side wing dressing or sauce. Enjoy!

Chile Chicken Thighs

Servings: 4
Cooking Time: 35 Minutes

Ingredients:
- 2 Tablespoon soy sauce
- 1/4 Cup honey
- 2 Clove garlic, minced
- 1/4 Teaspoon red pepper flakes
- 4 boneless, skinless chicken thighs
- 2 Tablespoon olive oil
- 2 Teaspoon Chicken Rub
- ancho chile powder
- 1/4 Teaspoon coarse ground black pepper

Directions:
1. Supply your smoker with wood pellets and follow the start-up procedure. Preheat the grill, with the lid closed, to 400° F.
2. In a small bowl, combine honey, soy sauce, garlic and red pepper chili flakes; blend well with wire whisk. Set aside.
3. Drizzle the chicken thighs with olive oil and season generously on both sides with the Traeger Chicken Rub and black pepper, then give each thigh a few shakes of ancho chili powder on both sides.
4. Place the seasoned chicken thighs directly on the grill grate and cook for about 15 minutes per side or until the internal temperature registers 165°F on an instant-read thermometer. Grill: 400 °F Probe: 165 °F
5. Brush with chili-honey glaze. Remove from grill. Serve with additional sauce. Enjoy!

Chicken Parmesan Sliders With Pesto Mayonnaise

Servings: 4
Cooking Time: 30 Minutes

Ingredients:
- 2 Pound Chicken, ground
- 1 Cup Parmesan cheese
- 1 Tablespoon Worcestershire sauce
- black pepper
- 1 Cup mayonnaise

- 2 Tablespoon Pesto Sauce
- 3 Roma tomatoes
- 1 red onion, sliced
- Baby Spinach

Directions:

1. Line a baking sheet with plastic wrap. In a large mixing bowl, combine the ground chicken, the Parmesan, the Worcestershire, and a few grinds of black pepper. Wet your hands with cold water, and use them to mix the ingredients.
2. Divide the meat mixture in half, then form six 2-inch patties out of each half. Place the patties on the baking sheet, cover with another sheet of plastic wrap, and refrigerate for at least 1 hour.
3. Combine the mayonnaise and pesto in a small bowl and whisk together. Cover and refrigerate until serving time.
4. Supply your smoker with wood pellets and follow the start-up procedure. Preheat the grill, with the lid closed, to 300° F.
5. Arrange the chicken patties on the grill grate and grill, turning once, until the patties are cooked through (165F), about 30 minutes. Grill: 300 °F Probe: 165 °F
6. To serve, put a chicken patty on the bottom of a slider bun and top with a dollop of the pesto mayonnaise. Add tomato, onion, and spinach as desired. Replace the top of the bun and skewer with a frilled toothpick, if desired.

Green Chile Chicken Enchiladas

Servings: 6
Cooking Time: 45 Minutes

Ingredients:

- 2 Cups Chicken, Shredded
- 1 (12 Oz) Package Colby Jack Cheese, Shredded
- 1 Enchilada Sauce, Can
- 1 Can Green Chile, Drained
- 1 Onion, Diced
- 1 Tablespoon Sweet Rib Rub
- 1 Cup Sour Cream
- 1 Package Flour Tortilla

Directions:

1. Supply your smoker with wood pellets and follow the start-up procedure. Preheat the grill, with the lid open, to 300° F.
2. In a bowl, mix - the chicken, green chiles, Sweet Heat seasoning, sour cream, diced onion, and half the bag of shredded cheese.
3. Place a large spoonful of the chicken mixture in the center of a tortilla and roll it up. Repeat with the remaining tortillas, then place in the baking pan, and pour the enchilada sauce over the tortilla pans. Top with the remainder of the shredded cheese.
4. Wrap the top of the pan tightly in aluminum foil and grill for 45 minutes or until the enchilada sauce is bubbly. Remove from the grill and serve.

Smoked Turkey Wings

Servings: 2
Cooking Time: 60 Minutes

Ingredients:

- 4 turkey wings
- 1 batch Sweet and Spicy Cinnamon Rub

Directions:

1. Supply your smoker with wood pellets and follow the start-up procedure. Preheat the grill, with the lid closed, to 180°F.
2. Using your hands, work the rub into the turkey wings, coating them completely.
3. Place the wings directly on the grill grate and cook for 30 minutes.
4. Increase the grill's temperature to 325°F and continue to cook until the turkey's internal temperature reaches 170°F. Remove the wings from the grill and serve immediately.

Grilled Chipotle Chicken Skewers

Servings: 4
Cooking Time: 25 Minutes

Ingredients:

- BBQ Sauce
- 1 cup spicy BBQ sauce
- 3 chipotle peppers
- 1 Tbsp adobo sauce

- Skewers
- Olive oil
- 2 lbs boneless skinless chicken breasts
- 10 thick-cut bacon strips
- 1 large green bell pepper, cut into 3/4 to 1 inch pieces
- 1 medium red onion, peeled and cut into 3/4 to 1 inch pieces
- Bamboo skewers
- Garnish: freshly chopped garnish

Directions:
1. Supply your smoker with wood pellets and follow the start-up procedure. Preheat the grill, with the lid closed.
2. Soak the wooden skewers in water for at least 10 to 15 minutes before skewering to avoid them burning as much.
3. Add all ingredients for the sauce to a blender. Blend until they are combined well.
4. Cut chicken into 3/4-inch bite-sized pieces. Cut bacon into 3/4-inch strips.
5. Thread bacon (folding the bacon in half before skewering), chicken, peppers, and onion onto the skewers, alternating as you go.
6. Arrange the skewers on the grill grate and cook for 10 minutes, turning every few minutes. Baste the skewers with BBQ sauce on all sides. Continue to baste and turn the skewers every minute or so to caramelize.
7. The chicken is cooked through when it reaches an internal temperature of 165 °F. The bacon should be nice and crispy at this point.
8. Remove the skewers from the grill and sprinkle with freshly chopped parsley.

Roasted Whole Chicken

Servings: 6-8
Cooking Time: 120 Minutes

Ingredients:
- 1 whole chicken
- 2 tablespoons olive oil
- 1 batch Chicken Rub

Directions:
1. Supply your smoker with wood pellets and follow the start-up procedure. Preheat the grill, with the lid closed, to 375°F.
2. Coat the chicken all over with olive oil and season it with the rub. Using your hands, work the rub into the meat.
3. Place the chicken directly on the grill grate and smoke until its internal temperature reaches 170°F.
4. Remove the chicken from the grill and let it rest for 10 minutes, before carving and serving.

Bbq Spatchcocked Chicken

Servings: 2
Cooking Time: 45 Minutes

Ingredients:
- 1 whole chicken
- 1/4 Cup Chicken Rub
- olive oil
- 1/2 Cup Sweet & Heat BBQ Sauce

Directions:
1. Supply your smoker with wood pellets and follow the start-up procedure. Preheat the grill, with the lid closed, to 375° F.
2. With a large knife or shears, cut the bird open along the backbone on both sides, through the ribs, and remove the backbone.
3. Brush chicken with olive oil and season both sides with Traeger Chicken rub.
4. Place the poultry on the Traeger, breast side up and cook for 35 to 40 minutes or until a thermometer inserted into the breast registers 160°F. Grill: 375 °F Probe: 160 °F
5. Remove from the grill and let rest 5 minutes before slicing. Enjoy!

Savory Smoked Turkey Legs

Servings: 4
Cooking Time: 150 Minutes

Ingredients:
- 1 Cup Chicken Stock
- 2 Tbsp Blackened Sriracha Rub
- 4 Turkey Legs (Drumsticks)

Directions:
1. Fire up your pellet grill on SMOKE mode. With the lid open, let it run for 10 minutes.
2. Supply your smoker with wood pellets and follow the start-up procedure. Preheat the grill, with the lid closed, to 225° F. If using a gas or charcoal grill, set it up for low, indirect heat.
3. Combine turkey stock with 2 teaspoons of Blackened Sriracha Rub.
4. Place turkey legs on a sheet tray, then inject each with seasoned stock. Season the outside of the legs with remaining Blackened Sriracha.
5. Place turkey legs directly on the grate of the smoking cabinet, and cook for 1 ½ hours.
6. Increase temperature to 325°F, then transfer turkey legs to the bottom grill and cook for another 45 to 60 minutes, until the internal temperature reaches 170°F.
7. Remove turkey from the grill, allow to rest for 10 minutes, then serve warm.

Grilled Garlic Chicken Kabobs

Servings: 6
Cooking Time: 15 Minutes

Ingredients:
- 3 (Cut Into 1 Inch Cubes) Chicken Breast, Raw
- 2 Cloves Garlic, Minced
- 2 Tablespoons Honey
- 1 Pound Of Button (Destemmed And Cut In Half) Mushroom
- 1/2 Cup Olive Oil
- 1 Red (Cut Into Quarters And Seperated) Onion
- 1 Green (Cut Into Large Chunks) Bell Pepper
- 2 Tablespoons Competition Smoked Seasoning
- 2 Tablespoons Soy Sauce

Directions:
1. To make the marinade: In a large bowl, combine the olive oil, soy sauce, honey, garlic and Competition Smoked. Add the chicken and mix well. When the chicken is covered completely, allow it to marinate for 2-12 hours.
2. In a large, shallow baking dish, soak the kabob skewers for a minimum of 2 hours and up to 12 hours.
3. Once the chicken has finished marinating and the skewers are finished soaking, drain the water from the skewers and remove the chicken from the marinade.
4. Supply your smoker with wood pellets and follow the start-up procedure. Preheat the grill, with the lid closed, to 350° F.
5. Thread a piece of chicken, followed by a piece of pepper, mushroom, and onion. Repeat until the skewers are full.
6. Grill the kabobs for 5 minutes on one side, then flip and grill for 5 more minutes or until the chicken reaches an internal temperature of 180°F. Remove from the grill and serve.

Hot Turkey Sandwich With Gravy

Servings: 4
Cooking Time: 10 Minutes

Ingredients:
- 8 Slices Bread, Sliced
- 1 Cup Gravy, Prepared
- 2 Cups Leftover Turkey, Shredded

Directions:
1. Supply your smoker with wood pellets and follow the start-up procedure. Preheat the grill, with the lid closed, to 400° F.
2. Place the BBQ Grill Mat on the grates of your preheated grill and lay the shredded turkey evenly across the mat to reheat for about 10 minutes.
3. Prepare or reheat the gravy. You"ll want to have the gravy warmed and ready as soon as the turkey is reheated and the bread is toasted.
4. Hold each slice of bread over the flame broiler to toast to your liking.
5. When all of your ingredients are hot, scoop 1/2 cup of the shredded turkey onto a piece of bread, generously cover with gravy and top with another piece of toasted bread. Serve immediately.

Grilled Parmesan Chicken Wings

Servings: 4
Cooking Time: 25 Minutes

Ingredients:
- 4 Tbsp Butter
- 4 Lbs Chicken Wings, Trimmed And Patted Dry
- 4 Garlic Cloves, Chopped
- 2 Tbsp Olive Oil
- 1/2 Cup Parmesan Cheese, Grated
- 2 Tbsp Parsley, Chopped
- Champion Chicken Seasoning

Directions:
1. Lay chicken wings out on a sheet tray, blot with paper towel, then season with Champion Chicken.
2. Supply your smoker with wood pellets and follow the start-up procedure. Preheat the grill, with the lid open, to 400° F. If using a gas or charcoal grill, set it up for medium-high heat.
3. Transfer wings to grill and cook for 20 to 25 minutes, turning every 5 minutes, until lightly browned. Remove wings from the grill and set on a sheet tray. Place in the smoking cabinet to keep warm while preparing the garlic butter.
4. Melt butter and olive oil in a cast iron skillet, then add garlic and simmer until fragrant. Remove from the grill.
5. Transfer chicken wings to a large bowl and pour garlic butter over the wings. Add cheese and parsley, then toss well to coat. Serve warm with additional sprinkling of parmesan cheese.

Turkey & Bacon Kebabs With Ranch-style Dressing

Servings: 8
Cooking Time: 25 Minutes

Ingredients:
- 1½lb (680g) skinless turkey tenders or boneless, skinless turkey breasts, cut into 1-inch (2.5cm) chunks
- 8 strips of thick-cut bacon
- 12 fresh bay leaves (optional)
- for the dressing
- 1 cup reduced-fat mayo
- 1 cup light sour cream
- ½ cup buttermilk or whole milk, plus more
- 2 tbsp minced fresh parsley
- 2 tbsp minced fresh chives
- 1 tbsp minced fresh dill
- 2 tsp freshly squeezed lemon juice
- 1 tsp Worcestershire sauce
- 1 tsp garlic salt
- 1 tsp onion powder
- ½ tsp coarse salt, plus more
- ½ tsp freshly ground black pepper, plus more

Directions:
1. In a large bowl, make the dressing by whisking together the mayo, sour cream, and buttermilk until smooth. Whisk in the remaining ingredients. Pour half the mixture into a small bowl. Cover and refrigerate.
2. Add the turkey to the mixture remaining in the bowl and toss to coat thoroughly. If the dressing seems too thick (dip-like), add more buttermilk 1 tablespoon at a time. Cover and refrigerate for 2 to 4 hours.
3. Supply your smoker with wood pellets and follow the start-up procedure. Preheat the grill, with the lid closed, to 375° F.
4. Place the bacon on the grate and cook until some of the fat has rendered and the bacon begins to brown, about 15 minutes. Remove the bacon from the grill to cool. Cut the bacon into 1-inch (2.5cm) squares. Set aside.
5. Drain the tenders and discard any excess dressing. Alternate threading the turkey, bacon pieces, and 3 bay leaves on a bamboo skewer. Repeat the threading with 3 more skewers.
6. Place the kebabs on the grate and grill until the turkey is cooked through, about 4 to 5 minutes per side, turning as needed.
7. Transfer the skewers to a platter. Serve with the reserved dressing.

Roasted Prosciutto Stuffed Chicken

Servings: 2
Cooking Time: 35 Minutes

Ingredients:
- 2 Whole boneless, skinless chicken breast
- salt and pepper
- 2 Tablespoon Dijon mustard
- 2 Slices Prosciutto Ham
- 4 Pieces mozzarella cheese
- 1 Large Tomatoes, sliced
- 4 Large basil leaves
- 2 Tablespoon olive oil
- Toothpicks

Directions:
1. Supply your smoker with wood pellets and follow the start-up procedure. Preheat the grill, with the lid closed, to 225° F.
2. While grill heats up, use a sharp knife to fillet each chicken breast in two. Open up each half, by pounding with a meat tenderizer.
3. Season each breast half with salt and pepper to taste. Rub mustard on both sides. Place a slice of proscuitto on the inside of the breast followed by a slice of mozzarella, a slice of tomato and a basil leaf. Drizzle olive oil on top.
4. Fold chicken breast back in half and secure with toothpicks. Brush outside of stuffed breast with olive oil.
5. Place directly on the grill grate. Cook for 6 to 7 minutes per side, or until chicken reaches an internal temperature of 160 degrees F.

Lemon Parmesan Chicken Wings

Servings: 4 -8
Cooking Time: 30 Minutes

Ingredients:
- 2 Tablespoons Unsalted Butter, Melted
- 2 Lbs Chicken Wings, Trimmed And Patted Dry
- 3 Cloves Garlic, Minced
- Juice Of 1 Lemon
- 2 Tablespoons Mustard, Dijon
- ¼ Cup Olive Oil
- ¼ Cup Shredded Parmesan Cheese
- 2 Tablespoons Parsley, Chopped
- 2 Tablespoons Champion Chicken Seasoning

Directions:
1. Supply your smoker with wood pellets and follow the start-up procedure. Preheat the grill, with the lid open, to 350° F. If you are using a charcoal or gas grill, set the temperature to medium high heat.
2. In a large resealable bag, combine the olive oil, minced garlic, lemon zest, lemon juice, Dijon mustard, Champion Chicken Seasoning, and chopped parsley. Seal the resealable bag and give it a good shake to mix the ingredients.
3. Once the chicken has finished marinating, remove the chicken from the marinade and drain. Place the chicken wings on the wing rack.
4. Place the wing rack on the grill and insert a temperature probe into the thickest part of one of the wings. Grill the wings for 5 minutes, then rotate, and grill for another 5-10 minutes, or until the internal temperature of the wings reaches 165°F.
5. Toss the wings in the large bowl with the melted butter and shredded Parmesan until well coated. Serve immediately.

Smoke Roasted Chicken With Herb Butter

Servings: 4
Cooking Time: 60 Minutes

Ingredients:
- 8 Tablespoon butter, room temperature
- 1 Scallions, minced
- 1 Clove garlic, minced
- 2 Tablespoon Fresh Herbs (Thyme, Rosemary, Oregano, Basil, Sage or Parsley, Minced)
- 1 1/2 Tablespoon Chicken Rub
- 1/2 Tablespoon fresh lemon juice
- 1 (4 to 4-1/2 lb) chicken
- Chicken Rub

Directions:
1. In a small bowl, combine butter, scallions, garlic, minced fresh herbs, Traeger Chicken Rub and lemon juice. Blend well with a wooden spoon.

2. Remove any giblets from the cavity of the chicken. Wash the chicken inside and out with cold running water. Dry thoroughly with paper towels.
3. Sprinkle a generous amount of Traeger Chicken Rub into the cavity of the chicken.
4. Gently loosen the skin around the chicken breast and slide in a few tablespoons of the herb butter and cover evenly. Smear the outside of the chicken with the remaining herb butter.
5. Tuck the chicken wings behind the back. Tie the legs together with butcher's twine.
6. Sprinkle the outside of the chicken with more Traeger Chicken Rub and insert sprigs of fresh herbs into the cavity of the chicken if desired.
7. Supply your smoker with wood pellets and follow the start-up procedure. Preheat the grill, with the lid closed, to 400° F.
8. When grill is hot, place chicken directly on the grill grate, breast side up. Cook for 1 to 1-1/4 hours or until the internal temperature registers 165°F. If the chicken is browning too quickly, loosely cover the breast and legs with foil and continue to cook. Grill: 400 °F Probe: 165 °F
9. Remove from the grill and let rest 15 minutes at room temperature before carving. Serve. Enjoy!

Smoked Avocado Turkey Tamale Pie

Servings: 6
Cooking Time: 240 Minutes

Ingredients:
- 1 Avocado, Diced (For Topping)
- 15 Oz Black Beans, Drained (For Filling)
- To Taste, Blackened Sriracha Rub Seasoning
- 2 Tsp Blackened Sriracha Rub Seasoning (For Filling)
- To Taste, Blackened Sriracha Rub Seasoning (For Polenta)
- 2 Tbsp Butter (For Polenta)
- 2 Tbsp Cilantro, Chopped (For Topping)
- 1 Cup Corn Kernels (For Filling)
- 2 Cups Enchilada Sauce (For Filling)
- 1/2 Jalapeño, Minced (For Topping)
- 2 Cups Milk Or Water (For Polenta)
- 1 Cup Polenta, Or Fine Cornmeal (For Polenta)
- 2 Scallions, Sliced (For Topping)
- 2 Cups Smoked Turkey Breast, Shredded (For Filling)
- 2 1/2 Lbs Split Turkey Breast, Bone-In
- 2 Cups Turkey Stock (For Polenta)
- 4 Oz White Cheddar, Shredded (For Polenta)
- 4 Oz White Cheddar, Shredded (For Topping)

Directions:
1. Supply your smoker with wood pellets and follow the start-up procedure. Preheat the grill, with the lid closed, to 225° F. If using a gas or charcoal grill, set it up for low, indirect heat.
2. Season the turkey breast with Blackened Sriracha, then transfer to the grill, on a rack, over indirect heat.
3. Smoke the turkey breast for 2 ½ to 3 hours, until an internal temperature of 160° F. Remove the turkey from the grill, allow to rest for 20 minutes, then shred with 2 forks.
4. While the turkey is resting, prepare the polenta:
5. Place a deep, cast iron skillet on the grill, then increase the temperature to 375° F. Add chicken broth and milk to a skillet and bring to a boil.
6. Whisk in the polenta, then reduce the heat to a simmer, stirring often for 5 minutes. Season with Blackened Sriracha, then stir in cheese and butter. Remove the skillet from the grill and smooth out the polenta in an even layer.
7. In a large glass measuring cup or mixing bowl, combine the turkey, enchilada sauce, black beans, corn and Blackened Sriracha.
8. Spoon the turkey mixture over the polenta, then top with 4 ounces of shredded cheese. Place on the grill, over indirect heat and bake for 20 to 25 minutes, until the filling is bubbling along the edge and the cheese is melted.
9. Remove the skillet from the grill and allow it to rest for 10 minutes. Serve warm, garnished with avocado, scallions, jalapeño, and fresh cilantro.

Spiced Cornish Hens With Cilantro Chutney

Servings: 2
Cooking Time: 60 Minutes

Ingredients:
- 2 Cornish game hens, each about 1 to 1¼lb (450 to 565g), thawed if frozen
- 1 small white onion, peeled and halved
- 4 slices of fresh ginger
- 4 garlic cloves, peeled
- 3 tbsp vegetable oil
- 2 tsp garam masala
- for the brine
- ½ gallon (1.9 liters) distilled water
- ½ cup kosher salt
- for the chutney
- 1 bunch of cilantro, washed and roughly chopped
- 4 scallions, trimmed and roughly chopped
- 2 garlic cloves, peeled and roughly chopped
- 2 small green chili peppers, deseeded and minced
- 1-inch (2.5cm) piece of fresh ginger, peeled and minced
- 1 tbsp dry-roasted peanuts
- 1 tsp coarse salt
- 1 tsp ground cumin
- ½ tsp ground coriander
- 3 tbsp freshly squeezed lemon juice
- ¼ cup extra virgin olive oil

Directions:
1. In a stockpot on the stovetop over medium-high heat, make the brine by bringing the water and salt to a boil. Stir until the salt dissolves. Remove the pot from the stovetop and let the brine cool to room temperature. Cover and refrigerate until cool.
2. Submerge the hens in the brine. If they float, place a resealable bag of ice on top. Cover and refrigerate for 4 hours or as long as 8 hours.
3. Supply your smoker with wood pellets and follow the start-up procedure. Preheat the grill, with the lid closed, to 350° F.
4. In a blender, make the chutney by combining all the ingredients except the olive oil. Blend until the ingredients begin to move, adding 1 tablespoon of water if they need help. When a paste has formed, add the olive oil in a thin stream until the chutney is smooth. If it seems too thick, add a small bit of water. If it's too thin, add a little more oil. Store in a covered container in the refrigerator until ready to use.
5. Remove the hens from the brine. Rinse inside and out under cold running water and pat dry with paper towels. Place half an onion, 2 slices of ginger, and 2 garlic cloves in the cavity of each hen. Tie the legs together with butcher's twine.
6. In a small bowl, combine the vegetable oil and garam masala. Rub the mixture thinly and evenly on the outside of the hens.
7. Place the hens on the grate and roast until they're nicely browned and the internal temperature in the thickest part of a thigh reaches 165°F (74°C), about 1 hour.
8. Transfer the hens to a platter. Serve with the chutney.

Spatchcocked Turkey

Servings: 10-14
Cooking Time: 120 Minutes

Ingredients:
- 1 whole turkey
- 2 tablespoons olive oil
- 1 batch Chicken Rub

Directions:
1. Supply your smoker with wood pellets and follow the start-up procedure. Preheat the grill, with the lid closed, to 350°F.
2. To remove the turkey's backbone, place the turkey on a work surface, on its breast. Using kitchen shears, cut along one side of the turkey's backbone and then the other. Pull out the bone.
3. Once the backbone is removed, turn the turkey breast-side up and flatten it.
4. Coat the turkey with olive oil and season it on both sides with the rub. Using your hands, work the rub into the meat and skin.

5. Place the turkey directly on the grill grate, breast-side up, and cook until its internal temperature reaches 170°F.
6. Remove the turkey from the grill and let it rest for 10 minutes, before carving and serving.

Bbq Chicken Tostada

Servings: 4
Cooking Time: 50 Minutes

Ingredients:
- 4 Whole boneless, skinless chicken thighs
- salt and pepper
- 8 Whole Corn Tostada
- Refried Beans
- lettuce
- green onion, coarsely chopped
- cilantro, chopped
- guacamole

Directions:
1. Supply your smoker with wood pellets and follow the start-up procedure. Preheat the grill, with the lid closed, to 350° F.
2. While grill heats, trim excess fat and skin from chicken thighs.
3. Season with a light layer of salt and pepper.
4. Place chicken thighs on the grill grate and cook for 35 minutes.
5. Check internal temperature; chicken is done when a thermometer inserted reads 175 degrees F. Remove from the grill and let rest for 10 minutes before shredding.
6. Place tostadas on grill while chicken is resting for 5 minutes.
7. Build tostadas starting with refried beans, sliced lettuce, shredded chicken, tomatoes, green onions, cilantro, guacamole. Enjoy!

Delicious Sweet And Sour Chicken Drumsticks

Servings: 4
Cooking Time: 150 Minutes

Ingredients:
- 3 Tbsp Brown Sugar
- 8 Chicken Drumsticks
- Garlic, Minced
- Ginger, Minced
- 2 Tbsp Honey
- 1 Cup Ketchup
- ½ Lemon Lemon, Juice
- 1/2 Lime, Juiced
- 2 Tbsp Rice Wine Vinegar
- ¼ Cup Soy Sauce
- 1 Tbsp Sweet Heat Rub

Directions:
1. In a mixing bowl, combine the ketchup, soy sauce, rice wine vinegar, brown sugar, honey, ginger, garlic, lemon, lime and Sweet Heat Rub. Reserve half of the mixture for dipping sauce and set aside. Use the remaining half and pour into a large resealable plastic bag. Add the drumsticks and seal bag. Refrigerate for at least 4-12 hours. Remove chicken from bag, discarding marinade.
2. Supply your smoker with wood pellets and follow the start-up procedure. Preheat the grill, with the lid open, to 225° F. If you're using a gas or charcoal grill, set it up for low-medium heat. Smoke the chicken over indirect heat with grill lid closed for 2 – 3 hours, turning once or twice, until the chicken reaches 180°F. During the last half hour, feel free to brush more glaze on.
3. Remove from grill, and let stand for 10 minutes. Feel free to add more sauce if desired or use it as a dipping sauce for the drumsticks.

The Grilled Chicken Challenge

Servings: 4
Cooking Time: 60 Minutes

Ingredients:
- 1 (4 lb) whole chicken
- Chicken Rub

Directions:
1. Supply your smoker with wood pellets and follow the start-up procedure. Preheat the grill, with the lid closed, to 375° F.

2. Rinse and pat dry the whole chicken (remove and discard giblets, if any). Lightly season the entire chicken, including the cavity with Traeger Chicken Rub (or similar rub of choice).

3. Place the chicken on the grill grate and cook for about 1 hour and 10 minutes. Remove chicken from grill when internal temperature of breast reaches 160°F. The temperature will continue to rise to 165°F as the chicken rests. Check temperature periodically throughout as cook times will vary based on the weight of the chicken. Grill: 375°F Probe: 160°F

4. Allow bird to rest until internal temperature of breast reaches 165°F, 15 to 20 minutes. Enjoy!

Chicken Egg Rolls With Buffalo Sauce

Servings: 4
Cooking Time: 75 Minutes

Ingredients:
- 1/4 Cup Bleu Cheese, Crumbled
- 1/4 Cup Buffalo Sauce
- 1 Lb Chicken Breasts - Boneless, Skinless
- 4 Oz Cream Cheese, Softened
- 8 Egg Roll Wrappers
- 1/2 Jalapeno Pepper, Minced
- Pinch Sweet Heat Rub
- 1/4 Red Bell Pepper, Chopped
- 4 Scallion, Sliced Thin
- 1/4 Cup Sour Cream
- 2 Cups Vegetable Oil

Directions:
1. Supply your smoker with wood pellets and follow the start-up procedure. Preheat the grill, with the lid open, to 200° F. If using a gas or charcoal grill, set it up for low, indirect heat.

2. Season chicken breasts with   Sweet Heat Rub, then place on the grill. Smoke for 1 hour, then remove from the grill, cool, shred, and set aside.

3. Prepare the filling: In a mixing bowl, use a hand mixer to blend cream cheese, bleu cheese, Buffalo sauce and sour cream.

4. Fold in scallions, jalapeño, red bell pepper, and shredded chicken.

5. Prepare egg rolls: Lay an egg roll wrapper on a flat surface and add 3 tablespoons of filling to the middle.

6. Fold the bottom of the wrapper over the top of the filling, then fold over each side. Brush the top point of the wrapper with warm water, then roll the wrapper tight. Transfer to a tray while filling the remaining wrappers.

7. Increase the temperature of the grill to 425°F, then set a cast iron Dutch oven on the grill. Add vegetable oil and heat for 5 minutes.

8. Place 3 egg rolls in heated oil and fry until golden, 1 to 2 minutes per side.

9. Transfer to a wire rack to cool, then fry the remaining egg rolls, in batches.

10. Cool egg rolls for 2 minutes, then slice in half and serve warm with celery sticks and extra Buffalo sauce for dipping.

Applewood-smoked Whole Turkey

Servings: 6-8
Cooking Time: 300 Minutes

Ingredients:
- 1 (10- to 12-pound) turkey, giblets removed
- Extra-virgin olive oil, for rubbing
- ¼ cup poultry seasoning
- 8 tablespoons (1 stick) unsalted butter, melted
- ½ cup apple juice
- 2 teaspoons dried sage
- 2 teaspoons dried thyme

Directions:
1. Supply your smoker with wood pellets and follow the start-up procedure. Preheat, with the lid closed, to 250°F.

2. Rub the turkey with oil and season with the poultry seasoning inside and out, getting under the skin.

3. In a bowl, combine the melted butter, apple juice, sage, and thyme to use for basting.

4. Put the turkey in a roasting pan, place on the grill, close the lid, and grill for 5 to 6 hours, basting every hour, until the skin is brown and crispy, or until a meat thermometer inserted in the thickest part of the thigh reads 165°F.

5. Let the bird rest for 15 to 20 minutes before carving.

Grilled Hand Pulled Chicken

Servings: 4
Cooking Time: 90 Minutes

Ingredients:
- 2 Tablespoons Apple Cider Vinegar
- 1 Clove Garlic, Minced
- Juice Of Half Of A Lemon
- 1 Cup Mayo
- 1 Tablespoon Olive Oil
- ½ Teaspoon Paprika, Powder
- 2 Tablespoons Sugar
- 1, 3-4 Pound Chicken, Giblets Removed And Patted Dry
- 4 Tablespoons Champion Chicken Seasoning

Directions:
1. Supply your smoker with wood pellets and follow the start-up procedure. Preheat the grill, with the lid open, to 350° F.
2. In a large bowl, mix all the ingredients for the sauce together. Divide the sauce between two bowls and set aside.
3. On a clean, flat surface, lay your chicken breast side down. Using the kitchen shears, remove the spine and discard. Open the chicken up and flip the chicken over so that it lays breast side up. Press the breastbone down with the heel of your hand to flatten the chicken.
4. Generously rub the chicken with the olive oil and Champion Chicken. Place on the grill, skin-side up, on the grates. Grill for 1 ½ hours, basting with half the reserved sauce every 20 minutes, until the internal temperature reaches 175°F. Remove the chicken from the grill and cover loosely for 10 minutes.
5. Shred the chicken with forks and discard the skin and bones. Serve the chicken with the remaining white BBQ sauce.

Chicken Cordon Bleu Rollups

Servings: 8
Cooking Time: 30 Minutes

Ingredients:
- 4 boneless, skinless chicken breasts, each about 6 to 8oz (170 to 225g)
- garlic salt
- freshly ground black pepper
- 8 thin slices of Swiss cheese
- 8 thin slices of deli ham or prosciutto
- 4 tbsp unsalted butter, melted
- minced fresh parsley or chives

Directions:
1. Supply your smoker with wood pellets and follow the start-up procedure. Preheat the grill, with the lid closed, to 400° F.
2. Place each chicken breast between two sheets of plastic wrap and pound with a meat mallet or a rolling pin until each breast is ¼ inch (.5cm) thick. Place the breasts smooth side down on a workspace and lightly season with garlic salt and pepper. Top each breast with 2 slices of cheese and 2 slices of ham. Roll up the breasts and secure them with toothpicks that have been coated with vegetable oil. Brush the outside of the breasts with butter and lightly season with garlic salt and pepper.
3. Place the chicken rollups on the grate at an angle to the bars. Smoke for 25 to 30 minutes.
4. Transfer the rollups to a platter and let rest for 3 minutes. Remove the toothpicks. Scatter parsley over the top before serving.

Asian Bbq Chicken

Servings: 4
Cooking Time: 60 Minutes

Ingredients:
- 1 Whole whole chicken
- Asian BBQ Rub
- 1 Whole ginger ale

Directions:
1. Rinse chicken in cold water and pat dry with paper towels. Cover the chicken all over with Traeger Asian BBQ rub; make sure to drop some in the inside too. Place in large bag or bowl and cover and refrigerate for 12 to 24 hours.
2. Supply your smoker with wood pellets and follow the start-up procedure. Preheat the grill, with the lid closed, to 375° F.

3. Open your can of ginger ale and take a few big gulps. Set the can of soda on a stable surface. Take the chicken out of the fridge and place the bird over top of the soda can. The base of the can and the two legs of the chicken should form a sort of tripod to hold the chicken upright.
4. Stand the chicken in the center of your hot grate and cook the chicken till the skin is golden brown and the internal temperature is about 165°F on a instant-read thermometer, approximately 40 minutes to 1 hour.
5. De-throne chicken. Enjoy!

Cornish Game Hen

Servings: 4
Cooking Time: 180 Minutes

Ingredients:
- 4 Cornish game hens
- Extra-virgin olive oil, for rubbing
- 2 teaspoons salt
- 1 teaspoon freshly ground black pepper
- 1 teaspoon celery seeds

Directions:
1. Supply your smoker with wood pellets and follow the start-up procedure. Preheat, with the lid closed, to 275°F.
2. Rub the game hens over and under the skin with olive oil and season all over with the salt, pepper, and celery seeds.
3. Place the birds directly on the grill grate, close the lid, and smoke for 2 to 3 hours, or until a meat thermometer inserted in each bird reads 170°F.
4. Serve the Cornish game hens hot.

Smoked Whiskey Peach Pulled Chicken

Servings: 6-8
Cooking Time: 45 Minutes

Ingredients:
- 3-4 pound whole chicken
- 1 cup peach juice
- 1/4 cup whiskey
- 1/4 cup melted butter
- 1/4 cup Hey Grill Hey's Sweet BBQ Rub
- 1/2 cup Whiskey Peach BBQ sauce

Directions:
1. Supply your smoker with wood pellets and follow the start-up procedure. Preheat the grill, with the lid closed, to 225°F, using a mild fruit wood like a peach.
2. Remove any giblets or neck from inside of the chicken and pat dry.
3. In a jar, combine the peach juice, whiskey, and melted butter. Inject this mixture into your chicken in several spots. Be sure to inject in at least 3 different places in each breast, 2 places in the thighs, and 1 time in each leg.
4. Season your chicken generously on all sides with the Sweet BBQ Rub. Place in the middle of your grill and close the lid. Smoke for 45 minutes per pound of chicken.
5. Brush liberally with the whiskey peach BBQ sauce once the internal temperature of your meat reaches 150 degrees.
6. Check the temperature in both the thighs and the breasts and when your internal temperature reads consistently 160 degrees F, remove the chicken to a rimmed serving platter or baking sheet and cover tightly with foil to allow the chicken to come up to 165 degrees F and rest for 20 minutes.
7. Shred the chicken and set it onto your serving platter. Discard the carcass or save for homemade stock. Drizzle your smoked pulled chicken with more of the Whiskey Peach Barbecue Sauce and serve on toasted buns.

Bacon Weaved Stuffed Turkey Breast

Servings: 8
Cooking Time: 60 Minutes

Ingredients:
- 1/2 Cup celery, diced
- 14 Ounce Stuffing Mix
- 2 Tablespoon chopped sage
- 4 Tablespoon Chicken Rub
- 1/2 Cup dried sweetened cranberries
- 2 Cup apple cider
- 20 Strips thick-cut bacon

Directions:

1. Prepare the stuffing: Add all stuffing ingredients into a large bowl and toss to mix together.
2. Create a bacon weave and lay it out in a 5x5 pattern on cutting board.
3. Using a long, thin knife, butterfly each of the turkey breasts. Stuff each breast with a generous amount of stuffing and close.
4. Place turkey breast on prepared bacon weave, carefully wrap turkey, and secure with tooth picks. Repeat for the second breast.
5. Supply your smoker with wood pellets and follow the start-up procedure. Preheat the grill, with the lid closed, to 375° F.
6. Place the breasts seam side down on a rimmed baking sheet. Transfer directly to grill.
7. Place the bacon wrapped turkey breasts directly to the Traeger and cook for approximately 45 mins to 1 hour or until an instant read thermometer inserted into the center of the stuffing reaches 165 degrees F. Grill: 375 °F Probe: 165 °F
8. If the bacon gets too dark, cover with foil. Slice and enjoy!

Cornish Game Hens

Servings: 4
Cooking Time: 60 Minutes

Ingredients:
- 4 Cornish game hens
- 4 Tablespoon butter, melted
- Chicken Rub
- 4 Sprig rosemary or sage, plus more for garnish

Directions:
1. Rinse the Cornish game hens under cold running water, inside and out. (Game hens do not usually come with giblets, but check the cavity for them before rinsing. If you find giblets, freeze them for chicken stock, if desired.)
2. Dry thoroughly with paper towels. Tuck the wings behind the backs and tie the legs together with butcher's string.
3. Rub the outside of each hen with the melted butter. Season with Traeger Chicken Rub. Slip a sprig of rosemary into the main cavity of each hen.
4. Supply your smoker with wood pellets and follow the start-up procedure. Preheat the grill, with the lid closed, to 375° F.
5. Roast the hens for 50 to 60 minutes, or until the juices run clear and the internal temperature of the thigh, when read on an instant-read meat thermometer, is 165°F. Grill: 375 °F Probe: 165 °F
6. Transfer the hens to a platter or plates and let rest for 5 minutes.
7. Garnish with a sprig of rosemary before serving. Enjoy!

Grilled Honey Chicken Kabobs

Servings: 4
Cooking Time: 14 Minutes

Ingredients:
- 1 pound boneless skinless chicken breasts (cut into 1 inch pieces)
- 1/4 cup olive oil
- 1/3 cup soy sauce
- 1/4 cup honey
- 1 teaspoon minced garlic
- salt and pepper to taste
- 1 red bell pepper (cut into 1 inch pieces)
- 1 yellow bell pepper (cut into 1 inch pieces)
- 2 small zucchini (cut into 1 inch slices)
- 1 red onion (cut into 1 inch pieces)
- 1 tablespoon chopped parsley

Directions:
1. In a large bowl combine the olive oil, soy sauce, honey, garlic and salt and pepper, and whisk.
2. Add the chicken, bell peppers, zucchini and red onion to the bowl, tossing to thoroughly coat.
3. Cover and refrigerate for 1 to 8 hours.
4. Soak wooden skewers in cold water for at least 30 minutes. Supply your smoker with wood pellets and follow the start-up procedure. Preheat the grill, with the lid closed, to high heat.
5. Thread the chicken and vegetables onto the skewers.
6. Cook for 5-7 minutes on each side or until chicken is cooked through.
7. To serve, sprinkle with parsley. Enjoy!

Fried Chicken Sliders

Servings: 8
Cooking Time: 30 Minutes

Ingredients:
- 8 Slider Buns
- ½ Cup Buttermilk
- 4 Horizontally Cut Chicken Breasts
- 2 Cups Flour, All-Purpose
- 1 Tablespoon Hot Sauce
- ¼ Cup Mayonnaise
- 2 Quarts Cooking Canola Or Soybean Oil
- ½ Cup Spicy Bread And Butter Pickle Slices
- ½ Tablespoon Champion Chicken Seasoning

Directions:
1. Supply your smoker with wood pellets and follow the start-up procedure. Preheat the grill, with the lid open, to 350° F. If you're using a gas or charcoal grill, set it up for medium heat.
2. Place a deep cast iron pan on the grill and fill it with about 3 inches of cooking oil. Place a temperature probe into the oil.
3. While the oil heats, combine the buttermilk, hot sauce and Champion Chicken seasoning in a resealable plastic bag. Seal and shake to mix, then place the chicken in the bag and turn to coat.
4. Place the flour on a plate and dip the chicken in the flour to coat. Place the chicken on a wire rack set on a baking sheet and allow the coated chicken to set for 10 minutes, then dip again in the flour.
5. Once the oil in the cast iron pan reaches 350°F, place a temperature probe in a piece of chicken and fry the chicken, 2-3 pieces at a time. The oil temperature in the pan will drop by 25-30 degrees, so make sure not to put more than 3 pieces of chicken in the pan or your chicken will be greasy.
6. Fry the chicken until golden brown, crispy, and the internal temperature of the chicken is 170°F. Remove the chicken and place on a plate lined with paper towels. Allow the chicken to drain and rest for 5 minutes. Fry the remaining chicken pieces, reinserting the temperature probe.
7. Once the chicken is all fried, place the chicken on the slider buns, top with spicy bread and butter pickles, and a swoop of mayo, serve immediately.

Roasted Honey Bourbon Glazed Turkey

Servings: 8
Cooking Time: 240 Minutes

Ingredients:
- 1 Whole (18-20 lb) turkey
- 1/4 Cup Fin & Feather Rub
- 1/2 Cup bourbon
- 1/2 Cup honey
- 1/4 Cup brown sugar
- 3 Tablespoon apple cider vinegar
- 1 Tablespoon Dijon mustard
- salt and pepper

Directions:
1. Supply your smoker with wood pellets and follow the start-up procedure. Preheat the grill, with the lid closed, to 375° F. Truss the turkey legs together. Season the exterior of the bird and the cavity with Traeger Fin and Feather Rub.
2. Place the turkey directly on the grill grate and cook for 20-30 minutes at 375°F or until the skin begins to brown. Grill: 375 °F
3. After 30 minutes, reduce the temperature to 325°F and continue to cook until internal temperature registers 165°F when an instant read thermometer is inserted into the thickest part of the breast, about 3-4 hours. Grill: 325 °F Probe: 165 °F
4. For the Whiskey Glaze: Combine all ingredients in a small saucepan and bring to a boil. Reduce the temperature and let simmer 15-20 minutes or until thick enough to coat the back of a spoon. Remove from heat and set aside.
5. During the last ten minutes of cooking, brush the glaze on the turkey while on the grill and cook until the glaze is set, about 10 minutes. Remove from grill and let rest 10-15 minutes before carving. Enjoy! *Cook times will vary depending on set and ambient temperatures.

Roasted Stuffed Turkey Breast

Servings: 6
Cooking Time: 40 Minutes

Ingredients:

- 1 (4-5 lb) boneless turkey breast
- 5 Slices thick-cut bacon, chopped
- 3/4 Cup assorted mushrooms
- 1 Bunch scallions, chopped
- 1/8 Cup white wine
- 3 Tablespoon panko breadcrumbs
- salt
- black pepper

Directions:

1. Supply your smoker with wood pellets and follow the start-up procedure. Preheat the grill, with the lid closed, to 375° F.
2. Slice the turkey breast horizontally, making sure not to slice all the way through. Lay breast open flat.
3. Cook bacon in a skillet over medium heat until crispy. Remove bacon and set aside. Sauté mushrooms in the bacon grease until browned. Add scallions and cook for an additional two minutes. Add white wine and cook down until no wine remains. Stir in breadcrumbs and bacon, adding salt and pepper to taste.
4. Transfer filling to fridge to cool for 15 to 20 minutes. Once chilled, spread the filling onto the turkey breast, pressing lightly to make sure it adheres. Roll the turkey breast tightly and tie with butcher's twine at about 1 inch intervals. Tuck the ends of the turkey breast under and tie with twine lengthwise.
5. Season the outside of the turkey breast with salt and pepper. Place in grill for 40 minutes. Check the internal temperature, desired temperature is 165°F. Once the finished temperature is reached, remove turkey from the grill and let rest for 10 minutes. Slice and serve. Enjoy!
Grill: 375 °F Probe: 165 °F

County Fair Turkey Legs

Servings: 4
Cooking Time: 90 Minutes

Ingredients:

- 4 turkey legs, each about 1lb (450g)
- for the brine
- ½ gallon (1.9 liters) distilled water
- ½ cup kosher salt
- ¼ cup light brown sugar or low-carb substitute
- 2½ tsp pink curing salt #1
- 1 tsp liquid smoke (optional)

Directions:

1. In a stockpot on the stovetop over medium-high heat, make the brine by combining the ingredients. Bring the mixture to a boil. Stir until the salts and sugar dissolve. Remove the pot from the stovetop and let the brine cool to room temperature. Cover and refrigerate until cool.
2. Submerge the turkey legs in the brine. If they float, place a resealable bag of ice on top. Refrigerate for 24 hours, turning from time to time so the legs cure evenly.
3. Supply your smoker with wood pellets and follow the start-up procedure. Preheat the grill, with the lid closed, to 325° F.
4. Remove the turkey legs from the brine and discard the liquid. Rinse the legs under cold running water and pat dry with paper towels.
5. Place the turkey legs on the grate and grill for 45 minutes. Turn and continue to cook until the turkey skin is nicely browned and the internal temperature in a leg reaches 170 to 175°F (77 to 79°C), about 45 minutes. (Turkey legs have a lot of connective tissue and they seem to turn out better when cooked to a slightly higher temperature.)
6. Remove the legs from the grill and serve warm or cold.

Texas Style Black Pepper Turkey

Servings: 6
Cooking Time: 240 Minutes

Ingredients:

- 1/2 Cup Coarse Black Pepper
- 1Lb Butter
- 1/2 Cup Salt, Kosher
- 1 Brined Turkey

Directions:

1. Supply your smoker with wood pellets and follow the start-up procedure. Preheat the grill, with the lid closed, to 300° F.
2. Liberally season Turkey with equal parts kosher salt and coarse black pepper.
3. Cook on grill until Internal temp reaches approximately 145°F or the skin has darkened to your liking.
4. Place turkey in a roasting pan topped with a pound of chopped butter and cover.
5. Return to the grill until internal temp of the thigh and breast reaches 165°F
6. Let rest for 30 minutes, carve and serve.

Carrot Celery Chicken Drumsticks

Servings: 4
Cooking Time: 30 Minutes

Ingredients:
- Buffalo Style Dry Rub
- Carrot, Stick
- Celery, Stick
- 12 Chicken, Drumsticks

Directions:
1. Supply your smoker with wood pellets and follow the start-up procedure. Preheat the grill, with the lid closed, to 350° F.
2. Generously sprinkle the Buffalo Wing Rub all over the drumsticks. Hang each drumstick by the bone on the Wing Rack. Place in the for about 30 minutes.
3. Serve hot with celery and carrot sticks. Enjoy!

Savory Cajun Bbq Chicken

Servings: 4
Cooking Time: 25 Minutes

Ingredients:
- ½ Cup Barbecue Sauce
- ¼ Cup Beer, Any Brand
- 1 Tablespoon Butter
- 1 Pound Boneless, Skinless Chicken Breasts
- 2 Cloves Garlic Clove, Minced
- ¼ Teaspoon Ground Thyme
- 1 Teaspoon Hot Sauce
- Juice Of 1 Lime
- 1 Tablespoon Olive Oil
- ½ Teaspoon Oregano
- 2 Tablespoons Sweet Heat Rub
- 1 Tablespoon Worcestershire Sauce

Directions:
1. In a small mixing bowl, mix together the Sweet Heat Rub, oregano, and ground thyme.
2. Rub the chicken breasts all over with olive oil, making sure to completely coat the meat. Generously season the chicken breasts on all sides with the Sweet Heat mixture.
3. Supply your smoker with wood pellets and follow the start-up procedure. Preheat the grill, with the lid closed, to 350° F. If you're using a gas or charcoal grill, set it up for medium heat. Insert a temperature probe into the thickest part of one of the chicken breasts and place the meat on the grill. Grill the meat on one side for 10-12 minutes, then flip and grill for another 5-7 minutes, or until the chicken breasts are golden brown and juicy and reaches an internal temperature of 165°F.
4. Remove the chicken from the grill and allow to rest for 10 minutes.
5. While the chicken rests, make the sauce. Combine the butter, barbecue sauce, beer, Worcestershire sauce, lime juice, and minced garlic in a heat proof saucepan and place on the grill. Bring the sauce to a boil. Once it boils, remove it from the heat, whisk it and serve with the chicken.

Whole Smoked Honey Chicken

Servings: 4
Cooking Time: 40 Minutes

Ingredients:
- 1 Tablespoon Honey
- 1 ½ Lemon
- 4 Tablespoons Champion Chicken Seasoning
- 4 Tablespoons Unsalted Butter
- 1, 4 Pound Chicken, Giblets Removed And Patted Dry

Directions:

1. Supply your smoker with wood pellets and follow the start-up procedure. Preheat the grill, with the lid open, to 225° F.
2. In a small saucepan, melt together the butter and honey over low heat. Squeeze ½ lemon into the honey mixture and remove from the heat.
3. Smoke the chicken, skin side down until the chicken is lightly browned and the skin releases from the grate without ripping, about 6-8 minutes.
4. Turn the chicken over and baste with the honey butter mixture.
5. Continue to smoke the chicken, basting every 45 minutes, until the thickest part of the chicken reaches 160°F.

Grilled Honey Garlic Wings

Servings: 4
Cooking Time: 60 Minutes

Ingredients:
- 2 1/2 Pound chicken wings
- Pork & Poultry Rub
- 4 Tablespoon butter
- 3 Clove garlic, minced
- 1/4 Cup honey
- 1/2 Cup hot sauce
- 1 1/2 Cup blue cheese or ranch dressing

Directions:
1. Start by segmenting the wings into three pieces, cutting through the joints. Discard the wing tips or save them to make a stock.
2. Lay out the remaining pieces on a rimmed baking sheet lined with nonstick foil or parchment paper. Season well with Traeger Pork & Poultry Rub.
3. Supply your smoker with wood pellets and follow the start-up procedure. Preheat the grill, with the lid closed, to 350° F.
4. Place the baking sheet with wings directly on the grill grate and cook for 45 to 50 minutes or until they are no longer pink at the bone. Grill: 350 °F
5. To make the sauce: Melt butter in a small saucepan. Add the garlic and sauté for 2 to 3 minutes. Add in the honey and hot sauce and cook for a few minutes until completely combined. Keep sauce warm while the wings are cooking.
6. After 45 minutes, pour the spicy honey-garlic sauce over the wings, turning with tongs to coat.
7. Place wings back on the grill and cook for an additional 10 to 15 minutes to set the sauce. Grill: 350 °F
8. Serve with ranch or blue cheese dressing. Enjoy!

Dry Brine Traeger Turkey

Servings: 6
Cooking Time: 360 Minutes

Ingredients:
- 1 farm fresh turkey, any size
- 1 Teaspoon kosher salt per pound of turkey
- fresh thyme
- fresh rosemary
- fresh sage
- fresh parsley

Directions:
1. Make sure to plan ahead, this recipe requires multiple days of brine time.
2. Combine desired amounts of thyme, rosemary, sage and/or parsley with kosher salt. Rub kosher salt and spice mixture over entire surface of the turkey, including the cavity.
3. Place turkey in a bag or plastic wrap and seal tight. Place turkey in the fridge for 2 days. On day 3, take the turkey out of the bag or unwrap plastic wrap. Place the turkey back in the fridge, uncovered for 24 hours.
4. Supply your smoker with wood pellets and follow the start-up procedure. Preheat the grill, with the lid closed, to 180° F.
5. Place the turkey on grill, breast up. Smoke the turkey for 3 to 4 hours. Grill: 180 °F
6. After 3 to 4 hours, increase the grill temperature to 325°F and continue to cook turkey until it reaches an internal temperature of 165°F. Enjoy!

Sweet Cajun Wings

Servings: 4
Cooking Time: 30 Minutes

Ingredients:
- 2 Pound chicken wings
- Pork & Poultry Rub
- Cajun Shake

Directions:
1. Coat wings in Traeger Sweet rub and Traeger Cajun shake.
2. Supply your smoker with wood pellets and follow the start-up procedure. Preheat the grill, with the lid closed, to 350° F.
3. Cook for 30 minutes or until skin is brown and center is juicy and an instant-read thermometer reads at least 165°F. Serve, enjoy! Grill: 350 °F Probe: 165 °F

Smoked Whole Chicken

Servings: 6-8
Cooking Time: 240 Minutes

Ingredients:
- 1 whole chicken
- 2 cups Tea Injectable (using Not-Just-for-Pork Rub)
- 2 tablespoons olive oil
- 1 batch Chicken Rub
- 2 tablespoons butter, melted

Directions:
1. Supply your smoker with wood pellets and follow the start-up procedure. Preheat the grill, with the lid closed, to 180°F.
2. Inject the chicken throughout with the tea injectable.
3. Coat the chicken all over with olive oil and season it with the rub. Using your hands, work the rub into the meat.
4. Place the chicken directly on the grill grate and smoke for 3 hours.
5. Baste the chicken with the butter and increase the grill's temperature to 375°F. Continue to cook the chicken until its internal temperature reaches 170°F.
6. Remove the chicken from the grill and let it rest for 10 minutes, before carving and serving.

Smoked Maple Syrup Thanksgiving Turkey

Servings: 8
Cooking Time: 375 Minutes

Ingredients:
- 1 Cup Butter, Room Temp
- 1/2 Cup Maple Syrup
- 2 Tablespoons Champion Chicken Seasoning
- 1, (Pre-Brined) Turkey, Whole

Directions:
1. Supply your smoker with wood pellets and follow the start-up procedure. Preheat the grill, with the lid closed, to 250° F.
2. Combine the melted butter and maple syrup in a bowl. With the Marinade Injector, fill with the butter and syrup mixture and pierce the meat with the needle while pushing on the plunger, injecting the flavor. You want to inject the marinade into the thickest part of the breast, thigh, and wings.
3. Next, combine the room temperature butter and Champion Chicken seasoning and spread all over the turkey, making sure that you get it under the skin as well.
4. Place the turkey in an aluminum pan to catch all the drippings (this makes incredible gravy) and place on the grill.
5. When the breast and thigh meat of the turkey reaches 165°F to 170°F, remove from grill and let rest 15 minutes before carving. Happy Thanksgiving!

Bbq Chicken Thighs

Servings: 4
Cooking Time: 35 Minutes

Ingredients:
- 6 bone-in, skin-on chicken thighs
- salt and ground black pepper
- Big Game Rub

Directions:
1. Supply your smoker with wood pellets and follow the start-up procedure. Preheat the grill, with the lid closed, to 350° F.

2. While grill is heating, trim excess fat and skin from chicken thighs. Season with a light layer of salt and pepper then a layer of Traeger Big Game Rub.

3. Place chicken thighs on the grill grate and cook for 35 minutes. Check internal temperature, chicken is done at 165°F, but there is enough fat that they will stay moist at an internal temperature of 180°F and the texture is better. Grill: 350 °F Probe: 165 °F

4. Remove from the grill and let rest for 5 minutes before serving. Enjoy!

Savory Grilled Chicken Burrito Bowls

Servings: 4
Cooking Time: 20 Minutes

Ingredients:
- 1 Avocado
- 1 Can Black Beans, Rinsed And Drained
- 1 ½ Pounds Boneless Skinless Chicken Strips
- 1 Tablespoon Cilantro, Chopped
- 1 Can Corn Kernels, Drained
- Juice From 1 Lime
- ½ Lime Lime Juice
- 1 ½ Cups Long Grain White Rice
- 2 Tablespoons Olive Oil
- 2 Tablespoons Sweet Heat Rub
- ¼ Cup Salsa
- 1 Teaspoon Salt
- ½ Cup Shredded Mexican Blend Cheese
- ¼ Cup Sour Cream

Directions:
1. Supply your smoker with wood pellets and follow the start-up procedure. Preheat the grill, with the lid open, to 350° F. If using a gas or charcoal grill, set it up for medium heat.

2. Place the rice in a fine mesh sieve and rinse under cold water for 2-5 minutes, or until the water runs clear. Add the rice to a pot with 2 cups of water and 1 teaspoon of salt and bring to a boil on the stove top. Once the rice boils, drop the temperature to a simmer, place the pot lid on top securely, and let the rice cook for 20-25 minutes.

3. Once the time is up, remove the rice from the heat, and allow it to steam with the lid on for a further 10 minutes. Remove the lid from the rice, add the lime juice and cilantro, and fluff the rice with a fork. Set aside.

4. Grill the chicken for 5-7 minutes, or until the chicken reaches an internal temperature of 165°F and is golden and charred in some spots. Remove the chicken from the grill and allow it to rest for 5 minutes before slicing into bite sized pieces.

5. To assemble the burrito bowls: place a large scoop of cilantro lime rice into a bowl. Top with slices of grilled chicken, a scoop of black beans, a scoop of corn, salsa, cheese, sour cream, and avocado. Serve immediately.

Bacon Wrapped Turkey Legs

Servings: 8
Cooking Time: 180 Minutes

Ingredients:
- 1 Gallon water
- 1/4 Cup Rub
- 3 Cup Morton Tender Quick Home Meat Cure
- 1/2 Cup brown sugar
- 6 Whole black peppercorns
- 2 Whole bay leaves
- 8 (1-1/2 lb each) turkey legs
- 8 Slices bacon

Directions:
1. Plan ahead, these turkey legs brine overnight. In a large stockpot, combine one gallon of water, Traeger Rub, curing salt, brown sugar, peppercorns and bay leaves.

2. Bring to a boil over high heat to dissolve the salt and sugar granules. Take off of the heat and add in 1/2 gallon of water and ice. Make sure the brine is at least to room temperature, if not colder. (You may need to refrigerate the brine for an hour or so.)

3. Add the turkey legs making sure they are completely submerged in the brine.

4. After 24 hours, drain the turkey legs and discard the brine. Rinse the brine off the legs with cold water, then dry thoroughly with paper towels.

5. Supply your smoker with wood pellets and follow the start-up procedure. Preheat the grill, with the lid closed, to 250° F.
6. Lay the turkey legs directly on the grill grate.
7. After 2-1/2 hours, wrap a piece of bacon around each leg and finish cooking them for the last 30 to 40 minutes. Grill: 250 °F
8. The total cooking time for the legs will be 3 hours, or until the internal temperature reaches 165°F on an instant-read meat thermometer. Serve and enjoy! Grill: 250 °F Probe: 165 °F

Bbq Chicken Legs

Servings: 6
Cooking Time: 60 Minutes

Ingredients:
- 8 chicken drumsticks
- 2 Tablespoon Chicken Rub
- 1 Cup Apricot BBQ Sauce
- 1 Cup 'Que BBQ Sauce
- 1 Cup apple jelly, melted

Directions:
1. Pat drumsticks dry with a paper towel and season generously Traeger Chicken Rub.
2. Supply your smoker with wood pellets and follow the start-up procedure. Preheat the grill, with the lid closed, to 180° F.
3. Arrange the chicken legs on the grill grate and smoke for 30 minutes. Grill: 180 °F
4. Increase the grill temperature to 350 degrees F and cook for an additional 30 minutes. Grill: 350 °F
5. While the drumsticks are cooking, combine the two BBQ sauces and the jelly in a small sauce pan. Bring to a simmer over medium heat then set aside until ready to use.
6. Brush the BBQ sauce on the chicken legs. Cook for an additional 10 minutes, or until an instant-read meat thermometer inserted into the thickest part of the leg (but not touching the bone) reaches 165 degrees F. Enjoy! Grill: 350 °F Probe: 165 °F

Bacon-wrapped Chicken Breasts

Servings: 4 - 6
Cooking Time: 270 Minutes

Ingredients:
- 5 Oz Frozen Spinach, Thawed, Strained
- 8 Bacon Slices
- 1 Tbsp Butter
- 4 Chicken Breasts, Boneless, Skinless, Butterflied
- 2 Garlic Clove, Minced
- 1 Cup Italian Cheese Blend, Shredded
- 8 Oz Mushrooms, Sliced Thin
- 1 Tbsp Olive Oil
- 1 Tbsp Hickory Bacon Rub
- 1 Yellow Onion, Chopped

Directions:
1. Supply your smoker with wood pellets and follow the start-up procedure. Preheat the grill, with the lid open, to 375° F. If using a gas or charcoal grill, set heat to medium heat. For all other grills, preheat cast iron skillet on grill grates.
2. Heat olive oil and butter on griddle, then add mushrooms and cook for about 3 minutes, stirring frequently. Add chopped onion and garlic and cook for 2 minutes. Add spinach and sauté another minute, then transfer vegetables to a heat-safe bowl to cool slightly.
3. Season the butterflied chicken breasts with Hickory Bacon, coating both sides. Sprinkle half of cheese over each butterflied chicken breast, followed by the sautéed vegetables, and the remaining half of the cheese.
4. On a metal sheet tray, lay out two bacon slices. Gently fold chicken breast halves together and place on top of bacon slices, then wrap tightly with bacon. To secure, tuck ends of bacon underneath, or insert a toothpick to hold it together. Repeat with remaining breasts.
5. Arrange the chicken breasts, bacon seam down, directly on the grill grate and grill, turning once or twice, until the bacon is crisp and golden brown, about 25 to 30 minutes, or until internal temperature reaches 165°F.
6. Remove from grill, allow to rest for 5 minutes, remove any toothpicks, then serve hot.

Nashville Spiced Smoked Chicken

Servings: 6
Cooking Time: 40 Minutes

Ingredients:
- 6 drumsticks
- 1 quart Butter Milk
- 1 tbsp Louisiana Hot Sauce
- 1 tbsp Ground Cumin
- 1/2 tbsp Chili powder
- 1 tbsp Onion Powder
- 1 tbsp Garlic Powder
- 1/2 tbsp White Pepper
- 1 tbsp Red Cayenne Pepper
- 1 tbsp Black Pepper
- 2 tbsp Brown Sugar

Directions:
1. Soak wings overnight in marinade.
2. Remove chicken from marinade. Dry off chicken and wash off buttermilk.
3. Drizzle chicken with olive oil.
4. Apply dry rub to drumsticks by rubbing thoroughly.
5. Let drumsticks rest in dry rub for at least 30 minutes.
6. Supply your smoker with wood pellets and follow the start-up procedure. Preheat the grill, with the lid closed, to 325° F, using Apple Wood Pellets.
7. Cook chicken on 325 degrees for 30-40 minutes or until internal temperature reach 160 degrees F.
8. Let chicken rest for 10 minutes before serving.

Grilled Chicken Wings

Servings: 6
Cooking Time: 50 Minutes

Ingredients:
- 4 Lbs Chicken Wings, Whole
- 1 Cup Cornmeal
- 2 Eggs
- 1 Cup Flour
- 2 Tbsp Champion Chicken Rub
- 1 Cup Milk

Directions:

1. Supply your smoker with wood pellets and follow the start-up procedure. Preheat the grill, with the lid open, to 300° F. If using a gas or charcoal grill, set it up for medium-low heat.
2. Place chicken wings on a sheet tray, then cut off the tip of each wing with a knife, or scissors. Pat dry with a paper towel.
3. In a mixing bowl, whisk together flour, cornmeal, and Champion Chicken. Set aside.
4. In another mixing bowl, whisk together milk and eggs. Set aside.
5. Form "breading" station: wings, egg wash, seasoned flour, sheet tray. Dunk each wing in egg wash, then coat in seasoned flour. Set aside on a sheet tray, while coating the remaining wings.
6. Place wings directly on the grill rack. Flip/rotate wings every 10 minutes for 45-55 minutes, until golden and "fried crisp."
7. Remove from the grill, rest for 10 minutes, then serve warm.

Beer Chicken

Servings: 4
Cooking Time: 75 Minutes

Ingredients:
- 1 Beer, Can
- 1 Chicken, Whole
- Lemon Pepper Garlic Seasoning

Directions:
1. Supply your smoker with wood pellets and follow the start-up procedure. Preheat the grill, with the lid open, to 400° F.
2. Season the chicken all over with spices. Open the can of your favorite pop/beer and place the opening of the chicken over the can. Make sure that the chicken can stand upright without falling over. Place on your Grill and barbecue until the internal temperature reaching 165 degrees F (about an hour).
3. Remove from grill, slice and serve hot.

Tandoori Chicken Leg Quarters

Servings: 4
Cooking Time: 40 Minutes

Ingredients:
- 4 skinless chicken leg quarters, about 2½lb (1.2kg) total
- juice of 2 lemons
- ¼ cup cold distilled water
- 1½ tsp coarse salt
- ½ tsp ground turmeric
- 3 tbsp vegetable oil, plus more
- 3 garlic cloves, peeled and minced
- 1½-inch (3.75cm) piece of fresh ginger, peeled and minced
- 2 tsp sweet paprika
- 1 tsp chili powder, preferably Kashmiri
- 1 tsp ground coriander
- 1 tsp ground cumin
- ½ tsp ground cayenne
- ¼ tsp ground nutmeg
- ½ cup plain Greek yogurt
- 4 tbsp unsalted butter, melted
- for serving
- 1 large red onion, peeled and thinly sliced crosswise
- ½ cup cilantro leaves
- lemon wedges

Directions:

1. Use a sharp, thin-bladed knife to cut several deep slashes in the fleshy side of each leg quarter to increase the surface area exposed to the marinade and to help the chicken cook faster. Place the chicken legs in a resealable plastic bag.
2. In a small bowl, combine the lemon juice, water, salt, and turmeric. Stir until the salt dissolves. Pour the mixture over the chicken legs and massage the bag to thoroughly coat the chicken, forcing the liquid into the slashes. Refrigerate for 15 minutes.
3. In a medium bowl, combine the vegetable oil, garlic, ginger, paprika, chili powder, coriander, cumin, cayenne, and nutmeg. Whisk in the yogurt. Add this mixture to the plastic bag and again massage the bag to thoroughly coat the chicken legs. Refrigerate for 4 to 8 hours.
4. Supply your smoker with wood pellets and follow the start-up procedure. Preheat the grill, with the lid closed, to 400° F.
5. Remove the chicken from the plastic bag and discard the marinade. Place the leg quarters fleshy side down on the grate and grill until the chicken is nicely browned and the temperature in the thickest part of the thigh reaches 170°F (77°C), about 35 to 40 minutes, turning once or twice.
6. Remove the chicken leg quarters from the grill and let rest for 2 minutes. Brush on both sides with butter. Place the legs on a platter. Scatter the red onion, cilantro leaves, and lemon wedges on the platter. Serve immediately.

BAKING RECIPES

Cornbread Chicken Stuffing

Servings: 6 - 8
Cooking Time: 95 Minutes

Ingredients:
- 2 Tbsp Butter
- 1 Cup Chicken Stock
- 6 Cups Cornbread, Cubed
- ½ Cup Dried Cranberries
- 1 Egg
- ½ Cup Heavy Whipping Cream
- 1 Lb. Italian Sausage
- 1 Diced Onion
- 1 ½ Tsp Pulled Pork Rub
- 2 Tbsp Sage, Fresh
- ½ Tsp Fresh Thyme

Directions:
1. Supply your smoker with wood pellets and follow the start-up procedure. Preheat the grill, with the lid closed, to 250° F. If using a gas or charcoal grill, set the temp to low heat.
2. Portion sausage into quarter-size pieces and place on mesh grate. Place grate on the grill and cook for 1 hour. Sausage pieces will have a smoky deep brown color. Move the mesh tray of sausage to the side of the grill with indirect heat.
3. Open the Flame Broiler Plate and increase the temperature to 350°F. Place a large cast iron skillet on the grill, over direct flame. Add butter and onions and cook until the onions caramelize lightly, stirring often. Add the sage and thyme and stir to combine.
4. Gently fold in the dried cranberries and cubed cornbread, then add sausage directly from mesh grate.
5. In a small mixing bowl, whisk together the heavy cream, chicken stock, egg, and Pulled Pork Rub. Pour mixture over the cornbread stuffing mix.
6. Cover grill and cook 30 minutes or until heated through and crispy on top.

Crème Brûlée

Servings: 2
Cooking Time: 45 minutes

Ingredients:
- 1 Quart heavy whipping cream
- 1 Pieces Vanilla Bean, split and scraped
- 6 Large egg yolk
- 1 Cup sugar

Directions:
1. Supply your smoker with wood pellets and follow the start-up procedure. Preheat the grill, with the lid closed, to 325° F.
2. Pour the cream into a saucepan over medium-high heat, add the vanilla bean and the scraped seeds. Bring to a boil. Remove from the heat and allow to steep (about 15 minutes). Remove the vanilla bean from saucepan and discard.
3. In a bowl, whisk together egg yolks and 1/2 cup (100 g) of the sugar until the mix starts to lighten in color. Add the cream a little at a time, stirring continually.
4. Pour the mixture into 6 (8 oz) ramekins and place the ramekins into a large roasting pan. Pour hot water into the pan so that it comes halfway up the sides of the ramekins.
5. Place water bath pan on the grill and bake until the Crème Brûlées still jiggle in the center, about 40 to 45 minutes. Grill: 325 °F
6. Remove the ramekins from the roasting pan and refrigerate for at least 2 hours and up to 2 days.
7. To serve, let the Crème Brûlée come to temperature (about 20 minutes) before torching the tops.
8. Sprinkle the remaining 1/2 cup (100 g) sugar equally on top of each ramekin. Using a torch in a circular motion, melt the sugar until it caramelizes and forms a crispy top.
9. Allow the Crème Brûlée to sit for a few minutes before serving. Enjoy!

Blueberry Pancakes

Servings: 4
Cooking Time: 10 Minutes

Ingredients:
- 2 Cups Blueberries, Fresh
- 1 Cup Pancake Mix
- 1/2 Cup Sugar
- 3/4 Cup Water, Warm

Directions:
1. Supply your smoker with wood pellets and follow the start-up procedure. Preheat the grill, with the lid closed, to 350° F.
2. Place the cast iron griddle on the grates of your grill.
3. In a large bowl, pour water, pancake mix and 1/2 cup of the blueberries and mix until combined.
4. Pour the batter onto the griddle in 4 equal parts. Cook with the lid closed for about 6 minutes, or until the edges of the pancakes are slightly cooked. Flip each pancake and continue cooking for another 4 minutes.
5. Pour the hot blueberry sauce over your freshly cooked pancakes and enjoy!

Skillet Buttermilk Cornbread

Servings: 6
Cooking Time: 25 Minutes

Ingredients:
- 1 Cup Cornmeal
- 1 Cup all-purpose flour
- 1/3 Cup granulated sugar
- 1 Teaspoon salt
- 1 Teaspoon baking powder
- 1 1/2 Cup buttermilk
- 2 Whole eggs
- 8 Tablespoon butter, melted

Directions:
1. Grease a cast iron skillet or 9-inch square baking pan with bacon fat. Put a 10-inch well-seasoned cast iron skillet on the grill grate. If using a regular baking pan, do not preheat.
2. Supply your smoker with wood pellets and follow the start-up procedure. Preheat the grill, with the lid closed, to 400° F.
3. In a large mixing bowl, combine the cornmeal, flour, sugar, salt, and baking powder and whisk to mix thoroughly. Make a well in the center of the dry ingredients.
4. In a separate mixing bowl, whisk together the buttermilk and eggs until well-combined. Add the melted butter. Pour into the dry ingredients and mix until the batter is fairly smooth. Do not overmix.
5. Carefully pour the batter into the preheated skillet. Bake for 20 to 25 minutes, or until the top is firm and a tester inserted in the center of the cornbread comes out clean. Be careful when removing the skillet from the grill as it will be very hot. Let the cornbread cool slightly on a trivet or cooling rack before slicing into wedges or squares.

Chili Cheese Fries

Servings: 6
Cooking Time: 10 Minutes

Ingredients:
- 1 Cup Cheddar Cheese, Shredded
- 1 Cup Chili Con Carne, Prepared
- 1 Bag French Fries
- 1 Tablespoon Olive Oil
- 1 Tablespoon Sweet Heat Rub

Directions:
1. Supply your smoker with wood pellets and follow the start-up procedure. Preheat the grill, with the lid closed, to 350° F. If you're using charcoal or gas, set it up for medium high heat.
2. Bake the fries according to manufacturer's instructions. Once the fries are done, place them in a large bowl and add the olive oil and Sweet Heat Rub. Toss the fries to coat. Once everything is well coated with the oil and seasoning, spread the fries on a baking sheet.
3. Top the fries with the chili and the shredded cheddar cheese. Place the baking sheet on the grill and grill for 7-10 minutes, or until the cheese is melted and bubbly, and the chili is warm all the way through.
4. Remove the baking sheet from the grill and serve the fries immediately.

Chocolate Peanut Cookies

Servings: 4
Cooking Time: 12 Minutes

Ingredients:

- 1/2 Tsp Baking Soda
- 1/2 Cup Brown Sugar
- 1/2 Cup + 1 Tbsp Butter, Unsalted
- 1/3 Cup Cocoa Powder, Dark And Unsweetened
- 2 Eggs, Beaten
- 1 1/2 Cups Flour, All-Purpose
- 1/3 Cup Miniature Chocolate Chips
- 2 Cups Peanut Butter Chips, Divided
- 1/4 Tsp Sea Salt
- 1/2 Cup Sugar, Granulated
- 1 Tsp Vanilla Extract

Directions:

1. Supply your smoker with wood pellets and follow the start-up procedure. Preheat the grill, with the lid closed, to medium-low heat. If using a gas or charcoal grill, preheat a cast iron skillet.
2. In a mixing bowl, whisk together the flour, cocoa powder, baking soda, and salt. Set aside.
3. Set a metal saucepan on the griddle, then add ½ cup of butter to melt. Whisk in the sugars and vanilla extract and cook for 2 minutes. Remove the pan from the griddle, and transfer contents to a large mixing bowl.
4. Slowly pour the beaten eggs into the sugar mixture, whisking constantly to temper the eggs.
5. Add the dry mixture to the wet ingredients until just combined. Fold in 1 cup of peanut butter chips and chocolate chips. Refrigerate mixture for 15 to 30 minutes.
6. Remove the dough from the refrigerator, then add an additional cup of peanut butter chips.
7. Portion dough into 16 to 18 cookie balls.
8. Melt 1 tablespoon of butter on the griddle, then transfer the cookie balls to the griddle. Press down gently on the cookies, then cook for 10 to 12 minutes, flipping halfway.
9. Transfer cookies to a cooling rack for 5 minutes before enjoying.

Pumpkin Bread

Servings: 6
Cooking Time: 60 Minutes

Ingredients:

- 1 Cup Pumpkin, canned
- 2 eggs
- 2/3 Cup vegetable oil
- 1/2 Cup sour cream
- 1 Teaspoon vanilla extract
- 2 1/2 Cup flour
- 1 1/2 Teaspoon baking soda
- 1 Teaspoon salt
- 1/2 Teaspoon ground cinnamon
- 1/4 Teaspoon ground nutmeg
- 1/4 Teaspoon ground cloves
- 1/4 Teaspoon ground ginger
- As Needed butter

Directions:

1. In a large mixing bowl, combine the pumpkin, eggs, vegetable oil, sour cream, and vanilla and whisk to blend.
2. In a separate bowl, combine the flour, baking soda, salt, cinnamon, nutmeg, cloves, and ginger. Add the dry ingredients to the wet ingredients and stir to combine. Do not overmix.
3. If desired, stir in one or more of the optional ingredients (walnuts, dried cranberries, raisins, or chocolate chips). Butter the interiors of two loaf pans.
4. Sprinkle with flour to coat the buttered surfaces, and tap out any excess. Divide the batter evenly between the two pans.
5. When ready to cook, set the smoker to 350°F and preheat, lid closed for 15 minutes.
6. Arrange the loaf pans directly on the grill grate. Bake for 45 to 50 minutes, or until a skewer or toothpick inserted in the center comes out clean. Also, the top of the loaf should spring back when pressed gently with a finger.
7. Transfer the loaf pans to a cooling rack and let cool for 10 minutes before carefully turning out the pumpkin bread. Let the loaves cool thoroughly before slicing. Wrap in aluminum foil or plastic wrap if not eating right away. Serve and enjoy!

Baked Irish Creme Cake

Servings: 4
Cooking Time: 60 Minutes

Ingredients:
- 1 Cup Pecans, pieces
- 1 Yellow Cake Mix, Boxed
- 1 Vanilla Pudding Mix, Instant Package (3.4oz)
- 4 Large eggs
- 1/2 Cup water
- 1/2 Cup vegetable oil
- 1 Cup Irish Cream Liquor
- 1/2 Cup butter
- 1 Cup sugar

Directions:
1. Grease and flour a 10" (25 cm) Bundt pan. Sprinkle pecans along the bottom.
2. In a large bowl, with a mixer, combine yellow cake mix, pudding mix, eggs, water, oil, and Irish Cream liquor. Pour batter over nuts in the pan.
3. Supply your smoker with wood pellets and follow the start-up procedure. Preheat the grill, with the lid closed, to 325° F.
4. Place Bundt pan on the Traeger and bake for 1 hour, or until a toothpick comes out clean. Remove from heat, cool for 10 minutes. Grill: 325 °F
5. While the cake is cooling, combine the butter, water and sugar and bring to a boil. Boil for 5 minutes, stirring constantly. Remove from heat and add Irish cream liquor.
6. Use a bamboo skewer to poke holes in the cooled cake. Spoon glaze over the cake. Allow cake to absorb the glaze. Enjoy!

Baked Cast Iron Berry Cobbler

Servings: 6
Cooking Time: 35 Minutes

Ingredients:
- 4 Cup Berries
- 12 Tablespoon sugar
- Cup orange juice
- 2/3 Cup Flour
- 3/4 Teaspoon baking powder
- 1 Pinch salt
- 1/2 Cup butter
- 1 Tablespoon Sugar, raw

Directions:
1. Supply your smoker with wood pellets and follow the start-up procedure. Preheat the grill, with the lid closed, to 350° F.
2. In a 10-inch (25-cm) cast iron or other baking pan, mix together the berries, 4 Tbsp sugar and the orange juice.
3. In a small bowl, mix together the flour, baking powder and salt. Set aside.
4. In a separate bowl, cream together the butter and granulated sugar. Add the egg and vanilla extract and mix to combine. Gradually fold in the flour mixture.
5. Spoon the batter on top of the berries and sprinkle raw sugar on top.
6. Bake the cobbler for approximately 35-45 minutes. Cool slightly and serve with whipped cream. Enjoy! Grill: 350 °F

Quick Baked Dinner Rolls

Servings: 8
Cooking Time: 30 Minutes

Ingredients:
- 2 Tablespoon quick-rise yeast
- 1 Teaspoon salt
- 1/4 Cup sugar
- 3 1/3 Cup flour
- 1/4 Cup unsalted butter, softened
- 1 egg
- cooking spray
- 1 egg, for egg wash

Directions:
1. Combine yeast and warm water in a small bowl to activate the yeast. Let sit until foamy, about 5-10 minutes.
2. Combine salt, sugar, and flour in the bowl of a stand mixer fitted with the dough hook. Pour water and yeast into the dry ingredients with the machine running on low.
3. Add butter and egg and mix for 10 minutes gradually increasing the speed from low to high.

4. Form the dough into a ball and place in a buttered bowl. Cover with a cloth and let the dough rise for approximately 40 minutes.
5. Transfer the risen dough to a lightly floured surface and divide into 8 pieces forming a ball with each.
6. Lightly spray a cast iron pan with cooking spray and arrange balls in the pan. Cover with a cloth and let rise 20 minutes.
7. Supply your smoker with wood pellets and follow the start-up procedure. Preheat the grill, with the lid closed, to 375° F.
8. Brush rolls with egg wash and then bake for 30 minutes until lightly browned. Serve hot. Enjoy! Grill: 375 °F

Traeger Baked Focaccia

Servings: 4
Cooking Time: 40 Minutes

Ingredients:
- 2 1/2 Cup all-purpose flour
- 1 Cup warm water (110°F to 115°F)
- 1 Tablespoon instant yeast
- 1 Teaspoon sugar
- 1 Teaspoon salt
- 3 Tablespoon olive oil, plus more as needed
- 1 Tablespoon fresh herbs such as thyme, rosemary and sage
- 2 Tablespoon freshly grated Parmesan, optional
- flaky sea salt

Directions:
1. Place the flour, water, yeast, sugar, salt and oil in the bowl of a stand mixer and mix for 60 seconds. You may also use a food processor by adding the flour, sugar, salt and yeast to the bowl and process while streaming in the warm water followed by the olive oil. Process until combined and a ball forms.
2. Gently form the sticky dough into a ball, if needed, and place in a well-oiled 12 inch cast iron skillet. Drizzle the top of the dough with more olive oil. Cover with plastic wrap and a kitchen towel and let rise in a warm spot for 45 to 60 minutes.
3. After the dough has risen, press the dough to the edges of the pan and cover it again. Let rise for 15 minutes.
4. Supply your smoker with wood pellets and follow the start-up procedure. Preheat the grill, with the lid closed, to 375° F.
5. Uncover the dough and press it again to the edges of the pan using your fingertips to create divots.
6. Drizzle with olive oil, then sprinkle with herbs, Parmesan and flaky salt.
7. Bake it on the Traeger for 30 to 40 minutes, or until golden brown and cooked through. Allow it to cool slightly before removing from cast iron and slicing. Enjoy! Grill: 375 °F

Pretzel Rolls

Servings: 6
Cooking Time: 20 Minutes

Ingredients:
- 2 3/4 Cup Bread Flour
- 1 Quick-Rising Yeast, envelope
- 1 Teaspoon salt
- 1 Teaspoon sugar
- 1/2 Teaspoon celery seed
- 1/2 Teaspoon Caraway Seeds
- 1 Cup hot water
- As Needed Cornmeal
- 8 Cup water
- 1/4 Cup baking soda
- 2 Tablespoon sugar
- 1 Whole Egg White
- Coarse salt

Directions:
1. Combine bread flour, 1 envelope yeast, salt, 1 teaspoon sugar, caraway seeds and celery seeds in food processor or standing mixer with dough hook and blend.
2. With machine running, gradually pour hot water, adding enough water to form smooth elastic dough. Process 1 minute to knead. (You could also knead it by hand for a few minutes.)
3. Grease medium bowl. Add dough to bowl, turning to coat. Cover bowl with plastic wrap, then towel; let

dough rise in warm draft-free area until doubled in volume, about 35 minutes.

4. Flour a large baking sheet. Punch dough down and knead on lightly floured surface until smooth. Divide into 8 pieces. Form each dough piece into a ball.

5. Place dough balls on prepared sheet, flattening each slightly. Using serrated knife, cut X in top center of each dough ball. Cover with towel and let dough balls rise until almost doubled in volume, about 20 minutes.

6. When ready to cook, start the smoker on Smoke with the lid open until a fire is established (4-5 minutes). Turn temperature to 375 F (190 C) and preheat, lid closed, for 10 to 15 minutes.

7. Grease another baking sheet and sprinkle with cornmeal. Bring water to boil in large saucepan. Add baking soda and sugar (water will foam up). Add 3 rolls (or however many will fit comfortably in the pot) and cook 30 seconds per side.

8. Using slotted spoon, transfer rolls to prepared sheet, arranging X side up. Repeat with remaining rolls. Brush rolls with egg white glaze. Sprinkle rolls generously with coarse salt.

9. Bake rolls until brown, about 20 to 25 minutes. Transfer to racks and cool 10 minutes. Serve rolls warm or at room temperature. Enjoy!

Baked Bourbon Maple Pumpkin Pie

Servings: 6-8
Cooking Time: 60 Minutes

Ingredients:
- 1/4 Cup Cocoa Powder, Unsweetened
- 1 Tablespoon Cocoa Powder, Unsweetened
- 3 1/2 Tablespoon sugar
- 1 Teaspoon salt
- 1 1/4 Cup all-purpose flour
- 1 Tablespoon all-purpose flour
- 6 Tablespoon butter
- 2 Tablespoon vegetable oil
- 1 Large Egg Yolk
- 1/2 Teaspoon apple cider vinegar
- 1/4 Cup ice water
- 1 Large egg, beaten
- 15 Ounce Pumpkin, canned
- 1/4 Cup sour cream
- 2 Tablespoon bourbon
- 1 Teaspoon ground cinnamon
- 1/2 Teaspoon salt
- 1/4 Teaspoon ground ginger
- 1/4 Teaspoon ground nutmeg
- 1/8 Teaspoon Allspice, ground
- 1/8 Teaspoon Mace, ground
- 3 Large eggs
- 3/4 Cup maple syrup
- 2 Tablespoon sugar
- 1/2 Vanilla Bean, halved
- 1 Cup heavy cream

Directions:
1. For the Chocolate Pie Dough: Pulse cocoa powder, granulated sugar, salt, and 1-1/4 cups plus 1 Tbsp flour in a food processor to combine. Add butter and shortening and pulse until mixture resembles coarse meal with a few pea-sized pieces of butter remaining. Transfer to a large bowl.

2. Whisk together the egg yolk, vinegar, and 1/4 cup ice water in a small bowl. Drizzle half of the egg mixture over flour mixture and, using a fork, mix gently just until combined. Add remaining egg mixture and mix until the dough just comes together (you will have some unincorporated pieces).

3. Turn out dough onto a lightly floured surface, flatten slightly, and cut into quarters. Stack pieces on top of one another. Placing unincorporated dry pieces of dough between layers, and press down to combine. Repeat process twice more (all pieces of dough should be incorporated at this point). Form dough into a 1" thick disk. Wrap in plastic; chill at least 1 hour.

4. Roll out a disk of dough on a lightly floured surface into a 14" round. Transfer to a 9" pie dish. Lift up the edge and allow the dough to slump down into the dish. Trim. Leaving about 1" overhang. Fold overhang under and crimp edge. Chill in freezer 15 minutes.

5. When ready to cook, set the smoker to 350°F and preheat, lid closed for 15 minutes.

6. Line pie with parchment paper or heavy-duty foil, leaving a 1-1/2" overhang. Fill with pie weights or dried

beans. Bake until crust is dry around the edge, about 20 minutes.

7. Remove paper and weights and bake until surface of the crust looks dry, 5-10 minutes.

8. Brush bottom and sides of crust with 1 beaten egg. Return to grill and bake until dry and set, about 3 minutes longer.

9. For the Pumpkin Maple Filling: Whisk together pumpkin puree, sour cream, bourbon, cinnamon, salt, ginger, nutmeg, allspice, mace (optional) and remaining 3 eggs in a large bowl; set aside.

10. Pour maple syrup and 2 tbsp sugar in a small saucepan. Scrape in the seeds from vanilla bean (reserve pod for another use) or add vanilla extract and bring syrup to a boil. Reduce heat to medium-high and simmer, stirring occasionally, until mixture is thickened and small puffs of steam start to release about 3 minutes.

11. Remove from heat and add cream in 3 additions, stirring with a wooden spoon after each addition until smooth. Gradually whisk hot maple cream into pumpkin mixture.

12. Place pie dish on a rimmed baking sheet and pour in pumpkin filling. Bake pie, rotating halfway through, until set around edge but center barely jiggles 50-60 minutes.

13. Transfer pie dish to a wire rack and let the pie cool. Slice and serve. Enjoy!

Crescent Rolls

Servings: 8
Cooking Time: 12 Minutes

Ingredients:

- 1 Crescent Dough, Can

Directions:

1. Supply your smoker with wood pellets and follow the start-up procedure. Preheat the grill, with the lid closed, to 375° F.

2. Unroll the dough and separate into triangles. Roll up the triangles and place on an ungreased nonstick cookie sheet. Bake for 10-12 minutes on your Grill. You will know that they are finished when the rolls are golden brown.

Anzac Coconut Biscuits

Servings: 4
Cooking Time: 30 Minutes

Ingredients:

- This recipe makes a dozen biscuits.
- 1 cup rolled oats
- 3/4 cup raw sugar
- 3/4 cup desiccated coconut
- 1 cup plain flour, sifted
- 125 g butter, melted
- 2 tablespoons Golden Syrup
- 1/2 tsp bicarb soda
- 3 tablespoons boiling water

Directions:

1. Combine and mix thoroughly sifted flour, oats, sugar and coconut in a large bowl.

2. Melt the butter and Golden Syrup over low heat.

3. Add boiling water to the bicarb soda, once dissolved add into the butter/syrup mix, it will bubble/fizz up a bit.

4. Add the liquid into the dry ingredients and mix throughly.

5. Rolls the mix into golf ball size balls and layout on grease proof paper on baking tray and flatten the tops just slightly.

6. Space the balls with about 3 fingers between each ball as they will flatten to about triple the diameter as they cook.

7. Supply your smoker with wood pellets and follow the start-up procedure. Preheat the grill, with the lid closed, to 350° F. Cook for 25-30 minutes until golden brown.

8. Rest on cooling rack until at room temperature then store in air-tight container.

Cherry Ice Cream Cobbler

Servings: 8
Cooking Time: 45 Minutes

Ingredients:

- 1 Tsp Baking Powder
- 3 Tbsp Butter, Melted
- 1 Cup Flour
- Ice Cream, Prepared

- 1/4 Tsp Salt
- 3/4 Cup Sugar
- 1/2 Cup Milk

Directions:

1. Supply your smoker with wood pellets and follow the start-up procedure. Preheat the grill, with the lid closed, to 350° F.
2. In a bowl, combine flour, sugar, baking powder, salt and mix to incorporate. Stir in butter and milk and mix until combined. In a cast iron pan, dump in cherry pie filling and pile on the prepared topping to cover.
3. Place in your Grill and bake for about 45 minutes, or until the topping is golden brown.
4. Let cool for a couple minutes and serve with ice cream.

S'mores Dip Skillet

Servings: 4-6
Cooking Time: 8 Minutes

Ingredients:

- 2 tablespoons salted butter, melted
- ¼ cup milk
- 12 ounces semisweet chocolate chips
- 16 ounces Jet-Puffed marshmallows
- Graham crackers and apple wedges, for serving

Directions:

1. Supply your smoker with wood pellets and follow the start-up procedure. Preheat, with the lid closed, to 450°F.
2. Place a cast iron skillet on the preheated grill grate and pour in the melted butter and milk, stirring for about 1 minute.
3. Once the mixture starts to heat, top with the chocolate chips in an even layer and arrange the marshmallows standing up to cover all of the chocolate.
4. Close the lid and smoke for 5 to 7 minutes, or until the marshmallows are lightly toasted.
5. Remove from the heat and serve immediately with graham crackers and apple wedges for dipping.

Chicken Pot Pie

Servings: 6
Cooking Time: 60 Minutes

Ingredients:

- 2 Chicken, Boneless/Skinless
- 1 Cream Of Chicken Soup, Can
- 1 Tsp Curry Powder
- 1/2 Cup Mayo
- 1 1/2 Cups Mixed Frozen Vegetables
- 1 Onion, Sliced
- 2 Frozen Pie Shell, Deep
- 1/2 Cup Sour Cream

Directions:

1. Supply your smoker with wood pellets and follow the start-up procedure. Preheat the grill, with the lid closed, to 425° F.
2. Cut the onion in half and place on the grates of the grill. If you"re using fresh chicken breasts, barbecue the chicken at the same time as the onions. The chicken is fully cooked when the internal temperature reached 170F. While the onion and chicken are cooking, prepare the pie crust by putting one crust in a pie plate. When the chicken and onions are done, shred chicken and chop onion into small pieces and place in the prepared pie plate along with the mixed vegetables.
3. Combine cream of chicken soup, mayo, sour cream, and curry powder in a bowl. Pour into the pie crust with the chicken and mix to combine. Wet the sides of the bottom crust with a small amount of water and top with the second pie crust. Push gently along the sides of the crust to seal the two pie crusts together.
4. Place in the and bake for 40 minutes, or until the crust is golden brown. Serve hot.

Strawberry Basil Daiquiri

Servings: 2
Cooking Time: 20 Minutes

Ingredients:

- 4 strawberries, stemmed
- 6 Tablespoon granulated sugar, divided
- 6 basil leaves
- 3 Ounce white rum
- 2 Ounce lime juice
- 1 Ounce Smoked Simple Syrup

- 2 fresh basil leaves, for garnish
- 2 lime slice, for garnish

Directions:

1. Supply your smoker with wood pellets and follow the start-up procedure. Preheat the grill, with the lid closed, to 375° F.
2. Cut strawberries in half and coat in 2 tablespoons granulated sugar. Place directly on grill grate and cook for 15 to 20 minutes. Remove from heat and cool. Grill: 375 °F
3. Add 1 tablespoon granulated sugar and basil leaves to shaking tin and lightly muddle. Add strawberries and muddle again.
4. Pour in white rum, lime juice and Smoked Simple Syrup. Shake with ice.
5. Strain contents into a chilled glass and garnish with large fresh basil leaf and sliced lime. Enjoy!

Cheese Mac

Servings: 6 - 10
Cooking Time: 60 Minutes

Ingredients:

- 5 Tbsp All-Purpose Flour
- 4 Strips Bacon
- Black Pepper
- 2 Cups Breadcrumbs
- 4 Oz Brie
- 4 Oz Brie Cheese
- ½ Cup Butter, Melted
- 12 Oz Cheddar Cheese, Grated
- 3 Cloves Garlic, Minced
- 2 Tbsp Extra Virgin Olive Oil
- 1 Tsp Fresh Grated Nutmeg
- 1 Tsp Ground Cayenne
- 8 Oz, Grated Gruyere Cheese
- 1 Cup Heavy Cream
- 1, Minced Jalapeno Pepper
- 4 Oz Mozzarella Cheese, Grated
- 2 Tbsp Parsley, Minced Fresh
- 12 Oz Raclette
- To Taste Salt
- 5 Tbsp Unsalted Butter
- 4 Oz Whole Milk, Warm
- 1 Yellow Onion, Diced

Directions:

1. Supply your smoker with wood pellets and follow the start-up procedure. Preheat the grill, with the lid closed, to 350° F. Bring a large saucepan of water to a boil. Add the pasta and cook according to the package instructions for al dente. Drain.
2. Heat the oil in a large saucepan over medium-high heat.
3. Add the onion and cook for about 5 minutes, stirring often, until lightly colored, then add the garlic and the jalapeño and cook for 2 more minutes.
4. Reduce the heat to medium, add the butter, and stir until melted. Add the flour and cook, stirring often, for 5 minutes to form a light roux.
5. Add the cheeses, the milk, and cream, reduce the heat to medium-low, and cook, stirring often, until the cheese is melted, and a smooth sauce comes together, about 7 minutes.
6. Stir in the cayenne and truffle oil, then add the pasta and stir to fully coat it in the sauce. Season with salt and pepper. Transfer the mixture to a 12-inch cast-iron skillet and cover with aluminum foil.
7. Place on the grill and bake for 20 minutes. Remove the foil and cover the mac and cheese with the breadcrumbs.
8. Return to the grill and bake for another 15 to 20 minutes, until the cheese is bubbling and the breadcrumbs are golden brown. Serve family style right out of the skillet.

Sopapilla Cheesecake By Doug Scheiding

Servings: 8
Cooking Time: 45 Minutes

Ingredients:

- 2 Tablespoon softened butter
- 24 Ounce cream cheese
- 2 Cup granulated sugar, divided
- 2 Teaspoon vanilla
- 2 Can Pillsbury Butter Flake Crescent Rolls

- 1/2 Cup butter, melted
- cinnamon

Directions:
1. Coat a 9x13 inch baking dish with 2 tablespoons softened butter and set aside.
2. Supply your smoker with wood pellets and follow the start-up procedure. Preheat the grill, with the lid closed, to 350° F.
3. In a mixer, combine cream cheese, 1 to 1-1/2 cups of sugar and vanilla. Mix for 60 to 90 seconds on high with paddle attachment.
4. Take crescents out of the refrigerator. Open one can and place into the buttered 9x13 inch rectangular metal pan or glass dish. Make sure to fill in the gaps in this bottom layer of crescents.
5. Put the cream cheese mixture on the top of the crescent layer using a spatula to make it level.
6. Open the second can of crescents and put on top of the cream cheese layer, again filling in the gaps in the crescents to cover middle.
7. Pour 1/2 cup of melted butter on the top of the last layer of crescent. Start on sides first then middle.
8. Then sprinkle 1/4 cup to 1/2 cup of sugar over the entire pan followed by a light, even dusting of cinnamon.
9. Place pan directly on the grill grate and bake for 40 to 50 minutes until top is brown and starting to get crusty. Grill: 350 °F
10. Remove from grill and let cool 5 to 10 minutes. This allows the cheesecake to set which makes portioning easier. This dessert can be served warm or cold. Enjoy!

Baked Pumpkin Pie

Servings: 6
Cooking Time: 50 Minutes

Ingredients:
- 4 Ounce cream cheese
- 15 Ounce pumpkin puree
- 1/3 Cup Cream, whipping
- 1/2 Cup brown sugar
- 1 Teaspoon pumpkin pie spice
- 3 Large eggs
- 1 frozen pie crust, thawed

Directions:
1. Supply your smoker with wood pellets and follow the start-up procedure. Preheat the grill, with the lid closed, to 325° F.
2. Mix cream cheese, puree, milk, sugar, and spice. One at a time, incorporate an egg to the mixture. Pour mixture into pie shell.
3. Bake for 50 minutes, edges should be golden and pie should be firm around edges with slight movement in middle. Let cool before whip cream is applied. Serve and enjoy! Grill: 325 °F

Savory Beaver Tails

Servings: 8
Cooking Time: 2 Minutes

Ingredients:
- 2 Tbsp Butter, Melted
- 1 Tbsp Cinnamon, Ground
- 1 Egg
- 2 1/2 Cups Flour, All-Purpose
- 1/2 Cup Milk, Warm
- 1/2 Tsp Salt
- 1 Tsp Sugar
- 1/2 Tsp Vanilla
- 1 L Vegetable Oil
- 1/4 Cup Water, Warm
- 2 1/2 Tsp Active Yeast, Instant

Directions:
1. In a small bowl, combine water, milk, yeast, and sugar. Let it sit for about 10 minutes or until frothy.
2. In another bowl, pour in the flour and make a well in the middle. Pour in butter, sugar, salt, vanilla and egg. Mix everything together until the dough is smooth. Knead for about 5 minutes and set the dough in a greased bowl. Cover with a towel and set aside for about an hour, or until the dough has doubled in size.
3. After one hour, supply your smoker with wood pellets and follow the start-up procedure. Preheat the grill, with the lid open, to 450° F.Pour 1L of vegetable oil into a cast iron pan and place on the grates of your Grill. Keep your flame broiler closed so as to prevent grease flareups. Preheat the oil so that it is 350 degrees F.

4. While you"re waiting for the oil to heat up, punch down the dough and separate into 8 small balls. Shape each piece of dough into a flat circle. Fry the dough in the preheated oil for about 1 minute per side, or until the dough is golden brown.

5. Sprinkle with cinnamon sugar immediately, or top with your desired toppings. Enjoy!

Sourdough Pizza

Servings: 4
Cooking Time: 12 Minutes

Ingredients:
- 1 1/2 Cup Fresh Sourdough Starter
- 1 Tablespoon olive oil
- 1 Teaspoon Jacobsen Salt Co. Pure Kosher Sea Salt
- 1 1/4 Cup all-purpose flour

Directions:
1. Supply your smoker with wood pellets and follow the start-up procedure. Preheat the grill, with the lid closed, to 450° F.
2. Mix together the fresh sourdough starter, one tablespoon of oil, Jacobsen salt and 1-1/4 cups of flour. Add more flour, a little at a time, as needed to form a pizza dough consistency.
3. Allow the dough to rest for 30 minutes, to allow for easier rolling. Roll the dough out into a circle, using a small amount of flour to prevent sticking.
4. Place on a pizza stone. Bake the crust for approximately 7 minutes Grill: 450 °F
5. Remove the crust from the grill; brush on remaining oil to prevent toppings from soaking into the crust. Add the desired toppings and return pizza to grill; bake until the crust browns and the cheese melts.

Chicken Pizza On The Grill

Servings: 4
Cooking Time: 10 Minutes

Ingredients:
- 3 Boneless, Skinless Chicken Breast
- 5 Cups Flour, Strong
- 3 Cups Georgia Style Bbq Sauce
- 3 Cups Mozzarella Cheese, Shredded
- 1 Tsp Olive Oil
- 3 Cups Georgia Style BBQ Sauce
- 1 1/2 Cups Red Bell Peppers, Diced
- 1 1/2 Cups Red Onion, Diced
- 1 Tsp Sugar
- 1/2 Cup Water, Hot
- 1 1/4 Cup Water, Warm
- 2 Tsb Active Yeast, Instant

Directions:
1. Roll your pizza dough so it forms a base about a 1/2 inch thick. To impress your friends and family, you'll want to aim for a nice, pizza like shape. HINT: use a sprinkle of cornmeal on the countertop to aid in moving the dough.
2. Now for the toppings! Start by spreading 1 cup of Georgia Style BBQ sauce onto each base. Make sure to leave a small portion for the crust! Next, load up with sliced, cooked chicken breasts, diced red onions and red bell peppers before finishing off with a two cups of shredded mozzarella cheese.
3. Supply your smoker with wood pellets and follow the start-up procedure. Preheat the grill, with the lid closed, to 500° F. Place the pizza stone in your grill. Pick up your pizza using a flat surface like a chopping board and slide the pizza carefully onto the hot stone. Close the lid and let your homemade wood-fired pizza bake for 10 - 12 minutes. Remove once your pizza has a golden crust and the cheese is bubbling. Cut and serve for pizza you'll hardly want to share.

Blueberry Bread Pudding

Servings: 4
Cooking Time: 60 Minutes

Ingredients:
- 5 eggs
- 3 Cup sugar
- 2 1/2 Cup milk
- 1 1/2 Teaspoon vanilla
- 1 Teaspoon cinnamon
- 1 Pinch salt
- 5 Cup Bread
- 3 Cup blueberries

Directions:
1. Beat the eggs in a large mixing bowl. Whisk in the sugar, milk, vanilla, cinnamon, and salt.
2. In another large bowl, combine the bread and 2 cups (200 g) of the blueberries.
3. Pour the egg mixture over the bread-blueberry mixture and let sit for 30 minutes. Meanwhile, place muffin liners in a muffin tin.
4. Supply your smoker with wood pellets and follow the start-up procedure. Preheat the grill, with the lid open.
5. Spoon the bread-blueberry mixture into the prepared cups; evenly top each with the remaining cup of blueberries, pressing them gently into the pudding with the back of a spoon.
6. Dust the top with sugar.
7. Arrange the pan directly on the grill grate and smoke for 30 minutes. Grill:180°F
8. Increase the temperature to 350F (180 C), and bake until the pudding is set and golden brown on top, about 25 minutes. Grill:350°F
9. Let cool slightly, then sift powdered sugar on top. Serve warm with sweetened whipped cream or vanilla ice cream, if desired.

Beer Bread

Servings: 4
Cooking Time: 60 Minutes

Ingredients:
- 400 g all-purpose flour
- 2 Tablespoon sugar
- 1 Tablespoon baking powder
- 1 Teaspoon salt
- 12 Ounce beer
- 2 Tablespoon honey
- 6 Tablespoon butter, melted

Directions:
1. Supply your smoker with wood pellets and follow the start-up procedure. Preheat the grill, with the lid closed, to 350° F.
2. Spray a loaf pan (9x5x3 inches) (55x12x20 cm) with nonstick cooking spray and set aside.
3. Put the flour, sugar, baking powder, and salt in a large mixing bowl. Whisk with a wire whisk to combine and aerate. Add the beer and honey and stir with a wooden spoon until the batter is just mixed. (Do not overmix.) If desired, gently stir in one or more of the optional add-ins.
4. Pour half of the melted butter in the prepared loaf pan and spoon in the batter. Pour the remainder of the butter over the top of the loaf.
5. Put the loaf pan directly on the grill grate and bake until a wooden skewer or toothpick inserted in the center of the loaf comes out clean, 50 to 60 minutes, and the bread is golden-brown. (Note: If using a glass loaf pan, the baking time might be shorter.)
6. Let the loaf cool slightly in the pan before removing from the pan. Leftovers make great toast.
7. Optional Add-ins: Bacon, cooked and crumbled, 1 cup (100 g) Grated Cheese, Red Bell Pepper and Onion, diced and sauted in Butter (1/4 cup each), Green Onions, minced, Dried Herbs such as Dill, Rosemary, Mixed Italian Herbs, etc,.Cracked Black Pepper, Your favorite Barbecue Rub, such as Traeger's Pork and Poultry Shake, Ground Cinnamon, Dry Ranch Dressing Mix, Coarse-grained Mustard.

Ultimate Baked Garlic Bread

Servings: 4
Cooking Time: 20 Minutes

Ingredients:
- 1 baguette
- 1/2 Cup softened butter
- 1/2 Cup mayonnaise
- 4 Tablespoon chopped Italian parsley
- 6 Clove garlic, minced
- salt
- chile flakes
- 1 Cup mozzarella cheese
- 1/2 Cup Parmesan cheese

Directions:
1. Supply your smoker with wood pellets and follow the start-up procedure. Preheat the grill, with the lid closed, to 375° F.

2. Lay baguette on a cutting board and cut it in half lengthwise.
3. In a bowl, add butter, mayonnaise, parsley, garlic, salt and chile flakes. Mix well.
4. Spread butter mixture on baguette halves and top with mozzarella and Parmesan cheese.
5. Place baguette on the grill (if you like the bread crisp, do not use foil and if you like it soft, wrap with foil). Grill for approximately 15 to 25 minutes. Serve warm. Enjoy! Grill: 375 °F

Grilled Beer Cheese Dip

Servings: 6
Cooking Time: 20 Minutes

Ingredients:
- 6 Oz Beer, Can
- 8 Oz Cream Cheese
- 1 Tsp Onion Powder
- ½ Tsp Pepper
- ½ Tsp Salt
- 2 Cups Shredded Cheese

Directions:
1. Supply your smoker with wood pellets and follow the start-up procedure. Preheat the grill, with the lid closed, to 350° F. If you're using a gas or charcoal grill, set it up for medium high heat. Preheat with lid closed for 10-15 minutes.
2. In the cast iron pan add cream cheese, shredded cheese, beer, onion powder, salt and pepper. Once grill is at 350°F place cast iron skillet onto the grill and cook for about 10 minutes, stir and cook for another 5-10 minutes.
3. Top with more shredded cheese and fresh parsley. Serve with fresh baked pretzels as well.

Grilled Apple Pie

Servings: 4
Cooking Time: 40 Minutes

Ingredients:
- 5 Whole Apples
- 1/4 Cup sugar
- 1 Tablespoon cornstarch
- 1 Whole refrigerated pie crust
- 1/4 Cup Peach, preserves

Directions:
1. Supply your smoker with wood pellets and follow the start-up procedure. Preheat the grill, with the lid closed, to 375° F. In a medium bowl, mix the apples, sugar, and cornstarch; set aside.
2. Unroll pie crust. Place in ungreased pie pan. With the back of a spoon, spread preserves evenly on crust. Arrange the apple slices in an even layer in the pie pan. Slightly fold crust over filling.
3. Place a baking sheet upside down on the grill grate to make an elevated surface. Put the pan with pie on top so it is elevated off grill. (This will help prevent the bottom from overcooking.) Cook the pie for 30 to 40 minutes or until crust is golden brown, the filling is bubbly. Grill: 375 °F
4. Remove from grill; cool 10 minutes before serving. Enjoy! *Cook times will vary depending on set and ambient temperatures.

The Dan Patrick Show Pull-apart Pesto Bread

Servings: 8
Cooking Time: 25 Minutes

Ingredients:
- 1 Sourdough Bread, loaf
- 1/2 Cup butter, melted
- 1 Cup Pesto Sauce
- 1 1/2 Cup Italian Cheese Blend

Directions:
1. Supply your smoker with wood pellets and follow the start-up procedure. Preheat the grill, with the lid closed, to 350° F.
2. Using a serrated knife, make 1" diagonal cuts through the bread leaving the bottom crust intact. Turn the bread and make diagonal cuts in the opposite direction, creating diamonds.
3. Place the bread on a sheet of foil large enough to wrap around the entire loaf. Pour the melted butter into the cracks in the bread. Using a spoon spread the pesto

into the cracks then follow with the cheese stuffing it down into each crack.
4. Fold up the edges of the foil to wrap up the loaf and transfer to a baking sheet. Place the baking sheet directly on the grill grate.
5. Bake for 15 minutes then unwrap the foil and cook for an additional 10 minutes. Remove from the grill and serve. Enjoy! Grill: 350 °F
6. Follow along as we give you a recipe each day this week from The Dan Patrick Show Game Day Recipes eBook.

Vanilla Chocolate Chip Cookies

Servings: 12
Cooking Time: 20 Minutes

Ingredients:
- 3/4 cup brown sugar
- 3/4 cup white sugar
- 1 stick butter, room temp
- 2 eggs
- 1 tsp vanilla
- 2 1/2 cups flour
- 1/2 tsp salt
- 1 tsp baking soda
- 1 cup Chocolate Chips

Directions:
1. Cream your butter and sugar together in a mixing bowl using a hand mixer or stand mixer on medium speed for about 4-5 minutes.
2. Once the butter is creamed, add the eggs and vanilla. Continue mixing for an additional minute.
3. Put flour, salt, and baking soda in a sifter. Sift it into your creamed butter mixture.
4. Scrape the sides of your mixing bowl with a rubber spatula, and then turn your mixer on to low speed.
5. Let it mix a little, and then scrape the sides again. Stop mixing when there are one or two streaks of flour left in the cookie dough.
6. Scrape the sides of your bowl and pour in a cup of chocolate chips, and turn the mixer to low again to mix the chocolate. It should take just a few turns for the chocolate pieces to be well incorporated.
7. Line a large baking sheet with parchment paper. Using a medium cookie scoop (about 1.5 tbsp), drop evenly spaced dollops of cookie dough onto the cookie sheet.
8. Supply your smoker with wood pellets and follow the start-up procedure. Preheat the grill, with the lid closed, to 350° F. Place the cookie sheet in your smoker, and let them cook for about 12 minutes.
9. Let them sit on a cooling rack while you continue to cook the additional cookies.
10. Cool for a few minutes to let cookies set.
11. Enjoy!

Bacon Chocolate Chip Cookies

Servings: 2
Cooking Time: 10-12 Minutes

Ingredients:
- 2¾ cups all-purpose flour
- 1½ teaspoons baking soda
- ½ teaspoon salt
- 12 tablespoons (1½ sticks) unsalted butter, softened
- 1 cup light brown sugar
- 1 cup granulated sugar
- 2 eggs, at room temperature
- 2½ teaspoons apple cider vinegar
- 1 teaspoon vanilla extract
- 2 cups semisweet chocolate chips
- 8 slices bacon, cooked and crumbled

Directions:
1. In a large bowl, combine the flour, baking soda, and salt, and mix well.
2. In a separate large bowl, using an electric mixer on medium speed, cream the butter and sugars. Reduce the speed to low and mix in the eggs, vinegar, and vanilla.
3. With the mixer speed still on low, slowly incorporate the dry ingredients, chocolate chips, and bacon pieces.
4. Supply your smoker with wood pellets and follow the start-up procedure. Preheat, with the lid closed, to 375°F.
5. Line a large baking sheet with parchment paper.
6. Drop rounded teaspoonfuls of cookie batter onto the prepared baking sheet and place on the grill grate. Close the lid and smoke for 10 to 12 minutes, or until the cookies are browned around the edges.

Spiced Carrot Cake

Servings: 10
Cooking Time: 35 Minutes

Ingredients:
- 1/2 Cup Apple Sauce, Unsweetened
- 2 Tsp Baking Powder
- 1 Tsp Baking Soda
- 1 1/2 Cups Brown Sugar
- 1/2 Cup Butter, Room Temp
- 3/4 Cup Canola Oil
- 3 Cups Carrot, Grated
- 1 1/2 Tsp Cinnamon, Ground
- 2 (8-Ounce) Packages Cream Cheese, Room Temperature
- 4 Egg
- 2 Cups Flour, All-Purpose
- 1/2 Tsp Ginger, Ground
- 1/4 Tsp Nutmeg, Ground
- 1/2 Tsp Salt
- 1/2 Cup Sugar
- 3 Cups Sugar, Icing

Directions:
1. Supply your smoker with wood pellets and follow the start-up procedure. Preheat the grill, with the lid closed, to 350° F.
2. Line the bottom of 2 9-inch cake pans with parchment paper and spray the sides with cooking spray. Set aside.
3. In a large bowl, combine flour, baking powder and soda, spices and salt.
4. In a smaller bowl, combine oil, eggs, sugars, and applesauce and whisk together. Add carrots and stir until well combined.
5. Pour the wet ingredients into the dry. Stir until combined but take care not to over mix. Pour the batter evenly between the two cake pans. Bake for about 35 minutes in your Grill, rotating the cake pans halfway between the cook. Remove once a toothpick is inserted in the middle of the cake and comes out clean.
6. While the cake is cooling, prepare the frosting. Beat the cream cheese until smooth with a hand mixer. Add the butter and icing sugar and mix until fully combined.
7. On a clean plate or cake stand, place one half of the cake and top with a good layer of cream cheese frosting. Place the second half on top and cover with the remaining frosting. Icing tip: try not to lift your knife while icing. Instead make long, smooth strokes. Lifting the knife often make cause crumbs to get into your icing. Top with pecans if desired.

Basil Margherita Pizza

Servings: 6
Cooking Time: 25 Minutes

Ingredients:
- Basil, Chopped
- 2 Cups Flour, All-Purpose
- Mozzarella Cheese, Sliced Rounds
- 1 Cup Pizza Sauce
- 1 Teaspoon Salt
- 1 Teaspoon Sugar
- 1 Tomato, Sliced
- 1 Cup Water, Warm
- 1 Teaspoon Yeast, Instant

Directions:
1. Combine the water, yeast, and sugar in a small bowl and let sit for about 5 minutes.
2. In a large bowl, stir together the flour and salt. Pour in the yeast mixture and mix until a soft dough forms. Knead for about 2 minutes. Place in an oiled bowl and cover with a cloth. Let the dough sit and rise for about 45 minutes or until the dough has doubled in size.
3. Roll out on a flat, floured surface (or on a pizza stone) until you"ve reached your desired shape and thickness.
4. Supply your smoker with wood pellets and follow the start-up procedure. Preheat the grill, with the lid closed, to 350° F.
5. On the rolled out dough, pour on the pizza sauce, cheese, and then tomatoes and basil. Place in your Grill and bake for about 25 minutes, or until the cheese is melted and slightly golden brown.

Baked Pear Tarte Tatin

Servings: 6
Cooking Time: 45 Minutes

Ingredients:
- 2 1/2 Cup all-purpose flour
- 2 Tablespoon sugar
- butter chilled
- 8 Tablespoon cold water
- 1/4 Cup granulated sugar
- 1/4 Cup butter
- 8 Whole Bartlett Pear

Directions:
1. Supply your smoker with wood pellets and follow the start-up procedure. Preheat the grill, with the lid closed, to 350° F.
2. For the crust: Place flour and sugar in a food processor and pulse to mix. Add butter a little at a time while pulsing. Once it starts to looks like cornmeal, add the water until dough start to come together.
3. Form a round with the dough, wrap in plastic and let it cool in the refrigerator.
4. While dough cools, make the caramel sauce. In a sauce pan, add 1/4 cup granulated sugar and 1/4 cup butter. Cook butter and sugar until it becomes a dark caramel, a couple minutes.
5. Pour caramel in the bottom of 10 inch deep cake pan. While the caramel is still hot, arrange pear wedges in a fan formation covering the caramel.
6. Roll the chilled pie dough into a circle big enough to cover the pan. Prick the pie dough with a fork and cover the pan with the pie dough. Trim the crust leaving room for shrinkage.
7. Place on the grill and bake for 45 minutes or until pears are soft. The pears will be soft and most of the juice will evaporate and thicken.
8. Let sit for 3 minutes. While pan is still hot, place a plate over pie and flip over. Slowly lift the plate.
9. Serve warm, topped with vanilla ice cream or whipped cream. Enjoy!

Onion Cheese Nachos

Servings: 6
Cooking Time: 10 Minutes

Ingredients:
- 1 Pound Beef, Ground
- 3 Cups Cheddar Cheese, Shredded
- 1 Green Bell Pepper, Diced
- 1/2 Cup Green Onion
- 1/2 Cup Red Onion, Diced
- 1 Large Bag Tortilla Chip

Directions:
1. Supply your smoker with wood pellets and follow the start-up procedure. Preheat the grill, with the lid closed, to 350° F.
2. While you're waiting, empty a large bag of nacho chips evenly onto a cast iron pan. Start loading up with toppings - cooked ground beef, red onion, red pepper, cheese, green onions. These are just the toppings we had on hand, so feel free to add anything you like! Make sure you do a couple layers of chips so everyone gets a good serving of nachos. And don't be skimpy with the cheese - lay it on heavy!
3. Place your loaded nachos on the grill and let the hot smoke melt your toppings into one cheesy creation. Heat at 350°F for 10 minutes or until the cheese has fully melted. Remove and serve with sour-cream and salsa.

Traeger Baked Protein Bars

Servings: 6
Cooking Time: 25 Minutes

Ingredients:
- 2 Cup Frozen Sweet Cherries
- 1 Cup Apricots, Frozen
- 1 Scoop Vanilla Protein Powder
- 2 Tablespoon honey
- 1 Teaspoon vanilla extract
- 1 Cup rolled oats

Directions:
1. Supply your smoker with wood pellets and follow the start-up procedure. Preheat the grill, with the lid closed, to 350° F.
2. In the bowl of a food processor, add cherries, apricots (revived in hot water for 5 minutes and drained), vanilla protein powder, honey, and vanilla. Pulse about

10 to 15 times, to break the fruit into smaller pieces and to mix all ingredients.
3. In a separate bowl, fold together oats and fruit mixture. Transfer mixture to a loaf pan or silicone mold and place in grill.
4. Bake for approximately 20 to 25 minutes. Grill: 350 °F
5. Let cool completely and cut into 8 pieces. Enjoy!

Green Bean Casserole Circa 1955

Servings: 6
Cooking Time: 30 Minutes

Ingredients:
- 1 1/2 Pound Green Beans, fresh
- 1 Can cream of mushroom soup
- 1/2 Cup milk
- 2 Teaspoon soy sauce
- 1/2 Teaspoon Worcestershire sauce
- 1/2 Teaspoon black pepper
- 1.334 Cup French's Original Crispy Fried Onions
- 1/4 Cup red bell pepper, diced

Directions:
1. In a mixing bowl, combine the beans (trimmed and cooked until tender, or may use 2 16 oz. cans), soup, milk, soy sauce, Worcestershire sauce, black pepper, 2/3 cup of the onion rings, and red pepper, if using. Transfer to a 1-1/2 quart casserole dish.
2. Supply your smoker with wood pellets and follow the start-up procedure. Preheat the grill, with the lid closed, to 375° F.
3. Cook the casserole until the filling is hot and bubbling, 25 to 30 minutes. Top with the remaining onions and cook for 5 to 10 minutes more, or until the onions are crisp and beginning to brown. Grill: 375 °F

Smoked Lemon Tea

Servings: 6 - 8
Cooking Time: 60 Minutes

Ingredients:
- 8 Black Tea Bags
- 4 Cups Boiling Water
- 2 Cups Ice
- 8 Lemons
- 2 Cups Sugar
- 2 Cups Water

Directions:
1. Place the tea bags in a heat-safe pitcher. Bring 4 Cups of water to a boil and pour over tea bags. Let steep for 5-10 minutes. Remove tea bags and set pitcher aside to cool.
2. Turn on your grill and set to smoke mode. Combine 2 cups of sugar and 2 cups water in a small aluminum pan. Smoke for about 45 minutes, stirring occasionally, or until the mixture reduces to a thick, simple syrup. Remove from the grill and let it cool.
3. Supply your smoker with wood pellets and follow the start-up procedure. Preheat the grill, with the lid closed, to 450° F. If using a charcoal or gas grill, set heat to high.
4. Cut the lemons in half and sear over the flame broiler until charred, about 7 minutes. Remove from grill and set aside to cool.
5. Juice the lemons into a medium bowl. Pour lemon juice through a metal strainer into the tea pitcher to remove seeds and pulp.
6. Pour the cooled simple syrup into pitcher and stir until fully incorporated with tea and lemons. Add 2 cups of ice and refrigerate until serving.

Smoky Apple Crepes

Servings: 6
Cooking Time: 60 Minutes

Ingredients:
- 1/2 Cup Apple Juice
- 2 Lbs Apples
- 2 Tbsp Brown Sugar
- 5 Tbsp Butter
- 3 Tbsp Butter, Melted
- Tt Caramel
- 3/4 Tsp Cinnamon, Ground
- Tt Cinnamon-Sugar
- 3/4 Tsp Cornstarch
- 2 Eggs
- 1 Cup Flour

- 2 Tsp Lemon Juice
- Tennessee Apple Butter Seasoning
- 1/2 Cup Water
- 3/4 Cup Milk

Directions:

1. Supply your smoker with wood pellets and follow the start-up procedure. Preheat the grill, with the lid closed, to 225° F. If using a gas or charcoal grill, set it up for low, indirect heat.
2. Peel, halve, and core apples.
3. Season apples with Tennessee Apple Butter then place directly on the grill grate, and smoke for 1 hour.
4. Meanwhile, prepare crêpe batter: combine eggs, milk, water, flour, and 3 tbsp of melted butter in a blender, and blend until smooth.
5. Refrigerate for 30 minutes.
6. Remove apples from grill, cool slightly, then slice thin.
7. Place a cast iron skillet on the grill and melt 3 tbsp butter with brown sugar, cinnamon, cornstarch, apple and lemon juices. Cook for 5 minutes until thick.
8. Add apples and cook for another 3 to 5 minutes, stirring to coat apples in sauce.
9. Remove from grill and set aside.
10. Preheat griddle to medium-low. If using a standard grill, preheat a cast iron skillet on medium-low heat.
11. Melt 1 teaspoon of butter on the griddle.
12. Then add ½ cup of batter, and spread with the bottom of a metal spatula, working quickly, as the batter cooks fast.
13. Cook one minute per side, until edges begin to brown. Remove from griddle, set aside, and repeat with remaining batter.
14. Spoon ¼ cup of apple filling into the center of each crêpe, then quarter-fold into a triangle.
15. Serve warm with additional apple filling, drizzle of warm caramel, and a dusting of cinnamon-sugar.

Donut Bread Pudding

Servings: 8
Cooking Time: 40 Minutes

Ingredients:

- 16 Cake Donuts
- 1/2 Cup Raisins, seedless
- 5 eggs
- 3/4 Cup sugar
- 2 Cup heavy cream
- 2 Teaspoon vanilla extract
- 1 Teaspoon ground cinnamon
- 3/4 Cup Butter, melted, cooled slightly
- Ice Cream

Directions:

1. Lightly butter a 9- by 13-inch baking pan. Layer the donuts in an even thickness in the pan. Distribute the raisins over the top, if using. Drizzle evenly with the butter.
2. Make the custard: In a medium bowl, whisk together the sugar, eggs, cream, vanilla, and cinnamon. Whisk in the butter. Pour over the donuts. Let sit for 10 to 15 minutes, periodically pushing the donuts down into the custard. Cover with foil.
3. Supply your smoker with wood pellets and follow the start-up procedure. Preheat the grill, with the lid closed, to 350° F.
4. Bake the bread pudding for 30 to 40 minutes, or until the custard is set. Remove the foil and continue to bake for 10 additional minutes to lightly brown the top. Grill: 350 °F
5. Let cool slightly before cutting into squares. Drizzle with melted ice cream, if desired. Enjoy!

Smoked Cheesy Alfredo Sauce

Servings: 2
Cooking Time: 40 Minutes

Ingredients:

- 1 Cup heavy cream
- 1 Stick butter
- 1 block Parmesan cheese
- 1 Sprig fresh sage
- 2 Pinch Nutmeg

Directions:

1. Supply your smoker with wood pellets and follow the start-up procedure. Preheat the grill, with the lid closed, to 180° F.

2. Pour the cream into a saucepan along with the butter and place on the Traeger grill grate to smoke along with the parmesan cheese.
3. Smoke for 30 minutes to 1 hour, depending on how much smoke flavor you want. Turn the heat on the Traeger up to 300°F. Grill: 180 °F
4. Shred the parmesan cheese and add it and the sage sprig into the pan with the cream and butter.
5. Whisk until the cheese has all melted and season to taste with the salt and pepper and a pinch or two of the ground nutmeg.
6. While warm, pour this sauce on anything. Enjoy!

Smoked, Salted Caramel Apple Pie

Servings: 4
Cooking Time: 60 Minutes

Ingredients:

- 1 Cup cream
- 1 Cup brown sugar
- 3/4 Cup Light Corn Syrup
- 6 Tablespoon butter
- 1 Teaspoon sea salt
- 1 Pastry for Double-Crust Pie
- 6 Granny Smith Apples, Cut Into Wedges

Directions:
1. Supply your smoker with wood pellets and follow the start-up procedure. Preheat the grill, with the lid closed, to 180° F.
2. Fill a large pan with ice and water. Pour the cream into a smaller, shallow pan. Place the pan with the cream in the ice bath and place them both on the Traeger to smoke for 15-20 minutes. Grill: 180 °F
3. To make the caramel, combine the sugar and corn syrup in a saucepan and cook over medium heat, stirring constantly until it coats the back of your spoon and starts to turn a copper color, then stir in butter, salt, and smoked cream.
4. To assemble the pie, gather the pie crust, salted caramel, and apples. Place one of the pie crusts into the pie plate and fill with apple slices. Pour caramel over the apples. Lay the top crust over the filling, then crimp the top and bottom crusts together.

5. Make slits in the top crust to release the steam and finish by brushing with egg or cream. Sprinkle with raw sugar and sea salt.
6. When ready to bake, set the Traeger to 375°F and preheat, lid closed for 15 minutes.
7. Place the pie on the grill and bake for 20 minutes. Grill: 375 °F
8. Reduce heat to 325°F and cook for 25 more minutes. When ready, the crust should be golden brown and the filling, bubbly. Grill: 325 °F
9. Remove the pie from the grill and let cool. Serve with vanilla ice cream. Enjoy!

Cake With Smoked Berry Sauce

Servings: 12
Cooking Time: 90 Minutes

Ingredients:

- 12 Oz Blackberries
- 18 Oz Blueberries, Fresh
- 1/4 Cup Brown Sugar
- 2 Tsp Cinnamon, Ground
- 4 Eggs
- 2 Tbsp Flour
- 1 3/4 Cup Granulated Sugar
- 1 Lemon, Juice & Zest
- 1/2 Cup Unsalted Butter
- 3.4 Ounce Box Vanilla Instant Pudding Mix
- 3/4 Cup Vegetable Oil
- 3/4 Cup Water
- 1 Cup White Wine
- 1 Box Yellow Cake Mix

Directions:
1. Fire up your Grill and set to Smoke mode. If using a gas or charcoal grill, set it up for low, indirect heat. Supply your smoker with wood pellets and follow the start-up procedure. Preheat the grill, with the lid closed, to 450° F.
2. Place blueberries and blackberries on a sheet tray, then transfer to upper shelf of smoking cabinet. Make sure that the sear slide and side dampers are open, then preheat the grill, with the lid closed, to 375° F, to ensure

the cabinet maintains temperature between 225° F and 250° F. Smoke for 30 to 45 minutes.

3. Place cast iron skillet on grill grate. Add sugar, lemon juice and zest, and wine to skillet. Stir with a wooden spoon until sugar dissolves, then add berries from smoking cabinet.

4. Simmer berries for 15 minutes, then remove sauce from grill to cool.

5. While berries are smoking, prepare cake pans and batter. Grease and flour 2 - 9-inch round cake pans. Set aside.

6. In a large mixing bowl, combine cake mix, brown sugar, granulated sugar, pudding mix, cinnamon, eggs, water, oil, and white wine. Using a hand mixer, mix on low speed for 1 minute, then slowly increase mixing speed to high, and beat an additional 2 to 3 minutes, or until batter is smooth.

7. Evenly distribute batter among cake pans, then place pans on grill shelf and bake at 350° F, for 25 to 30 minutes, or until a toothpick inserted comes out clean. Remove from grill and set aside to cool slightly.

8. While cake is cooling, prepare glaze. Melt butter with sugar in a sauce pot on the grill. Stir for 3 minutes, then add wine. Remove from grill and set aside.

9. Turn out cake onto a sheet tray lined with parchment. Use a toothpick to poke holes in the cake, then slowly pour hot glaze over cake.

10. Spread half of smoked berry sauce on top of one layer, then place second cake layer on top. Pour additional sauce on top of cake and dust with powdered sugar, if desired. Serve warm, or room temperature.

Spiced Lemon Cherry Pie

Servings: 6-8
Cooking Time: 60 Minutes

Ingredients:
- 1/2 Teaspoon Cinnamon, Ground
- 1/2 Teaspoon Cloves, Ground
- 1/2 Cup Cornstarch
- 1 Pound Frozen Sweet Dark Cherries, Thawed
- 1 Teaspoon Water (Beaten With Egg) 1 Egg
- 1 Lemon, Juice
- 1 Lemon, Zest
- 2 Prepared Store Bought Or Homemade Pie Crust
- 1 Teaspoon Hickory Honey Sea Salt Seasoning
- 1 Cup Sugar, Granulated
- 1 Teaspoon Vanilla Extract

Directions:

1. In a large bowl, mix together the thawed cherries and their juices, sugar, cornstarch, lemon zest, lemon juice, cinnamon, clove, vanilla extract and Hickory Honey Sea Salt. Allow to sit for 30 minutes.

2. Flour a work surface and roll out one of the prepared pie crusts so that it fits a 9 inch pie tin. Fill with the cherry pie filling and refrigerate. When the pie is chilled, roll out the second pie crust, brush the edge of the first pie crust with the egg mixture, top with the second pie crust, crimp the edge with a fork, and chill. Alternatively, cut the second pie crust into strips and form a lattice pattern, attaching the strips with the egg mixture. Chill the pie for 15-30 minutes, or until the dough is very cold and firm. Brush the top of the pie with the remaining egg mixture.

3. Supply your smoker with wood pellets and follow the start-up procedure. Preheat the grill, with the lid closed, to 350° F and grill for 45 minutes to 1 hour, or until the pie crust is golden and firm and the filling is bubbly. Remove from the grill and allow to cool at room temperature for at least 4 hours to set the filling, then serve and enjoy!

Baked Parker House Rolls

Servings: 8
Cooking Time: 15 Minutes

Ingredients:
- 1/2 Ounce (2 packets) active dry yeast
- 6 Tablespoon plus 1 teaspoon cane sugar
- 1 Cup warm water (110°F to 115°F)
- 5 Cup all-purpose flour, plus more as needed
- 2 Teaspoon salt
- 1 Cup warm milk (110°-115°F)
- 1 Large eggs
- oil
- 4 Tablespoon melted butter, divided

- 1 Tablespoon Maldon Sea Salt Flakes
- 2 Tablespoon poppy seeds
- 2 Tablespoon white sesame seeds
- 1 Tablespoon garlic flakes

Directions:
1. Place the yeast, 1 teaspoon of cane sugar and warm water in a mixing bowl or the base of a stand mixer. Stir to combine. Allow the yeast to proof for 5 minutes- it should start to bubble a bit, showing that the yeast is alive.
2. Sprinkle the flour, salt and remaining 6 tablespoons of sugar over the yeast mixture. Using a dough hook or a wooden spoon, stir for 30 seconds. Pour in the warm milk and egg.
3. Knead again on the medium-low setting, or on a floured work surface by hand until the dough is very soft, adding up to one more cup of flour so the dough is soft and smooth and has lost its sticky quality.
4. Coat the bowl with a small film of oil and place the dough in the bowl, turning to coat dough evenly with the oil. Cover the bowl with a clean cloth, place in a warm spot in the kitchen and allow to proof about 45 minutes. The dough will almost double in size.
5. Punch down the dough and place on a floured work surface. Divide the dough in half, then divide each half into 12 equal pieces.
6. Using your hands, tuck in the seams of each piece of dough then place the dough on a lightly floured surface.
7. Place your fingers around the piece of dough, and roll it in a circular motion to create a smooth, even ball. Alternately, roll the dough between your two hands to create a round ball shape. Repeat with the remaining 23 pieces.
8. Butter a 9x13 inch baking pan with a tablespoon of the melted butter. Place the dough balls evenly in the pan, creating rows of 4 pieces of dough across and 6 down. Cover again with a clean towel and allow the dough to rise in a warm spot, about 30 minutes longer.
9. While the dough is proofing, supply your smoker with wood pellets and follow the start-up procedure. Preheat the grill, with the lid closed, to 325° F. Brush the remaining 3 tablespoons of butter on the bread and sprinkle with the flake salt, seeds and garlic flakes.
10. Place the pan on the grill, cover and bake about 15 to 20 minutes, or until rolls are lightly browned on top and cooked through. When done, you should be able to pull apart two pieces and see that the dough is cooked and the bottoms are lightly browned. Grill: 325 °F

Eyeball Cookies

Servings: 20
Cooking Time: 35 Minutes

Ingredients:
- 2 Packages Candy Eyeballs
- Green, Blue And Purple Food Coloring
- 1 Box Of Yellow Gluten Free Cake Mix
- 1/2 Cup (Optional) Granulated Sugar
- 2 Large Eggs
- 1/3 Cup Powdered Sugar
- 1 Teaspoon Pure Vanilla Extract
- 6 Tablespoon Melted Vegan Butter (Unsalted)

Directions:
1. Supply your smoker with wood pellets and follow the start-up procedure. Preheat the grill, with the lid closed, to 350° F.
2. Line two large baking sheets with parchment paper. In a large bowl, combine cake mix, melted butter, eggs (or egg substitute), powdered sugar, sugar (optional), and vanilla and stir until combined. (substitute 2 flax eggs for Vegan – 1 tbsp flax seed meal and 5 tbsp water per egg).
3. Divide dough between 3 bowls and dye each bowl a different color.(We used green, blue and purple).
4. Roll dough into tablespoon-sized balls.
5. Place about 2" apart on the baking sheet and grill until tops have cracked and the tops look set, 8 to 10 minutes. – Turn half way through baking, after 4-5 minutes.
6. Immediately, while the cookies are still warm, stick candy eyeballs all over the cookies.
7. Let cool completely before serving.

Maple Syrup Pancake Casserole

Servings: 6
Cooking Time: 60 Minutes

Ingredients:
- 2 Tbsp Butter
- 1/2 Cup Chocolate Chips
- 4 Egg
- Maple Syrup
- 12 - 14 Pancakes
- Powdered Sugar
- 1/4 Cup Sugar, Granulated
- 1 Tsp Vanilla Extract
- 1 1/2 Cup Whole Milk

Directions:
1. In a mixing bowl, whisk together flour, baking powder, sugar, and salt. Then pour in the milk, egg and melted butter; mix until smooth.
2. Supply your smoker with wood pellets and follow the start-up procedure. Preheat the grill, with the lid closed, to medium-low heat. If using a gas or charcoal grill, preheat a large cast iron skillet over medium-low heat.
3. Lightly oil the griddle, then scoop the batter onto the griddle, using approximately ¼ cup for each pancake. Cook 1 to 2 minutes per side, until golden brown. Set aside to cool for 15 minutes, then assemble the casserole.

Baked Chocolate Coconut Brownies

Servings: 4
Cooking Time: 25 Minutes

Ingredients:
- 1/2 Cup gluten-free or all-purpose flour, such as Bob's Red Mill
- 1/4 Cup unsweetened alkalized cocoa powder
- 1/2 Teaspoon sea salt
- 4 Ounce semisweet chocolate, coarsely chopped
- 3/4 Cup unrefined coconut oil
- 1 Cup raw cane sugar
- 4 eggs
- 1 Teaspoon vanilla extract
- 4 Ounce semisweet chocolate chips, optional

Directions:
1. Supply your smoker with wood pellets and follow the start-up procedure. Preheat the grill, with the lid closed, to 350° F.
2. Grease a 9x9 inch baking pan and line with parchment paper.
3. Combine the flour, cocoa powder and salt in a medium bowl. Set aside.
4. In a double boiler or microwave, melt the chopped chocolate and coconut oil. Let cool slightly.
5. Add the sugar, eggs and vanilla. Whisking until well combined.
6. Whisk in the flour mixture and fold in the chocolate chips. Pour into the prepared pan.
7. Place on the grill and bake until a toothpick inserted in the center of the brownies comes out clean, about 20 to 25 minutes. This will yield a somewhat gooey brownie. Continue to bake for 5 to 10 minutes if you prefer a drier brownie. Grill: 350 °F
8. Let the brownies cool completely, then cut into squares. Store in an airtight container at room temperature for up to 3 days. Enjoy!

Garlic Cheese Pull Apart Bread

Servings: 2
Cooking Time: 20 Minutes

Ingredients:
- 1 Loaf Bread, Sourdough Round
- 2 1/2 Tbsp Butter, Salted
- 8 Oz Fontina Cheese
- 1 Grated Garlic, Roasted
- 1/4 Cup Parsley, Minced Fresh
- 1 Tsp Red Flakes Pepper
- 1 Pinch Salt

Directions:
1. Start your Grill on "smoke" with the lid open until a fire is established in the burn pot (3-7 minutes). Supply your smoker with wood pellets and follow the start-up procedure. Preheat the grill, with the lid closed, to 300° F.
2. In a small bowl, add the soft butter, grated garlic, red pepper flakes, sea salt, and ¼ cup of the chopped

parsley, and whisk together. With a bread serrated knife, cut 1-inch slices into the bread, not cutting all the way through the bottom of the load. With a butter knife, spread a thin layer of the butter mixture on each slice of the bread. Take the serrated knife again, and cut across the loaf to form 1 inch squares. Next, slice the cheese into small thin slices, then stuff one slice into each bread opening. Place the bread on a baking sheet, and cover tightly with aluminum foil. Place on the grill for about 10 minutes, remove the foil, and grill for a few more minutes until the top is nicely golden and the cheese is oozing. Remove from the grill, sprinkle with fresh parsley leaves, then serve.

Rosemary Cranberry Apple Sage Stuffing

Servings: 7
Cooking Time: 45 Minutes

Ingredients:

- 10 Cups Day Old Diced Bread, Sliced Loaf
- 2 1/2 Cups Broth, Chicken
- 1 Cup Butter, Unsalted
- 1 Cup Diced Celery, Cut
- 1 1/2 Cups Fresh Cranberries
- 1 Beaten Egg
- 1 Medium Granny Smith Apple, Peel, Core And Dice
- 2 Tbsp Minced Parsley, Fresh
- 1 Tbsp Minced Rosemary, Fresh
- 2 Tbsp Roughly Chopped Sage
- Salt And Pepper
- 1 Tbsp Minced Thyme
- 2 Cups Diced Yellow Onion, Sliced

Directions:

1. Supply your smoker with wood pellets and follow the start-up procedure. Preheat the grill, with the lid closed, to 350° F.
2. Melt butter over medium heat. Add onions then celery and cook until onions start to become translucent.
3. In a large bowl, mix together bread, apples, cranberries, cooked onion and celery mixture, and fresh herbs.
4. Add half of the chicken broth to the mixture and stir.
5. Beat together eggs and the rest of the chicken broth in a small bowl. Pour into the bread mixture and stir until completely combined.
6. Add salt and pepper to taste.
7. Pour stuffing into a cast iron pan or baking dish. Cover with foil and bake on the grill for 30 minutes. Remove the foil and cook for an additional 15 minutes.
8. Serve immediately and enjoy!

Smokin' Lemon Bars

Servings: 8-12
Cooking Time: 60 Minutes

Ingredients:

- 3/4 Cup lemon juice
- 1 1/2 Cup sugar
- 2 eggs
- 3 Egg Yolk
- 1 1/2 Teaspoon cornstarch
- Pinch sea salt
- 4 Tablespoon unsalted butter
- 1/4 Cup olive oil
- 1/2 Tablespoon lemon zest
- 1 1/4 Cup flour
- 1/4 Cup granulated sugar
- 3 Tablespoon Confectioner's Sugar
- 1 Teaspoon lemon zest
- 1/4 Teaspoon Sea Salt, Fine
- 10 Tablespoon Unsalted Butter, Cut Into Cubes

Directions:

1. When ready to cook, set grill temperature to 180°F and preheat, lid closed for 15 minutes.
2. In a small mixing bowl, whisk together lemon juice, sugar, eggs and yolks, cornstarch and fine sea salt. Pour into a sheet tray or cake pan and place on grill. Smoke for 30 minutes whisking mixture halfway through smoking. Remove from grill and set aside.
3. Pour mixture into a small saucepan. Place on stove top set to medium heat until boiling. Once boiling, boil for 60 seconds. Remove from heat and strain through a mesh strainer into a bowl. Whisk in cold butter, olive oil, and lemon zest.

4. To make a crust, pulse together the flour, granulated sugar, confectioners' sugar, lemon zest and salt in a food processor. Add butter and pulse until just mixed into a crumbly dough. Press dough into a prepared 9" by 9" baking dish lined with parchment paper that is long enough to hang over 2 of the sides.

5. When ready to cook, set the smoker to 350°F and preheat, lid closed for 15 minutes.

6. Bake until crust is very lightly golden brown, about 30 to 35 minutes.

7. Remove from grill and pour the lemon filling over the crust. Return to grill and continue to bake until filling is just set about 15 to 20 minutes.

8. Allow to cool at room temperature, then refrigerate until chilled before slicing into bars. Sprinkle with confectioners' sugar and flaky sea salt right before serving. Enjoy!

Dark Chocolate Brownies With Bacon-salted Caramel

Servings: 8
Cooking Time: 40 Minutes

Ingredients:
- 8 Strips bacon
- 1/2 Cup kosher salt
- 1 Whole Brownie Mix
- 1 Jar caramel sauce

Directions:
1. For the bacon salt: Cook a few strips of bacon (6 to 8) until very crisp: 350 degrees for about 25 minutes should do it. Let cool, then pulse in a food processor until finely chopped. Mix with 1/2 cup kosher salt. Store in the refrigerator until ready to use.

2. Supply your smoker with wood pellets and follow the start-up procedure. Preheat the grill, with the lid closed, to 350° F.

3. Mix the brownies according to package directions and pour into a greased pan. Drizzle approximately 2 tablespoons of the caramel sauce over the brownie batter. Sprinkle with approximately 1 teaspoon of the bacon salt. Place directly on the grill grate of your preheated Traeger.

4. Bake the brownies for 20-25 minutes, until the batter has started to set up. Remove from the grill and drizzle with 2 more tablespoons of caramel sauce and sprinkle with more bacon salt. Return to the grill for 20-25 more minutes, or until a toothpick inserted in the middle of the brownies comes out clean.

5. If you like extra caramel, drizzle another layer of caramel on the hot brownies and sprinkle with a final bit of bacon salt. Allow the brownies to cool completely before cutting them into squares. Clean your knife in between each slice to prevent the brownies from sticking to the knife. Enjoy!

Mexican Black Bean Cornbread Casserole

Servings: 6
Cooking Time: 30 Minutes

Ingredients:
- 1 Lb Beef, Ground
- 1 15Oz Drained Black Beans, Can
- 1 Box Corn Muffin Mix
- 1 15Oz Enchilada Sauce, Can
- 1 Onion, Chopped
- 1 15Oz Drained Pinto Beans, Can

Directions:
1. Supply your smoker with wood pellets and follow the start-up procedure. Preheat the grill, with the lid closed, to 300° F.

2. Mix corn muffin mix according to directions.

3. Place cast iron skillet over flame broiler and heat for a few minutes, leaving Grill lid open.

4. Add onion and ground beef/sausage to skillet and break up

5. Cook until meat is done about 5 to 10 minutes.

6. Add both cans of beans, and enchilada sauce, stir to combine.

7. Bring mixture to a simmer.

8. Carefully close flame broiler and turn Grill up to 400 degrees.

9. Spread prepared corn muffin mix over top of meat and bean mixture and bake for 15 minutes until cornbread mixture is lightly browned.

10. Let sit 15 minutes before serving.

Eggs Ham Benedict

Servings: 6
Cooking Time: 15 Minutes

Ingredients:
- 1 Biscuit Dough, Tube
- 6 Egg
- 16 Ham, Sliced
- 1 Packet Hollandaise Sauce, Package

Directions:
1. Supply your smoker with wood pellets and follow the start-up procedure. Preheat the grill, with the lid closed, to 350° F.
2. Grease a muffin tin and crack an egg in each cup. Place on the grate of the for about 10 minutes or until the whites are fully cooked.
3. At the same time, place your biscuit dough on a greased pan. Follow the directions on the packaging but bake on the . Place 2 slices of ham per biscuit on the pan as well.
4. While the ham, eggs, and biscuits are cooking, prepare the Hollandaise Sauce according to the directions on the packet.
5. When everything is fully cooked, cut a biscuit in half, and stack one or two slices of ham, 1 egg and a dollop of Hollandaise sauce. Repeat for each half biscuit. Serve with fresh fruit.

Pound Cake

Servings: 8
Cooking Time: 60 Minutes

Ingredients:
- 1 1/2 Cup butter
- 8 Ounce cream cheese
- 3 Cup sugar
- 6 eggs
- 3 Teaspoon Bourbon Vanilla
- 1 Tablespoon lemon zest
- fresh strawberries
- whipped cream

Directions:
1. In a large bowl, cream the butter, cream cheese, and sugar. Add eggs one at a time, whipping in between. Add vanilla and lemon zest, whip.
2. Pour batter into greased loaf pans, about halfway full to allow cake to rise.
3. Supply your smoker with wood pellets and follow the start-up procedure. Preheat the grill, with the lid closed, to 325° F.
4. Place loaf pans on grill and cook for 1 hour - 1 hour and 15 minutes. Check the cake at 45 minutes, if golden brown, cover loosely with foil and continue to cook until a toothpick inserted comes out clean. Grill: 325 °F
5. Cool loaf in pan for 10 minutes before removing to a wire rack.
6. Cut into 1 inch slices and serve with fresh sliced strawberries, top with smoked whip cream.

Mint Butter Chocolate Chip Cookies

Servings: 24
Cooking Time: 12 Minutes

Ingredients:
- 1/2 Cup Butter, Melted
- 1 Package Chocolate Chip Cookie Mix
- 8-10 Drop Food Coloring
- 1/2 Tsp Mint, Extract

Directions:
1. Supply your smoker with wood pellets and follow the start-up procedure. Preheat the grill, with the lid closed, to 350° F.
2. Follow the directions on the back of the Chocolate Chip Cookie mix and also add the mint extract and green food coloring. Mix until combined.
3. On a baking sheet lined with parchment paper, drop balls of dough about 2 tbsp in size onto the pan.
4. Place in your Grill and bake for 10-12 minutes. Let cool for a couple minutes before removing from the pan. Enjoy!

Smoked Lemon Cheesecake

Servings: 16
Cooking Time: 130 Minutes

Ingredients:
- For the crust
- Vegetable oil, for oiling the pan
- 12 ounces gingersnaps (about 36) or chocolate icebox cookies (about 36)
- 3 tablespoons light brown sugar
- 8 tablespoons (1 stick) unsalted butter, melted
- For the filling
- 4 packages (8 ounces each) cream cheese, at room temperature
- 1 cup firmly packed light brown sugar
- 2 teaspoons pure vanilla extract
- 2 teaspoons finely grated lemon zest
- 1 tablespoon fresh lemon juice
- 2 tablespoons (1/4 stick) unsalted butter, melted
- 5 large eggs
- Burnt Sugar Sauce (recipes follows, optional)

Directions:
1. Supply your smoker with wood pellets and follow the start-up procedure. Preheat the grill, with the lid closed, to 400° F. Lightly oil the springform pan with vegetable oil and wrap a sheet of aluminum foil around the outside.
2. Make the crust: Break the cookies into pieces and grind with the brown sugar to a fine powder in a food processor. You'll want about 1 3/4 cups of crumbs. Add the melted butter and run the processor in short bursts to obtain a crumbly dough. Press the mixture evenly across the bottom and halfway up the sides of the springform pan. Indirect-grill or bake the crust until lightly browned, 5 to 8 minutes. Transfer the pan to a wire rack and let cool.
3. Make the filling: Wipe out the food processor bowl. Add the cream cheese, brown sugar, vanilla, lemon zest, lemon juice, and butter, and process until smooth. Work in the eggs one by one, processing until smooth after each addition. (You can also use a stand mixer, beating the cream cheese mixture until smooth and beating in the eggs one at a time.) Pour the filling into the crust. Gently tap the pan on the countertop a few times to knock out any air bubbles.
4. Supply your smoker with wood pellets and follow the start-up procedure. Preheat the grill, with the lid closed, to 225 °F-250 °F.
5. Place the cheesecake in the smoker. Smoke until the top is bronzed with smoke and the filling is set, 1 1/2 to 2 hours. To test for doneness, gently poke the side of the pan—the filling will jiggle, not ripple. Alternatively, insert a slender metal skewer in the center of the cake; it should come out clean.
6. Transfer the cheesecake in its pan to a wire rack to cool to room temperature. Refrigerate until serving; the cheesecake can be made up to 8 hours ahead. Run a slender knife around the inside of the springform pan. Unclasp and remove the ring. (You'll serve the cheesecake off the bottom of the pan.) Let the cheesecake warm slightly at room temperature before serving.
7. If serving with the sauce, pour some of it over the cheesecake and the rest into a pitcher. Cut into wedges and pass the remaining sauce.

Double Chocolate Chip Brownie Pie

Servings: 8-12
Cooking Time: 45 Minutes

Ingredients:
- 1/2 Cup Semisweet Chocolate Chips
- 1 Cup butter
- 1 Cup brown sugar
- 1 Cup sugar
- 4 Whole eggs
- 2 Teaspoon vanilla extract
- 2 Cup all-purpose flour
- 333/500 Cup Cocoa Powder, Unsweetened
- 1 Teaspoon baking soda
- 1 Teaspoon salt
- 1 Cup Semisweet Chocolate Chips
- 3/4 Cup White Chocolate Chips
- 3/4 Cup Nuts (optional)
- 1 Whole Hot Fudge Sauce, 8oz
- 2 Tablespoon Guinness Beer

Directions:
1. Coat the inside of a 10-inch (25 cm) pie plate with non-stick cooking spray.
2. When ready to cook, set the grill temperature to 350°F (180 C)and preheat, lid closed for 15 minutes.
3. Melt 1/2 cup (100 g) of the semi sweet chocolate chips in the microwave. Cream together butter, brown sugar and granulated sugar. Beat in the eggs, adding one at a time and mixing after each egg, and the vanilla. Add in the melted chocolate chips.
4. On a large piece of wax paper, sift together the cocoa powder, flour, baking soda and salt. Lift up the corners of the paper and pour slowly into the butter mixture.
5. Beat until the dry ingredients are just incorporated. Stir in the remaining semi sweet chocolate chips, white chocolate chips, and the nuts. Press the dough into the prepared pie pan.
6. Place the brownie pie on the grill and bake for 45-50 minutes or until the pie is set in the middle. Rotate the pan halfway through cooking. If the top or edges begin to brown, cover the top with a piece of aluminum foil.
7. In a microwave-safe measuring cup, heat the fudge sauce in the microwave. Stir in the Guinness.
8. Once the brownie pie is done, allow to sit for 20 minutes. Slice into wedges and top with the fudge sauce. Enjoy.

Pineapple Cake

Servings: 4
Cooking Time: 30 Minutes

Ingredients:
- 2/3 cup of vegetable oil (olive oil works great, not virgin)
- 3 eggs
- 1/3 cup brown sugar (not too sweet)
- 3/4 cup self raising plain flour
- 1/4 cup wholemeal self raising flour
- 1/3 cup saltanas
- 1/3 cup diced canned pineapple (drained)
- 1/3 cup diced raw walnuts
- 2 large carrots grated
- Icing Ingredients

- 250 grams cream cheese
- 35 grams icing sugar (not too sweet)
- Whole lemon or orange zest

Directions:
1. Mix all ingredients in a large bowl.
2. Place into 6″ greased baking tray or un-greased silicone tray.
3. Supply your smoker with wood pellets and follow the start-up procedure. Preheat the grill, with the lid closed, to 190 °F. Cook for 25-30min until golden brown and no dough when probed.
4. Let cool on rack (not directly on plate or board) then apply icing.
5. Whip icing ingredients and place in fridge until ready to coat the cake.

Pizza Bites

Servings: 6
Cooking Time: 20 Minutes

Ingredients:
- 4 1/2 Cup Bread Flour
- 1 1/2 Tablespoon sugar
- 2 Teaspoon Instant Yeast
- 2 Teaspoon kosher salt
- 3 Tablespoon extra-virgin olive oil
- 15 Fluid Ounce Water, Lukewarm
- 8 Ounce Pepperoni, sliced
- 1 Cup pizza sauce
- 1 Cup mozzarella cheese
- 1 Whole egg, for egg wash
- 1 As Needed salt

Directions:
1. For the Pizza Dough: Combine flour, sugar, salt, and yeast in food processor. Pulse 3 to 4 times until incorporated evenly. Add olive oil and water. Run food processor until mixture forms ball that rides around the bowl above the blade, about 15 seconds. Continue processing 15 seconds longer.
2. Transfer dough ball to lightly floured surface and knead once or twice by hand until smooth ball is formed. Divide dough into three even parts and place each into a

1 gallon zip top bag. Place in refrigerator and allow to rise at least one day.

3. At least two hours before baking, remove dough from refrigerator and shape into balls by gathering dough towards bottom and pinching shut. Flour well and place each one in a separate medium mixing bowl. Cover tightly with plastic wrap and allow to rise at warm room temperature until roughly doubled in volume.

4. When ready to cook, set the grill temperature to 350°F and preheat, lid closed for 15 minutes.

5. After the first rise remove the dough from the fridge and let come to room temperature. Roll dough on a flat surface. Cut dough into long strips 3" wide by 18" long.

6. Slice pepperoni into strips.

7. In a medium bowl combine the pizza sauce, mozzarella and pepperoni.

8. Spoon 1 TBSP of the pizza filling onto the pizza dough every two inches, about halfway down the length of the dough. Dip a pastry brush into the egg wash and brush around pizza filling. Fold the half side of the dough (without the pizza filling) over the other the half that contains the pizza filling.

9. Press down between each pizza bite slightly with your fingers. With a ravioli or pizza cutter, cut around each filling- creating a rectangle shape and sealing the crust in.

10. Transfer each pizza bite onto a parchment lined cookie sheet. Cover with a kitchen towel and let them rise for 30 minutes.

11. When ready to cook, preheat the grill to 350°F with the lid closed for 10-15 minutes.

12. Brush the bites with remaining egg wash, sprinkle with salt and place directly on the sheet tray. Bake 10-15 minutes until the exterior is golden brown.

13. Remove from grill and transfer to a serving dish. Serve with extra pizza sauce for dipping and enjoy!

Baked Peach Cobbler Cupcakes

Servings: 8
Cooking Time: 30 Minutes

Ingredients:
- 2 Large Peaches, fresh
- 3/4 Cup sugar
- 2 Teaspoon lemon juice
- 1/2 Teaspoon ground cinnamon
- Yellow Cake Mix, Boxed
- 1 Can vanilla icing

Directions:
1. Bring a pot of water to a boil. Turn peaches upside down and cut a small shallow X across the bottom. Put peaches in boiling water and boil for 1 minute to help loosen the skin.

2. Drain the peaches into a colander and rinse off with cold water. Peel skin off peaches.

3. Filling: Dice peaches and place into a large pan. Cook peaches over medium heat. As it starts to sizzle, add sugar, lemon and cinnamon. Cook mixture on medium heat for 10-15 minutes until a majority of the juice from the peaches evaporates leaving a thick syrup.

4. Transfer to a bowl to cool.

5. Supply your smoker with wood pellets and follow the start-up procedure. Preheat the grill, with the lid closed, to 350° F.

6. Cupcakes: Follow the directions on box cake mix and put the mixture into cupcake pan with liners.

7. When grill has preheated, bake cupcakes for 13-16 minutes, until a light golden brown. Grill: 350 °F

8. When cupcakes have cooled, use a piping bag to pipe the peach cobbler mixture into the middle of the cupcake.

9. Ice with your favorite vanilla icing. Enjoy!

Irish Soda Bread

Servings: 8-12
Cooking Time: 45 Minutes

Ingredients:
- As Needed Cornmeal
- 3 1/2 Cup all-purpose flour
- 1 1/2 Teaspoon sugar
- 1 1/4 Teaspoon baking soda
- 1 Teaspoon salt
- 1 Cup buttermilk
- To Taste butter

Directions:

1. When ready to cook, set the temperature to 400F (205 C) and preheat, lid closed, for 10 to 15 minutes.
2. Lightly dust the bottom of an 8-inch (20-cm) round cake pan with cornmeal and set aside.
3. Tear off a large sheet of wax paper and lay it on your work surface.
4. Combine the flour, sugar, soda, and salt in a large sifter and sift onto the wax paper. Carefully lift up the sides of the wax paper and tip the flour mixture back into the sifter. Re-sift into a large mixing bowl.
5. Lightly flour your work surface. Make a well in the middle of the flour mixture in the bowl and pour in 1 cup (240 mL) of buttermilk. Stir with a wooden spoon. Work quickly and gently as the carbon dioxide bubbles formed when the buttermilk hits the dry ingredients will deflate, the dough will look somewhat shaggy. If the dough seems dryish, add a little more buttermilk.
6. Turn out onto the floured surface, and with floured hands, knead gently for 10 to 20 seconds - just long enough to bring the dough bits together. (It will look more like biscuit dough than bread dough.)
7. Form into a flattish round and transfer to the prepared pan. Flour a sharp knife, and deeply cut a cross in the top of the loaf all the way to the edge of the bread. Quickly get it in to bake, if it sits too long, it will deflate.
8. Bake the bread for 45 to 50 minutes, or until it is browned and the bottom of the loaf sounds hollow when rapped with your knuckles.
9. Remove the bread from the baking pan and cool on a cooling rack. Just be-fore serving, cut the loaf in half and then slice each half into thin slices.
10. Serve with butter. Wrap leftovers tightly in plastic wrap or foil. This bread makes great toast. Enjoy!

Pull-apart Dinner Rolls

Servings: 8
Cooking Time: 10 Minutes

Ingredients:

- 1/4 Cup warm water (110°F to 115°F)
- 1/3 Cup vegetable oil
- 2 Tablespoon active dry yeast
- 1/4 Cup sugar
- 1/2 Teaspoon salt
- 1 egg
- 3 1/2 Cup all-purpose flour
- cooking spray

Directions:

1. Supply your smoker with wood pellets and follow the start-up procedure. Preheat the grill, with the lid closed, to 400° F.
2. In the bowl of a stand mixer, combine warm water, oil, yeast and sugar. Let mixture rest for 5 to 10 minutes, or until frothy and bubbly.
3. With a dough hook, mix in salt, egg and 2 cups of flour until combined. Add remaining flour 1/2 cup at a time (dough will be sticky).
4. Prepare a cast iron pan with cooking spray and set aside.
5. Spray your hands with cooking spray and shape the dough into 12 balls.
6. After shaped, place in the prepared cast iron pan and let rest for 10 minutes. Bake in Traeger for about 10 to 12 minutes, or until tops are lightly golden. Enjoy! Grill: 400 °F

Double Vanilla Chocolate Cake

Servings: 12
Cooking Time: 40 Minutes

Ingredients:

- 1 1/2 Tsp Baking Soda
- 1/2 Cup Butter, Melted
- 1 Cup Buttermilk, Low Fat
- 1 Jar Chocolate Icing, Prepared
- 3/4 Cup Cocoa, Powder
- 1 Cup Coffee, Hot
- 2 Large Egg
- 1 3/4 Cups Flour, All-Purpose
- 3/4 Tsp Salt
- 2 Cups Sugar
- 1 Tbsp Vanilla

Directions:

1. Supply your smoker with wood pellets and follow the start-up procedure. Preheat the grill, with the lid closed, to 350° F.

2. Stir together flour, sugar, cocoa, baking soda and salt in a large bowl. Combine eggs, buttermilk, butter and coffee and mix until smooth. Add in hot coffee and stir until combined and the dough is runny.
3. Pour the batter into two prepared baking pans and bake on the top rack of your for 40 minutes, turning the pans 180 degrees halfway through.
4. Allow to cool and then frost with chocolate icing.

Smoked Vanilla Apple Pie

Servings: 6
Cooking Time: 45 Minutes

Ingredients:
- 1 1/2 cups of self-raising flour
- 3/4 cup of sugar
- 0.3 lbs of butter melted
- 1 tsp of vanilla extract
- 1 egg
- 0.9-lb tin of pie apples
- sugar & cinnamon for dusting

Directions:
1. Supply your smoker with wood pellets and follow the start-up procedure. Preheat the grill, with the lid closed, to 350° F.
2. Combine the self-raising flour, sugar, melted butter, vanilla, and egg in a large bowl until a golden dough texture is formed.
3. Spread half the mixture in a pie dish and press the bottoms and up the sides of the dish.
4. Pour pie apple tin into the pie and spread out evenly.
5. Sprinkle the remaining mixture over the top of the apple evenly and place in the smoker.
6. Leave for 45 minutes or until the golden crust forms on the top.
7. Dust with cinnamon and a little sugar if desired.
8. Serve warm with custard, ice cream, or both.

Savory Cheesecake With Bourbon Pecan Topping

Servings: 6
Cooking Time: 75 Minutes

Ingredients:
- Crust
- 12 ounce Oreos
- 6 ounce melted butter
- Filling
- 24 ounces cream cheese - room temperature
- 1 cup granulated sugar
- 3 tbs cornstarch
- 2 large eggs
- 2/3 cup heavy cream
- 1 tbs vanilla
- 1 1/2 tbs bourbon
- Topping
- 3 large eggs beaten
- 1/3 cup granulated sugar
- 1/3 cup brown sugar
- 8 tbsp corn syrup dark corn syrup recommended
- 2 tbsp bourbon
- 1/2 tbsp vanilla
- 1/8 tbsp salt
- 3/4 cup rough chopped pecans (smoked pecans recommended)

Directions:
1. Supply your smoker with wood pellets and follow the start-up procedure. Preheat the grill, with the lid closed, to 350 °F.
2. Wrap foil on the bottom and up the sides of a 9" spring-form pan (outside of pan).
3. Butter the bottom & insides of the pan.
4. Crust
5. Throw ingredients in a food processor until they are finely ground.
6. Spread in 9" cheesecake pan on bottom & about ½ way upsides.
7. Filling
8. Place 8 oz of cream cheese in mixer bowl with 1/3 of sugar & cornstarch. Mix until smooth andcreamy.
9. Add another 8 oz cream cheese andbeat until smooth, then add remaining cream cheese,beating until smooth.
10. Then mix in the rest of the sugar, bourbon & vanilla.
11. Add eggs one at a time beating well after each one.

12. Add the heavy cream and mix just until smooth. Reminder: Do not over mix.
13. Pour batter into the prepared crust.
14. Topping
15. Mix all together except pecans.
16. Sprinkle pecans on top of cheesecake batter.
17. Pour topping over cheesecake batter.
18. Place in a pan big enough to hold a spring-form pan. Pour boiling water in the roasting pan to come up about ½ way up the spring-form pan.
19. Bake at 350 °F for 75 minutes until the top just barely jiggles. Carefully take the pan out of water-bath and put on cooling rack.
20. Let cool for 2 hours in pan. After 2 hours put in fridge until totally chilled then serve.

Bananas Rum Foster

Servings: 4
Cooking Time: 10 Minutes

Ingredients:
- 1/3 Cup Banana Nectar
- 4 Bananas, Quartered
- 3/4 Cup Brown Sugar
- 1/4 Cup Butter
- 1/2 Tsp Cinnamon, Ground
- 1/3 Cup Dark Rum
- Vanilla Ice Cream

Directions:
1. Supply your smoker with wood pellets and follow the start-up procedure. Preheat the grill, with the lid closed, to medium heat. If using a gas or charcoal grill, preheat a cast iron skillet.
2. Place a large skillet on the griddle, then melt butter in the skillet. Whisk in brown sugar and cinnamon, stirring until sugar dissolves.
3. Add the banana nectar and bananas. Stir to coat
4. Once the bananas begin to soften and turn brown, add the rum. Stir, then ignite the sauce with a stick lighter. After the flames subside, simmer the sauce for 2 minutes.
5. Divide the bananas among 4 scoops/bowls of vanilla ice cream, then spoon the warm sauce over the top of the ice cream. Serve immediately.

Baked Chocolate Brownie Cookies With Egg Nog

Servings: 6
Cooking Time: 12 Minutes

Ingredients:
- 16 Ounce Bar bittersweet chocolate, finely chopped
- 4 Tablespoon unsalted butter, room temperature
- 4 eggs
- 1 1/3 Cup granulated sugar
- 1 Teaspoon vanilla extract
- 1 1/2 Cup all-purpose flour
- 1/2 Teaspoon baking powder
- 1 Cup semisweet chocolate chips

Directions:
1. Supply your smoker with wood pellets and follow the start-up procedure. Preheat the grill, with the lid closed, to 350° F.
2. Line two baking sheets with parchment paper.
3. Put the finely chopped chocolate and butter in a heatproof bowl and set over a saucepan of barely simmering water; stir occasionally until chocolate is completely melted and smooth. Set aside and allow to cool to room temperature.
4. Whisk together eggs, sugar and vanilla extract in a medium bowl. Set aside.
5. Sift together the flour and baking powder in a small bowl. Add the melted chocolate mixture to the egg mixture and stir with a rubber spatula until completely combined.
6. Add the flour mixture in three batches, folding gently into the batter with a spatula. Once all of the flour has been incorporated, stir in the chocolate chips.
7. Scoop 1-1/2 tablespoons of dough onto prepared baking sheets. Bake for 10 to 12 minutes or until they are firm on the outside. Do not over bake. Grill:350° F
8. Leave to cool completely on the baking sheets. Enjoy!

Lemon Chicken, Broccoli, String Beans Foil Packs

Servings: 4
Cooking Time: 20 Minutes

Ingredients:
- 2 Cups Broccoli
- 3 Tbsp Butter, Melted
- 4 Chicken, Boneless/Skinless
- 1 Garlic, Minced
- 1 1/2 Tsp Italian Seasoning, Dried
- 1 Lemon, Sliced
- Pepper
- Salt
- 1 Cup String Beans

Directions:
1. Supply your smoker with wood pellets and follow the start-up procedure. Preheat the grill, with the lid closed, to 450° F.
2. Lay four 12 x 12 inch pieces of foil out on a flat surface, then place one chicken breast in the middle of each foil.
3. Divide the broccoli and string beans between the four foil packs. Thinly slice the lemon, split them between each foil pack, and place the slices on, in and around the chicken and vegetables.
4. Mix the butter, garlic, juice of the remaining lemon, and Italian seasoning together, and then brush over the chicken and vegetables. Sprinkle with salt and pepper to taste.
5. Fold the foil over the chicken and vegetables to close the pack, and pinch the ends together so the pack will remain closed.
6. Grill for 7-9 minutes on each side. Turn off grill, remove the foil packets, and serve immediately.

Baked Potatoes & Celery Root Au Gratin

Servings: 2
Cooking Time: 60 Minutes

Ingredients:
- 5 Tablespoon butter, softened
- 2 Large leeks, white parts only, cleaned and sliced into half moons
- kosher salt
- freshly ground black pepper
- 5 Small Yukon Gold potatoes, sliced 1/4 inch thick
- 2 Whole celery root, peeled and sliced 1/4 inch thick
- 2 Cup cream
- 1 Tablespoon minced sage
- 1 Cup shredded Gruyere or other hearty Swiss cheese, divided

Directions:
1. Supply your smoker with wood pellets and follow the start-up procedure. Preheat the grill, with the lid closed, to 400° F.
2. Butter a 9x13 baking dish with 1 tablespoon of the softened butter. In a medium frying pan over medium heat, melt the remaining butter. Add the leeks and a generous pinch of salt and pepper and cook, stirring often until softened, about 5 minutes.
3. Remove from the heat and allow to cool. Place the potato and celery root slices into a large mixing bowl. Add the cream, leek mixture, minced sage, 1 teaspoon salt, 1/2 teaspoon pepper and 1 cup cheese. Stir gently to coat.
4. Arrange a layer of potato and celery root slices so they're slightly overlapping in the prepared baking dish. Repeat two more times so there are three layers of potatoes. Pour remaining cream from the bowl over the gratin, then sprinkle the top with the remaining cup of cheese.
5. Cover the dish loosely with foil and bake on the grill for 45 minutes. Remove the foil and continue baking until the top is golden and bubbly and the potatoes are tender when pierced, about 30 to 45 minutes longer. Let stand for 10 minutes before serving. Enjoy!

Easy Smoked Cornbread

Servings: 4
Cooking Time: 75 Minutes

Ingredients:
- 2 cups self rising flour
- 1 1/2 cups white corn meal
- 2 cups sharp cheddar cheese
- 1/2 cup sour cream
- 1/2 cup sugar
- 1 Tbsp baking powder
- 1 teaspoon sea salt
- 1 12 oz can of evaporated milk
- 1/2 cup vegetable oil
- 2 large eggs beaten

Directions:
1. Mix all ingredients together well and fold into a greased baking pan (such as a round cake Pan).
2. Supply your smoker with wood pellets and follow the start-up procedure. Preheat the grill, with the lid closed, to 375° F. Smoke on 375 °F for 1 hour and 15 minutes or until toothpick comes clean and edges look brown.
3. Rub some butter on top and sprinkle a little Fred's Butt Rub on top before serving.
4. Enjoy!

Cinnamon Pull-aparts

Servings: 6
Cooking Time: 20 Minutes

Ingredients:
- 16.3 Ounce Biscuits, Homestyle, Canned
- 1 Cup packed brown sugar
- 1/2 Cup butter
- 1/4 Cup water
- 1 Teaspoon ground cinnamon
- 1/2 Cup Nuts (optional)

Directions:
1. Cut each biscuit into 4 pieces and peel each piece in half; set aside.
2. Combine brown sugar, butter and water in a large saucepan and bring to a boil; reduce heat and simmer for 1 minute. Stir in cinnamon and nuts; add biscuit quarters and mix to coat. Pour into greased 13 by 9 inch casserole dish and spread evenly in the dish.
3. Supply your smoker with wood pellets and follow the start-up procedure. Preheat the grill, with the lid closed, to 350° F.
4. Place the casserole dish on the grill; close lid and cook for 20 to 25 minutes or until the biscuits are done. Grill: 350 °F
5. Remove from the grill and transfer to a serving platter making sure to get all the gooey syrup onto the biscuits. Serve warm. Enjoy!

Smoky Pimento Cheese Cornbread

Servings: 4
Cooking Time: 30 Minutes

Ingredients:
- 2 Tsp Baking Powder
- 2 Cups Buttermilk, Low Fat
- 1/2 Cup Cornmeal, Yellow
- 2 Egg
- 1 1/2 Cups Flour, All-Purpose
- 16 Oz Pimento Cheese Spread
- 2 Tbsp Bacon Cheddar Seasoning
- 1/4 Cup Sugar

Directions:
1. Supply your smoker with wood pellets and follow the start-up procedure. Preheat the grill, with the lid closed, to 350° F. Place a cast iron skillet in the grill to preheat.
2. In a bowl, mix together the eggs, buttermilk, Bacon Cheddar Seasoning, and pimento cheese spread. Add in the sugar, baking powder, cornmeal and flour. Mix until well combined.
3. With cooking gloves, carefully remove the cast iron skillet from the grill, grease it, and add the cornbread batter.
4. Grill for 25-30 minutes, or until the cornbread is golden and pulling away from the edges of the skillet.

Chocolate Lava Cake With Smoked Whipped Cream

Servings: 4
Cooking Time: 45 Minutes

Ingredients:
- 1 Pint heavy whipping cream
- 9 Tablespoon Butter
- 220 G Semisweet Chocolate
- 1 1/4 Cup powdered sugar
- 2 Large eggs
- 2 egg yolk
- 6 Tablespoon flour
- 1 Tablespoon Bourbon Vanilla
- Powdered Sugar
- cocoa powder

Directions:
1. Supply your smoker with wood pellets and follow the start-up procedure. Preheat the grill, with the lid closed, to 180° F.
2. For the Smoked Whipped Cream: Add cream to a shallow, aluminum baking pan. Place the pan on the grill and smoke for 30 minutes.
3. Pour the smoked cream into a large mixing bowl and refrigerate for later use. Grill: 180 °F
4. Increase the grill temperature to 375°F and preheat. Grill: 375 °F
5. Brush 4 small soufflé cups with 1 tablespoon melted butter.
6. Melt the chocolate and remaining butter in a heatproof bowl over simmering water, stir until smooth.
7. Stir in powdered sugar. Add eggs and egg yolks, stirring continuously. Whisk in flour until blended completely.
8. Pour batter into the prepared soufflé cups. Place them on the Traeger and bake for 13-14 minutes, or until the sides are set. Grill: 375 °F
9. For the Whipped Cream: Remove the chilled smoked cream from the refrigerator, add the bourbon vanilla and whip until airy.
10. Add confectioners sugar and continue whipping until whipped cream forms stiff peaks.
11. Dust lava cakes with confectioners sugar and cocoa, top with a dollop of smoke-infused whipped cream. Enjoy!

Baked Cheesy Parmesan Grits

Servings: 4
Cooking Time: 60 Minutes

Ingredients:
- 4 Cup chicken stock
- 3 Tablespoon butter
- 3/4 Teaspoon salt
- 1 Cup quick grits
- 1 Cup shredded cheddar cheese
- pepper
- 1/2 Cup Monterey Jack cheese, shredded
- 1/2 Cup whole milk
- 2 Large eggs

Directions:
1. Supply your smoker with wood pellets and follow the start-up procedure. Preheat the grill, with the lid closed, to 350° F.
2. Butter an 8" baking dish or a 10" cast iron pan.
3. Bring the chicken stock, butter, and salt to boil in medium saucepan. Gradually whisk in grits.
4. Reduce heat to medium and cook until mixture thickens slightly, stirring often about 8 minutes. Remove from heat.
5. Add cheeses and stir until melted. Season with pepper and salt to taste.
6. Whisk together milk and eggs in small bowl. Gradually whisk mixture into grits.
7. Pour the cheese grits into the buttered cast iron pan. Bake until grits feel firm to touch, about 1 hour. Grill: 350 °F
8. Remove from grill and let stand 10 minutes before serving. Enjoy!

Garlic Lemon Pepper Chicken Wings

Servings: 4
Cooking Time: 30 Minutes

Ingredients:
- 1/4 Cup Black Peppercorns, Ground
- 4 Pounds Chicken, Wing
- 2 Tsp Coriander, Ground
- 2 Tsp Garlic Powder
- 2-3 Tbsp Lemon, Zest
- 1 Tsp Salt, Kosher
- 3 Tsp Dried Thyme, Fresh Sprigs

Directions:
1. Supply your smoker with wood pellets and follow the start-up procedure. Preheat the grill, with the lid closed, to 400° F.
2. In a bowl, begin to mix the ground pepper and zest of the lemon together, then add the rest of the ingredients.
3. Place the wings in a bowl and toss with a little olive oil, add a few tablespoons of the seasoning, toss with your hands, then repeat until the wings are well seasoned to your liking.
4. Place the wings on the grill, and cook them for about 15 minutes, then flip and grill for another 15 minutes.
5. Continue to flip the wings, until they are done and crispy. Remove the wings from the grill, and serve.

Cast Iron Pineapple Upside Down Cake

Servings: 6
Cooking Time: 40 Minutes

Ingredients:
- 1/4 Cup butter, melted
- 1 Cup brown sugar
- 20 Ounce Pineapple, sliced
- 6 Ounce maraschino cherries
- 1 Whole Yellow Cake Mix, Boxed
- vegetable oil
- eggs

Directions:
1. Supply your smoker with wood pellets and follow the start-up procedure. Preheat the grill, with the lid closed, to 350° F.
2. Pour melted butter into a 12-inch cast iron pan. Sprinkle brown sugar on top of the butter. Arrange pineapple slices on brown sugar, squeezing in as many slices as possible. Place a cherry in center of each pineapple slice; press gently into brown sugar.
3. Make cake batter as directed on box, substituting pineapple juice mixture for as much of the water as possible, and adding in required oil and eggs. Pour batter into cast iron dish, over pineapple and cherries.
4. Place the cast iron pan on the grill grate and cook for 20 minutes. Rotate the pan a half turn to ensure it cooks evenly. Cook for an additional 20 minutes, or until toothpick inserted in center comes out clean.
5. Immediately run knife around side of pan to loosen cake. Place heatproof serving plate upside down onto pan; turn plate and pan over.
6. Leave pan over cake 5 minutes so brown sugar topping can drizzle over cake. Cool 30 minutes. Enjoy!

Smoker Wheat Bread

Servings: 6
Cooking Time: 60 Minutes

Ingredients:
- As Needed extra-virgin olive oil
- 2 Cup all-purpose flour
- 1 Cup whole wheat flour
- 1 1/4 Ounce Packet, Active Dry Yeast
- 1 1/4 Teaspoon salt
- 1 1/2 Cup water
- As Needed Cornmeal

Directions:
1. Oil a large mixing bowl and set aside. In a second mixing bowl, combine the flours, yeast, and salt.
2. Push your sleeve up to your elbow and form your fingers into a claw. Mix the dry ingredients until well-combined.
3. Add the water and mix until blended. The dough will be wet, shaggy, and somewhat stringy.

4. Tip the dough into the oiled mixing bowl and cover with plastic wrap.

5. Allow the dough to rise at room temperature-- about 70 degrees-- for 2 hours, or until the surface is bubbled.

6. Turn the dough out onto a lightly floured work surface and lightly flour the top. With floured hands, fold the dough over on itself twice. Cover loosely with plastic wrap and allow the dough to rest for 15 minutes.

7. Dust a clean lint-free cotton towel with cornmeal, wheat bran, or flour. With floured hands, gently form the dough into a ball and place it, seam side down, on the towel.

8. Dust the top of the ball with cornmeal, wheat bran, or flour, and cover the dough with a second towel. Let the dough rise until doubled in size; the dough will not spring back when poked with a finger.

9. In the meantime, start the smoker grill and set temperature to 450 F. Preheat, lid closed, for 10-15 minutes.

10. Put a lidded 6- to 8-quart cast iron Dutch oven - preferably one coated with enamel, on the grill grate.

11. When the dough has risen, remove the top towel, slide your hand under the bottom towel to support the dough, then carefully tip the dough, seam side up, into the preheated pot.

12. Remove the towel. Shake the pot a couple of times if the dough looks lopsided: It will straighten out as it bakes.

13. Cover the pot with the lid and bake the bread for 30 minutes. Remove the lid and continue to bake the bread for 15 to 30 minutes more, or until it is nicely browned and sounds hollow when rapped with your knuckles.

14. Turn onto a wire rack to cool. Slice with a serrated knife. Enjoy!

Blueberry Sour Cream Muffins

Servings: 8
Cooking Time: 25 Minutes

Ingredients:
- 2 Cup flour
- 1/2 Teaspoon salt
- 1/2 Teaspoon baking soda
- 1/2 Cup butter
- 3/4 Cup sugar, plus more for muffin tops
- 2 Large eggs
- 3/4 Cup sour cream
- 1 1/2 Teaspoon vanilla extract
- 1 1/2 Cup blueberries, fresh or thawed

Directions:

1. In a small mixing bowl, whisk together the flour, salt and baking soda.

2. In another bowl, using a wooden spoon or a mixer, beat the butter and sugar until light-colored and fluffy. Beat in the eggs, one at a time. Stir in sour cream and vanilla.

3. Add the flour mixture gradually and mix just until incorporated. Using a rubber spatula, gently fold in the blueberries.

4. Line a 12-cup muffin tin with the cupcake liners. Using an ice cream scoop or spoon, fill each muffin cup two-thirds full with the batter. Sprinkle sugar evenly over the top of each muffin.

5. Supply your smoker with wood pellets and follow the start-up procedure. Preheat the grill, with the lid closed, to 375° F.

6. Bake the muffins 25 to 30 minutes, or until a toothpick inserted comes out clean. Served warm and with butter. Grill: 375 °F

SEAFOOD RECIPES

Roasted Halibut With Spring Vegetables

Servings: 4
Cooking Time: 20 Minutes

Ingredients:
- 4 thick-cut halibut fillets
- 2 Tablespoon Fin & Feather Rub
- Butcher Paper
- 1 Pound Carrots, Peeled and Cut into 3/4" Inch Slices
- 1 Pound asparagus, ends trimmed
- 1/2 Pound Oyster Mushrooms
- 2 Tablespoon butter
- salt and pepper
- 1/2 Cup white wine

Directions:
1. Season the halibut fillets with Traeger Fin and Feather Rub.
2. To build the packets: Start with four sheets of parchment paper about twenty inches long. Fold in half, then open it back up.
3. Divide the carrots, asparagus, and mushrooms between the four pieces of parchment and top each with a little bit of butter. Season with salt and pepper. Place a halibut fillet on top of the vegetables in each packet.
4. Next, fold the paper over so the two ends meet, enclosing the food. Beginning at either end of the center crease, make small, overlapping diagonal folds around the filling, sealing the packet tight. Before finishing the final fold, pour a little bit of wine in each packet then seal completely.
5. Supply your smoker with wood pellets and follow the start-up procedure. Preheat the grill, with the lid closed, to 500° F.
6. Place all four packets on a sheet tray and place in the grill. Cook for 7-10 minutes or until the internal temperature of the fish reaches 145°F. Remove from the grill and place packet on a serving dish. Grill: 500 °F Probe: 145 °F
7. Using a knife or scissors, cut open each packet and fold the edges back. Finish with a little bit of lemon juice if desired. Enjoy!

Bacon Wrapped Shrimp

Servings: 6
Cooking Time: 20 Minutes

Ingredients:
- 1 1/2 Pound Jumbo Shrimp, Peeled And Deveined
- 10 Strips Bacon
- Cheesy Grits, For Serving
- 1/4 Cup extra-virgin olive oil
- 2 Tablespoon lemon juice
- 1 Teaspoon Fresh Chopped Parsley
- 1 Tablespoon lemon zest
- 1 Teaspoon garlic, minced
- 1 Teaspoon salt
- 1/2 Teaspoon black pepper

Directions:
1. Rinse the shrimp under cold running water and dry thoroughly on paper towels.
2. Transfer to a re-sealable plastic bag or a bowl.
3. For the marinade: Combine the olive oil, lemon juice, lemon zest, garlic, salt, pepper, and parsley in a small jar with a tight-fitting lid and shake vigorously until combined.
4. Pour over the shrimp and refrigerate for 30 minutes to 1 hour.
5. Supply your smoker with wood pellets and follow the start-up procedure. Preheat the grill, with the lid closed, to 400° F.
6. Lay the bacon strips diagonally on the grill grate and grill for 10 to 12 minutes, or until the bacon is partially cooked but still very pliable.
7. Cut each strip in half width-wise. Leave the grill on.
8. Drain the shrimp, discarding the marinade. Wrap a strip of bacon around the body of each shrimp, securing with a toothpick. Grill for 4 minutes per side, turning once. Enjoy! Grill: 400 °F
9. Wrap a strip of bacon around the body of each shrimp, securing with a toothpick.
10. Grill for 4 minutes per side, turning once. Serve over cheesy grits, if desired. Enjoy!

Spicy Crab Poppers

Servings: 8
Cooking Time: 30 Minutes

Ingredients:
- 18 Whole jalapeño
- 8 Ounce cream cheese, softened
- 1 Cup Canned Corn, drained
- 1/2 Cup Crab meat, lump
- 1 1/4 Teaspoon Old Bay Seasoning
- 2 Scallions, minced

Directions:
1. Cut each jalapeño in half lengthwise through the stem and remove the ribs and seeds.
2. Filling: In a mixing bowl, combine the cream cheese, corn, crab meat, scallions, and Old Bay Seasoning and stir until blended. Stir in the scallions. Spoon the filling into the jalapeño halves, mounding it slightly.
3. Arrange the poppers on a baking sheet covered with foil or parchment paper.
4. Supply your smoker with wood pellets and follow the start-up procedure. Preheat the grill, with the lid closed, to 350° F.
5. Roast the jalapeños for 25 to 30 minutes, or until the peppers have softened and the filling is hot and bubbling.
6. Let cool slightly before serving. Enjoy!

Hot-smoked Salmon

Servings: 4
Cooking Time: 180minutes

Ingredients:
- 1½lb (680g) skinless center-cut salmon fillet, preferably wild caught
- for the brine
- 1 quart (1 liter) distilled water
- ¼ cup coarse salt
- ¼ cup light brown sugar or low-carb equivalent
- ¼ cup gin (optional)

Directions:
1. In a saucepan on the stovetop over medium-high heat, make the brine by combining the water, salt, brown sugar, and gin (if using). Bring the mixture to a boil. Stir until the salt and sugar dissolve. Remove the pan from the stovetop and let the brine cool to room temperature. Refrigerate until cool.
2. Run your fingers over the salmon fillet, feeling for bones. Remove any with kitchen tweezers or needle-nosed pliers. Rinse the salmon under cold running water. Place the salmon in a resealable plastic bag and pour the brine over it. Refrigerate for 4 to 8 hours.
3. Place a wire rack on a rimmed sheet pan. Remove the salmon from the brine and rinse under cold running water. Pat dry with paper towels and then place the salmon on the wire rack. Place the pan in a cool area with good air circulation (such as near a fan). In 2 to 4 hours, you'll notice the salmon has developed a pellicle—a kind of sticky skin or coating that will help the smoke adhere to the fish. (Don't skip this step.)
4. Supply your smoker with wood pellets and follow the start-up procedure. Preheat the grill, with the lid closed, to 150° F.
5. Place the salmon on the grate and smoke until the fish flakes easily when pressed with a fork and the internal temperature reaches 140°F (60°C), about 3 hours. If albumin (a harmless white protein) appears on top of the fillet as it smokes, gently remove it with a paper towel.
6. Remove the salmon from the grill and let rest for 10 minutes. (You can also transfer the fish to a clean wire rack and let it cool to room temperature. Cover and refrigerate if not using immediately. The salmon will keep for up to 5 days.)
7. Serve the salmon with eggs, on salads, with Mustard Caviar, or with its traditional accompaniments: cream cheese, capers, chopped hard-boiled eggs, diced red onion, and dark bread.

Grilled Pepper Lobster Tails

Servings: 3
Cooking Time: 10 Minutes

Ingredients:
- Tt Black Pepper
- 3/4 Stick Butter, Room Temp
- 2 Tablespoons Chives, Chopped

- 1 Clove Garlic, Minced
- Lemon, Sliced
- 3 (7-Ounce) Lobster, Tail
- Tt Salt, Kosher

Directions:
1. Start your Grill on "SMOKE" with the lid open until a fire is established in the burn pot (3-7 minutes).
2. Supply your smoker with wood pellets and follow the start-up procedure. Preheat the grill, with the lid closed, to 350° F.
3. Blend butter, chives, minced garlic, and black pepper in a small bowl. Cover with plastic wrap and set aside.
4. Butterfly the tails down the middle of the softer underside of the shell. Don't cut entirely through the center of the meat. Brush the tails with olive oil and season with salt, to your liking.
5. Grill lobsters cut side down about 5 minutes until the shells are bright red in color. Flip the tails over and top with a generous tablespoon of herb butter. Grill for another 4 minutes, or until the lobster meat is an opaque white color.
6. Remove from the grill and serve with more herb butter and lemon wedges.

Peper Fish Tacos

Servings: 12
Cooking Time: 10 Minutes

Ingredients:
- 1 Tsp Black Pepper
- 1/4 Tsp Cayenne Pepper
- 1 1/2 Lbs Cod Fish
- 1/2 Tsp Cumin
- 1 Tsp Garlic Powder
- 1 Tsp Oregano
- 1 1/2 Tsp Paprika, Smoked
- 1/2 Tsp Salt

Directions:
1. Supply your smoker with wood pellets and follow the start-up procedure. Preheat the grill, with the lid closed, to 350° F.
2. Mix together paprika, garlic powder, oregano, cumin, cayenne, salt and pepper. Sprinkle over cod.
3. Place the cod on your preheated for about 5 minutes per side. Toast tortillas over heat, if desired.
4. Break the cod into pieces, smash the avocado, slice the tomatoes in half and place evenly among the tortillas. Top with red onion, lettuce, jalapenos, sour cream, and cilantro. Spritz with lime juice and enjoy!

Grilled Maple Syrup Salmon

Servings: 6
Cooking Time: 30 Minutes

Ingredients:
- 1 large salmon fillet (around 3 pounds)
- 1/2 cup salted butter (melted)
- 2 tablespoons soy sauce
- Salt and pepper
- 1/4 cup maple syrup

Directions:
1. Supply your smoker with wood pellets and follow the start-up procedure. Preheat the grill, with the lid closed, to 400° F.
2. Place the salmon fillet in a baking pan lined with parchment paper.
3. Sprinkle the fish with salt and pepper.
4. Add half of the melted butter to the salmon and place the baking pan on the grill.
5. Grill for 15-20 minutes or until fish is roughly 70% cooked. It will feel still gelatinous in the thickest parts of the salmon.
6. Combine the remaining melted butter, soy sauce, and maple syrup and pour over the salmon.It will run off the sides so use a spoon to pour it back over the fish. It's also perfectly fine that some will be left on the sides of the pan.
7. Cook for 5 to 10 additional minutes or until the fish is cooked through. The fish should be firm to the touch but still moist and soft when pressed on,and the ridges will flake or pull apart if pressed on.

Lemon Shrimp Scampi

Servings: 3
Cooking Time: 10 Minutes

Ingredients:
- 2 Tsp Blackened Sriracha Rub Seasoning
- 1/2 Cup Butter, Cubed, Divided
- 1/2 Tsp Chili Pepper Flakes
- 3 Garlic Cloves, Minced
- To Taste, Lemon Wedges, For Serving
- 1 Lemon, Juice & Zest
- Linguine, Cooked
- 3 Tbsp Parsley, Chopped
- 1 1/2 Lbs Shrimp, Peeled & Deveined
- Toasted Baguette, For Serving

Directions:
1. Supply your smoker with wood pellets and follow the start-up procedure. Preheat the grill, with the lid closed, to medium-high heat. If using a gas or charcoal grill, set it up for medium-high heat.
2. Add half of the butter to the griddle, then sauté the garlic, Blackened Sriracha, and chili flakes for 1 minute, until fragrant.
3. Add the shrimp, turning occasionally for 2 minutes, until opaque.
4. Add the remaining butter, parsley, lemon zest and juice. Toss the shrimp to coat in lemon butter, then remove from the griddle, and transfer to a serving bowl.
5. Serve immediately, with fresh lemon wedges, and toasted baguette. Serve over linguine, spaghetti or zucchini noodles, if desired.

Alder Smoked Scallops With Citrus & Garlic Butter Sauce

Servings: 4
Cooking Time: 35 Minutes

Ingredients:
- 2 Pound large dry sea scallops
- kosher salt
- freshly ground black pepper
- 8 Tablespoon salted butter, melted
- 1 Clove garlic, minced
- 1 Small orange
- 1/4 Teaspoon Worcestershire sauce
- 1 1/2 Teaspoon fresh chopped parsley or tarragon
- flat-leaf parsley, for serving

Directions:
1. Wash the scallops under cold running water and thoroughly pat dry on paper towels. Remove any tags of abductor muscle tissue you find on the sides of the scallops.
2. Arrange the scallops on a baking sheet fitted with a cooling rack, and season with salt and pepper.
3. Supply your smoker with wood pellets and follow the start-up procedure. Preheat the grill, with the lid closed, to 165° F.
4. Place the baking sheet with the scallops on the grill grate and smoke for 20 minutes.
5. While your scallops are smoking, make your sauce. Melt the butter in a small saucepan over medium-low heat. Add a pinch of salt, garlic, Worcestershire sauce, zest and juice from half of the orange, and parsley. Simmer for 5 minutes. Keep warm.
6. Remove the baking sheet with the scallops from the grill and set aside. Increase the temperature to 400°F and preheat, lid closed. Optional: Place an oyster bed or oyster pan in the grill to preheat. These heavy iron pans are a great way to sear the scallops. Grill: 400 °F
7. Return the baking sheet with the scallops to the grill, brush with the butter sauce, reserving some for serving. Roast until just opaque and tender, 10 to 15 minutes. The time will depend on how thick the scallops are. Do not overcook. If you are using an oyster pan, brush each compartment lightly with olive oil to prevent sticking. Spoon butter sauce on each of the scallops, reserving some for serving.
8. Serve the scallops hot with a little more orange zest, fresh parsley and the the warm citrus and garlic butter sauce. Enjoy!

Traeger Jerk Shrimp

Servings: 8
Cooking Time: 10 Minutes

Ingredients:
- 1 Tablespoon brown sugar
- 1 Tablespoon smoked paprika
- 1 Teaspoon garlic powder
- 1/4 Teaspoon Thyme, ground
- 1/4 Teaspoon ground cayenne pepper
- 1 Teaspoon sea salt
- 1 lime zest
- 2 Pound shrimp in shell
- 3 Tablespoon olive oil

Directions:
1. Combine spices, salt, and lime zest in a small bowl and mix. Place shrimp into a large bowl, then drizzle in the olive oil, Add the spice mixture and toss to combine, making sure every shrimp is kissed with deliciousness.
2. Supply your smoker with wood pellets and follow the start-up procedure. Preheat the grill, with the lid closed, to 450° F.
3. Arrange the shrimp on the grill and cook for 2 – 3 minutes per side, until firm, opaque, and cooked through. Grill: 450 °F
4. Serve with lime wedges, fresh cilantro, mint, and Caribbean Hot Pepper Sauce. Enjoy!

Smoked Mango Shrimp

Servings: 4
Cooking Time: 5 Minutes

Ingredients:
- 2 Tablespoon Olive Oil
- 1 Pound Raw Tail-On, Thawed And Deveined Shrimp, Uncooked

Directions:
1. Supply your smoker with wood pellets and follow the start-up procedure. Preheat the grill, with the lid closed, to 425° F. Rinse shrimp off in sink with cold water. Place in bowl and season generously with Mango Magic seasoning and olive oil. Toss well in bowl.
2. Thread several shrimp onto a skewer, so that they are all just touching each other. Repeat with other skewers and remaining shrimp.
3. Grill shrimp for 2 - 3 minutes on each side, or until pink and opaque all the way through. Remove from grill and serve immediately.

Prosciutto-wrapped Scallops

Servings: 4
Cooking Time: 10 Minutes

Ingredients:
- 1½lb (680g) jumbo sea or diver scallops (size U-10)
- 8 to 10 thin slices of prosciutto, each halved lengthwise
- coarse salt
- freshly ground black pepper
- for the butter
- 8oz (225g) unsalted butter
- 2 tsp minced fresh curly or flat-leaf parsley
- 1½ tsp finely grated orange zest
- 1 tbsp freshly squeezed orange juice
- 1 tsp finely grated lemon zest
- 1 tsp finely grated lime zest
- ½ tsp coarse salt

Directions:
1. Supply your smoker with wood pellets and follow the start-up procedure. Preheat the grill, with the lid closed, to 450° F.
2. In a small saucepan on the stovetop over medium-low heat, make the citrus butter by melting the butter. Add the remaining ingredients and simmer for 3 to 5 minutes to blend the flavors. Keep warm.
3. Rinse the scallops under cold running water and dry with paper towels. Place each scallop on its side at the end of a piece of prosciutto and wrap the prosciutto around the scallop. Secure with a toothpick. Season the exposed sides of the scallop with salt and pepper.
4. Place the scallops exposed sides down on the grate and grill until the edges of the prosciutto begin to frizzle and the scallop is warm inside, about 3 to 5 minutes per side.
5. Transfer the scallops to a platter. Brush with some of the warm citrus butter before serving. Serve the remaining butter on the side.

Grilled Lobster Tails With Smoked Paprika Butter

Servings: 4
Cooking Time: 10-12 Minutes

Ingredients:
- 4 lobster tails, each about 8 to 10oz (225 to 285g), thawed if frozen
- 3 lemons, 1 quartered lengthwise, 2 halved through their equators
- for the butter
- 1¼ cup unsalted butter, at room temperature
- 2 garlic cloves, peeled and finely minced
- 3 tbsp chopped fresh parsley
- 2 tbsp chopped fresh chives
- 1 tbsp freshly squeezed lemon juice
- 2 tsp finely chopped lemon zest
- 2 tsp smoked paprika
- 1 tsp coarse salt

Directions:
1. Supply your smoker with wood pellets and follow the start-up procedure. Preheat the grill, with the lid closed, to 450° F.
2. In a medium bowl, make the paprika butter by combining the ingredients. Beat with a wooden spoon until well blended.
3. Use a sharp, heavy knife or sturdy kitchen shears to cut lengthwise through the top shell of each lobster tail in a straight line toward the tail fin. Gently loosen the meat from the bottom shell and sides. Lift the meat through the slit you just made so the meat sits on top of the shell. Slip a lemon quarter underneath the meat (between the meat and the bottom shell) to keep it elevated. Spread 1 tablespoon of paprika butter on top of each lobster. Melt the remaining butter and keep it warm.
4. Place the lobster tails flesh side up and lemon halves cut sides down on the grate. Grill the lobsters until the flesh is white and opaque and the internal temperature of the lobster meat reaches 135 to 140°F (57 to 60°C), about 10 to 12 minutes, basting at least once with some of the melted butter. (Don't overcook or the lobster will become unpleasantly rubbery.)
5. Transfer the lobsters and the lemon halves to a platter. Divide the remaining melted butter between 4 ramekins before serving.

Barbecued Scallops

Servings: 4
Cooking Time: 10 Minutes

Ingredients:
- 1 pound large scallops
- 2 tablespoons olive oil
- 1 batch Dill Seafood Rub

Directions:
1. Supply your smoker with wood pellets and follow the start-up procedure. Preheat the grill, with the lid closed, to 375°F.
2. Coat the scallops all over with olive oil and season all sides with the rub.
3. Place the scallops directly on the grill grate and grill for 5 minutes per side. Remove the scallops from the grill and serve immediately.

Lobster Tail

Servings: 2
Cooking Time: 25 Minutes

Ingredients:
- 2 lobster tails
- Salt
- Freshly ground black pepper
- 1 batch Lemon Butter Mop for Seafood

Directions:
1. Supply your smoker with wood pellets and follow the start-up procedure. Preheat the grill, with the lid closed, to 375°F.
2. Using kitchen shears, slit the top of the lobster shells, through the center, nearly to the tail. Once cut, expose as much meat as you can through the cut shell.
3. Season the lobster tails all over with salt and pepper.
4. Place the tails directly on the grill grate and grill until their internal temperature reaches 145°F. Remove the lobster from the grill and serve with the mop on the side for dipping.

Swordfish With Sicilian Olive Oil Sauce

Servings: 4
Cooking Time: 10 Minutes

Ingredients:

- 1/2 Cup extra-virgin olive oil, plus 2 tablespoons for oiling the fish
- 1 Whole lemon, juiced
- 2 Clove garlic, minced
- 3 Tablespoon finely chopped fresh parsley
- 1 Tablespoon finely chopped fresh oregano or 1 teaspoon dried oregano
- 1 Tablespoon brined capers, drained (optional)
- 4 (6 to 8 oz) swordfish, halibut, tuna or salmon steaks, 1 inch thick
- salt and pepper

Directions:

1. Put 1/2 cup of olive oil in a small saucepan and warm over low heat.
2. Whisk in lemon juice and 2 tablespoons hot water. Stir in garlic, parsley, oregano, capers (if using), and salt and pepper to taste (go easy on the salt if you're using capers). Keep warm.
3. Supply your smoker with wood pellets and follow the start-up procedure. Preheat the grill, with the lid closed, to 400° F.
4. Brush the fish steaks with 2 tablespoons of olive oil and season with salt and pepper. Grill: 400 °F
5. Arrange on the grill grate and grill until the fish is opaque and flakes easily when pressed with a fork, about 18 minutes. (If you prefer your tuna or salmon on the rare side, cook them for less time.) Grill: 400 °F
6. Transfer the fish steaks to a platter or plates and drizzle with the warm olive oil sauce.
7. Serve the remaining sauce on the side. Enjoy!

Citrus-smoked Trout

Servings: 6
Cooking Time: 120 Minutes

Ingredients:

- 6 to 8 skin-on rainbow trout, cleaned and scaled
- 1 gallon orange juice
- ½ cup packed light brown sugar
- ¼ cup salt
- 1 tablespoon freshly ground black pepper
- Nonstick spray, oil, or butter, for greasing
- 1 tablespoon chopped fresh parsley
- 1 lemon, sliced

Directions:

1. Fillet the fish and pat dry with paper towels.
2. Pour the orange juice into a large container with a lid and stir in the brown sugar, salt, and pepper.
3. Place the trout in the brine, cover, and refrigerate for 1 hour.
4. Cover the grill grate with heavy-duty aluminum foil. Poke holes in the foil and spray with cooking spray (see Tip).
5. Supply your smoker with wood pellets and follow the start-up procedure. Preheat, with the lid closed, to 225°F.
6. Remove the trout from the brine and pat dry. Arrange the fish on the foil-covered grill grate, close the lid, and smoke for 1 hour 30 minutes to 2 hours, or until flaky.
7. Remove the fish from the heat. Serve garnished with the fresh parsley and lemon slices.

Cider Hot-smoked Salmon

Servings: 4
Cooking Time: 60 Minutes

Ingredients:

- 1 1/2 Pound Wild Caught Salmon Fillet, skinned, pin bones removed
- 12 Ounce apple juice or cider
- 4 Pieces juniper berries
- 1 Pieces Star Anise, Broken
- 1 Pieces bay leaf, coarsely crumbled
- 1/2 Cup kosher salt
- 1/4 Cup brown sugar
- 2 Teaspoon Blackened Saskatchewan Rub
- 1 Teaspoon coarse ground black pepper, divided

Directions:

1. Rinse the salmon fillet under cold running water and check for pin bones by running a finger over the fleshy part of the fillet. If you feel a bone, remove it with kitchen tweezers or a needle-nose pliers.
2. In a sturdy resealable plastic bag, combine the cider, crushed juniper berries, star anise, and bay leaf. Add the salmon fillet and put the bag in a bowl or pan in the refrigerator. Let sit for at least 8 hours, or overnight.
3. Remove the salmon from the bag and discard the cider mixture. Dry the salmon well on paper towels. Make the cure: In a small mixing bowl, combine the kosher salt, brown sugar, and Traeger rub.
4. Pour half into a shallow plate, or baking dish. Put the salmon fillet, skin-side down, on top of the cure. Generously sprinkle the top with the remaining cure, cover with plastic wrap, and refrigerate for 1 to 1-1/2 hours. Any longer, and the fish will get too salty.
5. Remove the salmon from the cure and pat dry with paper towels. Sprinkle the black pepper on top of the fillet.
6. Supply your smoker with wood pellets and follow the start-up procedure. Preheat the grill, with the lid closed, to 200° F.
7. Lay the salmon skin-side down on the grill grate. Cook for 1 hour, or until the internal temperature in the thickest part of the fish reaches 150 or the fish flakes easily when pressed with a finger or fork. Grill: 200 °F Probe: 150 °F
8. Let cool slightly. Turn the fillet over and remove the skin; it should come off in one piece.
9. If not serving immediately, let the salmon cool completely, then wrap in plastic wrap and refrigerate for up to 2 days. Transfer to a platter and serve with some or all of the suggested accompaniments. Enjoy!

Lime Mahi Mahi Fillets

Servings: 4
Cooking Time: 8 Minutes

Ingredients:
- 3/4 cup extra-virgin olive oil
- 1 clove garlic, minced
- 1/8 teaspoon ground black pepper
- 1/2 teaspoon cayenne pepper
- 2 tablespoons dill weed.
- 1 pinch salt
- 2 tablespoons lime juice
- 1/8 teaspoon grated lime peel
- 2 (4 ounce) mahi mahi fillets

Directions:
1. Supply your smoker with wood pellets and follow the start-up procedure. Preheat the grill, with the lid closed, to 325° F.
2. Lightly oil the grate.
3. Combine in a bowl the extra-virgin olive oil, minced garlic, black pepper, cayenne pepper, salt, lime juice, and grated lime zest.
4. Wisk to prepare the marinade.
5. Place the mahi mahi fillets in the marinade and turn to coat.
6. Allow to marinate at least 15 minutes.
7. Cook on preheated grill until fish flakes easily with a fork and is lightly browned (Typically 3 to 4 minutes per side).
8. Garnish with the twists of lime zest to serve.

Smoked Honey Salmon

Servings: 2
Cooking Time: 25 Minutes

Ingredients:
- 1 lb. salmon fillets
- 1/2 tsp. pepper
- 1/4 tsp. salt
- 2 tbsp. sriracha
- 2 tsp. honey
- 2 tsp. chili sauce
- 1 tsp. lime juice
- 1/2 tsp. fish sauce

Directions:
1. Supply your smoker with wood pellets and follow the start-up procedure. Preheat the grill, with the lid closed, to 350° F.
2. Sprinkle the salmon with salt and pepper.
3. In a bowl, whisk together the sriracha, honey, chili sauce, lime juice, and fish sauce.

4. Once the grill is hot, place the salmon on the grill and leave for 15 minutes.

5. After 15 minutes, brush the salmon with the sriracha chili sauce and keep cooking for 5-10minutes. The salmon should be firm to the touch and crispy on the edges.

6. Serve hot!

Grilled Garlic Lobster Tails

Servings: 2
Cooking Time: 11 Minutes

Ingredients:
- 4 Lobster Tails (8 oz Each)
- 3 Sticks Unsalted Butter
- 4 Cloves Garlic Minced
- ½ Cup Fresh Parsley Chopped
- Juice of 1 Lemon
- 2 Tablespoons Fresh Lemon Zest
- 2 Teaspoons Crushed Red Pepper
- ¼ Cup Olive Oil
- 1 TBS Kosher Salt
- 1 TBS Cracked Black Pepper

Directions:
1. Supply your smoker with wood pellets and follow the start-up procedure. Preheat the grill, with the lid closed, to 375° F.
2. Split lobster tails in half lengthwise and season with salt, pepper, and olive oil.
3. Place butter in an aluminum pan and put the pan on the hot side of the grill to melt the butter.
4. Add garlic, parsley, lemon zest, lemon juice, and red pepper to butter and simmer for 5 minutes.
5. Place lobster tails meat side down on the grill and cook for 6 minutes. Baste the shell side with the butter mixture.
6. Dunk each tail in the butter mixture and then transfer to the grill, shell side down. Baste meat again with butter mixture.
7. Cook for an additional 5 minutes or until the lobster meat turns opaque and shells are bright pink.
8. Serve with remaining butter mixture, fresh parsley, and lemon wedges.

Traeger Smoked Salmon

Servings: 6
Cooking Time: 240 Minutes

Ingredients:
- 1 (2-1/2 to 3 lb) salmon fillet
- 1/2 Cup kosher salt
- 1 Cup brown sugar, firmly packed
- 1 Tablespoon ground black pepper

Directions:
1. Remove all pin bones from salmon.
2. In a small bowl, combine salt, sugar and black pepper. Lay a large piece of plastic wrap on a flat surface that is at least 6 inches longer than the fillet. Spread 1/2 of the mixture on top of the plastic and lay the fillet skin side down on top of the cure. Top with the other 1/2 of the cure spreading it evenly over the top of the fillet. Fold up the edges of the plastic and wrap tightly.
3. Place the wrapped salmon fillet in the bottom of a flat, rectangle baking dish or hotel pan. Place another identical pan on top of the fillet. Place a couple of cans or something heavy inside the top pan to weigh it down making sure the weight is distributed evenly.
4. Transfer the weighted salmon to the refrigerator and cure for 4 to 6 hours.
5. Remove the salmon from the plastic wrap and rinse the cure thoroughly (not rinsing thoroughly will result in a salty finished product). Place skin side down on a wire rack atop a sheet tray and pat dry. Place the sheet tray in the refrigerator and allow the salmon to dry overnight. This allows a tacky film called a pellicle to form on the surface of the salmon. The pellicle helps smoke adhere to the fish.
6. Supply your smoker with wood pellets and follow the start-up procedure. Preheat the grill, with the lid closed, to 180° F.
7. Place the salmon skin side down directly on the grill grate and smoke for 3 to 4 hours or until the internal temperature of the fish registers 140°F. Enjoy warm or chilled. Grill: 180 °F Probe: 140 °F

Smoky Crab Dip

Servings: 6
Cooking Time: 20 Minutes

Ingredients:
- 1/3 Cup mayonnaise
- 3 Ounce sour cream
- 1 Teaspoon smoked paprika
- 1/4 Teaspoon cayenne pepper
- 1 1/2 Pound Crab meat, lump
- salt and pepper
- scallions, chopped
- butter crackers

Directions:
1. Supply your smoker with wood pellets and follow the start-up procedure. Preheat the grill, with the lid closed, to 350° F.
2. Meanwhile, in a large bowl gently stir together all of the ingredients except the crackers, garnish scallions and the crab meat until thoroughly combined. Gently fold in the crab meat, being careful not to break it up too much.
3. Season to taste and transfer to an oven-safe serving dish.
4. Bake for 20 to 25 minutes, until bubbly and golden on top. Grill: 350 °F
5. Garnish with the additional chopped scallions and serve warm with butter crackers. Enjoy!

Vodka Brined Smoked Wild Salmon

Servings: 4
Cooking Time: 60 Minutes

Ingredients:
- 1 Cup brown sugar
- 1 Tablespoon black pepper
- 1/2 Cup coarse salt
- 1 Cup vodka
- 1 (1-1/2 to 2 lb) wild caught salmon
- 1 lemon wedges
- capers

Directions:
1. In a small bowl, whisk together brown sugar, pepper, salt and vodka.
2. Place the salmon in a large resealable bag. Pour in marinade and massage into the salmon. Refrigerate for 2 to 4 hours.
3. Remove from bag, rinse and dry with paper towels.
4. Supply your smoker with wood pellets and follow the start-up procedure. Preheat the grill, with the lid closed, to 180° F.
5. Smoke the salmon, skin-side down for 30 minutes.
6. Increase grill temperature to 225°F and continue to cook salmon for an additional 45 to 60 minutes or until the internal temperature in the thickest part of the fish reaches 140°F or the fish flakes easily when pressed with a finger or fork. Grill: 225 °F Probe: 140 °F
7. Serve with lemons and capers. Enjoy!

Grilled Shrimp Brochette

Servings: 6
Cooking Time: 20 Minutes

Ingredients:
- 1 Pound extra-large shrimp, peeled and deveined
- 6 Whole fresh jalapeños
- 8 Ounce block Monterey Jack cheese
- 1 Pound bacon
- 2 Tablespoon Meat Church The Gospel All-Purpose Rub
- oil

Directions:
1. Fillet shrimp open slightly and set aside. Core the jalapeños and cut them into small slivers. Slice the cheese into similar-sized slivers as the peppers. Cut the bacon slices in half.
2. Place one slice of jalapeño and one slice of cheese inside each shrimp. Wrap stuffed shrimp in a half piece of bacon and secure with a toothpick.
3. After you have constructed all of the shrimp, season lightly with Meat Church The Gospel All-Purpose Rub.
4. Supply your smoker with wood pellets and follow the start-up procedure. Preheat the grill, with the lid closed, to 425° F.
5. Lightly oil the grill grate then place shrimp directly on the grate. Cook for about 20 minutes, turning at least once halfway through. Shrimp should turn pink and bacon will begin to crisp up. Grill: 425 °F
6. Remove from the grill and let rest for at least 10 minutes. Enjoy!

Cajun-blackened Shrimp

Servings: 4
Cooking Time: 20 Minutes

Ingredients:
- 1 pound peeled and deveined shrimp, with tails on
- 1 batch Cajun Rub
- 8 tablespoons (1 stick) butter
- ¼ cup Worcestershire sauce

Directions:
1. Supply your smoker with wood pellets and follow the start-up procedure. Preheat the grill, with the lid closed, to 450°F and place a cast-iron skillet on the grill grate. Wait about 10 minutes after your grill has reached temperature, allowing the skillet to get hot.
2. Meanwhile, season the shrimp all over with the rub.
3. When the skillet is hot, place the butter in it to melt. Once the butter melts, stir in the Worcestershire sauce.
4. Add the shrimp and gently stir to coat. Smoke-braise the shrimp for about 10 minutes per side, until opaque and cooked through. Remove the shrimp from the grill and serve immediately.

Flavour Fire Spiced Shrimp

Servings: 2
Cooking Time: 8 Minutes

Ingredients:
- 1 pound of extra large raw whole wild shrimp
- 1 tablespoon vegetable oil
- 1 tablespoon chili powder
- 1 teaspoon garlic powder
- 1/2 teaspoon onion powder
- 1/2 teaspoon cayenne pepper
- 1/4 teaspoon paprika
- 1/4 teaspoon dried oregano
- Pinch of Kosher salt

Directions:
1. Supply your smoker with wood pellets and follow the start-up procedure. Preheat the grill, with the lid closed, to High heat.
2. While grill is preheating, remove the shrimp shells, leaving the heads.
3. Butterfly shrimp by using a knife to cut each shrimp down the middle, from the head down to the tail.
4. Remove the vein, rinse off the shrimp and lightly dry off with paper towels.
5. Place the shrimp in a large bowl, sprinkle with all the seasonings and the oil.
6. Mix together, ensuring the mixture evenly covers each shrimp.
7. Using a skewer, impale the whole body of a shrimp, from head to tail. (Wrap them in aluminum foil if using wooden skewers).
8. Place the whole shrimp on the grill and cook for 3-4 minutes on each side (Or until shells turns pink and the shrimp is opaque).
9. Serve with your favorite sauce or condiment.

Smoked Crab Legs

Servings: 4
Cooking Time: 30 Minutes

Ingredients:
- 4 Whole crab legs
- 4 Tablespoon butter, melted
- 1/2 Cup Texas Spicy BBQ Sauce
- salt and pepper
- 1 Tablespoon Fin & Feather Rub

Directions:
1. Supply your smoker with wood pellets and follow the start-up procedure. Preheat the grill, with the lid closed, to 250° F.
2. Place the crab legs directly on the grill grate and smoke for 20 minutes. Grill: 250 °F
3. While the crab is smoking, make the sauce. In a medium bowl, combine melted butter, Traeger Texas Spicy BBQ sauce, salt, pepper and Traeger Fin & Feather Rub.
4. After 20 minutes of cooking, brush the crab legs with the BBQ sauce mixture. Continue to cook for another 10 minutes reserving the remaining sauce to serve. Remove crab legs from the grill, and serve with melted butter and BBQ sauce mixture. Enjoy!

Simple Glazed Salmon Fillets

Servings: 2
Cooking Time: 25 Minutes

Ingredients:
- 4 (6-8 oz) center-cut salmon fillets, skin on
- Fin & Feather Rub
- 1/2 Cup mayonnaise
- 2 Tablespoon Dijon mustard
- 1 Tablespoon fresh lemon juice
- 1 Tablespoon fresh chopped tarragon or dill
- lemon wedges

Directions:
1. Season the fillets with the Traeger Fin & Feather Rub.
2. Make the Glaze: Combine the mayonnaise and mustard in a small bowl. Stir in the lemon juice and dill or tarragon.
3. Spread the flesh-side of the fillets with the glaze.
4. Supply your smoker with wood pellets and follow the start-up procedure. Preheat the grill, with the lid closed, to 350° F.
5. Arrange the salmon fillets on the grill grate, skin-side down. Grill for 25 to 30 minutes, or until the salmon is opaque and flakes easily with a fork. Grill: 350 °F
6. Transfer to a platter or plates, garnish with sliced lemons and chopped dill and serve immediately. Enjoy!

Grilled Oysters With Mignonette

Servings: 2
Cooking Time: 15 Minutes

Ingredients:
- 4 Cup rock salt
- 18 Large oysters
- 4 Tablespoon unsalted butter
- 2 Clove garlic, minced
- kosher salt
- 12 Medium lemon wedges, for serving
- 2 Tablespoon minced shallot
- 1/4 Cup red wine vinegar
- 1/2 Teaspoon freshly ground black pepper

Directions:
1. Choose a shallow serving platter that will hold all of the oysters. Pour the rock salt onto the platter to create a 1/2 inch base. This will steady the oysters for serving.
2. To prepare the oysters, check to ensure they are completely closed. Discard oysters that are not. Wash and lightly scrub the oysters to ensure there is no grit on the surface. This will prevent the grit from entering the oyster once shucked.
3. Using a thick glove or kitchen towel, sturdy the oyster in the hand opposite of the one holding the knife. Using an oyster knife or very sturdy paring knife, locate the "hinge" on each oyster. Place the point of the knife in the hinge, and wiggle the tip of the knife into the oyster until it feels sturdy. Firmly turn the knife to apply a torquing pressure to gently open the oyster.
4. Remove the top shell of the oyster. Using the tip of the knife, loosen the oyster from its shell, leaving the juices intact. Place each loosened oyster on its half shell on a baking sheet.
5. Supply your smoker with wood pellets and follow the start-up procedure. Preheat the grill, with the lid closed, to 450° F.
6. In a small saucepan, melt the butter over medium-low heat. Add the garlic and a generous pinch of salt, and cook until fragrant but not burned, about 1 minute. Remove from the heat. Grill: 450 °F
7. For the Mignonette: Combine the minced shallot, red wine vinegar and 1/2 teaspoon freshly ground black pepper. Set aside.
8. Spoon 1 teaspoon of the garlic butter sauce onto each oyster in its half shell. Carefully place each oyster directly on the grill grates, ensuring they don't slip. Close the lid and allow them to cook for 3 to 4 minutes, until the edges of the oysters have pulled away from the shell. Remove carefully with tongs to keep the juices and butter in the shells. Place directly on the rock salt to balance them. Serve immediately with the mignonette and lemon wedges to squeeze onto the oysters. Enjoy!

Smoked Sugar Halibut

Servings: 8
Cooking Time: 120 Minutes

Ingredients:
- 1/4 cup granulated sugar
- 1/4 cup brown sugar
- 1/2 cup kosher salt
- 1 tsp ground coriander
- 2 lbs fresh halibut

Directions:
1. In a small bowl, mix the sugars, salt, and coriander together. Season the halibut on all sides.
2. Wrap the halibut in plastic wrap, place on a rimmed sheet pan, and brine in the fridge for 3 hours.
3. Remove the plastic wrap and rinse the fish. Pat it dry. Set it on a drying rack over a sheet pan for 1-2 hours in the fridge.
4. Supply your smoker with wood pellets and follow the start-up procedure. Preheat the grill, with the lid closed, to 200° F. Smoke the fish for 2 hours or until its internal temperature reaches 140 °F.
5. Serve your preferred sauce with the fish.

Kimi's Simple Grilled Fresh Fish

Servings: 2
Cooking Time: 45 Minutes

Ingredients:
- 1 Cup soy sauce
- 1/3 Cup extra-virgin olive oil
- 1 Tablespoon garlic, minced
- 2 lemons, juiced
- fresh basil
- 4 Pound Fresh Fish, cut into portion-sized pieces

Directions:
1. Mix all ingredients to create sauce and cover fish in marinade for 45 minutes.
2. Supply your smoker with wood pellets and follow the start-up procedure. Preheat the grill, with the lid closed, to 140° F. Grill the marinated fish on the grill until it reaches an internal temperature of 140-145°F. Serve immediately, enjoy! Grill: 350 °F Probe: 145 °F

Lemon Lobster Rolls

Servings: 4
Cooking Time: 35 Minutes

Ingredients:
- 1/2 Cup Butter
- 4 Hot Dog Bun(S)
- 1 Lemon, Whole
- 4 Lobster, Tail
- 1/4 Cup Mayo
- Pepper

Directions:
1. Supply your smoker with wood pellets and follow the start-up procedure. Preheat the grill, with the lid closed, to 300° F.
2. Using kitchen shears, cut the shell of the tail and crack in half so that the meat is exposed. Pour in butter and season with pepper. Place the tails meat side up on the grill and cook until the shell has turned red and the meat is white, about 35 minutes.
3. Remove from the grill and separate the shell from the meat. Place the meat in a bowl with mayo, lemon juice and rind and season with pepper. Stir to combine and evenly distribute into the hot dog buns.

Florentine Shrimp Al Cartoccio

Servings: 4
Cooking Time: 13 Minutes

Ingredients:
- 6 tbsp unsalted butter, melted
- ½ cup heavy whipping cream
- ½ cup grated Parmesan cheese
- 2 garlic cloves, peeled and minced
- 1 cup thinly sliced button mushrooms, cleaned and destemmed
- 1 cup baby spinach leaves
- 2 tbsp chopped sun-dried, oil-packed tomatoes
- ½ tsp dried oregano
- ½ tsp dried basil
- ½ tsp crushed red pepper flakes, plus more
- ½ tsp coarse salt
- ½ tsp freshly ground black pepper

- 20 to 24 jumbo shrimp, about 1lb (450g) total, peeled and deveined
- sprigs of fresh rosemary, basil, thyme, or oregano

Directions:
1. Supply your smoker with wood pellets and follow the start-up procedure. Preheat the grill, with the lid closed, to 400° F.
2. In a large bowl, combine the butter and whipping cream. Stir in the Parmesan, garlic, mushrooms, spinach, tomatoes, oregano, basil, red pepper flakes, and salt and pepper. Add the shrimp and stir gently to coat.
3. Place four 12-inch (30.5cm) sheets of wide heavy-duty aluminum foil on a workspace and pull up the sides. Divide the shrimp mixture evenly between the sheets of foil. Roll and crimp the top and sides of the foil to create sealed packages.
4. Place the packets seam side up on the grate and grill until the shrimp are cooked through, about 10 to 13 minutes. (You can carefully open one package to check on the shrimp.)
5. Transfer the packets to plates. Carefully open the packets to avoid any steam. Scatter fresh herbs over the shrimp before serving.

Lemon Herb Grilled Salmon

Servings: 4
Cooking Time: 25 Minutes

Ingredients:
- 1 1/2 pounds salmon with skin
- 1/2 tablespoon lemon zest
- 1 tablespoon lemon juice
- 1 tablespoon unsalted butter
- 1/2 teaspoon sea salt
- 1/2 teaspoon ground black pepper
- 2 teaspoons freshly chopped dill
- 1 teaspoon freshly chopped parsley
- lemon slices for the garnish

Directions:
1. Supply your smoker with wood pellets and follow the start-up procedure. Preheat the grill, with the lid closed, to 325° F.
2. In a small bowl, combine the lemon zest, lemon juice, softened unsalted butter, dill, parsley, sea salt, and ground black pepper.
3. Generously slather the top of the salmon fillet with the mixture and top with a slice of lemon. You may allow marinating for about 10 minutes or so to absorb the mixture.
4. Place the salmon fillets on the hot grill grate, skin-side facing down.
5. Cook the salmon for 20 to 25 minutes, until it reaches an internal temperature of 145 °F and flakes easily, or until the salmon is cooked to your preferred taste.
6. Serve with lemon slices. Enjoy!

Smoked Lobster Scampi

Servings: 2
Cooking Time: 30 Minutes

Ingredients:
- 1 Lobster Tail
- 1 Handful Pasta, Angel Hair
- 2 Tablespoon butter
- 1 Teaspoon garlic, minced
- 1/2 Teaspoon lemon juice
- 2 Teaspoon Parmesan cheese, grated
- 2 Tablespoon Sun Dried Tomato Pesto
- fresh parsley

Directions:
1. Supply your smoker with wood pellets and follow the start-up procedure. Preheat the grill, with the lid closed, to 180° F.
2. Use kitchen shears to cut along the top of the lobster on both sides to expose the meat. Place the lobster directly on the grill for 20-25 minutes, depending on the size of the lobster. Grill: 180 °F
3. While lobster smokes, cook pasta according to packaged directions.
4. After 20-25 minutes, take lobster off the grill and remove the meat from the tail. Cut meat into chunks.
5. While the pasta is boiling, melt butter over medium high heat. Once butter starts to brown, add the garlic

and lobster chunks. Toss in pan a few times then add lemon and parmesan. Set aside.
6. When pasta has finished, place 1 tbsp of the sun dried tomato pesto on the bottom of a bowl or plate. Top with pasta, then finish with the lobster scampi. Garnish with parsley. Enjoy!

Whole Vermillion Red Snapper

Servings: 6
Cooking Time: 20 Minutes

Ingredients:
- 1 Whole Vermillion Red Snapper, scaled & gutted
- 4 Clove garlic, chopped
- 1 Whole lemon, thinly sliced
- 2 Sprig rosemary sprigs
- sea salt and freshly ground black pepper

Directions:
1. Supply your smoker with wood pellets and follow the start-up procedure. Preheat the grill, with the lid closed, to High heat.
2. Stuff the cavity of the fish with chopped garlic. Sprinkle the fish with sea salt, pepper, rosemary, and lemon.
3. Grill fish directly on the grill grate. Cook for 20-25 minutes. Serve. Enjoy!

Sweet Smoked Salmon Jerky

Servings: 6
Cooking Time: 300 Minutes

Ingredients:
- 2 Quart water
- 3/4 Cup kosher salt
- 1 Cup Morton Tender Quick Home Meat Cure, optional
- 4 Cup dark brown sugar
- 2 Cup maple syrup, divided
- 1 (2-3 lb) wild caught salmon fillet, skinned and pin bones removed

Directions:
1. In a large nonreactive bowl, combine 2 quarts water, salt, curing salt (if using), brown sugar and 1 cup of the maple syrup. Stir with a long-handled spoon to dissolve the salts and sugar.
2. With a sharp, serrated knife, slice the salmon into 1/2 inch thick slices with the short side parallel to you on the cutting board. In other words, make your cuts from the head end to the tail end. (This is considerably easier if the fish is frozen.) Cut each strip crosswise into 4 or 5 inch lengths.
3. Immerse the strips in the brine, weighing down with a plate or a bag of ice. Cover with plastic wrap and refrigerate for 12 hours.
4. Supply your smoker with wood pellets and follow the start-up procedure. Preheat the grill, with the lid closed, to 180° F.
5. Drain the salmon strips and discard the brine. Arrange the salmon strips in a single layer directly on the grill grate. Smoke for several hours (5 to 6), or until the jerky is dry but not rock-hard. You want it to yield when you bite into it. Halfway through the smoking time, mix the remaining cup of maple syrup with 1/4 cup of warm water and brush the salmon strips on all sides with the mixture. Grill: 180 °F
6. Transfer to a resealable bag while the jerky is still warm. Let the jerky rest for an hour at room temperature. Squeeze any air from the bag, and refrigerate the jerky. Enjoy!

Baked Whole Fish In Sea Salt

Servings: 4
Cooking Time: 30 Minutes

Ingredients:
- 3 Pound Whole Branzino, (1.5 each)
- 10 Sprig thyme sprigs
- 1 Medium lemon, thinly sliced
- 5 Cup sea salt
- 10 Whole egg white
- olive oil
- 1 Whole lemon juice

Directions:
1. Supply your smoker with wood pellets and follow the start-up procedure. Preheat the grill, with the lid closed, to High heat.

2. Clip the fins and remove the gills from the fish. Stuff cavity with thyme and lemon slices. Whip the egg whites to soft peaks and fold in the sea salt.
3. Place directly on the grill grate and bake for 30 minutes or until a thermometer poked through the salt crust and into the flesh of the fish registers an internal temperature of 135-140 degrees F. Remove fish from the grill and let stand 10 minutes.
4. Using a wooden spoon, strike the crust to crack it open and brush remaining salt from the surface of the fish.
5. Remove the skin and drizzle fish with good olive oil and a squeeze of lemon. Enjoy!

Spiced Smoked Swordfish

Servings: 4
Cooking Time: 60 Minutes

Ingredients:
- 4 swordfish fillets (about 4 ounces each)
- For the brine:
- 1 gallon water
- ½ cup kosher salt
- ½ cup brown sugar
- For the rub:
- 1 tablespoon olive oil
- 1 tablespoon kosher salt
- 1 tablespoon coarse ground black pepper
- 1 tablespoon garlic powder
- 1 tablespoon onion powder

Directions:
1. Make the brine by mixing the water, salt, and sugar in a large pot and stir. Add swordfish fillets to the bowl and refrigerate overnight in the mixture.
2. Supply your smoker with wood pellets and follow the start-up procedure. Preheat the grill, with the lid closed, to 225° F.
3. Remove the fillets from the brine, rinse, and blot dry.
4. Brush a coat of olive oil on each fillet and mix salt, pepper, garlic powder, and onion powder in a small bowl for the rub. Apply the rub liberally to each fillet.
5. Put the fillets skin-side down on the smoker and cook for about 1 hour or until the internal temperature in the thickest part of the fillets reaches 145 °F.
6. Enjoy.

Grilled Salmon Steaks With Dill Sauce

Servings: 4
Cooking Time: 8 Minutes

Ingredients:
- 4 salmon steaks, each about 6 to 8oz (170 to 225g) and 1 inch (2.5cm) thick
- extra virgin olive oil
- coarse salt
- freshly ground rainbow peppercorns or freshly ground black pepper
- lemon wedges
- for the sauce
- 1 cup reduced-fat mayo
- ⅓ cup light sour cream
- ¼ cup chopped fresh dill
- 2 tbsp freshly squeezed lemon juice
- coarse salt
- freshly ground black pepper
- sprigs of fresh dill

Directions:
1. Supply your smoker with wood pellets and follow the start-up procedure. Preheat the grill, with the lid closed, to 450° F.
2. In a small bowl, make the dill sauce by combining the mayo, sour cream, dill, and lemon juice. Mix until smooth. Season with salt and pepper to taste. Transfer to a serving bowl. Scatter the dill sprigs over the top. Cover and refrigerate until ready to serve.
3. Brush the salmon with olive oil and season with salt and pepper. Place the salmon on the grate at an angle to the bars. Grill until grill marks begin to appear, about 4 minutes. Use a thin-bladed spatula to turn the salmon. Grill until the internal temperature reaches 140°F (60°C), about 4 minutes more.
4. Transfer the salmon to a platter. Serve immediately with the lemon wedges and dill sauce.

Spicy Lime Shrimp

Servings: 4
Cooking Time: 10 Minutes

Ingredients:
- 2 Tsp Chili Paste
- 1/2 Tsp Cumin
- 2 Cloves Garlic, Minced
- 1 Large Lime, Juiced
- 1/4 Tsp Paprika, Powder
- 1/4 Tsp Red Flakes Pepper
- 1/2 Tsp Salt

Directions:
1. In a bowl, whisk together the lime juice, olive oil, garlic, chili powder, cumin, paprika, salt, pepper, and red pepper flakes.
2. Then pour it into a resealable bag, add the shrimp, toss the coat, let it marinate for 30 minutes.
3. Supply your smoker with wood pellets and follow the start-up procedure. Preheat the grill, with the lid closed, to 400° F.
4. Next place the shrimp on skewers, place on the grill, and grill each side for about two minutes until it's done. One finished, remove the shrimp from the grill and enjoy!
5. Place the skewers directly on the grill grate and grill the shrimp for 5 minutes per side. Remove the skewers from the grill and serve immediately.

Grilled Artichoke Cheese Salmon

Servings: 12
Cooking Time: 270 Minutes

Ingredients:
- 28 Oz Artichoke Hearts, Whole, Canned
- 1/2 Cup Breadcrumbs
- 1/2 Cup Brown Sugar
- 8 Oz Cream Cheese
- 1 Tbsp Garlic Powder
- 1 Cup Italian Cheese Blend, Shredded
- 1/4 Cup Kosher Salt
- 1 Cup Mayonnaise
- 2 Tsp Olive Oil
- 1 Tbsp Onion Powder
- 1/2 Cup Parmesan Cheese
- 2 Tbsp Parsley, Chopped
- Blackened Sriracha Rub
- 1 1/4 Lbs Salmon, Fillet, Scaled And Deboned
- Sour Cream
- 1/2 Tsp White Pepper, Ground

Directions:
1. In a small mixing bowl, whisk together the brown sugar, salt, garlic powder, onion powder, and white pepper. This will make twice the cure needed, so be sure and place the remaining half in a resealable plastic bag and save for smoking fish at a later date.
2. Lay a sheet of plastic wrap on a sheet tray and sprinkle a thin layer of the cure on it. Place the salmon skin-side down on top of the cure, then sprinkle a couple tablespoons of cure on top. Gently press the cure on top of the salmon flesh, then wrap in plastic wrap.
3. Refrigerate for 8 hours, or overnight.
4. Remove salmon from the refrigerator and wash off the cure in the sink, under cold water.
5. Blot salmon with a paper towel, then set salmon skin side on a wire rack. Dry at room temperature for two hours, or until a yellowish shimmer appears on the salmon.

Barbecued Shrimp

Servings: 4
Cooking Time: 10 Minutes

Ingredients:
- 1 pound peeled and deveined shrimp, with tails on
- 2 tablespoons olive oil
- 1 batch Dill Seafood Rub

Directions:
1. Soak wooden skewers in water for 30 minutes.
2. Supply your smoker with wood pellets and follow the start-up procedure. Preheat the grill, with the lid closed, to 375°F.
3. Thread 4 or 5 shrimp per skewer.
4. Coat the shrimp all over with olive oil and season each side of the skewers with the rub.

6. Supply your smoker with wood pellets and follow the start-up procedure. Preheat the grill, with the lid closed, to 250° F. If using a gas, charcoal or other grill, set it to low, indirect heat.
7. Place the salmon in the upper cabinet. Smoke for 2 hours, then increase the grill temperature to 350° F to maintain a cabinet temperature of 225°F and smoke another 1 to 2 hours, until salmon reaches an internal temperature of 145° F.
8. Remove salmon from the cabinet and set aside to rest for 15 minutes, then flake apart. Reserve ½ cup to top dip after grilling.
9. While the salmon is resting, drain the artichokes, then skewer onto metal skewers (if using wooden skewers, make sure to soak in water for 1 hour prior to grilling, or you can use a grill basket as well).
10. Season with Blackened Sriracha, then set on the grill. Grill for 2 to 3 minutes, until lightly browned.
11. Remove from the grill, cool slightly, then roughly chop. Set aside.
12. In a mixing bowl, combine shredded Italian cheese, grated parmesan, breadcrumbs and parsley. Set aside.
13. Place cream cheese, mayonnaise, and sour cream in a cast iron skillet. Stir frequently, with a wooden spoon, for about 5 minutes, until the mixture is smooth.
14. Carefully fold in flaked salmon and grilled artichoke hearts, then spread breadcrumb mixture over dip.
15. Drizzle with olive oil, then close the grill lid and bake for 25 to 30 minutes, until dip begins to bubble around the edges, and cheese begins to caramelize on top.
16. Remove dip from the grill, top with reserved salmon and a pinch of parsley. Serve warm with bagel chips, crackers, or crusty bread.

Garlic Blackened Salmon

Servings: 4
Cooking Time: 10 Minutes

Ingredients:
- 1 Tablespoon, Optional Cayenne Pepper
- 2 Cloves Garlic, Minced
- 2 Tablespoons Olive Oil
- 4 Tablespoons Sweet Rib Rub
- 2 Pound Salmon, Fillet, Scaled And Deboned

Directions:
1. Supply your smoker with wood pellets and follow the start-up procedure. Preheat the grill, with the lid closed, to 350° F.
2. Remove the skin from the salmon and discard. Brush the salmon on both sides with olive oil, then rub the salmon fillet with the minced garlic, cayenne pepper and Sweet Rib Rub.
3. Grill the salmon for 5 minutes on one side. Flip the salmon and then grill for another 5 minutes, or until the salmon reaches an internal temperature of 145°F. Remove from the grill and serve.

Grilled Salmon Gravlax

Servings: 4
Cooking Time: 10 Minutes

Ingredients:
- 1 center-cut salmon fillet, about 2lb (1kg), preferably wild caught, skin on
- ½ cup aquavit or vodka
- 4 whole juniper berries
- ¼ cup finely chopped fresh dill, plus more
- lemon wedges
- for the rub
- 3 tbsp granulated light brown sugar or low-carb substitute
- 2 tbsp coarse salt
- 2 tsp freshly ground black pepper
- 1 tsp freshly ground white pepper
- 1 tsp ground coriander

Directions:
1. Run your fingers over the fillet, feeling for bones. Remove them with kitchen tweezers or needle-nosed pliers. Rinse the salmon under cold running water and pat dry with paper towels.
2. Place the salmon skin side down in a nonreactive baking dish and pour the aquavit over it. Crush the berries with the flat of a chef's knife and add them to the dish. Cover and refrigerate for 1 hour.
3. In a small bowl, make the rub by combining the ingredients.

4. Remove the salmon from the aquavit and pat dry with paper towels. Discard the soaking liquid and juniper berries. Rinse out the baking dish and place the salmon in the dish. Lightly but evenly sprinkle the rub on the flesh side of the fillet and gently distribute it with your fingertips. Scatter the dill over the top. Cover the dish and refrigerate for 4 hours.

5. Supply your smoker with wood pellets and follow the start-up procedure. Preheat the grill, with the lid closed, to 400° F.

6. With a sharp knife, slice the fillet into 4 equal portions. Place the fillets on the grate and grill until the fish is somewhat opaque but still translucent in the center and the internal temperature reaches 125°F (52°C), about 3 to 5 minutes per side.

7. Transfer the fillets to a platter. Scatter more dill over the top. Serve with lemon wedges.

Oysters Margarita

Servings: 4
Cooking Time: 10minutes

Ingredients:

- 24 fresh oysters in the shell
- 4oz (120ml) freshly squeezed lime juice
- 2oz (60ml) tequila
- 2oz (60ml) orange liqueur, such as triple sec
- 6 tbsp cold butter, cut into 24 cubes
- crunchy salt, such as margarita rimming salt
- lime wedges
- hot sauce (optional)

Directions:

1. Supply your smoker with wood pellets and follow the start-up procedure. Preheat the grill, with the lid closed, to 450° F.

2. Carefully shuck each oyster to remove the top shell. Run your shucking knife under the oyster to release it from the bottom shell, but don't spill the juices. Discard the top shells, but keep the oysters in the bottom shells. Balance each oyster on a wire rack placed on a rimmed sheet pan.

3. Place 1 teaspoon of lime juice, ½ teaspoon of tequila, ½ teaspoon of orange liqueur, and 1 cube of butter on each oyster.

4. Place the pan on the grate and smoke until the butter has melted and the juices are bubbling, about 8 to 10 minutes. (The oysters should be just barely cooked.)

5. Remove the pan from the grill. Sprinkle a pinch of salt on each oyster. Serve immediately with lime wedges and hot sauce (if using).

Traeger Baked Rainbow Trout

Servings: 2
Cooking Time: 20 Minutes

Ingredients:

- 2 Tablespoon olive oil, divided
- 2 Whole rainbow trout, gutted and cleaned, heads and tails still on
- 1/2 Teaspoon fresh dill
- 1/2 Teaspoon fresh thyme
- 1 Teaspoon Jacobsen Salt Co. Pure Kosher Sea Salt
- 1/2 Large onion, sliced
- 1 Large lemon, thinly sliced
- 1 Teaspoon freshly ground black pepper

Directions:

1. Supply your smoker with wood pellets and follow the start-up procedure. Preheat the grill, with the lid closed, to 400° F.

2. Grease a 9x13 inch baking dish with 1 tablespoon olive oil.

3. Place trout in the prepared baking dish and coat fish with remaining olive oil. Season the inside and outside of fish with dill, thyme and salt. Stuff each fish with onion and lemon slices then grind pepper over the top. Place 1 lemon slice on each fish.

4. Bake in the Traeger for 10 minutes. Add 2 tablespoons hot water to the baking dish. Continue baking until fish flakes easily with a fork, about 10 more minutes. Enjoy! Grill: 400 °F

Grilled Fresh Fish

Servings: 2
Cooking Time: 15 Minutes

Ingredients:
- 1 Whole fillet of firm white fish: sea bass, halibut or cod
- Fin & Feather Rub
- 2 Whole lemons

Directions:
1. Supply your smoker with wood pellets and follow the start-up procedure. Preheat the grill, with the lid closed, to 325° F.
2. Season fish with Traeger Fin & Feather Rub and let sit for 30 minutes. Slice lemons in half.
3. Place the fish and the lemons (cut side down) directly on the grill grates. Cook for 10 to 15 minutes until the fish is flaky and is at least 145°F in the thickest part of fish. Be careful not to over cook.
4. Serve with the grilled lemons. Enjoy!

Grilled Lemon Shrimp Scampi

Servings: 4
Cooking Time: 6 Minutes

Ingredients:
- 1 ½ pounds medium shrimp, peeled and deveined
- ¼ cup olive oil
- ¼ cup lemon juice
- 3 tablespoons chopped fresh parsley
- 1 tablespoon minced garlic
- ground black pepper to taste
- ¼ teaspoon crushed red pepper flakes to taste

Directions:
1. In a large, non-reactive bowl, stir together the olive oil, lemon juice, parsley, garlic, and black pepper. Season with crushed red pepper, if desired. Add shrimp, and toss to coat. Marinate in the refrigerator for 30 minutes.
2. Supply your smoker with wood pellets and follow the start-up procedure. Preheat the grill, with the lid closed, to high heat.
3. Thread shrimp onto skewers, piercing once near the tail and once near the head. Discard any remaining marinade.
4. Lightly oil grill grate. Place the shrimp skewers on the grill grates.
5. Grill for 2 to 3 minutes per side, or until opaque.

Cedar Smoked Garlic Salmon

Servings: 6
Cooking Time: 60 Minutes

Ingredients:
- 1 Tsp Black Pepper
- 3 Cedar Plank, Untreated
- 1 Tsp Garlic, Minced
- 1/3 Cup Olive Oil
- 1 Tsp Onion, Salt
- 1 Tsp Parsley, Minced Fresh
- 1 1/2 Tbsp Rice Vinegar
- 2 Salmon, Fillets (Skin Removed)
- 1 Tsp Sesame Oil
- 1/3 Cup Soy Sauce

Directions:
1. Soak the cedar planks in warm water for an hour or more.
2. In a bowl, mix together the olive oil, rice vinegar, sesame oil, soy sauce, and minced garlic.
3. Add in the salmon and let it marinate for about 30 minutes.
4. Start your grill on smoke with the lid open until a fire is established in the burn pot (3-7 minutes).
5. Supply your smoker with wood pellets and follow the start-up procedure. Preheat the grill, with the lid closed, to 225° F.
6. Place the planks on the grate. Once the boards start to smoke and crackle a little, it's ready for the fish.
7. Remove the fish from the marinade, season it with the onion powder, parsley and black pepper, then discard the marinade.
8. Place the salmon on the planks and grill until it reaches 140°F internal temperature (start checking temp after the salmon has been on the grill for 30 minutes).
9. Remove from the grill, let it rest for 10 minutes, then serve.

Thai-style Swordfish Steaks With Peanut Sauce

Servings: 4
Cooking Time: 8 Minutes

Ingredients:
- 4 center-cut swordfish steaks, each about 6oz (170g) and 1 inch (2.5cm) thick
- Peanut Sauce
- lime wedges
- for the marinade
- 1/2 cup light Thai-style unsweetened coconut milk
- 2 garlic cloves, peeled and smashed with a chef's knife
- juice and zest of 1 lime
- 1-inch (2.5cm) piece of fresh ginger, peeled and roughly chopped
- 1/2 Thai bird's eye chili pepper or serrano pepper, deseeded and thinly sliced, plus more
- 2 tbsp fresh cilantro leaves, coarsely chopped
- 1 tbsp Asian fish sauce
- 1 tbsp light soy sauce or liquid aminos
- 1 tbsp light brown sugar or low-carb substitute
- 1 tsp ground coriander
- 1/2 tsp ground turmeric

Directions:
1. In a medium bowl, make the marinade by whisking together the ingredients. Whisk until the brown sugar dissolves.
2. Place the swordfish steaks in a single layer in a nonreactive baking dish and pour the marinade over them, turning the steaks to coat thoroughly. Refrigerate for 1 hour.
3. Supply your smoker with wood pellets and follow the start-up procedure. Preheat the grill, with the lid closed, to 450° F.
4. Remove the swordfish from the marinade and scrape off any solids. (Discard the marinade.) Place the steaks on the grate and grill until the fish easily flakes when pressed with a fork, about 3 to 4 minutes per side, turning with a thin-bladed spatula.
5. Transfer the swordfish steaks to a platter. Serve with the peanut sauce and lime wedges.

Cajun Catfish

Servings: 6
Cooking Time: 15 Minutes

Ingredients:
- 2½ pounds catfish fillets
- 2 tablespoons olive oil
- 1 batch Cajun Rub

Directions:
1. Supply your smoker with wood pellets and follow the start-up procedure. Preheat the grill, with the lid closed, to 300°F.
2. Coat the catfish fillets all over with olive oil and season with the rub. Using your hands, work the rub into the flesh.
3. Place the fillets directly on the grill grate and smoke until their internal temperature reaches 145°F. Remove the catfish from the grill and serve immediately

Delicious Smoked Trout

Servings: 8
Cooking Time: 120 Minutes

Ingredients:
- 6 rainbow trout fillets
- Brine:
- 2 Tablespoons kosher salt
- 2 Tablespoons brown sugar
- 4 cups cool water

Directions:
1. For the brine, dissolve the kosher salt and brown sugar in water.
2. Place the trout fillets in the brine, skin side up, and brine the fillets for 15 minutes.
3. Supply your smoker with wood pellets and follow the start-up procedure. Preheat the grill, with the lid closed, to 180° F.
4. Remove the trout from the brine and transfer it to the grill grates.
5. Smoke the trout for 1.5 to 2 hours with the lid closed, depending on the thickness of your fillets.
6. Smoke until the trout reaches an internal temperature of 145 °F, or until the trout flakes easily.
7. Remove the trout from the smoker and serve warm, or let it cool completely and serve chilled with your favorite accouterments.

Shrimp Cabbage Tacos With Lime Cream

Servings: 4
Cooking Time: 10 Minutes

Ingredients:
- 1/4 Cabbage, Shredded
- 2 Tsp Cilantro, Chopped
- Corn Tortillas
- 1/2 Lime, Wedges
- 1/4 Cup Mayonnaise
- Blackened Sriracha Rub
- 1/4 Red Bell Pepper, Chopped
- 1 Lb Shrimp, Peeled & Deveined
- 1/4 Cup Sour Cream
- 2 Tsp Vegetable Oil
- 1/2 White Onion, Chopped

Directions:
1. Place shrimp In a medium bowl. Season with Blackened Sriracha Rub, then drizzle with vegetable oil. Toss by hand to coat well then set aside.
2. In a small mixing bowl, stir together mayonnaise, sour cream, and fresh lime juice. Season to taste with Blackened Sriracha. Set aside.
3. In a small mixing bowl, combine jalapeño, onion, red bell pepper, and cilantro. Set aside.
4. Supply your smoker with wood pellets and follow the start-up procedure. Preheat the grill, with the lid closed, till over medium heat. If using a grill, preheat a cast iron skillet over medium-heat.
5. Place tortillas on the griddle to warm each side, then turn off the burner below.
6. Transfer shrimp to the hot griddle, and cook for 4 to 6 minutes, tossing occasionally, until opaque. For spicier shrimp, season with additional Blackened Sriracha.
7. Assemble tacos: shredded cabbage, shrimp, pepper mixture, then drizzle with sauce. Serve warm with fresh lime wedges.

Smoked Salt Cured Lox

Servings: 8
Cooking Time: 30 Minutes

Ingredients:
- 1 Cup kosher salt
- 1 Cup sugar
- 1 Tablespoon cracked black pepper
- 1 Whole lemon zest
- 1 Whole orange zest
- 1 Whole Packaged Dill, roughly chopped including stems
- 2 Pound salmon fillet, skin on

Directions:
1. Mix together salt, sugar, black pepper, lemon zest, orange zest, and dill.
2. Slice salmon in half. Coat all flesh of salmon completely with salt sugar mixture. Sandwich the 2 pieces together, flesh to flesh and completely cover with salt sugar mixture.
3. Wrap tightly with plastic wrap and place into a gallon zip top bag. Squeeze out as much air as possible. Place wrapped salmon into a baking dish and place something heavy on top like a pot filled with water or a brick wrapped in foil. Place into the refrigerator for 10 hours. After 10 hours, flip over and put the weight back on top. Refrigerate for another 10 hours.
4. Remove from refrigerator, unwrap and rinse of remaining salt with cold water. Pat dry and leave on counter for 1 hour.
5. Supply your smoker with wood pellets and follow the start-up procedure. Preheat the grill, with the lid closed, to 180° F.
6. Place salmon onto a baking pan. Fill another baking pan with ice and place baking pan with salmon over ice.
7. Place onto grill and smoke for 30 minutes. Remove from grill and slice thin. Grill: 180 °F
8. Serve with bagels, cream cheese, capers, dill, lemon wedges, sliced tomatoes, and red onion. Enjoy!

Teriyaki Smoked Honey Tilapia

Servings: 4
Cooking Time: 120 Minutes

Ingredients:
- 4 tilapia fillets
- 1 cup teriyaki sauce
- 2/3 cup honey
- 1 tbsp sriracha sauce
- Green onions (optional)

Directions:
1. In a large bowl, make the marinade by mixing together the teriyaki sauce, honey, and sriracha. Make sure honey is dissolved and well blended.
2. Place the tilapia fillets in the marinade. Turn the fillets so they are completely coated. Cover with a plastic wrap and marinate in the fridge for about 2 hours.
3. Supply your smoker with wood pellets and follow the start-up procedure. Preheat the grill, with the lid closed, to 275° F.
4. Remove the tilapia fillets from the marinade and transfer them to the grill. Smoke the fillets until they reach an internal temperature of 145°F, about 2 hours.
5. Sprinkle with green onions if desired.

Oysters In The Shell

Servings: 4
Cooking Time: 20 Minutes

Ingredients:
- 8 medium oysters, unopened, in the shell, rinsed and scrubbed
- 1 batch Lemon Butter Mop for Seafood

Directions:
1. Supply your smoker with wood pellets and follow the start-up procedure. Preheat the grill, with the lid closed, to 375°F.
2. Place the unopened oysters directly on the grill grate and grill for about 20 minutes, or until the oysters are done and their shells open.
3. Discard any oysters that do not open. Shuck the remaining oysters, transfer them to a bowl, and add the mop. Serve immediately.

Garlic Blackened Catfish

Servings: 4
Cooking Time: 10 Minutes

Ingredients:
- ½ Cup Cajun Seasoning
- ¼ Tsp Cayenne Pepper
- 1 Tsp Granulated Garlic
- 1 Tsp Ground Thyme
- 1 Tsp Onion Powder
- 1 Tsp Ground Oregano
- 1 Tsp Pepper
- 4 (5-Oz.) Skinless Catfish Fillets
- 1 Tbsp Smoked Paprika
- 1 Stick Unsalted Butter

Directions:
1. In a small bowl, combine the Cajun seasoning, smoked paprika, onion powder, granulated garlic, ground oregano, ground thyme, pepper and cayenne pepper.
2. Sprinkle fish with salt and let rest for 20 minutes.
3. Supply your smoker with wood pellets and follow the start-up procedure. Preheat the grill, with the lid closed, to 450° F. If you're using a gas or charcoal grill, set it up for medium-high heat. Place cast iron skillet on the grill and let it preheat.
4. While grill is preheating, sprinkle catfish fillets with seasoning mixture, pressing gently to adhere. Add half the butter to preheated cast iron skillet and swirl to coat, add more butter if needed. Place fillets in hot skillet and cook 3-5 minutes or until a dark crust has been formed. Flip and cook an additional 3-5 minutes or until the fish flakes apart when pressed gently with your finger.
5. Remove fish from grill and sprinkle evenly with fresh parsley. Serve with lemon wedges and enjoy!

Wood-fired Halibut

Servings: 4
Cooking Time: 20 Minutes

Ingredients:
- 1 pound halibut fillet
- 1 batch Dill Seafood Rub

Directions:
1. Supply your smoker with wood pellets and follow the start-up procedure. Preheat the grill, with the lid closed, to 325°F.
2. Sprinkle the halibut fillet on all sides with the rub. Using your hands, work the rub into the meat.
3. Place the halibut directly on the grill grate and grill until its internal temperature reaches 145°F. Remove the halibut from the grill and serve immediately.

Garlic Pepper Shrimp Pesto Bruschetta

Servings: 12
Cooking Time: 15 Minutes

Ingredients:
- 12 Slices Bread, Baguette
- 1/2 Tsp Chili Pepper Flakes
- 1/2 Tsp Garlic Powder
- 4 Cloves Garlic, Minced
- 2 Tbsp Olive Oil
- 1/2 Tsp Paprika, Smoked
- 1/4 Tsp Parsley, Leaves
- Pepper
- Pesto
- Salt
- 12 Shrimp, Jumbo

Directions:
1. Supply your smoker with wood pellets and follow the start-up procedure. Preheat the grill, with the lid closed, to 350° F. Place the baguette slices on a baking sheet lined with foil. Stir together the olive oil, and minced garlic, then brush both sides of the baguette slices with the mix. Place the pan inside the grill, and bake for about 10-15 minutes.
2. In a skillet, add a splash of olive oil, shrimp, chili powder, garlic powder, smoked paprika, salt pepper, and grill on medium-high heat for about 5 minutes (until the shrimp is pink). Be sure to stir often. Once pink, remove pan from heat. Once the baguettes are toasted, let them cool for 5 minutes, then spread a layer of pesto onto each one, then top with a shrimp, and serve.

Grilled Blackened Saskatchewan Salmon

Servings: 4
Cooking Time: 30 Minutes

Ingredients:
- 1 salmon fillets
- zesty Italian dressing
- Blackened Saskatchewan Rub
- lemon wedges

Directions:
1. Brush salmon with Italian dressing and season with Traeger Blackened Saskatchewan Rub.
2. Supply your smoker with wood pellets and follow the start-up procedure. Preheat the grill, with the lid closed, to 325° F.
3. Place salmon on the grill and cook for 20 to 30 minutes, until it reaches an internal temperature of 145°F and flakes easily. Remove salmon from grill. Serve with lemon wedges. Enjoy! Grill: 325 °F Probe: 145 °F

Grilled Mussels With Lemon Butter

Servings: 4
Cooking Time: 15 Minutes

Ingredients:
- 2 Pound Mussels, debearded, washed
- 5 Quart water
- 1/3 Cup salt
- 2 Clove garlic, minced
- 1/3 Cup white wine
- 1 Whole lemon juice
- 3 Tablespoon parsley, chopped
- 1 loaf French country bread

Directions:
1. Supply your smoker with wood pellets and follow the start-up procedure. Preheat the grill, with the lid closed, to 375° F.
2. Scrub mussels well in running water making sure to remove all dirt and barnacles.
3. Place clean mussels in a large bowl with 5 quarts (5 L) water and 1/3 cup (91 g) of salt for about 15 minutes.

4. Drain, rinse and repeat soaking method two more times to purge and remove all sand.
5. Melt butter in a saute pan over medium high heat. Add garlic and cook for 1 minute until fragrant. Add wine and bring to a simmer. Add mussels and lemon juice to the pan and toss to coat.
6. Cover with a tight fitting lid and transfer to the grill. Let the mussels steam 8-10 minutes. Remove from the grill and discard any unopened mussels.
7. Sprinkle with chopped parsley and transfer to a serving dish. Serve with sliced bread. Enjoy!

Bbq Roasted Salmon

Servings: 4
Cooking Time: 15 Minutes

Ingredients:
- 1/3 Cup honey
- 3 Tablespoon Mustard, whole-grain
- 1 Cup ketchup
- 1/2 Cup dark brown sugar
- 1 Teaspoon Cider Vinegar
- 1/2 Teaspoon Thyme Leaves, finely chopped
- 1/8 Teaspoon Jacobsen Salt Co. Pure Kosher Sea Salt
- 1/8 Teaspoon freshly ground black pepper
- 4 Whole Salmon Fillets, 6oz each, skin-on

Directions:
1. Combine all sauce ingredients in a large bowl, preferably one day prior to making the salmon.
2. Rub salmon fillets on both sides with sauce. Reserve any extra, unused sauce.
3. Supply your smoker with wood pellets and follow the start-up procedure. Preheat the grill, with the lid closed, to 350° F.
4. Place fillets on grill, skin-side down, and cook for 15 minutes. Grill: 350 °F
5. Let the fish rest for about 3-5 minutes. Serve with extra sauce. Enjoy!

Bbq Oysters

Servings: 4
Cooking Time: 6 Minutes

Ingredients:
- 1 Pound unsalted butter, softened
- 1 Tablespoon Meat Church Holy Gospel BBQ Rub
- 1 Bunch green onions, chopped
- 2 Clove garlic, minced
- 12 oysters
- 1/4 Cup seasoned breadcrumbs
- 8 Ounce shredded pepper jack cheese
- Sweet & Heat BBQ Sauce
- 1/2 Bunch green onions, minced

Directions:
1. Supply your smoker with wood pellets and follow the start-up procedure. Preheat the grill, with the lid closed, to 375° F.
2. For the compound butter: Combine butter, garlic, onion and Meat Church Rub thoroughly.
3. Lay the butter on parchment paper or plastic wrap. Roll it up to form a log and tie each end with butcher's twine. Place in the freezer for an hour to solidify. You can use this butter on any grilled meat to enhance the flavor. You can also use a high-quality butter to replace the compound butter.
4. Shuck the oysters, keeping all of the juice in the shell. Sprinkle the oysters with breadcrumbs and place directly on the Traeger. Cook them for 5 minutes. You will be looking for the edge of the oyster to start to curl slightly.
5. After 5 minutes, place a spoonful of compound butter in the oysters. After the butter melts, add a pinch of pepper jack cheese.
6. Remove the oysters after 6 minutes on the grill total. Top oysters with a squirt of Traeger Sweet & Heat BBQ Sauce and a few chopped onions. Allow to cool for 5 minutes, then enjoy!

Moules Marinières With Garlic Butter Sauce

Servings: 4
Cooking Time: 12 Minutes

Ingredients:
- 3lb (1.4kg) fresh mussels, scrubbed under cold running water and debearded
- lemon wedges

- crusty bread (optional)
- for the sauce
- 6 tbsp unsalted butter
- 3 garlic cloves, peeled and minced
- 1 cup dry white wine or hard cider
- 1 tbsp freshly squeezed lemon juice
- 2 tsp hot sauce, plus more
- coarse salt
- freshly ground black pepper
- 2 tbsp chopped fresh curly parsley or tarragon

Directions:
1. Supply your smoker with wood pellets and follow the start-up procedure. Preheat the grill, with the lid closed, to 450° F.
2. In a small saucepan on the stovetop over medium-low heat, make the sauce by melting the butter. Add the garlic and sauté for 1 to 2 minutes. Add the wine, lemon juice, and hot sauce. Season with salt and pepper to taste. Simmer for 5 minutes. Remove the saucepan from the heat and stir in the parsley. Keep warm.
3. Discard any mussels that are cracked or don't snap shut when tapped. Place the mussels in a large aluminum foil roasting pan and cover tightly with heavy-duty aluminum foil.
4. Place the pan on the grate and steam the mussels until the shells open, about 10 to 12 minutes. Remove the pan from the grill and use long-handled tongs to remove the foil from the pan. (Be careful of escaping steam.) Use the tongs to discard any mussels that don't open.
5. Pour the reserved garlic butter sauce over the mussels. Serve from the pan or transfer the mussels to a shallow serving bowl. Serve immediately with lemon wedges, additional hot sauce, and crusty bread (if using) to sop up the juices.

Garlic Grilled Shrimp Skewers

Servings: 3
Cooking Time: 6 Minutes

Ingredients:
- 1 pound large shrimp
- 1/4 cup olive oil
- 1/4 cup fresh cilantro, finely chopped
- 1/4 cup fresh parsley, finely chopped
- 4 cloves garlic, minced
- 1 tablespoon lemon juice
- 1/2 teaspoon salt
- 1/4 teaspoon black pepper
- Pinch cayenne pepper, adjust to spice preference

Directions:
1. Add the olive oil, herbs, and spices to a small mixing bowl and whisk together.
2. Place the shrimp in a bowl and pour 3/4 of the marinade on top of the shrimp. Mix together gently to coat the shrimp evenly.
3. Cover the bowl and marinate the shrimp for 30 minutes to an hour.
4. Thread the shrimp on the skewers and make sure to get all the good garlic and herbs from the bowl and spread on to the shrimp.
5. Supply your smoker with wood pellets and follow the start-up procedure. Preheat the grill, with the lid closed, to medium high heat.
6. Once the grill is hot, arrange the shrimp skewers on the grill and cook for 2-3 minutes per side, or until they turn pink and opaque.
7. Remove the shrimp skewers to a plate and spoon the remaining marinade on top before serving.

Planked Trout With Fennel, Bacon & Orange

Servings: 4
Cooking Time: 40minutes

Ingredients:
- 4 whole trout, each about 14 to 16oz (400 to 450g), cleaned and gutted, fins removed
- coarse salt
- freshly ground black pepper
- for the filling
- 1 large navel orange
- 4 slices of thick-cut bacon, diced
- 1 large fennel bulb, trimmed, halved, decored, and diced, green fronds reserved
- 4oz (110g) baby spinach, about 6 cups

- coarse salt
- freshly ground black pepper

Directions:

1. Supply your smoker with wood pellets and follow the start-up procedure. Preheat the grill, with the lid closed, to 450° F. Place 4 cedar planks on the grate and allow them to singe slightly on both sides. Remove them from the grill and place them on a heatproof surface to cool.
2. Lower the temperature to 300°F (149°C).
3. Slice 4 thin rounds from the center of the orange and then slice each in half for 8 pieces total. Zest the remainder of the orange and set aside.
4. In a cold skillet on the stovetop over medium heat, sauté the bacon, until the fat has rendered and the bacon is golden brown, about 6 to 8 minutes, stirring frequently. Use a slotted spoon to transfer the bacon to paper towels to drain. Add the fennel to the fat in the skillet and cook until tender crisp, about 5 minutes. Add the spinach and stir until it wilts, about 1 to 2 minutes. Squeeze the juice of one of the reserved orange ends over the mixture. Add the drained bacon. Season with salt and pepper and then stir. Remove the skillet from the stovetop and set aside.
5. Rinse each trout inside and out under cold running water and pat dry with paper towels. Place three 12-inch (30.5cm) pieces of butcher's twine on each plank and place a trout on top. Season the inside of each fish with salt and pepper. Place two half-rounds of orange in each belly, rind side facing out. Top with some of the filling. Tie the trout with the butcher's twine and trim any ends. Repeat with the remaining trout.
6. Place the planks on the grate and cook the trout until they're cooked through, about 30 to 40 minutes.
7. Remove the planks from the grill and remove the twine. Top each trout with a few curls of orange zest and some reserved fennel fronds. Serve the trout on the planks.

Lemon Scallops Wrapped In Bacon

Servings: 4
Cooking Time: 20 Minutes

Ingredients:

- 3 Tbsp Lemon, Juice
- Pepper
- 12 Scallop

Directions:

1. Start your grill on smoke with the lid open until a fire is established in the burn pot (3-7 minutes).
2. Supply your smoker with wood pellets and follow the start-up procedure. Preheat the grill, with the lid closed, to 400° F.Cut the bacon rashers in half, wrap each half around a scallop and use a toothpick to keep it in place.
3. Next drizzle the lemon juice over the scallops, and then place them on a baking tray.
4. Place in the grill, and grill for about 15-20 minutes, or until the bacon is crisp, remove from the grill, then serve.

Seared Ahi Tuna Steak With Soy Sauce

Servings: 2
Cooking Time: 60 Minutes

Ingredients:

- 1/2 Cup Gluten Free Soy Sauce
- 1 Large Sushi Grade Ahi Tuna Steak, Patted Dry
- 1/4 Cup Lime Juice
- 2 Tablespoons Rice Wine Vinegar
- 2 Tablespoons Sesame Oil, Divided
- 2 Tablespoons Sriracha Sauce
- 4 Tablespoons Sweet Heat Rub
- 2 Cups Water

Directions:

1. Supply your smoker with wood pellets and follow the start-up procedure. Preheat the grill, with the lid closed, to 400° F. If using gas or charcoal, set it up for high heat over direct heat.
2. In the glass baking dish, pour in the water, soy sauce, lime juice, rice wine vinegar, 1 tablespoon sesame oil, sriracha sauce, and mirin. Whisk the marinade together with the whisk until everything is well combine. Place the ahi steak into the marinade and place the glass baking dish with the ahi steak in the refrigerator for 30 minutes. After 30 minutes, flip the ahi steak over so that

the ahi has the chance to fully marinate on all sides, and allow to marinate for 30 more minutes.

3. After the tuna steak has finished marinating, drain off the marinade and pat the steak dry with paper towels on all sides. Pour the Sweet Heat Rub onto the plate and rub the remaining tablespoon of sesame oil generously on all sides of the tuna steak, and then gently place the tuna steak into the seasoning on the plate, turning on all sides to coat evenly.

4. Insert a temperature probe into the thickest part of the ahi steak and place the steak on the hottest part of the grill. Grill the ahi tuna steak for 45 seconds on each side, or just until the outside is opaque and has grill marks. Flip the steak and allow it to grill for another 45 seconds until the outside is just cooked through. The ahi tuna steak's internal temperature should be just at 115°F.

5. Remove the steak from the grill once it reaches 115°F, and immediately slice and serve. The inside of the steak should still be cool and ruby pink.

Grilled Whole Steelhead Fillet

Servings: 6
Cooking Time: 30 Minutes

Ingredients:
- (2-1/2 to 3 lb) steelhead or salmon fillet, skin-on
- 2 Tablespoon Montana Mex Sweet Seasoning
- 1 Teaspoon Montana Mex Jalapeño Seasoning Blend
- 1 Teaspoon Montana Mex Mild Chile Seasoning Blend
- 2 Tablespoon Montana Mex Avocado Oil
- 2 Tablespoon freshly grated ginger
- 1 lemon, thinly sliced

Directions:
1. Coat fillet evenly with all three dry seasonings, avocado oil, grated ginger and thinly sliced lemon.
2. Supply your smoker with wood pellets and follow the start-up procedure. Preheat the grill, with the lid closed, to 380° F.
3. Place the fish skin-side down on the grill grate and cook for 20 minutes. Grill: 380 °F
4. Remove fillet from grill and let rest for 5 minutes. Enjoy!

Tequila & Lime Shrimp With Smoked Tomato Sauce

Servings: 4
Cooking Time: 6 Minutes

Ingredients:
- 24 to 28 jumbo shrimp, about 2lb (1kg) total, peeled and deveined
- 1 lime, quartered
- Smoked Tomato Sauce
- for the marinade
- ½ cup tequila or mezcal
- juice and zest of 1 lime
- 2 garlic cloves, peeled and roughly chopped
- ½ cup freshly squeezed orange juice
- ¼ cup extra virgin olive oil
- 2 tsp agave, light brown sugar, or low-carb substitute
- 2 tsp Mexican hot sauce, plus more
- 1½ tsp coarse salt
- 1 tsp baking soda
- 1 tsp chili powder
- ½ tsp ground cumin

Directions:
1. In a medium bowl, make the marinade by whisking together the ingredients. Whisk until the salt dissolves. Taste for seasoning, adding more hot sauce if desired.
2. Place the shrimp in a resealable plastic bag and pour the marinade over them, turning the bag several times to coat thoroughly. Refrigerate for 30 minutes.
3. Supply your smoker with wood pellets and follow the start-up procedure. Preheat the grill, with the lid closed, to 450° F.
4. Drain the shrimp and discard the marinade. Pat the shrimp dry with paper towels. Thread the shrimp on 4 bamboo skewers (preferably flat ones). Make sure all the shrimp face the same direction. Finish each skewer with a lime wedge.
5. Place the skewers on the grate and grill until the shrimp are white and opaque, about 2 to 3 minutes per side, turning once. (Don't overcook.)
6. Remove the shrimp from the grill. Serve immediately with the warm tomato sauce.

Smoked Cedar Plank Salmon

Servings: 4
Cooking Time: 20 Minutes

Ingredients:
- 1/4 Cup Brown Sugar
- 1/2 Tablespoon Olive Oil
- Competition Smoked Seasoning
- 4 Salmon Fillets, Skin Off

Directions:
1. Soak the untreated cedar plank in water for 24 hours before grilling. When ready to grill, remove and wipe down.
2. Supply your smoker with wood pellets and follow the start-up procedure. Preheat the grill, with the lid closed, to 350° F.
3. In a small bowl, mix the brown sugar, oil, and Lemon Pepper, Garlic, and Herb seasoning. Rub generously over the salmon fillets.
4. Place the plank over indirect heat, then lay the salmon on the plank and grill for 15-20 minutes, or until the salmon is cooked through and flakes easily with a fork. Remove from the heat and serve immediately.

Grilled Lemon Lobster Tails

Servings: 3
Cooking Time: 7 Minutes

Ingredients:
- 6 lobster tails
- 1/4 cup melted butter
- 1/4 cup fresh lemon juice
- 1 tablespoon fresh dill
- 1 teaspoon salt
- 6 lime wedges

Directions:
1. Supply your smoker with wood pellets and follow the start-up procedure. Preheat the grill, with the lid closed, to 375° F.
2. Split the lobster tails in half place then back side down.
3. Cut down through the center to the shell the whole length of each tail.
4. Pull the shell back, exposing the meat.
5. Pat the lobster tails with paper towel to dry.
6. Combine in a small mixing bowl the butter, lemon juice, dill, and salt until the salt has dissolved.
7. Brush the mixture onto the flesh side of each lobster tail.
8. Place the lobster tails onto the grill and cook for 5 to 7 minutes, turning them once during the cooking process. (The shells should turn a bright pink).
9. Remove the heat.
10. Serve with lime wedges!

Pacific Northwest Salmon

Servings: 4
Cooking Time: 75 Minutes

Ingredients:
- 1 (2-pound) half salmon fillet
- 1 batch Dill Seafood Rub
- 2 tablespoons butter, cut into 3 or 4 slices

Directions:
1. Supply your smoker with wood pellets and follow the start-up procedure. Preheat the grill, with the lid closed, to 180°F.
2. Season the salmon all over with the rub. Using your hands, work the rub into the flesh.
3. Place the salmon directly on the grill grate, skin-side down, and smoke for 1 hour.
4. Place the butter slices on the salmon, equally spaced. Increase the grill's temperature to 300°F and continue to cook until the salmon's internal temperature reaches 145°F. Remove the salmon from the grill and serve immediately.

Smoked Salmon Candy

Servings: 4
Cooking Time: 180 Minutes

Ingredients:
- 2 Cup gin
- 1 Cup dark brown sugar
- 1/2 Cup kosher salt
- 1 Cup maple syrup
- 1 Tablespoon black pepper

- 3 Pound salmon
- vegetable oil
- dark brown sugar

Directions:
1. In a large bowl, combine all ingredients for the cure.
2. Cut the salmon into 2 ounce pieces and place in the cure.
3. Cover and refrigerate overnight.
4. Supply your smoker with wood pellets and follow the start-up procedure. Preheat the grill, with the lid closed, to 180° F.
5. Spray foil with vegetable oil. Place salmon on foil and sprinkle with additional brown sugar.
6. Place foil directly on the grill grate. Close the lid and smoke the salmon for 3 to 4 hours or until fully cooked. Grill: 180 °F
7. Serve hot or chilled. Enjoy!

Traeger Crab Legs

Servings: 4
Cooking Time: 30 Minutes

Ingredients:
- 3 Pound crab legs, thawed and halved
- 1 Cup butter, melted
- 2 Tablespoon fresh lemon juice
- 2 Clove garlic, minced
- 1 Tablespoon Fin & Feather Rub or Old Bay Seasoning, plus more to taste
- lemon wedges
- Italian Parsley, chopped

Directions:
1. If the crab legs are too long to fit in the roasting pan, break them down at the joints by twisting, or use a heavy knife or cleaver. Split the shells open lengthwise. Transfer to the roasting pan.
2. Combine the butter, lemon juice and garlic; whisk to mix. Pour mixture over the crab legs, turning the legs to coat. Sprinkle the Traeger Fin & Feather Rub or Old Bay Seasoning over the legs.
3. Supply your smoker with wood pellets and follow the start-up procedure. Preheat the grill, with the lid closed, to 350° F.
4. Cook the crab legs, basting once or twice with the butter sauce from the bottom of the pan, for 20 to 30 minutes (depending on the size of the crab legs) or until warmed through. Grill: 350 °F
5. Transfer the crab legs to a large platter and divide the sauce and accumulated juices between 4 dipping bowls. Enjoy!

Baked Steelhead

Servings: 4
Cooking Time: 20 Minutes

Ingredients:
- 1 steelhead fillet
- 16-oz bottle Italian dressing
- 3 Tablespoon unsalted butter
- Blackened Saskatchewan Rub
- 1/2 shallot, minced
- 2 Clove garlic, minced
- 1 lemon

Directions:
1. Supply your smoker with wood pellets and follow the start-up procedure. Preheat the grill, with the lid closed, to 350° F.
2. Put butter in a small cast iron pan and place inside Traeger while preheating to soften. Pour Italian dressing over fillet to evenly coat.
3. Shake Traeger Blackened Saskatchewan rub evenly in a thin layer to cover dressing. Mince shallot and garlic.
4. Remove butter from pre-heated grill, careful as the cast iron will be hot. Stir in shallots and garlic.
5. Spread a nice thick layer of mixture on the top-middle of the fillet. Cut lemon into thin slices and place on top of butter mix.
6. Place steelhead on the grill and cook for 20 to 30 minutes, until fish is flaky, being careful not to over cook.
7. Remove fillet from the grill. Enjoy!

Smoked Fish Chowder

Servings: 4
Cooking Time: 60 Minutes

Ingredients:
- 12 Ounce (1-1/2 to 2 lb) skin-on salmon fillet, preferably wild-caught
- Fin & Feather Rub
- 2 Corn Husks
- 3 Slices Bacon, sliced
- 4 Can Cream of Potato Soup, Condensed
- 3 Cup whole milk
- 8 Ounce cream cheese
- 3 green onions, thinly sliced
- 2 Teaspoon hot sauce

Directions:
1. Supply your smoker with wood pellets and follow the start-up procedure. Preheat the grill, with the lid closed, to 180° F.
2. Sprinkle Traeger Fin & Feather rub as needed on salmon. Arrange the salmon skin-side down on the grill grate. Smoke for 30 minutes. Grill: 180 °F
3. Increase the grill temperature to 350°F. Grill: 350 °F
4. Cook the salmon for 30 minutes, or until the fish flakes easily with a fork. (The exact time will depend on the thickness of the fillet.) There is no need to turn the fish. Using a large thin spatula, transfer the salmon to a wire rack to cool. Remove the skin. (The salmon can be made a day ahead, wrapped in plastic wrap and refrigerated.) Break into flakes and set aside.
5. Arrange the corn and bacon strips on the grill grate. (The salmon will be roasting while you do this.) Roast the corn and the bacon until the corn is cooked through and browned in spots, turning as needed, and the bacon is crisp, about 15 minutes.
6. In the meantime, bring the cream of potato soup and the milk to a simmer over medium heat in a large saucepan or Dutch oven on the stovetop. Gradually stir in the cream cheese and whisk to blend. Chop the bacon into bits and slice the corn off the cobs using long strokes of a chef's knife.
7. Add to the soup along with the green onions. Stir in the salmon. Heat gently for 5 to 10 minutes. Add the hot sauce to taste. If the chowder is too thick, add more milk. Serve at once. Enjoy!

Salmon Cakes With Homemade Tartar Sauce

Servings: 4
Cooking Time: 15 Minutes

Ingredients:
- 1 1/2 Cups Breadcrumb, Dry
- 1/2 Tablespoon Capers, Diced
- 1/4 Cup Dill Pickle Relish
- 2 Eggs
- 1 1/4 Cup Mayonnaise, Divided
- 1 Tablespoon Mustard, Grainy
- 1/2 Tablespoon Olive Oil
- 1/2 Red Pepper, Diced Finely
- 1/2 Tablespoon Sweet Rib Rub
- 1 Cup Cooked Salmon, Flaked

Directions:
1. In a large bowl, mix together the salmon, eggs, ¼ cup mayonnaise, breadcrumbs, red bell pepper, Sweet Rib Rub, and mustard. Allow the mixture to sit for 15 minutes to hydrate the breadcrumbs.
2. Supply your smoker with wood pellets and follow the start-up procedure. Preheat the grill, with the lid closed, to 350° F.
3. In a small bowl, mix together the remaining mayonnaise, dill pickle relish, and diced capers. Set aside.
4. Place the baking sheet on the grill to preheat. Once the baking sheet is hot, drizzle the olive oil over the pan and drop rounded tablespoons of the salmon mixture onto the sheet pan. Press the mixture down into a flat patty with a spatula. Allow to grill for 3 to 5 minutes, then flip and grill for 1 to 2 more minutes. Remove from the grill and serve with the reserved tartar sauce.

VEGETABLES RECIPES

Grilled Beer Cabbage

Servings: 4
Cooking Time: 50 Minutes

Ingredients:
- 2 Cabbage, head
- 1 Tablespoon extra-virgin olive oil
- 1 Teaspoon salt
- 1 Teaspoon freshly ground black pepper
- 14 Fluid Ounce Guinness Extra Stout

Directions:
1. Clean and core cabbages. Drizzle with olive oil and salt and pepper. Rub into the cabbage.
2. Supply your smoker with wood pellets and follow the start-up procedure. Preheat the grill, with the lid closed, to 180° F.
3. Place cabbages directly on grill grate; smoke for 15 to 20 minutes. Remove from grill and thickly slice cabbage. Grill: 180 °F
4. Place sliced cabbage in cast-iron skillet. Pour beer over cabbage and return to grill.
5. Increase temperature to 375°F and cook for 30 minutes, or until cabbage has reached desired softness. Grill: 375 °F
6. Serve with corned beef. Enjoy!

Braised Creamed Green Beans

Servings: 4
Cooking Time: 25 Minutes

Ingredients:
- 6 Tablespoon butter
- 2 Clove garlic, pressed or minced
- 1 shallot, thinly sliced
- 1 Cup heavy cream
- 1 Pinch ground nutmeg
- salt
- 3 Pound mixed greens such as kale, chard or collards; washed, stems removed and torn into bite sized pieces

Directions:
1. Supply your smoker with wood pellets and follow the start-up procedure. Preheat the grill, with the lid closed, to 325° F.
2. In a saucepan, heat 2 tablespoons of the butter over high heat until it foams. Add the garlic and shallot and cook over medium-low heat, stirring, until softened and golden, about 5 minutes.
3. Add the cream, bring to a simmer and cook until slightly thickened, about 10 minutes.
4. Add the nutmeg and salt to taste. Using a hand blender, purée until smooth.
5. In a cast iron pan, heat the remaining 4 tablespoons butter over high heat until it foams.
6. Add the greens and cook until tender but still bright green, about 5 minutes.
7. Sprinkle with salt and add the cream mixture. Cover and transfer to the grill.
8. Braise greens for 15-20 minutes until the cream is bubbling and greens are tender. Grill: 325 °F
9. Season to taste with nutmeg and salt. Serve hot. Enjoy!

Smoked Pickled Green Beans

Servings: 4
Cooking Time: 45 Minutes

Ingredients:
- 1 Pound Green Beans, blanched
- 1/2 Cup salt
- 1/2 Cup sugar
- 1 Tablespoon red pepper flakes
- 2 Cup white wine vinegar
- 2 Cup ice water

Directions:
1. Supply your smoker with wood pellets and follow the start-up procedure. Preheat the grill, with the lid closed, to 180° F.
2. Place the blanched green beans on a mesh grill mat and place mat directly on the grill grate. Smoke the green beans for 30-45 minutes until they've picked up

the desired amount of smoke. Remove from grill and set aside until the brine is ready. Grill: 180 °F
3. In a medium sized saucepan, bring all remaining ingredients, except ice water, to a boil over medium high heat on the stove. Simmer for 5-10 minutes then remove from heat and steep 20 minutes more. Pour brine over ice water to cool.
4. Once brine has cooled, pour over the green beans and weigh them down with a few plates to ensure they are completely submerged. Let sit 24 hours before use. Enjoy!

Roasted Pickled Beets

Servings: 8
Cooking Time: 60 Minutes

Ingredients:
- 6 Medium Red Beets, scrubbed and trimmed
- 1 Cup red wine vinegar
- 1/2 Cup sugar
- 10 Whole peppercorns
- 1 Cup water
- 1 1/2 Teaspoon coarse salt
- 8 whole cloves
- 2 Pieces Star Anise, Broken
- 1 cinnamon stick, broken in half

Directions:
1. Make a foil pouch large enough to enclose the beets. Poke a few holes in the top to allow steam to escape.
2. Supply your smoker with wood pellets and follow the start-up procedure. Preheat the grill, with the lid closed, to 350° F.
3. Roast the beets until they are tender, 50 to 60 minutes. Carefully remove the foil and allow the beets to cool until they can be comfortably handled. Grill: 350 °F
4. Slip the skins off with your fingers. (You may wish to wear latex gloves to avoid staining your hands.) Cut the beets into quarters or slices. (Candy cane beets are especially pretty when sliced.)
5. In the meantime, make the brine: Bring the vinegar, sugar, salt, and water to a boil in a small saucepan over high heat.
6. Put the cloves, peppercorns, star anise, and cinnamon in a clean lidded jar, such as a canning jar
7. Add the beets to the jar. Pour the hot brine over the beets. Put the lid on the jar. Cool the beets to room temperature, then refrigerate for 3 to 5 days before serving. Enjoy!

Bacon Wrapped Corn On The Cob

Servings: 4
Cooking Time: 21 Minutes

Ingredients:
- 4 Whole Corn, ears
- 8 Slices bacon
- 1 Teaspoon freshly ground black pepper
- 1 Teaspoon chili powder
- 1 To Taste Parmesan cheese, grated

Directions:
1. Peel back the corn husks, remove silk strings and rinse corn under cold water.
2. Wrap 2 pieces of bacon around each ear of corn, securing with toothpicks.
3. Dust each ear of corn with some chili powder and cracked black pepper.
4. Supply your smoker with wood pellets and follow the start-up procedure. Preheat the grill, with the lid closed, to 375° F.
5. Place the ears of corn directly on the Traeger and grill for approximately 20 minutes or until the bacon is cooked crisp. Grill: 375 °F
6. Take the corn off the Traeger. Carefully remove the toothpicks and season with a little more chili powder and a grating of parmesan cheese, if desired. Serve & enjoy!

Traeger Smoked Coleslaw

Servings: 8
Cooking Time: 20 Minutes

Ingredients:
- 1 Head purple cabbage, shredded
- 1 Head green cabbage, shredded
- 1 Cup shredded carrots
- 2 scallions, thinly sliced
- 1 1/2 Cup mayonnaise

- 1/8 Cup white wine vinegar
- 1 Teaspoon celery seed
- 1 Teaspoon sugar
- salt and pepper

Directions:
1. Supply your smoker with wood pellets and follow the start-up procedure. Preheat the grill, with the lid closed, to 180° F.
2. Spread cabbage and carrots out on a sheet tray and place directly on the grill grates. Smoke for 20 to 25 minutes or until cabbage picks up desired amount of smoke. Grill: 180 °F
3. Remove from grill and transfer to the refrigerator immediately to cool. While cabbage is cooling, make the dressing.
4. For the dressing, combine all ingredients in a small bowl and mix well.
5. Place smoked cabbage and carrots in a large bowl and pour dressing over them. Stir to coat well.
6. Transfer to a serving dish and sprinkle with scallions. Enjoy!

Cast Iron Potatoes

Servings: 4
Cooking Time: 60 Minutes

Ingredients:
- 4 Tablespoon butter, cut into cubes
- 2 1/2 Pound potatoes, peeled and cut into 1/8 inch slices
- 1/2 Large sweet onion, thinly sliced
- salt
- black pepper
- 1 1/2 Cup grated mild cheddar or jack cheese
- 2 Cup milk
- paprika

Directions:
1. Butter the inside of a cast iron skillet and layer half the potato slices on the bottom. Top with half the onions. Season with salt and pepper.
2. Sprinkle 1 cup of the cheese over the potatoes and onions and dot with half the butter. Layer the remaining potatoes and onions on top. Dot with remaining butter.
3. Pour the milk into the skillet. Cover the skillet tightly with aluminum foil.
4. Supply your smoker with wood pellets and follow the start-up procedure. Preheat the grill, with the lid closed, to 350° F.
5. Bake for 1 hour, or until the potatoes are very tender. Grill: 350 °F
6. Remove the foil and top with the remaining 1/2 cup of cheese. Bake for 30 minutes more (uncovered) until the cheese is lightly browned. Dust the top with paprika and serve immediately.

Roasted Potato Poutine

Servings: 6
Cooking Time: 40 Minutes

Ingredients:
- 4 Large russet potatoes
- Tablespoon olive oil or vegetable oil
- Prime Rib Rub
- Cup chicken or beef gravy (homemade or jarred)
- 1 1/2 Cup white or yellow cheddar cheese curds
- freshly ground black pepper
- 2 Tablespoon scallions

Directions:
1. Supply your smoker with wood pellets and follow the start-up procedure. Preheat the grill, with the lid closed, to 500° F.
2. Scrub the potatoes and slice into fries, wedges or preferred shape.
3. Put potatoes into a large mixing bowl and coat with oil. Season generously with Traeger Prime Rib rub.
4. Tip the potatoes onto a rimmed baking sheet and spread in a single layer, cut sides down.
5. Roast for 20 minutes, then using a spatula, turn the potatoes to the other cut side. Continue to roast until the potatoes are tender and golden brown, about 15 to 20 minutes more.
6. While potatoes cook, warm the gravy on the stovetop or in a heat-proof saucepan on your Traeger.
7. To assemble the poutine, arrange the potatoes in a large shallow bowl or on a serving platter. Distribute the

cheese curds on top. Pour the hot gravy evenly over the potatoes and cheese curds.

8. Season with black pepper and garnish with thinly sliced scallions. Serve immediately. Enjoy!

Mashed Red Potatoes

Servings: 4
Cooking Time: 40 Minutes

Ingredients:

- 8 Large red potatoes
- salt
- black pepper
- 1/2 Cup heavy cream
- 1/4 Cup butter

Directions:

1. Supply your smoker with wood pellets and follow the start-up procedure. Preheat the grill, with the lid closed, to 180° F.
2. Slice red potatoes in half, lengthwise then cut in half again to make quarters. Season potatoes with salt and pepper.
3. Increase the heat to High and preheat. Once the grill is hot, set potatoes directly on the grill grate. Grill: 450 °F
4. Every 15 minutes flip potatoes to ensure all sides get color. Continue to do this until potatoes are fork tender.
5. When tender, mash potatoes with cream, butter, salt, and pepper to taste. Serve warm, enjoy!

Grilled Chili-lime Corn

Servings: 8
Cooking Time: 45 Minutes

Ingredients:

- 12 Corn, ears
- 1 Teaspoon chili powder
- 1/2 Teaspoon onion powder
- 1 Teaspoon Leinenkugel's Summer Shandy Rub
- 2 lime, juiced
- 1 Tablespoon lime zest

Directions:

1. Soak the ears of corn, still in their husk, in water for 4 to 8 hours.
2. Supply your smoker with wood pellets and follow the start-up procedure. Preheat the grill, with the lid closed, to 350° F.
3. Place corn directly on grill grates. Turn corn every 15 minutes for 45 minutes total cooking time. Grill: 350 °F
4. Combine chili powder, onion powder, Summer Shandy rub, lime juice, lime zest and butter in an oven safe dish and place in grill for 10 minutes. Remove corn and butter from the grill.
5. Pull corn husk back, but not off and remove corn silk. Using the corn husk as a handle, brush the corn with the melted chili-lime butter. Enjoy!

Carolina Baked Beans

Servings: 12-15
Cooking Time: 180 Minutes

Ingredients:

- 3 (28-ounce) cans baked beans (I like Bush's brand)
- 1 large onion, finely chopped
- 1 cup The Ultimate BBQ Sauce
- ½ cup light brown sugar
- ¼ cup Worcestershire sauce
- 3 tablespoons yellow mustard
- Nonstick cooking spray or butter, for greasing
- 1 large bell pepper, cut into thin rings
- ½ pound thick-cut bacon, partially cooked and cut into quarters

Directions:

1. Supply your smoker with wood pellets and follow the start-up procedure. Preheat, with the lid closed, to 300°F.
2. In a large mixing bowl, stir together the beans, onion, barbecue sauce, brown sugar, Worcestershire sauce, and mustard until well combined
3. Coat a 9-by-13-inch aluminum pan with cooking spray or butter.
4. Pour the beans into the pan and top with the bell pepper rings and bacon pieces, pressing them down slightly into the sauce.
5. Place a layer of heavy-duty foil on the grill grate to catch drips, and place the pan on top of the foil. Close the lid and cook for 2 hours 30 minutes to 3 hours, or until the beans are hot, thick, and bubbly.
6. Let the beans rest for 5 minutes before serving.

Baked Garlic Duchess Potatoes

Servings: 8
Cooking Time: 60 Minutes

Ingredients:
- 12 Medium Potatoes, Yukon gold
- salt
- 5 Large Egg Yolk
- 2 Clove garlic, minced
- 1.24 Cup heavy cream
- 3/4 Cup sour cream
- 10 Tablespoon butter, melted
- black pepper

Directions:
1. Place potatoes in a large pot and fill with water. Season with salt. Bring to a boil over medium-high heat.
2. Reduce heat and simmer until a paring knife easily slides through potatoes, about 25 to 35 minutes. Drain and let cool slightly.
3. Supply your smoker with wood pellets and follow the start-up procedure. Preheat the grill, with the lid closed, to 450° F.
4. Whisk together egg yolks, garlic, cream, sour cream, butter, and pepper in a large bowl. Season with salt.
5. Peel potatoes and push flesh through a ricer or a food mill directly into bowl with egg mixture. Fold in the egg mixture being careful not to overmix.
6. Transfer to a 3-quart baking dish and bake until golden brown and slightly puffed, about 30–40 minutes. Enjoy! Grill: 450 °F

Roasted Pumpkin Seeds

Servings: 8
Cooking Time: 40 Minutes

Ingredients:
- 1 Whole Pumpkin, seeds
- olive oil or vegetable oil
- Jacobsen Salt Co. Pure Kosher Sea Salt

Directions:
1. As soon as possible after removing the seeds from the pumpkin, rinse pumpkin seeds under cold water in a colander and pick out the pulp and strings.
2. Place the pumpkin seeds in a single layer on an oiled baking sheet, stirring to coat. Supply your smoker with wood pellets and follow the start-up procedure. Preheat the grill, with the lid closed, to 180° F.
3. Place the baking sheet with the seeds on the grill grate, close the lid, and smoke for 20 minutes. Grill: 180 °F
4. Sprinkle your seeds with salt and turn the temperature on your grill up to 325°F. Roast the seeds until toasted, about 20 minutes. Check and stir seeds after the first 10 minutes. Grill: 325 °F
5. Seeds will be brown because they were smoked before being roasted. Enjoy!

Baked Sweet And Savory Yams By Bennie Kendrick

Servings: 6
Cooking Time: 60 Minutes

Ingredients:
- 3 Medium Yams
- 3 Tablespoon extra-virgin olive oil
- honey
- Goat Cheese
- 1/2 Cup brown sugar
- 1/2 Cup Pecans, pieces

Directions:
1. Supply your smoker with wood pellets and follow the start-up procedure. Preheat the grill, with the lid closed, to 350° F.
2. While Traeger comes to temperature, wash yams and poke a few holes all over. Wrap yams in foil.
3. Bake for 45-60 minutes or until knife tender. You don't want to overcook and get the yams too soft because you want to be able to cut each yam into rounds.
4. Once yams have cooled to the touch, cut each into 1/4" rounds. Lightly coat each round with oil olive and place on sheet tray.
5. Sprinkle each top with brown sugar. Using a teaspoon, place desired amount of goat cheese on each round. Next top with chopped pecans. Finally, drizzle Bee Local honey over each round.
6. Based on how sweet you like your yams, you can add more brown sugar and honey.
7. After complete, place your sheet tray back in the grill and cook, lid closed, for another 20 minutes. Enjoy!

Grilled Fingerling Potato Salad

Servings: 6
Cooking Time: 15 Minutes

Ingredients:
- 10 Whole scallions
- 2/3 Cup extra-virgin olive oil, divided
- 1 1/2 Pound fingerling potatoes, cut in half lengthwise
- pepper
- 2 Teaspoon kosher salt, divided, plus more as needed
- 2 Tablespoon rice vinegar
- 2 Teaspoon lemon juice
- 1 Small jalapeño, sliced

Directions:
1. Supply your smoker with wood pellets and follow the start-up procedure. Preheat the grill, with the lid closed, to 450° F.
2. Brush the scallions with oil and place on the grill.
3. Cook until lightly charred, about 2 to 3 minutes. Remove and let cool. Grill: 450 °F
4. Once the scallions have cooled, slice and set aside.
5. Brush the fingerling potatoes with oil (reserving 1/3 cup for later use), then salt and pepper. Place cut-side down on the grill until cooked through, about 4 to 5 minutes. Grill: 450 °F
6. In a bowl, whisk the remaining 1/3 cup olive oil, 1 teaspoon salt, rice vinegar and lemon juice. Next mix in the scallions, potatoes and sliced jalapeño.
7. Season with salt and pepper, and serve. Enjoy!

Sweet Potato Marshmallow Casserole

Servings: 6
Cooking Time: 60 Minutes

Ingredients:
- 5 Yams
- 1 1/2 Stick butter
- 1/2 Cup brown sugar
- 1 Teaspoon vanilla
- 1 Teaspoon kosher salt
- 1 Teaspoon cracked black pepper
- 1 Marshmallows, miniature
- 1/4 Unsalted Butter, Softened

Directions:
1. Supply your smoker with wood pellets and follow the start-up procedure. Preheat the grill, with the lid closed, to 375° F.
2. Pierce the skin of the yams with a fork a few times. Place on a baking sheet or foil tin inside the grill and let roast for 50 minutes or until extremely softened. Grill: 375 °F
3. Remove yams from the grill and set aside until cool enough to handle. While the potatoes cool, with a stiff whisk, whip together 1/2 cup softened butter, the brown sugar, vanilla, salt and pepper.
4. Remove and discard skins from sweet potatoes and mash until smooth. Fold in the butter mixture and transfer to a cast iron pan.
5. Place cast iron on the grill and bake for 15-20 minutes. Remove from the grill, top with marshmallows and dot with remaining 1/4 cup butter.
6. Place back in the grill for 15 minutes until warm and the marshmallows are golden. Enjoy! Grill: 375 °F

Grilled Broccoli Rabe

Servings: 4
Cooking Time: 10 Minutes

Ingredients:
- 4 Tablespoon extra-virgin olive oil
- 4 Bunch broccoli rabe or broccolini
- kosher salt
- 1 lemon, halved

Directions:
1. Supply your smoker with wood pellets and follow the start-up procedure. Preheat the grill, with the lid closed, to 450° F.
2. On a platter or in a mixing bowl, drizzle the olive oil over the broccoli rabe. Use your hands to mix thoroughly, coating the vegetables evenly with the oil. Season with sea salt.
3. Place the broccoli rabe in one layer directly on the lowest grill grate. Close the lid and cook for 5 to 10 minutes. You want there to be some color and slight char

on the first side. Flip and cook for a few more minutes. Grill: 450 °F
4. Transfer the broccoli rabe to a serving platter and squeeze the juice of half a lemon evenly over the top.
5. Serve with more lemon wedges on the side. Enjoy!

Grilled Asparagus & Honey-glazed Carrots

Servings: 4
Cooking Time: 35 Minutes

Ingredients:
- 1 Bunch asparagus, woody ends removed
- 1 Pound Carrots, peeled
- 2 Tablespoon olive oil
- sea salt
- 2 Tablespoon honey
- lemon zest

Directions:
1. Rinse all vegetables under cold water. Drizzle asparagus with olive oil and a generous sprinkling of sea salt. Generously drizzle carrots with honey and lightly sprinkle with sea salt.
2. Supply your smoker with wood pellets and follow the start-up procedure. Preheat the grill, with the lid closed, to 350° F.
3. Place carrots on the grill first and cook for 10-15 minutes, then add asparagus and cook both for another 15 to 20 minutes, or until they're done to your liking. Grill: 350 °F
4. Top the asparagus with some fresh lemon zest. Enjoy!

Christmas Brussel Sprouts

Servings: 6
Cooking Time: 50 Minutes

Ingredients:
- 1/2 Pound thick-cut bacon
- 1 Medium onion, diced
- 2 Pound fresh Brussels sprouts
- 2 Tablespoon olive oil
- salt and pepper

Directions:
1. Supply your smoker with wood pellets and follow the start-up procedure. Preheat the grill, with the lid closed, to 350° F.
2. Place bacon directly on grill grate and cook for 15-20 minutes, or until lightly browned. Remove from grill and set aside on paper towel lined plate.
3. Slice onion in half and then slice into 1/4 inch moons and add to large mixing bowl. Slice brussels sprouts in half lengthwise and add to bowl.
4. Cut reserved bacon into 1/2 inch pieces and add to bowl. Drizzle with olive oil and sprinkle with salt and pepper. Toss to coat and pour into baking pan.
5. Turn the temperature on grill to 375 and place baking pan on grill. Roast for 30 minutes mixing halfway through cooking. Grill: 375 °F

Baked Bacon Green Bean Casserole

Servings: 6
Cooking Time: 50 Minutes

Ingredients:
- 1 1/2 Pound Green Beans, fresh
- 1 Can cream of mushroom soup
- 1/2 Cup milk
- 1/2 Teaspoon Worcestershire sauce
- 1/2 Teaspoon black pepper
- 2/3 Cup French's Original Crispy Fried Onions
- 8 Slices bacon
- 1/4 Cup red bell pepper, diced
- 2/3 French's Original Crispy Fried Onions

Directions:
1. In a mixing bowl, combine beans, soup, milk, Worcestershire sauce, black pepper, 2/3 cup of the onions, 6 of the slices of crumbled bacon, and red bell pepper. Transfer to a 1-1/2 quart casserole dish.
2. Supply your smoker with wood pellets and follow the start-up procedure. Preheat the grill, with the lid closed, to 350° F.
3. Cook casserole until the filling is hot and bubbling, 35 to 40 minutes. Grill: 350 °F
4. Top with remaining onions and the last 2 slices of crumbled bacon and cook for 5 to 10 minutes more, or until the onions are crisp and beginning to brown. Serve, enjoy! Grill: 350 °F

Roasted Tomatoes

Servings: 2
Cooking Time: 180 Minutes

Ingredients:
- 3 Large ripe tomatoes
- 1/2 Tablespoon kosher salt
- 1 Teaspoon coarse ground black pepper
- 1/4 Teaspoon sugar
- 1/4 Teaspoon thyme or basil
- olive oil

Directions:
1. Line a rimmed baking sheet with parchment paper.
2. Supply your smoker with wood pellets and follow the start-up procedure. Preheat the grill, with the lid closed, to 225° F.
3. Remove the stem end from each tomato and cut the tomatoes into 1/2 inch thick slices.
4. Combine the salt, pepper, sugar and thyme or basil in a small bowl and mix.
5. Pour olive oil into the well of a dinner plate.
6. Dip one side of each tomato slice in the olive oil and arrange on the baking sheet. Dust the tomato slices with the seasoning mixture.
7. Arrange the pan directly on the grill grate and roast the tomatoes until the juices stop running and the edges have contracted, about 3 hours. Remove from grill and enjoy!

Sicilian Stuffed Mushrooms

Servings: 6
Cooking Time: 25 Minutes

Ingredients:
- 12 Medium Fresh Mushrooms, about 1-1/2 inches in diameter
- 4 Ounce cream cheese, room temperature
- 1/4 Cup Parmesan cheese, grated
- 1/4 Cup shredded mozzarella cheese
- 8 Whole Pimento Stuffed Green Olives, chopped
- 3 Tablespoon Pepperoni, finely diced
- 1 1/2 Tablespoon Sun Dried Tomatoes, drained & minced
- 1/4 Teaspoon freshly ground black pepper

Directions:
1. Dampen a paper towel and wipe the outside of the mushrooms clean. Remove the stem. Using a small spoon, scoop out the inside of the mushroom leaving a shell.
2. Filling: In a small mixing bowl, beat together the cream cheese, Parmesan, and mozzarella. Stir in olives, pepperoni, tomatoes, basil, and pepper.
3. Mound the filling in the mushroom caps. Set each filled cap into the well of a muffin tin.
4. Supply your smoker with wood pellets and follow the start-up procedure. Preheat the grill, with the lid closed, to 350° F.
5. Arrange the muffin tin on the grill grate and bake the mushrooms for 25 to 30 minutes, or until the mushrooms are tender and the filling is beginning to brown.
6. Transfer to a serving plate or platter. Enjoy!

Smoked Mashed Potatoes

Servings: 6
Cooking Time: 45 Minutes

Ingredients:
- 2 Pound red bliss potatoes, washed and diced medium
- chicken stock or water
- 1/2 Stick salted butter
- 1 Cup whole milk
- 1/2 Cup sour cream
- 1/2 Cup shredded or grated Parmesan cheese
- kosher salt
- freshly ground black pepper
- 1/2 Cup fresh sliced green onions

Directions:
1. Place the diced red potatoes into a small saucepan or stockpot and cover with chicken stock or water.
2. Bring to a boil and cook on a simmer until fork tender, then cook 4 to 5 minutes past that until soft.
3. Supply your smoker with wood pellets and follow the start-up procedure. Preheat the grill, with the lid closed, to 400° F.

4. In a separate ovenproof pan, such as a cast iron skillet, add butter and milk and place in the Traeger during start up, until melted (approximately 7 to 10 minutes). Grill: 400 °F

5. Carefully remove the butter/milk mixture from the Traeger using heatproof gloves.

6. Drain the potatoes and place into a large bowl. Add the melted butter/milk mixture and slowly mash.

7. Add sour cream, cheese and green onions, then season to taste with salt and pepper.

8. Place into the cast iron skillet, then place the skillet back into the Traeger and cook until the potatoes have a slight crust and are bubbling, about 15 minutes. Grill: 400 °F

9. Carefully remove the mashed potatoes from the Traeger using heatproof gloves. Allow to cool for 5 minutes. Scoop and enjoy!

Baked Sweet Potato Casserole With Marshmallow Fluff

Servings: 6
Cooking Time: 60 Minutes

Ingredients:
- 3 Pound sweet potatoes
- 1/2 Cup milk
- 1 Cup brown sugar
- 3 eggs
- 4 Tablespoon butter
- 1/2 Teaspoon salt
- 3 egg white
- 1 Pinch salt
- 1 Pinch ground cinnamon

Directions:
1. Supply your smoker with wood pellets and follow the start-up procedure. Preheat the grill, with the lid closed, to 375° F.

2. Rinse, dry and pierce the sweet potatoes and place in grill whole. Cook for 45 minutes or until fork tender. Remove from grill and peel. Grill: 375 °F

3. Once peeled, mash the sweet potatoes in a large bowl with the milk, brown sugar, eggs, butter and salt. Place mashed potatoes in a baking dish and cook for 35 minutes. Grill: 375 °F

4. While the potatoes bake, make the fluff. Make a double boiler by bringing a small pot of water to a simmer, then placing the bowl of your stand mixer or another large stainless steel bowl atop the water.

5. Add the 3 egg whites, 2/3 cup brown sugar, a pinch of salt and a pinch of cinnamon to the bowl and whisk continuously until the sugar dissolves and the liquid is warm to the touch.

6. Transfer the bowl from the stovetop to your stand mixer and use the whisk attachment to whip the whites on medium-high speed until it turns glossy with stiff peaks, about 5-8 minutes.

7. Once the casserole has finished baking, use a rubber spatula to cover the sweet potato mixture with the fluff. Use the back of the spatula to create dramatic peaks.

8. Return to the grill for 5-7 minutes, or until the fluff starts to turn golden and the peaks are just shy of burnt. Remove from grill and enjoy!

Tater Tot Bake

Servings: 4
Cooking Time: 15 Minutes

Ingredients:
- 1 Whole frozen tater tots
- salt and pepper
- 1 Cup sour cream
- 1 Cup shredded cheddar cheese, divided
- 1/2 Cup bacon, chopped
- 1/4 Cup green onion, diced

Directions:
1. Supply your smoker with wood pellets and follow the start-up procedure. Preheat the grill, with the lid closed, to 375° F.

2. Line a baking sheet with aluminum foil for easy clean up and spread frozen tater tots onto sheet.

3. Sprinkle with Veggie Shake or salt and pepper to taste.

4. Place the baking sheet on the preheated grill grate and cook the tater tots for 10 minutes.

5. Drizzle sour cream over cooked tater tots.

6. Sprinkle the cheese, bacon bits and green onions on top of the tater tots.
7. Turn heat up to High heat and cook for 5 more minutes until the cheese melts and serve immediately. Enjoy!

Baked Breakfast Mini Quiches

Servings: 8
Cooking Time: 15 Minutes

Ingredients:
- cooking spray
- 1 Tablespoon extra-virgin olive oil
- 1/2 yellow onion, diced
- 3 Cup Spinach, fresh
- 10 eggs
- 4 Ounce shredded cheddar, mozzarella or Swiss cheese
- 1/4 Cup fresh basil
- 1 Teaspoon kosher salt
- 1/2 Teaspoon black pepper

Directions:
1. Spray a 12-cup muffin tin generously with cooking spray.
2. In a small skillet over medium heat, warm the oil. Add the onion and cook, stirring frequently, until softened, about 7 minutes. Add the spinach and cook until wilted, about 1 minute longer.
3. Transfer to a cutting board to cool, then chop the mixture so the spinach if broken up a little.
4. Supply your smoker with wood pellets and follow the start-up procedure. Preheat the grill, with the lid closed, to 350° F.
5. In a large bowl, whisk the eggs until frothy. Add the cooled onions and spinach, cheese, basil, 1 tsp salt and 1/2 tsp pepper. Stir to combine. Divide egg mixture evenly among the muffin cups.
6. Place tray on the grill and bake until the eggs have puffed up, are set, and are beginning to brown, about 18 to 20 minutes. Grill: 350 °F
7. Serve immediately, or allow to cool on a wire rack, then refrigerate in an air tight container for up to 4 days. Enjoy!

Grilled Street Corn

Servings: 6
Cooking Time: 10 Minutes

Ingredients:
- 6 ears corn, husked
- 1 As Needed extra-virgin olive oil
- 1/4 Cup mayonnaise
- 1 Tablespoon ancho or guajillo chile powder
- 1/2 Cup chopped cilantro, plus more for serving
- 1 lime, zested and juiced
- salt
- 1/2 Cup Cotija cheese
- 1 As Needed cilantro, finely chopped

Directions:
1. Supply your smoker with wood pellets and follow the start-up procedure. Preheat the grill, with the lid closed, to 450° F.
2. Brush corn with oil and place on grill, turning occasionally.
3. While corn is on the grill, mix mayonnaise with chile powder, cilantro, lime juice and zest in a bowl. Season with salt.
4. After about 10 minutes corn should be cooked through and slightly charred on the outside. Remove from grill.
5. Top corn with chile mayonnaise then sprinkle on the Cotija cheese and chopped cilantro. Enjoy!

Portobello Marinated Mushroom

Servings: 2
Cooking Time: 15 Minutes

Ingredients:
- 1 Teaspoon chopped thyme
- 1 Teaspoon rosemary, chopped
- 1 Teaspoon Oregano, chopped
- 3 Tablespoon extra-virgin olive oil
- 1 To Taste Jacobsen Salt Co. Pure Kosher Sea Salt
- 1 To Taste pepper
- 6 Whole Portobello Mushroom
- 2 Whole russet potatoes

Directions:

1. Supply your smoker with wood pellets and follow the start-up procedure. Preheat the grill, with the lid closed, to 450° F.
2. Mix fresh herbs, olive oil, salt, and pepper together in a bowl. Rub over mushrooms. Grill both sides of mushrooms for approximately 2-3 minutes on each side. Grill: 450 °F
3. Clean the potatoes and slice into long strips.
4. Heat the oil on the Traeger in a sauce pan; drop the potatoes in the hot oil and fry for 7-8 minutes. Let the potatoes cool slightly on a sheet pan. Enjoy! Grill: 450 °F

Broccoli-cauliflower Salad

Servings: 4
Cooking Time: 25 Minutes

Ingredients:
- 1½ cups mayonnaise
- ½ cup sour cream
- ¼ cup sugar
- 1 bunch broccoli, cut into small pieces
- 1 head cauliflower, cut into small pieces
- 1 small red onion, chopped
- 6 slices bacon, cooked and crumbled (precooked bacon works well)
- 1 cup shredded Cheddar cheese

Directions:
1. In a small bowl, whisk together the mayonnaise, sour cream, and sugar to make a dressing.
2. In a large bowl, combine the broccoli, cauliflower, onion, bacon, and Cheddar cheese.
3. Pour the dressing over the vegetable mixture and toss well to coat.
4. Serve the salad chilled.

Smoked Jalapeño Poppers

Servings: 4
Cooking Time: 60 Minutes

Ingredients:
- 12 Medium jalapeño
- 6 Slices bacon, cut in half
- 8 Ounce cream cheese
- 2 Tablespoon Pork & Poultry Rub
- 1 Cup grated cheese

Directions:
1. Supply your smoker with wood pellets and follow the start-up procedure. Preheat the grill, with the lid closed, to 180° F. For optimal flavor, use Super Smoke if available.
2. Slice the jalapeños in half lengthwise. Scrape out any seeds and ribs with a small spoon or paring knife. Mix softened cream cheese with Traeger Pork & Poultry rub and grated cheese. Spoon mixture onto each jalapeño half. Wrap with bacon and secure with a toothpick.
3. Place the jalapeños on a rimmed baking sheet. Place on grill and smoke for 30 minutes. Grill: 180 °F
4. Increase the grill temperature to 375°F and cook an additional 30 minutes or until bacon is cooked to desired doneness. Serve warm, enjoy! Grill: 375 °F

Butternut Squash

Servings: 4
Cooking Time: 45 Minutes

Ingredients:
- 1 Whole butternut squash
- Veggie Rub
- Blackened Saskatchewan Rub
- olive oil

Directions:
1. Cut squash in half and lightly coat with mixture of olive oil, Traeger Veggie Shake, and Traeger Blackened Saskatchewan.
2. Wrap in foil with 1/2 cup (120mL) of water.
3. Supply your smoker with wood pellets and follow the start-up procedure. Preheat the grill, with the lid closed, to 450° F.
4. Place squash on grill for 45 minutes. Remove from grill and unwrap. Enjoy!

Roasted Artichokes With Garlic Butter

Servings: 2
Cooking Time: 60 Minutes

Ingredients:
- 2 Large artichokes
- 3 Tablespoon olive oil

- sea salt
- 1 Stick unsalted butter
- 2 Clove garlic, chopped
- 2 Tablespoon chives, parsley, tarragon or cilantro
- 1 lemon

Directions:

1. Supply your smoker with wood pellets and follow the start-up procedure. Preheat the grill, with the lid closed, to 375° F.
2. Meanwhile, break off and discard any small outer leaves on the artichokes. Use a knife to slice off the tops of the artichokes, then using scissors, cut off any thorns on the remaining artichoke leaves. Trim the very bottom of the stem, then peel the tough and fibrous outer layer of the stem. Finally, cut artichokes in half and rinse off.
3. Transfer artichokes to a large mixing bowl, drizzle with olive oil and generously sprinkle with sea salt. Toss to coat the artichokes thoroughly. Grill: 375 °F
4. Add the artichokes to the grill, cut side down, and roast at 375°F until the artichoke bottoms are tender when poked with a fork or knife, about 50 to 60 minutes. Grill: 375 °F
5. When artichokes are almost done, add butter, chopped garlic and a pinch of sea salt to a small sauce pan and melt slowly over medium-low heat. Once the butter melts all the way and starts to bubble slightly, add the herbs.
6. When the artichokes are done, transfer to a butcher paper lined tray with the cut sides up. Drizzle half the garlic butter and squeeze half of the lemon over the artichokes. Add a small sprinkle of sea salt over the artichokes.
7. Serve with a ramekin of the remaining butter for dipping and extra wedges of lemon. Enjoy! Chef Tip: You can also serve with a ramekin of good mayonnaise mixed with a bit of hot sauce.

Butter Braised Green Beans

Servings: 6
Cooking Time: 60 Minutes

Ingredients:

- 24 Ounce thin fresh green beans, trimmed or whole frozen green beans, thawed
- 8 Tablespoon butter, melted
- Veggie Rub or coarse salt
- freshly ground black pepper

Directions:

1. Supply your smoker with wood pellets and follow the start-up procedure. Preheat the grill, with the lid closed, to 325° F.
2. Put the green beans in a pile on a rimmed baking sheet and pour the melted butter over them. Using tongs, spread the beans out in the pan and season with Traeger Veggie Rub and black pepper.
3. Roast the beans for about 1 hour, stirring and lifting with tongs every 20 minutes or so. The beans should be very tender, shriveled, and lightly browned in places. Transfer to a serving bowl and serve while hot. Enjoy!

Smoked Bbq Onion Brussels Sprout

Servings: 4
Cooking Time: 110 Minutes

Ingredients:

- 4 strip bacon
- 1 onion minced
- 2 cloves garlic minced
- 1 lb brussels sprouts stems trimmed and cut in half
- 1 tbsp BBQ Spice Blend
- 1/2 cup Apple Habanero Bar-B-Que Sauce (or other BBQ sauce)

Directions:

1. Supply your smoker with wood pellets and follow the start-up procedure. Preheat the grill, with the lid closed, to High heat. Place a cast iron skillet over the highest heat spot and cook the bacon until crisp.
2. Remove the bacon from pan and drain, reserving the bacon fat in the pan.
3. Reduce the heat on your smoker to 250°F.
4. Add the onions, garlic, and brussels to the pan and toss to coat in the bacon drippings. Sprinkle the BBQ spice blend over top.
5. Cover the lid and allow to smoke for 1 to 1 1/2 hours, until the sprouts are fork tender.

6. For the last 20 minutes of smoking, toss the brussels sprouts in half of the barbecue sauce.
7. Remove the sprouts from the smoker.
8. Chop the bacon and add it and the remaining barbecue sauce to the pan of sprouts, tossing to coat.
9. Serve hot.

Salt Crusted Baked Potatoes

Servings: 4
Cooking Time: 60 Minutes

Ingredients:
- 6 russet potatoes, scrubbed and dried
- 3 Tablespoon canola oil
- 1 Tablespoon kosher salt
- butter
- sour cream
- Chives, fresh
- Bacon Bits
- cheddar cheese

Directions:
1. In a large bowl, coat the potatoes in canola oil and sprinkle heavily with salt.
2. Supply your smoker with wood pellets and follow the start-up procedure. Preheat the grill, with the lid closed, to 450° F.
3. Place the potatoes directly on the grill grate and bake for 30-40 minutes, or until soft in the middle when pricked with a fork. Serve loaded with your favorite toppings. Enjoy! Grill: 450 °F

Baked Kale Chips

Servings: 4
Cooking Time: 20 Minutes

Ingredients:
- 2 Bunch kale, leaves washed and stems removed
- 1 As Needed extra-virgin olive oil
- 1 To Taste sea salt

Directions:
1. Dry the kale leaves well and lay them out on a sheet tray. Drizzle lightly with olive oil and sprinkle with sea salt.
2. Supply your smoker with wood pellets and follow the start-up procedure. Preheat the grill, with the lid closed, to 250° F.
3. Place the sheet tray directly on the grill grate and cook until kale is lightly browned and crispy, about 20 minutes. Enjoy! Grill: 250 °F

Roasted Hasselback Potatoes By Doug Scheiding

Servings: 6
Cooking Time: 120 Minutes

Ingredients:
- 6 Large russet potatoes
- 1 Pound bacon
- 1/2 Cup butter
- salt
- black pepper
- 1 Cup cheddar cheese
- 3 Whole scallions

Directions:
1. To cut potatoes, place two wooden spoons on either side of the potato (this prevents your knife from going all the way through). Slice potato into thin chips leaving about 1/4" attached on the bottom.
2. Freeze bacon slices for about 30 minutes then cut into small pieces about the size of a stamp. Place these in the cracks between every other slice.
3. Place the potato in a large cast iron skillet. Top the potato with slices of hard butter (you can also place thin slivers of cold butter between the potato slices with the bacon if desired). Season with salt and pepper.
4. Supply your smoker with wood pellets and follow the start-up procedure. Preheat the grill, with the lid closed, to 350° F.
5. Place the cast iron directly on the grill grate and cook for two hours. Top potatoes with more butter and baste with melted butter every 30 minutes.
6. In the last 10 minutes of cooking, sprinkle with cheddar and return to grill to melt.
7. To finish, top with chives or scallions. Enjoy!

Traeger Grilled Whole Corn

Servings: 4
Cooking Time: 25 Minutes

Ingredients:
- 3 green onions
- 6 Tablespoon butter, softened
- 1 Teaspoon chile powder
- 1 Teaspoon toasted sesame seeds
- 4 ears corn, in husk

Directions:
1. Supply your smoker with wood pellets and follow the start-up procedure. Preheat the grill, with the lid closed, to 325° F.
2. Place green onions directly on the grill grate and cook 15 minutes until lightly charred. Remove from grill and set aside.
3. Sesame-Chile Butter: Take butter out of fridge and let soften. Chop up charred green onions and add to butter along with chile powder and sesame seeds. Mash all ingredients together.
4. Grill corn, rotating occasionally, until husks are blackened (some will flake and fall off) and kernels are tender with some browned and charred spots, about 25 to 35 minutes. Grill: 325 °F
5. Let corn cool slightly, then shuck. Serve with the Sesame-Chile Butter. Enjoy

Baked Artichoke Parmesan Mushrooms

Servings: 8
Cooking Time: 30 Minutes

Ingredients:
- 8 Cremini Mushroom Caps
- 6 1/2 Ounce artichoke hearts
- 1/3 Cup Parmesan cheese, grated
- 1/4 Cup mayonnaise
- 1/2 Teaspoon garlic salt
- your favorite hot sauce
- paprika

Directions:
1. Clean the mushrooms with a damp paper towel. Remove the stems and discard or save for another use.
2. Using a small spoon, scoop out the inside (gills, etc.). Combine the artichoke hearts, parmesan, mayonnaise, garlic salt, and hot sauce and mix well.
3. Mound the filling in the mushroom caps. Dust the tops with paprika.
4. Arrange the mushrooms in an oven-safe baking dish.
5. Supply your smoker with wood pellets and follow the start-up procedure. Preheat the grill, with the lid closed, to 350° F.
6. Bake the mushrooms (uncovered) until the filling is bubbling and just beginning to brown, about 25 to 30 minutes. Serve immediately. Grill: 350 °F
7. For a simple variation, stuff the mushrooms with your favorite bulk sausage and bake on your Traeger as directed above. Enjoy!

Whole Roasted Cauliflower With Garlic Parmesan Butter

Servings: 4
Cooking Time: 45 Minutes

Ingredients:
- 1 Whole head cauliflower
- 1/4 Cup olive oil
- salt and pepper
- 1/2 Cup butter, melted
- 1/4 Cup shredded Parmesan cheese
- 2 Clove garlic, minced
- 1/2 Tablespoon chopped parsley

Directions:
1. Supply your smoker with wood pellets and follow the start-up procedure. Preheat the grill, with the lid closed, to 450° F.
2. Brush the cauliflower with olive oil and season liberally with salt and pepper.
3. Put cauliflower in a cast iron skillet, place directly on the grill grate and cook for 45 minutes until golden brown and the center is tender.
4. While the cauliflower is cooking, combine the melted butter, parmesan, garlic and parsley in a small bowl.

5. During the last 20 minutes of cooking, baste the cauliflower with the melted butter mixture.
6. Remove the cauliflower from the grill and top with extra parmesan and parsley if desired. Enjoy!

Roasted Fall Vegetables

Servings: 6
Cooking Time: 30 Minutes

Ingredients:
- 1/2 Pound Potatoes, new
- 2 Tablespoon olive oil
- salt and pepper
- 1/2 Pound Butternut Squash, diced
- 1/2 Pound fresh Brussels sprouts
- 1 Pint mushrooms, sliced

Directions:
1. Supply your smoker with wood pellets and follow the start-up procedure. Preheat the grill, with the lid closed, to 200° F.
2. Toss potatoes and squash with olive oil, salt and pepper and spread out on a sheet tray.
3. Place directly on the grill grate and cook for 15 minutes. Add brussels sprouts and mushrooms and toss to coat.
4. Cook another 15-20 minutes until veggies are lightly browned and cooked through.
5. Adjust seasoning as needed. Enjoy!

Steak Fries With Horseradish Creme

Servings: 6
Cooking Time: 25 Minutes

Ingredients:
- 5 Potatoes, Baking
- 2 Tablespoon extra-virgin olive oil
- 1 Teaspoon butter
- 3 Clove garlic, crushed
- 1 Teaspoon onion powder
- 2 Teaspoon Jacobsen Salt Co. Pure Kosher Sea Salt
- 1 Teaspoon black pepper

Directions:
1. Wash the potatoes thoroughly, and cut them in eighths, then toss them in the olive oil, butter, crushed garlic, onion powder, salt, and pepper.
2. Supply your smoker with wood pellets and follow the start-up procedure. Preheat the grill, with the lid closed, to 450° F.
3. In order to get great grill marks, line up the wedges on the front of the grill and the back of the grill, turning to get grill marks on all sides.
4. Once they have been seared, move them to the center of the grill and finish cooking about ten more minutes, serve hot with the horseradish mayo. Enjoy!

Red Potato Grilled Lollipops

Servings: 4
Cooking Time: 25 Minutes

Ingredients:
- 8 Large red bliss potatoes, halved
- 2 Clove garlic, minced
- 2 Sprig rosemary, minced
- 2 Tablespoon olive oil
- 1 Teaspoon salt
- 1/2 Teaspoon black pepper
- 5 Wooden Skewers, soaked in water
- 1/4 Cup Parmesan cheese, grated

Directions:
1. Supply your smoker with wood pellets and follow the start-up procedure. Preheat the grill, with the lid closed, to 450° F.
2. Halve potatoes and poke each several times with a fork.
3. Put the potatoes in a large bowl and toss with the minced garlic, rosemary leaves, a few tablespoons of olive oil, kosher salt, and pepper. Microwave the potatoes for 4 minutes. Gently toss potatoes and microwave for another 3 minutes.
4. Skewer potato halves threading about 4 or 5 potato halves on each skewer. Brush potatoes with olive oil.
5. Place the potato skewers on the Traeger, cut side down, and grill until the sides begin to brown (4-7 minutes).

6. Flip and grill skin side down for another 7-10 minutes.

7. They are done when a sharp knife tip easily penetrates the sides. Remove potatoes from grill and top with grated parmesan cheese. Enjoy!

Roasted New Potatoes

Servings: 4
Cooking Time: 25 Minutes

Ingredients:
- 2 Pound small new potatoes
- 3 Tablespoon butter, melted
- 2 Tablespoon olive oil
- 2 Tablespoon whole mustard seeds
- salt and pepper
- 2 Tablespoon freshly minced chives
- 2 Tablespoon freshly minced parsley

Directions:
1. Place potatoes in a colander and rinse with cold water. Dry on paper towels and transfer to a rimmed baking sheet large enough to hold them in a single layer.
2. Drizzle the potatoes with butter and olive oil, then sprinkle them with the mustard seeds. Season with salt and pepper.
3. Supply your smoker with wood pellets and follow the start-up procedure. Preheat the grill, with the lid closed, to 400° F.
4. Place the baking sheet with the potatoes on the grill grate. Roast for about 25 minutes shaking the pan once or twice, until potatoes are tender and the skins are slightly wrinkled. Grill: 400 °F
5. Transfer potatoes to a bowl or platter. Top with fresh chives and parsley. Enjoy!

Baked Heirloom Tomato Tart

Servings: 4
Cooking Time: 45 Minutes

Ingredients:
- 1 Whole Puff Pastry Sheet
- 2 Pound heirloom tomatoes, various shapes and sizes
- 1/2 Tablespoon kosher salt
- 1/2 Cup Ricotta Cheese
- 5 Whole eggs
- 1 To Taste salt and pepper
- 1/2 Teaspoon thyme leaves
- 1/2 Teaspoon red pepper flakes
- 4 Sprig thyme

Directions:
1. Supply your smoker with wood pellets and follow the start-up procedure. Preheat the grill, with the lid closed, to 350° F.
2. Place the puff pastry on a parchment lined sheet tray, and make a cut ¾ of the way through the pastry, ½" from the edge.
3. Slice the tomatoes and season with salt. Place on a sheet tray lined with paper towels.
4. In a small bowl combine the ricotta, 4 of the eggs, salt, thyme leaves, red pepper flakes and black pepper. Whisk together until combined. Spread the ricotta mixture over the puff pastry, staying within ½" from the edge.
5. In a small bowl whisk the last egg. Brush the egg wash onto the exposed edges of the pastry.
6. Place the sheet tray directly on the grill grate and bake for 45 minutes, rotating half-way through. Grill: 350 °F
7. When the edges are browned and the moisture from the tomatoes has evaporated, remove from the grill and let cool 5-7 minutes before serving. Enjoy!

Smoked & Loaded Baked Potato

Servings: 4
Cooking Time: 60 Minutes

Ingredients:
- 6 Yukon Gold or russet potatoes
- 8 Slices bacon
- 1/2 Cup butter, melted
- 1 Cup sour cream
- 1 1/2 Cup shredded cheddar cheese, divided
- salt and pepper
- 1 Bunch green onions, thinly sliced

Directions:

1. Supply your smoker with wood pellets and follow the start-up procedure. Preheat the grill, with the lid closed, to 375° F.
2. Poke potatoes with a fork, then place straight onto the grill. Cook for 1 hour. Grill: 375 °F
3. At the same time, cook bacon on a baking sheet on the grill for about 20 minutes; remove, cool and crumble. Grill: 375 °F
4. Once potatoes are done, remove and allow to cool for 15 minutes.
5. Cut each potato lengthwise, creating long halves. Use a small spoon to scoop out about 70% of the potato to make a boat, keeping a thick layer of potato near skin.
6. Place excess potato in a bowl and reserve. Lightly mash extra potato with a fork; add butter, sour cream, 1/2 cup cheese and season with salt and pepper.
7. Take the potato skins and fill with potato mixture, then sprinkle with extra cheese and bacon.
8. Place back on grill for about 10 minutes or until warm and cheese has melted. Garnish with green onions and extra sour cream. Enjoy! Grill: 375 °F

Baked Stuffed Avocados

Servings: 6
Cooking Time: 15 Minutes

Ingredients:
- 4 avocados, halved and pit removed
- 8 eggs
- 2 Cup shredded cheddar cheese
- 1/4 Cup cherry tomatoes, halved
- 4 Slices Bacon, cooked & chopped
- salt and pepper
- 1 scallion, thinly sliced

Directions:
1. Supply your smoker with wood pellets and follow the start-up procedure. Preheat the grill, with the lid closed, to 450° F.
2. After removing the pit from the avocado, scoop out a little of the flesh to make enough room to fit 1 egg per half.
3. Fill the bottom of a cast iron pan with kosher salt and nestle the avocado halves into the salt, cut side up. The salt helps to keep them in place while cooking, like ice with oysters.
4. Crack one egg into each half, top with shredded cheddar cheese, cherry tomatoes and bacon. Season with salt and pepper to taste.
5. Place the cast iron pan directly on the grill grate and bake the avocados for 12 to 15 minutes until the cheese is melted and the egg is just set. Grill: 450 °F
6. Remove from the grill and let rest 5 to 10 minutes. Top with sliced scallions and enjoy!

Roasted Garlic Herb Fries

Servings: 4
Cooking Time: 45 Minutes

Ingredients:
- 4 Whole russet potatoes
- 1 Teaspoon salt
- 2 Tablespoon avocado oil
- 1 Teaspoon fresh chopped rosemary
- 1 Teaspoon fresh chopped thyme
- 2 Clove garlic, minced
- 2 Teaspoon flake salt
- 1 Teaspoon chopped parsley, for garnish

Directions:
1. Supply your smoker with wood pellets and follow the start-up procedure. Preheat the grill, with the lid closed, to 425° F.
2. Chop potatoes into fries, (a mandolin works great for this) and place directly into an ice water bath with 1 teaspoon salt for 15 to 30 minutes.
3. Combine oil, rosemary, thyme and garlic in a big bowl. Remove potatoes from ice water and dry thoroughly with paper towels.
4. Toss potatoes in the oil mixture and place them on 2 to 3 parchment-lined baking sheets in a single layer. Sprinkle the flake salt over the fries.
5. Place baking sheets on the grill and roast for 30 minutes, flip the fries, then cook for an additional 15 minutes until golden and crispy. Dust with parsley. Grill: 425 °F
6. Serve with your favorite dipping sauce, side dish or as a nacho base.

Roasted Olives

Servings: 4
Cooking Time: 45 Minutes

Ingredients:
- 2 Cup mixed olives
- 3 Sprig fresh rosemary
- 2 Clove garlic, minced
- 2 Tablespoon orange zest
- 1/3 Cup extra-virgin olive oil
- 2 Tablespoon orange juice
- 1/2 Teaspoon red pepper flakes

Directions:
1. Combine the olives, rosemary, garlic, orange zest, red pepper flakes, olive oil, and orange juice in a glass oven-safe pie plate or baking dish. Cover with foil.
2. Supply your smoker with wood pellets and follow the start-up procedure. Preheat the grill, with the lid closed, to 300° F.
3. Roast the olives for 45 minutes, stirring once or twice. Serve warm in an attractive bowl. Enjoy! Grill: 300 °F

Green Bean Casserole

Servings: 6
Cooking Time: 25 Minutes

Ingredients:
- 1/2 Stick butter
- 1 Small onion
- 1/2 Cup sliced button mushrooms
- 4 Can green beans, drained
- 2 Can cream of mushroom soup
- 1 Teaspoon Lawry's Seasoned Salt
- pepper
- 1 Can French's Original Crispy Fried Onions
- 1 Cup grated sharp cheddar cheese

Directions:
1. Supply your smoker with wood pellets and follow the start-up procedure. Preheat the grill, with the lid closed, to 375° F.
2. Melt butter in a cast iron skillet and add onions and mushrooms, stirring occasionally until softened.
3. Add drained green beans and cream of mushroom soup and stir gently to combine.
4. Season with seasoned salt and pepper and sprinkle the top with grated cheddar cheese and fried onions.
5. Bake for 25 minutes. Serve warm, enjoy! Grill: 375 °F

Baked Sweet Potatoes

Servings: 8
Cooking Time: 60 Minutes

Ingredients:
- 1 Cup butter, softened
- 1/4 Cup pure maple syrup
- 1/2 Teaspoon ground cinnamon
- 8 Medium sweet potatoes

Directions:
1. Make the Maple-Cinnamon Butter: In a mixing bowl, combine the butter, maple syrup, and cinnamon and whip with a wooden spoon. (Alternatively, blend the ingredients using a hand-held mixer or a stand mixer.) Transfer to a small bowl, cover, and chill until serving time.
2. Supply your smoker with wood pellets and follow the start-up procedure. Preheat the grill, with the lid closed, to 375° F. Arrange the sweet potatoes on the grill grate and bake until soft, 1 to 1-1/2 hours, depending on the size of the potatoes. Make a slit in the side of each, and squeeze the ends gently to fluff.
3. Serve hot with the Maple-Cinnamon Butter. Enjoy!

Chef Curtis' Famous Chimichurri Sauce

Servings: 4
Cooking Time: 5 Minutes

Ingredients:
- 2 Whole lemon, halved
- 2 Medium flat-leaf Italian parsley, washed and chopped with the majority of stems cut off
- 4 Clove garlic, diced
- 1/4 Cup red wine vinegar
- 1/2 Teaspoon black pepper

- 1/4 Cup extra-virgin olive oil
- 1 Teaspoon salt

Directions:
1. Supply your smoker with wood pellets and follow the start-up procedure. Preheat the grill, with the lid closed, to 450° F.
2. Place lemon halves directly on the grill grate and cook for 5 minutes or until grill marks appear. Grill: 450 °F
3. Take lemons off grill and juice. Combine all of the ingredients in a food processor or blender and purée until smooth, or leave slightly chunky for some texture.
4. Add additional olive oil to taste for a milder flavor if preferred. Serve on protein or as a dip. Enjoy!

Roasted Jalapeño Poppers

Servings: 2
Cooking Time: 30 Minutes

Ingredients:
- 8 Slices Bacon, Center Cut
- 2 Cup cream cheese
- 2 Ounce Cheese, sharp cheddar
- 1/2 Cup green onions, minced
- 2 Teaspoon fresh squeezed lime juice
- 4 Tablespoon Seeded Tomato, Chopped
- 4 Tablespoon cilantro, chopped
- 1/2 Teaspoon kosher salt
- 2 Small garlic clove, minced
- 12 Whole Jalapeños

Directions:
1. Supply your smoker with wood pellets and follow the start-up procedure. Preheat the grill, with the lid closed, to 350° F.
2. Place 2 bacon slices directly on the grill grate and cook 10-15 minutes until cooked through and crispy flipping halfway through. Remove from grill, but leave the grill on. When cool enough to handle, coarsely chop the bacon and reserve. Grill: 350 °F
3. In the bowl of a stand mixer, combine cream cheese, cheddar cheese, green onions, chopped bacon, lime juice, tomatoes, cilantro, salt and garlic. Mix on medium speed with a paddle until combined. Transfer mixture to a piping bag.
4. Cut the tops off the jalapeños and remove the seeds and ribs with a small paring knife.
5. Pipe the filling into each pepper so that the filling comes up a 1/4" over the top of the pepper. Place the tops back on each pepper.
6. With a rolling pin, flatten out the remaining six slices of bacon until they are 1/8" thick. Cut each slice in half. Wrap 1/2 a bacon slice around each pepper and secure with a toothpick.
7. Place the peppers in the Traeger Jalapeno Popper Tray. Place the tray directly on the grill grate and cook for 30-40 minutes until the peppers are tender, bacon is crispy, and cheese is melted. Enjoy! Grill: 350 °F

Roasted Sweet Potato Steak Fries

Servings: 4
Cooking Time: 40 Minutes

Ingredients:
- 3 Whole sweet potatoes
- 4 Tablespoon extra-virgin olive oil
- salt and pepper
- 2 Tablespoon fresh chopped rosemary

Directions:
1. Supply your smoker with wood pellets and follow the start-up procedure. Preheat the grill, with the lid closed, to 450° F.
2. Cut sweet potatoes into wedges and toss with olive oil, salt, pepper and rosemary. Spread on a parchment lined baking sheet and put in the grill. Cook for 15 minutes then flip and continue to cook until lightly browned and cooked through, about 40 to 45 minutes total. Grill: 450 °F
3. Serve with your favorite dipping sauce. Enjoy! Grill: 450 °F

Roasted Tomatoes With Hot Pepper Sauce

Servings: 4
Cooking Time: 60 Minutes

Ingredients:

- 2 Pound fresh Roma tomatoes
- 3 Tablespoon parsley, chopped
- 2 Tablespoon garlic, chopped
- salt and pepper
- 1/2 Cup extra-virgin olive oil
- 1 Pound Spaghetti
- Hot peppers

Directions:

1. Supply your smoker with wood pellets and follow the start-up procedure. Preheat the grill, with the lid closed, to 400° F.
2. Wash tomatoes and cut them in half, lengthwise. Place them in a baking dish cut side up.
3. Sprinkle with chopped parsley, garlic, add salt and black pepper and pour 1/4 cup (100 mL) of olive oil over them.
4. Place on pre-heated grill and bake for 1 1/2 hours. Tomatoes will shrink and the skins will be partly blackened. Grill: 400 °F
5. Remove tomatoes from baking dish and place in a food processor leaving the cooked oil, and puree them.
6. Drop pasta into boiling salted water and cook until tender. Drain and toss immediately with the pureed tomatoes.
7. Add the remaining 1/4 cup (60mL) of raw olive oil and crumbled hot red pepper to taste. Toss and serve. Enjoy!

Smoked Asparagus Soup

Servings: 4
Cooking Time: 40 Minutes

Ingredients:

- Pound Asparagus Spears
- 1 Tablespoon olive oil
- salt and pepper
- 1/2 yellow onion, diced
- 1 Tablespoon butter
- 2 Clove garlic, minced
- 1 1/2 Cup chicken stock
- 1 1/2 Cup cream
- 2 Stalk Raw Asparagus, Shaved

Directions:

1. Supply your smoker with wood pellets and follow the start-up procedure. Preheat the grill, with the lid closed, to 180° F.
2. Drizzle 1 pound of asparagus with olive oil and season with salt and pepper. Place directly on the grill grate and smoke for 20-30 minutes. Taste along the way to assess smoke level pulling earlier if needed. Grill: 180 °F
3. Place 1 Tbsp butter in a saucepan and melt over medium heat. Add onion and garlic and saute for 2-3 minutes or until onion is translucent.
4. Remove asparagus from the grill and cut into 1" pieces. Place asparagus in the pan with the onions and add stock and cream. Bring to a simmer.
5. Remove from heat and puree using a blender or immersion blender until smooth.
6. Season with salt and pepper and serve. Top with fresh shaved asparagus, sprinkle with salt, pepper, and smoked paprika if desired. Enjoy!

Smoked Parmesan Herb Popcorn

Servings: 2
Cooking Time: 15 Minutes

Ingredients:

- 4 Tablespoon butter
- 2 Teaspoon Italian Seasoning
- 1 Teaspoon garlic powder
- 1 Teaspoon salt
- 1/4 Cup popcorn kernels
- 1/2 Cup Parmesan cheese, grated

Directions:

1. Supply your smoker with wood pellets and follow the start-up procedure. Preheat the grill, with the lid closed, to 250° F.

2. In a small saucepan, melt the butter over medium heat. Add Italian seasoning, garlic powder, and salt and stir to combine. Remove from heat and set aside.

3. Add 1/4 cup of popcorn to a brown paper lunch bag. Fold the top of the bag over twice to close. Place the bag in the microwave and microwave on high for 1 to 2 minutes, or until there are about 5 seconds between pops. Open the bag with care and dump into a large mixing bowl.

4. Pour butter mixture of popcorn in a bowl and toss to combine. Dump popcorn onto a baking sheet and place in grill.

5. Smoke for 10 minutes; remove from grill. Toss with parmesan cheese to serve. Enjoy! Grill: 250 °F

Roasted Mashed Potatoes

Servings: 8
Cooking Time: 40 Minutes

Ingredients:
- 5 Pound Yukon Gold potatoes
- 1 1/2 Stick butter, softened
- 1 1/2 Cup heavy whipping cream, room temperature
- kosher salt
- white pepper

Directions:
1. Supply your smoker with wood pellets and follow the start-up procedure. Preheat the grill, with the lid closed, to 300° F.
2. Peel and cut potatoes into 1/2 inch cubes. Place the potatoes in a shallow baking dish with 1/2 cup water and cover. Bake until tender, about 40 minutes. Grill: 300 °F
3. In a medium saucepan, combine cream and butter. Cook over medium heat until butter is melted.
4. Remove potatoes from the grill and drain water.
5. Transfer potatoes to a bowl and mash using a potato masher. Gradually add in cream and butter mixture and mix using the masher. Be careful not to overwork or the potatoes will becomes gluey. Season with salt and pepper to taste. Enjoy!

Roasted Do-ahead Mashed Potatoes

Servings: 6
Cooking Time: 50 Minutes

Ingredients:
- 5 Pound Yukon Gold or russet potatoes
- 9 Tablespoon butter
- 8 Ounce cream cheese
- 1/2 Cup milk
- salt and pepper

Directions:
1. Peel the potatoes and cut into chunks that are roughly the same size. Cover with cold water and add a teaspoon of salt. Bring to a boil over high heat, then reduce the heat to medium and simmer the potatoes until they are tender.
2. Drain the potatoes and return them to the pot. Stir over low heat for 2 to 3 minutes to evaporate any excess moisture.
3. Mash the potatoes with a hand-held potato masher. (Alternative, rice the potatoes using a ricer.) Incorporate 8 tbsp butter and cream cheese. Add milk until the potatoes are of a good consistency. Stir in salt and pepper to taste.
4. Butter the inside of a casserole dish. Spread the potatoes out in an even layer in the casserole dish, smoothing the top with a spatula. Cool, cover, and refrigerate if not cooking right away. Before cooking, let the potatoes warm to room temperature (about an hour).
5. Supply your smoker with wood pellets and follow the start-up procedure. Preheat the grill, with the lid closed, to 350° F.
6. Bake the potatoes for 45 to 50 minutes, or until hot through. Grill: 350 °F

Roasted Sheet Pan Vegetables

Servings: 4
Cooking Time: 25 Minutes

Ingredients:
- 1 Small head purple cauliflower, stemmed and cut into 2 inch florets
- 1 Small head yellow cauliflower, stemmed and cut into 2 inch florets
- 4 Cup butternut squash

- 2 Cup oyster or shiitake mushrooms, rinsed and sliced
- 3 Tablespoon olive oil
- 2 Teaspoon kosher salt
- freshly ground black pepper
- 1/4 Cup chopped flat-leaf parsley

Directions:
1. Supply your smoker with wood pellets and follow the start-up procedure. Preheat the grill, with the lid closed, to 450° F.
2. In a large mixing bowl, combine all of the vegetables. Drizzle olive oil over the top, along with kosher salt and a generous grinding of black pepper.
3. Using your hands, toss the vegetables until they are evenly coated.
4. Spread out onto 1 or 2 half sheet pans or baking sheets, ensuring there is a little space between the veggies. (If they are too crowded, the vegetables will steam instead of roast and you won't get that crispy texture.)
5. Place the sheet pans on the grill and cook for 15 minutes. Open and stir, then close the lid and continue to cook until the vegetables are brown around the edges, about 5 to 15 minutes longer. Grill: 450 °F
6. Toss with parsley and serve immediately. The vegetables are also delicious at room temperature. Enjoy!

Smoked Pico De Gallo

Servings: 4
Cooking Time: 30 Minutes

Ingredients:
- 3 Cup diced Roma tomatoes
- 1 jalapeño, diced
- 1/2 red onion, diced
- 1/2 Bunch cilantro, finely chopped
- 2 lime, juiced
- salt
- olive oil

Directions:
1. Supply your smoker with wood pellets and follow the start-up procedure. Preheat the grill, with the lid closed, to 180° F.
2. Place the diced tomatoes on a small sheet pan spreading them into a thin layer. Place the sheet pan directly on the grill and smoke for 30 minutes. Grill: 180 °F
3. When the tomatoes are finished, toss all ingredients in a medium bowl and finish with lime juice, salt and olive oil to taste. Serve and enjoy!

Roasted New Potatoes With Compound Butter

Servings: 4
Cooking Time: 45 Minutes

Ingredients:
- 2 Pound Small Red, White or Purple Potatoes (or Combination of All Three)
- 3 Tablespoon olive oil
- salt and pepper
- 2 Stick Butter, unsalted
- 1 Tablespoon shallot, minced
- 3 Tablespoon Finely Chopped Herbs, Such As Tarragon, Parsley, Basil or Combination
- 2 Teaspoon kosher salt

Directions:
1. Supply your smoker with wood pellets and follow the start-up procedure. Preheat the grill, with the lid closed, to 400° F. Cut the potatoes in half and place in a large mixing bowl. Cover with the olive oil, a teaspoon of salt and generous grinding of pepper.
2. Place on a large baking sheet so there is space between the potatoes. Place on the grill and roast for 45 minutes to 1 hour, until crispy skinned. Toss once during cooking. Grill: 400 °F
3. To make the butter: Place it in a medium sized shallow mixing bowl. Use a wooden spoon or strong spatula to break it up and soften it even more. Sprinkle the shallot, herbs, and salt over the butter, then use the spoon to combine the ingredients. Taste, adding more salt or herbs if necessary. Reserve a few tablespoons of the butter to serve on the potatoes.
4. To freeze the butter for future use, place a foot long piece of plastic wrap on the counter. Spread the butter out into a 6" log across the long direction of the plastic

wrap towards the bottom. Begin to roll the plastic wrap away from you to roll it into a log, twisting the sides of the plastic wrap like a candy wrapper to secure.

5. Using your hands, shape the log into an even cylinder. Once it's wrapped tightly, place in the freezer. Then when more is needed, simply slice off coins of it to serve over grilled steak, chicken, veggies, or roasted potatoes. The butter holds well in the freezer for up to one month. Enjoy! *Cook times will vary depending on set and ambient temperatures.

Roasted Beet & Bacon Salad

Servings: 4
Cooking Time: 45 Minutes

Ingredients:

- 2 Medium raw beets, peeled and thinly sliced
- 8 Slices bacon
- 1/4 Cup raw pecans or walnuts
- 2 Medium ripe pears, sliced
- 2 Large avocados, diced
- 1 Head red leaf lettuce or baby spinach, torn into bite-size pieces
- 1/4 Cup champagne vinaigrette

Directions:

1. Supply your smoker with wood pellets and follow the start-up procedure. Preheat the grill, with the lid closed, to 400° F.
2. Place beets on a foil-lined baking sheet and top with bacon. Place baking sheet directly on the grill grate (while preheating) and cook for 25 minutes. Grill: 400 °F
3. Toss to coat beets in rendered bacon fat.
4. Spread everything out in a single layer and continue to cook for another 15 minutes, or until beets are tender and bacon is crispy. Grill: 400 °F
5. Add pecans or walnuts and roast for 5 more minutes. Spoon out nuts and place on paper towels to drain and cool.
6. Once bacon is cool to the touch, roughly chop into medium pieces.
7. Place bacon, beets, nuts, pears, avocado and lettuce in a large salad bowl. Drizzle with champagne vinaigrette, toss to coat, and serve. Enjoy!

Grilled Corn On The Cob With Parmesan And Garlic

Servings: 6
Cooking Time: 30 Minutes

Ingredients:

- 4 Tablespoon butter, melted
- 2 Clove garlic, minced
- salt and pepper
- 8 ears fresh corn
- 1/2 Cup shaved Parmesan
- 1 Tablespoon chopped parsley

Directions:

1. Supply your smoker with wood pellets and follow the start-up procedure. Preheat the grill, with the lid closed, to 450° F.
2. Place butter, garlic, salt and pepper in a medium bowl and mix well.
3. Peel back corn husks and remove the silk. Rub corn with half of the garlic butter mixture.
4. Close husks and place directly on the grill grate. Cook for 25 to 30 minutes, turning occasionally until corn is tender. Grill: 450 °F
5. Remove from grill, peel and discard husks. Place corn on serving tray, drizzle with remaining butter and top with Parmesan and parsley.

Traeger Baked Potato Torte

Servings: 6
Cooking Time: 25 Minutes

Ingredients:

- 6 Yukon Gold potatoes, sliced 1/4 inch thick
- 2 Stick butter, melted
- 3 Clove garlic, crushed
- 2 Tablespoon rosemary, chopped
- 1 Cup Parmesan cheese, grated
- salt and pepper

Directions:

1. Supply your smoker with wood pellets and follow the start-up procedure. Preheat the grill, with the lid closed, to 375° F.

2. While the Traeger is heating up, peel and slice the potatoes (make sure to put them in water so they will not oxidize). Melt the butter and combine it with the crushed garlic.

3. Grease a 12" cast iron pan with butter and start to layer the torte. The layers should go as follows, potatoes, butter garlic mixture, rosemary, parmesan, continue layering to the top of the pan, about 4 to 5 layers.

4. Place the pan in the Traeger and bake for 20 to 25 minutes, or until the potatoes are fully cooked. If the top of the torte starts to darken before it is finished cooking, reduce the heat to 325°F. Serve hot and enjoy! Grill: 375 °F

Roasted Red Pepper White Bean Dip

Servings: 4
Cooking Time: 40 Minutes

Ingredients:

- 4 Whole garlic
- 4 Tablespoon extra-virgin olive oil
- 2 Bell Pepper, Red
- 3 Tablespoon Dill Weed, fresh
- 3 Tablespoon chopped flat-leaf parsley
- 2 Can cannellini beans, mashed
- 4 Teaspoon lemon juice
- 1 1/2 Teaspoon salt

Directions:

1. Roasting the garlic and red peppers:
2. Supply your smoker with wood pellets and follow the start-up procedure. Preheat the grill, with the lid closed, to 400° F.
3. Peel away the outside layers of the garlic husk. Cut off the top of the garlic bulb, exposing each of the individual cloves. Drizzle olive oil over the top of the head of garlic and rub it in. Wrap the garlic in foil, completely covering it. Put the head of garlic and the two red peppers (washed and dried) on the Traeger.
4. Roast the garlic for 25-30 minutes and the peppers for about 40 minutes. Rotate the peppers a quarter-turn every 10 minutes until the exterior is blistered and blackened. Grill: 400 °F

5. Pull the peppers off the grill and put them in a bowl. Cover the bowl with plastic wrap and leave them for 15 minutes. The steam will loosen the skins so that they slip off like a drumstick covered in barbecue sauce.
6. Peel off the pepper skin. Cut off the stems and scrape out the seeds and they're ready to use.
7. As for the garlic, let it cool and then pull out the individual cloves as needed.
8. The dip:
9. In a blender put the roasted red peppers, 4 cloves of roasted garlic, dill, parsley, drained and rinsed beans, olive oil, lemon juice and salt.
10. Blend until the dip is smooth and creamy. You may need to scrape down the sides of the blender a couple of times. If it's having difficulty blending or looks too thick add more olive oil or lemon juice. (Add more lemon juice if it tastes like it needs more acid or brightness.) Enjoy!

Twice-smoked Potatoes

Servings: 16
Cooking Time: 95 Minutes

Ingredients:

- 8 Idaho, Russet, or Yukon Gold potatoes
- 1 (12-ounce) can evaporated milk, heated
- 1 cup (2 sticks) butter, melted
- ½ cup sour cream, at room temperature
- 1 cup grated Parmesan cheese
- ½ pound bacon, cooked and crumbled
- ¼ cup chopped scallions
- Salt
- Freshly ground black pepper
- 1 cup shredded Cheddar cheese

Directions:

1. Supply your smoker with wood pellets and follow the start-up procedure. Preheat, with the lid closed, to 400°F.
2. Poke the potatoes all over with a fork. Arrange them directly on the grill grate, close the lid, and smoke for 1 hour and 15 minutes, or until cooked through and they have some give when pinched.

3. Let the potatoes cool for 10 minutes, then cut in half lengthwise.
4. Into a medium bowl, scoop out the potato flesh, leaving ¼ inch in the shells; place the shells on a baking sheet.
5. Using an electric mixer on medium speed, beat the potatoes, milk, butter, and sour cream until smooth.
6. Stir in the Parmesan cheese, bacon, and scallions, and season with salt and pepper.
7. Generously stuff each shell with the potato mixture and top with Cheddar cheese.
8. Place the baking sheet on the grill grate, close the lid, and smoke for 20 minutes, or until the cheese is melted.

Skillet Potato Cake

Servings: 4
Cooking Time: 40 Minutes

Ingredients:
- 8 Tablespoon butter, melted
- 2 Pound russet potatoes, peeled and thinly sliced
- 3 Tablespoon kosher salt
- 2 Tablespoon freshly ground black pepper
- thyme

Directions:
1. Supply your smoker with wood pellets and follow the start-up procedure. Preheat the grill, with the lid closed, to 375° F.
2. Brush the bottom of a cast iron skillet with part of the melted butter. Place potato slices vertically around the outer edges then fill in the middle in the same fashion.
3. Pour additional melted butter over the top of the layers and sprinkle with salt and pepper.
4. Place skillet in grill and cook for 35 to 40 minutes or until potatoes are fork tender and golden brown.
5. Garnish with a sprinkle of fresh thyme over the top of the potatoes. Enjoy!

Baked Loaded Tater Tots

Servings: 6
Cooking Time: 35 Minutes

Ingredients:
- 2 Pound frozen tater tots
- 1 Can Black Beans
- 1 1/2 Cup leftover chili
- 1 Cup leftover queso
- 1 red onion, finely diced
- 1/2 Cup chopped cilantro
- 1/2 Cup sour cream
- 1 jalapeños, sliced

Directions:
1. Supply your smoker with wood pellets and follow the start-up procedure. Preheat the grill, with the lid closed, to 375° F.
2. Spread frozen tots out on a sheet tray and place directly on the grill grate.
3. Cook for 20 to 25 minutes or until tots are crispy. Grill: 375 °F
4. Top with warmed chili, queso and beans. Place back on the grill for 15 minutes. Grill: 375 °F
5. Remove from grill and top with red onion, cilantro, sour cream and jalapeño. Enjoy!

Roasted Vegetable Napoleon

Servings: 4
Cooking Time: 30 Minutes

Ingredients:
- 2 Whole sweet potatoes
- 2 Whole zucchini
- 2 Whole Squash
- 1 Whole red onion
- 2 Whole Bell Pepper, Red
- salt and pepper

Directions:
1. Supply your smoker with wood pellets and follow the start-up procedure. Preheat the grill, with the lid closed, to High heat.
2. Salt and pepper all vegetables and grill them on both sides. Begin with the peppers and onions as they will take a little longer to cook. Grill: 450 °F

Grilled Asparagus And Hollandaise Sauce

Servings: 4
Cooking Time: 10 Minutes

Ingredients:
- 1 Pound asparagus
- 2 Teaspoon red pepper flakes
- 2 Tablespoon olive oil
- salt and pepper
- 4 egg yolk
- 1 Tablespoon lemon juice
- 1/2 Cup butter, melted
- cayenne pepper
- salt

Directions:
1. Supply your smoker with wood pellets and follow the start-up procedure. Preheat the grill, with the lid closed, to 375° F.
2. In a large bowl, mix asparagus with olive oil, red pepper flakes and salt. Arrange asparagus on a cooking sheet and take to the grill. Cook for approximately 10 to 15 minutes. Grill: 375 °F
3. In an aluminum bowl, whisk the egg yolks well. Add the lemon juice and whisk until creamy.
4. Place bowl over a double boiler, over low heat, making sure that it does not touches the water.
5. While whisking, add the melted butter slowly. Whisk until it doubles the volume. Take off the heat, still whisking and add the cayenne pepper and salt.
6. Arrange asparagus over a serving plater. Pour hollandaise sauce over asparagus and serve. Enjoy!

Grilled Zucchini Squash Spears

Servings: 4
Cooking Time: 10 Minutes

Ingredients:
- 4 Medium zucchini
- 2 Tablespoon olive oil
- 1 Tablespoon sherry vinegar
- 2 thyme, leaves pulled
- salt and pepper

Directions:
1. Clean the zucchini and cut the ends off. Cut each in half lengthwise, then each half into thirds.
2. Combine remaining ingredients in a medium Ziplock bag and add the spears. Toss and mix well to coat the zucchini.
3. Supply your smoker with wood pellets and follow the start-up procedure. Preheat the grill, with the lid closed, to 350° F.
4. Remove the spears from the bag and place directly on the grill grate cut side down.
5. Cook for 3-4 minutes per side, until grill marks appear and zucchini is tender. Grill: 350 °F
6. Remove from grill and finish with more thyme leaves if desired. Enjoy!

Roasted Asparagus

Servings: 4
Cooking Time: 30 Minutes

Ingredients:
- 1 Bunch asparagus
- 2 Tablespoon olive oil, plus more as needed
- Veggie Rub

Directions:
1. Coat asparagus with olive oil and Veggie Rub, stirring to coat all pieces.
2. Supply your smoker with wood pellets and follow the start-up procedure. Preheat the grill, with the lid closed, to 350° F.
3. Place asparagus directly on the grill grate for 15-20 minutes.
4. Remove from grill and enjoy!

Smoked Beet-pickled Eggs

Servings: 4
Cooking Time: 30 Minutes

Ingredients:
- 6 Eggs, hard boiled
- 1 Red Beets, scrubbed and trimmed
- 1 Cup apple cider vinegar
- 1 Cup Beet, juice
- 1/4 Onion, Sliced

- 1/3 Cup granulated sugar
- 3 Cardamom
- 1 star anise

Directions:
1. Supply your smoker with wood pellets and follow the start-up procedure. Preheat the grill, with the lid closed, to 275° F.
2. Place the peeled hard boiled eggs directly on the grill and smoke for 30 minutes. Grill: 275 °F
3. Put the smoked eggs in a quart size glass jar with the cooked/chopped beets in the bottom.
4. In a medium sauce pan, add the vinegar, beet juice, onion, sugar, cardamom and anise.
5. Bring to a boil and cook, uncovered, until sugar has dissolved and the onions are translucent (about 5 minutes).
6. Remove from the heat and let cool for a few minutes.
7. Pour the vinegar and onions mixture over the eggs and beets in the jar, covering the eggs completely.
8. Securely close with the jar lid. Refrigerate up to a month. Enjoy!

Parmesan Roasted Cauliflower

Servings: 4
Cooking Time: 40 Minutes

Ingredients:
- 1 Head cauliflower, cut into florets
- 1 Medium onion, sliced
- 4 Clove garlic, unpeeled
- 4 Tablespoon olive oil
- salt
- black pepper
- 1 Teaspoon fresh thyme
- 1/2 Cup Parmesan cheese, grated

Directions:
1. Supply your smoker with wood pellets and follow the start-up procedure. Preheat the grill, with the lid closed, to 400° F.
2. On a baking tray, mix together cauliflower, onion, thyme, garlic, olive oil, salt and pepper.
3. Place tray on preheated grill and cook until cauliflower is firm and almost tender (about 25 minutes). Grill: 400 °F
4. Sprinkle cauliflower with Parmesan cheese and continue to cook on the Traeger for another 10 to 15 minutes. Cauliflower should be tender and the Parmesan crisp. Serve immediately, enjoy!

Grilled Asparagus And Spinach Salad

Servings: 8
Cooking Time: 10 Minutes

Ingredients:
- 4 Fluid Ounce apple cider vinegar
- 8 Fluid Ounce Honey Bourbon BBQ Sauce
- 2 Bunch asparagus, ends trimmed
- 3 Fluid Ounce extra-virgin olive oil
- 2 Ounce Beef Rub
- 24 Ounce Spinach, fresh
- 4 Ounce candied pecans
- 4 Ounce feta cheese

Directions:
1. Combine apple cider vinegar and Traeger Apricot BBQ Sauce to create salad dressing.
2. Supply your smoker with wood pellets and follow the start-up procedure. Preheat the grill, with the lid closed, to High heat.
3. Toss the asparagus with Olive Oil and the Beef Shake. Put asparagus in the Traeger Grilling Basket and move the basket to the grill grate.
4. Grill for about 10 minutes. Remove the asparagus once it is cooked. Grill: 350 °F
5. Place the hot asparagus right on top of the bowl of spinach.
6. Add candied pecans, feta cheese & salad dressing then toss and serve. Enjoy!

Double-smoked Cheese Potatoes

Servings: 12
Cooking Time: 35 Minutes

Ingredients:
- 4 large baking potatoes (12 to 14 ounces each—preferably organic)

- 1 1/2 tablespoons bacon fat or butter, melted, or extra virgin olive oil
- Coarse salt (sea or kosher) and freshly ground black pepper
- 4 strips artisanal bacon (like Nueske's), cut crosswise into 1/4-inch slivers
- 6 tablespoons (3/4 stick) cold unsalted butter, thinly sliced
- 2 scallions, trimmed, white and green parts finely chopped (about 4 tablespoons)
- 2 cups coarsely grated smoked or regular white cheddar cheese (about 8 ounces)
- 1/2 cup sour cream
- Spanish smoked paprika (pimentón) or sweet paprika, for sprinkling

Directions:

1. Supply your smoker with wood pellets and follow the start-up procedure. Preheat the grill, with the lid closed, to 400° F. Add enough wood for 1 hour of smoking as specified by the manufacturer.

2. Scrub the potatoes on all sides with a vegetable brush. Rinse well under cold running water and blot dry with paper towels. Prick each potato several times with a fork (this keeps the spud from exploding and facilitates the smoke absorption). Brush or rub the potato on all sides with the bacon fat and season generously with salt and pepper.

3. Place the potatoes on the smoker rack. Smoke until the skins are crisp and the potatoes are tender in the center (they'll be easy to pierce with a slender metal skewer), about 1 hour.

4. Meanwhile, place the bacon in a cold skillet and fry over medium heat until browned and crisp, 3 to 4 minutes. Drain off the bacon fat (save the fat for future potatoes).

5. Transfer the potatoes to a cutting board and let cool slightly. Cut each potato in half lengthwise. Using a spoon, scrape out most of the potato flesh, leaving a 1/4-inch-thick shell. (It's easier to scoop the potatoes when warm.) Cut the potato flesh into 1/2-inch dice and place in a bowl.

6. Add the bacon, 4 tablespoons of the butter, the scallions, and cheese to the potato flesh and gently stir to mix. Stir in the sour cream and salt and pepper to taste; the mixture should be highly seasoned. Stir as little and as gently as possible so as to leave some texture to the potatoes.

7. Spoon the potato mixture back into the potato shells, mounding it in the center. Top each potato half with a thin slice of the remaining butter and sprinkle with paprika. The potatoes can be prepared up to 24 hours ahead to this stage, covered, and refrigerated.

8. Just before serving, preheat your smoker to 400 °F. Add enough wood for 30 minutes of smoking. Place the potatoes in a shallow aluminum foil pan and re-smoke them until browned and bubbling, 15 to 20 minutes.

Spicy Asian Brussels Sprouts

Servings: 4
Cooking Time: 10 Minutes

Ingredients:
- 2 Cup fresh Brussels sprouts
- 2 Tablespoon vegetable oil
- 1 Tablespoon Asian BBQ Rub
- 1/4 Cup Thai sweet chile sauce

Directions:

1. Supply your smoker with wood pellets and follow the start-up procedure. Preheat the grill, with the lid closed, to 350° F.

2. Spread the halved brussel sprouts in a single layer on a lined cookie sheet. Drizzle with the oil and toss to coat.

3. Sprinkle the brussel sprouts evenly with an Asian BBQ rub and put the cookie sheet on the grill. Close the lid and cook for 7-8 minutes. Grill: 350 °F

4. Toss the brussels sprouts in the Thai Chili Sauce and return to the grill for an additional 3-4 minutes, or until the sprouts are crisp-tender. Grill: 350 °F

5. Serve immediately. Enjoy!

Potluck Salad With Smoked Cornbread

Servings: 6
Cooking Time: 45 Minutes

Ingredients:
- 1 cup all-purpose flour
- 1 cup yellow cornmeal
- 1 tablespoon sugar
- 2 teaspoons baking powder
- 1 teaspoon salt
- 1 cup milk
- 1 egg, beaten, at room temperature
- 4 tablespoons (½ stick) unsalted butter, melted and cooled
- Nonstick cooking spray or butter, for greasing
- ½ cup milk
- ½ cup sour cream
- 2 tablespoons dry ranch dressing mix
- 1 pound bacon, cooked and crumbled
- 3 tomatoes, chopped
- 1 bell pepper, chopped
- 1 cucumber, seeded and chopped
- 2 stalks celery, chopped (about 1 cup)
- ½ cup chopped scallions

Directions:
1. For the cornbread:
2. In a medium bowl, combine the flour, cornmeal, sugar, baking powder, and salt.
3. In a small bowl, whisk together the milk and egg. Pour in the butter, then slowly fold this mixture into the dry ingredients.
4. Supply your smoker with wood pellets and follow the start-up procedure. Preheat, with the lid closed, to 375°F.
5. Coat a cast iron skillet with cooking spray or butter.
6. Pour the batter into the skillet, place on the grill grate, close the lid, and smoke for 35 to 45 minutes, or until the cornbread is browned and pulls away from the side of the skillet.
7. Remove the cornbread from the grill and let cool, then coarsely crumble.
8. For the salad:
9. In a small bowl, whisk together the milk, sour cream, and ranch dressing mix.
10. In a medium bowl, combine the crumbled bacon, tomatoes, bell pepper, cucumber, celery, and scallions.
11. In a large serving bowl, layer half of the crumbled cornbread, half of the bacon-veggie mixture, and half of the dressing. Toss lightly.
12. Repeat the layering with the remaining cornbread, bacon-veggie mixture, and dressing. Toss again.
13. Refrigerate the salad for at least 1 hour. Serve cold.

Stuffed Jalapenos

Servings: 8
Cooking Time: 60 Minutes

Ingredients:
- 40 Whole jalapeño
- 8 Ounce cream cheese, room temperature
- 1 Cup Sharp Cheddar Grated
- 1 1/2 Teaspoon Pork & Poultry Rub
- 2 Tablespoon sour cream
- 1 Whole (14 oz) cocktail sausages
- 20 Whole Slices of Smoked Bacon, Cut in Half

Directions:
1. Wash and dry the peppers. Cut the stem ends off with a paring knife, and using the same knife or a small metal spoon, carefully scrape the seeds and ribs out of each pepper. Set aside.
2. In a small bowl, combine the cream cheese, grated cheese, Traeger Pork and Poultry Rub, and the sour cream.
3. Transfer the mixture to a sturdy resealable plastic bag and trim 1/2-inch off one of the lower corners with a scissors. Squeeze the cream cheese mixture into each pepper, filling each a little over the halfway point.
4. Stuff one sausage into each pepper. Wrap the outside of each with a piece of bacon, securing with 1 or 2 toothpicks.
5. Arrange the peppers on a foil-lined baking sheet. Supply your smoker with wood pellets and follow the start-up procedure. Preheat the grill, with the lid closed, to 180° F, and smoke the peppers for 1 to 1-1/2 hours.
6. Increase the heat to 350 degrees F and continue to cook for 20 to 30 minutes, or until the bacon begins to render its fat and crisp. Enjoy! Grill: 350 °F

Grilled Cabbage Steaks With Warm Bacon Vinaigrette

Servings: 4
Cooking Time: 10 Minutes

Ingredients:
- 3 Strips thick-cut lean bacon, cut into 1/4 inch strips
- 1 Large shallot, minced
- 2 Tablespoon sherry vinegar
- 1 Tablespoon whole grain mustard
- 1 Teaspoon chopped thyme
- 2 Tablespoon olive oil, plus more as needed
- 1 Head green cabbage, cut into 3/4 inch thick slices (about 6 steaks)
- salt and pepper

Directions:
1. Supply your smoker with wood pellets and follow the start-up procedure. Preheat the grill, with the lid closed, to 450° F.
2. For the Vinaigrette: In a large skillet, cook the bacon in 2 tablespoons olive oil over medium-high heat until browned and crisp. Remove bacon from heat and stir in the shallot, vinegar, mustard and thyme then set aside.
3. Brush cabbage steaks with olive oil and season with salt and pepper. Place cabbage steaks directly on grill grate and grill for 5 minutes per side. Grill: 450 °F
4. Remove cabbage steaks from grill and drizzle with bacon vinaigrette. Enjoy!

BEEF LAMB AND GAME RECIPES

Cheddar Bacon Beef Burgers

Servings: 12
Cooking Time: 30 Minutes

Ingredients:
- Bacon Cheddar Burger Seasoning
- 3/4 Cup Bacon, Chopped
- 3 Lbs Beef, Ground
- 1 Jalapeno, Chopped
- Pepper
- 1/2 Cup Ranch Dressing
- Salt
- 1 1/2 Cups Shredded Cheddar Cheese

Directions:
1. Supply your smoker with wood pellets and follow the start-up procedure. Preheat the grill, with the lid closed, to 350° F.
2. In a small bowl, combine cheese, bacon, jalapeno and ranch dressing.
3. In a clean, large bowl, combine ground beef with enough salt and pepper to taste.
4. Form meat into patties and place on a pan. A good rule of thumb is for each patty to be about the size of the palm of your hand.
5. Using a clean glass, press into each patty, leaving the imprint of the bottom of the glass in the patty. Stuff the filling into the indent. Grill for 25 minutes or until the ground beef reaches an internal temperature of 160°F. Serve hot.

Roasted Duck

Servings: 4
Cooking Time: 180 Minutes

Ingredients:
- 1 (5-6 lb) duck, defrosted
- Pork & Poultry Rub
- 1 Small onion, peeled and quartered
- 1 orange, quartered
- fresh herbs, such as parsley, sage or rosemary

Directions:
1. Remove the giblets and discard or save for another use. Trim any loose skin at the neck and remove excess fat from around the main cavity. Remove the wing tips if desired.
2. Rinse the duck under cold running water, inside and out, and dry with paper towels.
3. Prick the skin all over with the tip of a knife or the tines of a fork; do not pierce the meat. This helps to render the fat and crisp the skin.
4. Season the bird, inside and out, with Traeger Pork and Poultry Rub. Tuck the onion, orange, and fresh herbs into the cavity.
5. Tie the legs together with butcher's string.
6. Supply your smoker with wood pellets and follow the start-up procedure. Preheat the grill, with the lid closed, to 225° F.
7. Place the duck directly on the grill grate. Roast for 2-1/2 to 3 hours, or until the skin is brown and crisp. The internal temperature should register 160°F in the thigh (be sure to avoid the bone as this will give you an inaccurate reading). Grill: 225 °F Probe: 160 °F
8. If the duck is not browned to your liking, increase the grill temperature to 375°F and roast for several minutes at the higher temperature. Grill: 375 °F
9. Tent the duck loosely with foil and allow it to rest for 30 minutes.
10. Remove the butcher's twine and carve. Enjoy!

Smoked Bacon Brisket Flat

Servings: 4
Cooking Time: 480 Minutes

Ingredients:
- 1/2 lbs bacon
- 4 lbs brisket flat, trimmed
- tt lonestar brisket rub

Directions:
1. Supply your smoker with wood pellets and follow the start-up procedure. Preheat the grill, with the lid open, to 250° F. If using a gas or charcoal grill, set it up for low, indirect heat.

2. Place the brisket in a foil-lined aluminum pan. Season the fat side of the brisket with Lonestar Brisket Rub, then flip and season the meat side with additional rub.

3. Transfer the brisket to the grill and smoke for 1 hour.

4. Use tongs to flip the brisket over, so the fat side is up, then drape half the bacon slices over the brisket. Smoke for 2 hours, then remove the browned bacon, and set aside.

5. Lay the remaining raw bacon strips over the brisket, and continue cooking until these new bacon strips are browned and the internal temperature of the brisket reads 202°F, which will likely take an additional 3 to 4 hours cook time.

6. Remove the brisket from the grill, and rest for 1 hour, then slice thin. Serve warm.

The Perfect T-bones

Servings: 4
Cooking Time: 30 Minutes

Ingredients:
- 4 (1½- to 2-inch-thick) T-bone steaks
- 2 tablespoons olive oil
- 1 batch Espresso Brisket Rub or Chili-Coffee Rub

Directions:
1. Supply your smoker with wood pellets and follow the start-up procedure. Preheat the grill, with the lid closed, to 500°F.
2. Coat the steaks all over with olive oil and season both sides with the rub. Using your hands, work the rub into the meat.
3. Place the steaks directly on a grill grate and smoke until their internal temperature reaches 135°F for rare, 145°F for medium-rare, and 155°F for well-done. Remove the steaks from the grill and serve hot.

Burnt Beer Beef Brisket

Servings: 10-12
Cooking Time: 1440 Minutes

Ingredients:
- 1 Cup Apple Cider Vinegar
- 1 Jar Barbecue Sauce
- 1/2 (Any Brand) Beer, Can
- Beef And Brisket Rub
- 10 - 12 Pound Whole Beef Brisket
- 2 Tablespoons Worcestershire Sauce

Directions:
1. Remove the brisket from the refrigerator. Trimming a cold brisket is easier than trimming a room temperature brisket. Flip the brisket over so that the pointed end of the meat is facing under. Cut away any silver skin or excess fat from the flat muscle and discard. Next, there will be a large, crescent shaped fat section on the flat of the meat. Trim that fat until it is smooth against the meat so that it looks like a seamless transition between the point and flat. Flip the brisket over and trim the fat cap to ¼ inch thick.

2. Generously season the trimmed brisket on all sides with the Beef and Brisket Seasoning.

3. In a bowl, mix together the beer (for a gluten free brisket, be sure to use GF beer), apple cider vinegar and Worcestershire sauce to make mop sauce.

4. Supply your smoker with wood pellets and follow the start-up procedure. Preheat the grill, with the lid closed, to 225° F. Place the brisket in the smoker, insert a temperature probe, and smoke until the internal temperature reads 165°F, about 8 hours. Baste the brisket with the mop sauce every 2 hours to keep it moist. Once the brisket reaches 165°F, remove from the smoker, wrap in butcher paper, folding the edges over to form a leak proof seal, and return to the smoker seam-side down for another 5-8 hours, or until the brisket reaches 202°F.

5. Remove from the smoker, place in an insulated cooler, and allow to rest for 3 hours. Once the brisket has finished resting, heat your smoker to 275°F. Unwrap the brisket and cut the flat from the point. Re wrap the flat and save for another recipe. Cut the point into chunks, coat in barbecue sauce, and sprinkle with Beef and Brisket seasoning.

6. Smoke the burnt ends for 1 hour, or until deeply burnished and glazed. Serve and enjoy!

Baked Venison Tater Tot Casserole

Servings: 4
Cooking Time: 40 Minutes

Ingredients:
- 2 Pound Venison, ground
- 2 Can Peas, canned
- 2 Can cream of mushroom soup
- 28 Ounce frozen tater tots

Directions:
1. Cook ground venison in a medium sauté pan over medium high until browned. Drain off excess fat and set venison aside.
2. In a 13x9 pan, combine venison, peas and soup. Top with tater tots.
3. Supply your smoker with wood pellets and follow the start-up procedure. Preheat the grill, with the lid closed, to 350° F.
4. Place casserole dish directly on grill grate and cook for 30 minutes. Serve hot, enjoy!

Grilled Tomahawk Steak

Servings: 4
Cooking Time: 60 Minutes

Ingredients:
- 2 Large tomahawk steaks
- 2 Tablespoon kosher salt
- 2 Tablespoon ground black pepper
- 1 Tablespoon paprika
- 1/2 Tablespoon garlic powder
- 1/2 Tablespoon onion powder
- 1/2 Tablespoon brown sugar
- 1 Teaspoon ground mustard
- 1/4 Teaspoon cayenne pepper

Directions:
1. In a small bowl, combine all ingredients for the rub. Season the steaks liberally with the rub and set steaks aside while the grill preheats.
2. Supply your smoker with wood pellets and follow the start-up procedure. Preheat the grill, with the lid closed, to 225° F.
3. Place the steaks directly on the grill grate and smoke for 45 minutes to 1 hour, until the internal temperature reaches 120°F. Grill: 225 °F
4. Remove steaks from the grill and set aside to rest.
5. Increase the grill temperature to 450°F. Grill: 450 °F
6. Place the steaks directly on the grill grate and cook 7 to 10 minutes per side, or until the internal temperature reaches 130°F. Grill: 450 °F Probe: 130 °F
7. Remove from grill and let rest 5 minutes before serving. Enjoy!

Grilled Garlic Tri Tip

Servings: 2
Cooking Time: 20 Minutes

Ingredients:
- 4 Tablespoons Beef & Brisket Rub
- 1/3 Cup Brown Sugar
- 1 Stick Unsalted Softened Butter
- 1/2 Tsp Cayenne Pepper
- 1 Garlic Clove, Minced
- 2 Tablespoons Olive Oil
- Juice From 1 Orange
- 1 Tbsp Paprika, Powder
- 1/3 Cup Soy Sauce
- 3 - 4 Pounds Trimmed Tri Tip Roast
- 2 Tablespoons Worcestershire Sauce

Directions:
1. Add the brown sugar, orange juice, Worcestershire sauce, minced garlic and soy sauce to a resealable plastic bag. Add the tri tip to the bag, seal it, and massage the meat to help coat it evenly with the marinade. Place the bag in the refrigerator and allow the tri tip to marinate for 2 hours.
2. Remove the bag from the refrigerator and drain the marinade. Remove the steak from the bag and pat dry with paper towels.
3. In a small mixing bowl, combine the softened butter with 2 tablespoons of Beef & Brisket Seasoning, paprika, and cayenne. Mix the butter until well combined. Set aside.
4. Rub the tri tip down with the olive oil and season generously with the remaining Beef & Brisket Seasoning.

5. Supply your smoker with wood pellets and follow the start-up procedure. Preheat the grill, with the lid closed, to 450° F. If you're using a gas or charcoal grill, set it up for high heat. Insert a temperature probe into the thickest part of the steak and place it on the grill. Sear the tri tip on the grill for 3-5 minutes, then flip it and sear for another 3-5 minutes.

6. Turn the temperature down to 250°F, then grill the tri tip for 15 more minutes until the internal temperature reaches 135°F.

Bbq Beef Ribs

Servings: 4
Cooking Time: 480 Minutes

Ingredients:
- 2 Rack (5-7 lb) 3-bone beef ribs
- 3/4 Cup Meat Church Holy Cow BBQ Rub
- 2 Cup beef broth, for spritzing

Directions:
1. Supply your smoker with wood pellets and follow the start-up procedure. Preheat the grill, with the lid closed, to 275° F.
2. Flip the ribs so they are meat side down and remove the membrane off the back of the rack. One trick to do this is to grab the membrane with a paper towel and and pull it off.
3. Apply a heavy coat of Meat Church Holy Cow BBQ Rub on the bone side, thoroughly covering the meat, repeat with second rack. Allow the rub to adhere for 10 minutes. Flip over the rack of ribs and repeat the process.
4. Place the ribs meat side up on the Traeger. You can spritz the ribs every hour or so with a liquid such as beef broth or water to keep them moist.
5. Continue smoking the ribs until probe tender. This is often beyond 210ºF internal temperature. To speed up the process, wrap the ribs after the meat has reached in internal temperature of at least 160ºF. Grill: 275 °F Probe: 210 °F
6. Remove the ribs from the grill and allow to rest and cool while lightly tented in aluminum foil for 15 to 20 minutes. To serve the ribs whole, make two long cuts or slice the meat off the bone and cube it up for more folks to enjoy.

Smoked Brisket With Traeger Coffee Rub

Servings: 8
Cooking Time: 540 Minutes

Ingredients:
- 1 (15 lb) beef brisket
- 1/4 Cup Coffee Rub, divided
- 15 Ounce beef broth
- 4 Tablespoon salt, divided

Directions:
1. Supply your smoker with wood pellets and follow the start-up procedure. Preheat the grill, with the lid closed, to 225° F.
2. Trim brisket of all excess fat.
3. To make the beef broth injection, combine 2 tablespoons Traeger Coffee Rub, beef broth and 2 tablespoons salt in a small bowl, stirring until the salt is dissolved. Inject the brisket by inserting the needle parallel to the grain about 1 inch apart in a checker pattern over the entire brisket. Pull it back out as you press the plunger. Inject in a high-sided aluminum pan or bus tub and hold your hand over where you are injecting to contain the mess.
4. Season the exterior of the brisket with remaining rub and remaining salt.
5. Place brisket directly on the grill grate and cook for about 6 hours or until the internal temperature reaches 160°F . Grill: 225 °F Probe: 160 °F
6. Wrap the brisket tightly in two layers of foil or butcher paper. Return to grill.
7. Cook an additional 3 hours or until the internal temperature reaches 204°F . Remove brisket from the grill and make a small opening in the foil to let steam escape. Grill: 225 °F Probe: 204 °F
8. Close the opening after 10 minutes and allow meat to rest 60 minutes before slicing. Slice and enjoy!

Herb Chipotle Lamb

Servings: 6
Cooking Time: 120 Minutes

Ingredients:
- Black Pepper
- 1 Tbsp Chipotle Peppers, Crushed
- 3/4 Cup Extra-Virgin Olive Oil
- 3 Garlic, Cloves
- 2 Tbsp Italian Parsley
- 1 Rack Lamb Ribs
- ¼ Cup Applewood Bacon Rub
- 2 Tbsp Rosemary, Fresh
- 2 Tbsp Sage, Fresh
- 2 Tbsp Thyme, Fresh Sprigs

Directions:
1. For the dry rub: baste the lamb ribs with olive oil and season with the chipotle powder and black pepper. Let the lamb ribs rest for at least 15 minutes in the refrigerator.
2. Supply your smoker with wood pellets and follow the start-up procedure. Preheat the grill, with the lid closed, to 275° F.
3. For the wet rub: Blend rosemary, cilantro, Italian parsley, sage, thyme, and oregano with ¼ cup Extra Virgin Olive Oil, ¼ cup of Smoke Infused Applewood Bacon and 2-3 garlic cloves.
4. Apply the wet rub all over the lamb ribs.
5. Lay your lamb ribs bone side down on the grill and smoke until they reach an internal temp of 120-125°F.
6. Turn your grill temp up to 425°F and sear until it of 135-145°F.
7. Rest 10-15 minutes. Carve and enjoy!

Lemon Tomahawk Steak

Servings: 2 – 4
Cooking Time: 215 Minutes

Ingredients:
- Apple Corer Or Metal Spoon
- 3 Lbs Gala Apples
- 1 Lemon
- Chop House Steak Rub
- 1 Tbsp Tennessee Apple Butter Rub
- Sugar
- 4 Cups Water

Directions:
1. Supply your smoker with wood pellets and follow the start-up procedure. Preheat the grill, with the lid closed, to 400° F. If using a gas or charcoal grill, set heat to medium-high heat.
2. Core and halve the apples. Place apples skin-side down on a sheet tray and season with Tennessee Apple Butter and set aside.
3. In a cast iron pot, combine the apple cores with the juice and zest from one lemon. Cover the mixture with water, transfer to the grill and bring to a boil. Reduce heat to 225° F. Place the apples directly on the grill grate (skin-side down) and cook for 1 hour.
4. After 1 hour, remove cast iron pot from the grill. Strain liquid, discard cores, return liquid to pot, and whisk in sugar. Cover with lid and return to grill. Allow to simmer for another hour.
5. Add smoked apples to the pot and continue to simmer for 20 minutes. Remove pot from grill and purée apple mixture in a blender. Pour apple purée back into pot and return to grill. Increase heat to 375° F and simmer for 20 minutes. Remove from grill and allow to cool slightly.
6. Reduce heat on grill to 225° F. Season the tomahawk steak with Chop House Steak Rub on both sides. Place the steak on the grill grates, insert a temperature probe, and grill, undisturbed, for 45 minutes, or until the steak reaches an internal temperature of 120°F
7. Remove steak from grill and set aside. Open the Sear Slide on your and increase temperature to 400°F. Return tomahawk to grill and sear over open flames, about 2-3 minutes per side.
8. Pull the steak off the grill and allow it to rest for 10 minutes. Ladle reserved apple butter over steak and serve.

Garlic Beef Meatballs

Servings: 6
Cooking Time: 15 Minutes

Ingredients:
- 1 1/2 Pounds Beef, Ground Round
- 1/2 Cup Breadcrumb, Dry
- 2 Cloves Garlic, Crushed
- 3/4 Tsp Italian Seasoning, Dried
- 1 Tsp Mustard, Dry
- 1/4 Cup Parmesan Cheese, Shredded
- 1/3 Cup Parsley, Minced Fresh
- 1/4 Tsp Crushed Red Red Bell Peppers
- 1/4 Tsp Salt
- 1/4 Cup Tomato Sauce

Directions:
1. Start your Grill on "smoke" with the lid open until a fire is established in the burn pot (3-7 minutes).
2. Supply your smoker with wood pellets and follow the start-up procedure. Preheat the grill, with the lid closed, to 400° F.
3. Place all ingredients in a bowl, combine them and stir well. Shape the mixture into 30 meatballs (1 ½ inches in width).
4. Spray a broiler pan with cooking spray, place on the grill, and bake for 15 minutes until fully cooked and browned.
5. Remove from grill, cool for 5 minutes, and serve.

Spiced Cowboy Steak

Servings: x
Cooking Time: 53 Minutes

Ingredients:
- 2 cowboy steaks about 1 3/4 inches to 2 inches thick
- Rub:
- 1 1/2 tablespoon olive oil
- 2 cloves garlic minced
- 1 tablespoon coarse salt kosher or sea salt
- 1 teaspoon black pepper
- 1 teaspoon dried thyme
- 1/2 teaspoon onion powder
- 1/2 teaspoon marjoram
- 1/4 teaspoon smoked paprika

Directions:
1. Combine all the rub ingredients and slather onto both sides of the cowboy steaks.
2. Supply your smoker with wood pellets and follow the start-up procedure. Preheat the grill, with the lid closed, to 225 °F.
3. Place steaks on the cooking grate and cook until the internal temperature reaches 120 degrees F (about 45 minutes).
4. Remove steaks from grill, cover it and set aside. Turn pellet grill to the HIGH setting.
5. Place steaks back on the hot grill. After 4 minutes, rotate 45 degrees to create a diamond pattern of sear marks. After 4 minutes turn it over and repeat on the other side.
6. Once seared to perfection, remove steaks from grill and place onto a clean cutting board. Let rest for 5-7 minutes and serve with a dollop of flavored butter on top, or carve and share.

Texas Hill Country Brisket With Mustard Barbecue Sauce

Servings: 10-12
Cooking Time: 660 Minutes

Ingredients:
- 1 whole packer brisket, about 12 to 14lb (5.4 to 6.4kg)
- for the sauce
- ½ cup yellow mustard
- ½ cup brown mustard
- ½ cup apple cider vinegar
- ¼ cup light brown sugar or low-carb substitute, plus more
- 1 tbsp ketchup
- 1 tbsp Worcestershire sauce
- 1 tbsp hot sauce
- 1 tsp beef bouillon granules
- 1 tsp granulated garlic
- 1 tsp coarse salt, plus more
- ½ tsp freshly ground black pepper
- for the rub
- ¼ cup coarse salt

- ¼ cup fresh coarsely ground black pepper
- 1 tbsp granulated garlic
- 1 tbsp chili powder

Directions:

1. Place a pan of water on the grate. Supply your smoker with wood pellets and follow the start-up procedure. Preheat the grill, with the lid closed, to 250° F.

2. In a medium saucepan on the stovetop over medium-low heat, make the sauce by whisking together the ingredients. Bring the mixture to a simmer, stirring occasionally. Simmer for 10 minutes. Taste, adding brown sugar or salt. Transfer the sauce to a covered jar and refrigerate until ready to use.

3. In a small bowl, make the rub by combining the ingredients. Trim some of the excess exterior fat off the brisket, leaving a cap of at least ¼ inch (.5cm). Place the brisket on a rimmed baking sheet. Evenly but conservatively season the meat on all sides with the rub.

4. Place the brisket fat side down on the grate and smoke until the internal temperature reaches 165°F (74°C), about 5 to 6 hours.

5. Remove the brisket from the grill and wrap it fat side up in unlined butcher paper, crimping the seams. (You can also use aluminum foil—many well-known Texas pitmasters do—but it's not as porous.) Return the brisket seam side up to the grate. Continue to cook until the internal temperature reaches 203°F (95°C), about 6 to 8 hours more. The meat should be very tender, with the melted collagen making it almost jiggly.

6. Transfer the brisket to an insulated cooler lined with clean towels or a thick layer of newspapers. Let the meat rest for 1 to 2 hours.

7. Place the brisket on a cutting board and unwrap it. Separate the point from the flat following the seam of fat that runs between them. Use a serrated knife to slice the meat against the grain into pencil-thick pieces. (The grain in the point runs perpendicular to the grain in the flat.)

8. Shingle the meat on a platter. Drizzle with any meat juices from the cutting board. Serve with the barbecue sauce.

Flavour Tri Tip Burnt Ends

Servings: 3
Cooking Time: 420 Minutes

Ingredients:

- 1/2 cup bbq sauce
- to taste, beef & brisket rub
- 1 1/2 tbsp brown sugar
- 1 1/2 tbsp butter, cubed
- 1/2 cup dr. pepper soda
- 1/2 tbsp honey
- 2 tbsp mustard
- 2 lbs tri tip steak
- 1/2 tbsp worcestershire sauce

Directions:

1. Supply your smoker with wood pellets and follow the start-up procedure. Preheat the grill, with the lid closed, to 225° F. If using a gas or charcoal grill, set it up for low, indirect heat.

2. Rub the mustard all over the tri tip, then season with Beef & Brisket rub.

3. Place the tri tip directly on the grill grates and smoke until the internal temperature reaches 165° F (about 2 1/2 hours).

4. Remove the tri tip from the grill and wrap it in butcher paper. Return the tri tip to the grill and continue to smoke until the internal temperature reaches 200° F (an additional 2 ½ to 3 hours).

5. Remove the tri tip from the grill, and rest for 30 minutes, or rest and refrigerate overnight.

6. Increase the grill temperature to 275° F.

7. Cube into ½ inch to ¾ inch pieces, then place cubed tri tip in a large cast iron skillet.

8. Stir together BBQ sauce, Dr. Pepper, honey, and worcestershire sauce in a jar or mixing bowl, then pour over the cubed tri tip. Dot with butter, then sprinkle brown sugar over the top.

9. Place skillet on the grill grate, over indirect heat. Cook for 1 ½ to 2 hours, rotating pieces halfway through cooking. Sauce will have reduced, coated and slightly char the tri tip. Remove from the grill and serve warm.

Grass-fed Beef Burgers

Servings: 4
Cooking Time: 30 Minutes

Ingredients:
- 2 Pound grass-fed ground beef
- 4 Teaspoon kosher salt
- 4 Slices provolone cheese
- 4 brioche burger buns
- 4 Slices Tomato
- Burger Toppings Of Your Choice

Directions:
1. Divide grassfed beef into four portions. To not overwork the meat, remove from the package and directly shape into burger patties about 5" (12cm) across- do not knead the meat. Sprinkle each burger with one teaspoon Kosher salt divided one half on each side.
2. Supply your smoker with wood pellets and follow the start-up procedure. Preheat the grill, with the lid closed, to 415° F.
3. Lay the hamburgers on the grill grate. Cook for 12 minutes for medium rarer- the exterior should be nicely browned. Thermometer should be placed into the center of the burger and should register 130°F(55 C). Grill: 415 °F Probe: 130 °F
4. During the last few minutes of cooking, add provolone slices to burgers and place buns on the grill to toast. Serve with condiments. Enjoy!

Jalapeno Pepper Jack Cheese Bacon Burgers

Servings: 4
Cooking Time: 30 Minutes

Ingredients:
- 4 Slices, Raw Bacon
- 1/2 Cup Prepared Barbecue Sauce
- 1 Pound Ground Beef
- Hickory Bacon Seasoning, Plus More For Sprinkling
- 2 Thinly Sliced Jalapeno Peppers
- 1/2 Cup Olive Oil
- 4 Onion Burger Buns
- Onion, Crispy
- 4 Pepper Jack Cheese, Sliced

Directions:
1. Supply your smoker with wood pellets and follow the start-up procedure. Preheat the grill, with the lid closed, to 350° F. If using a gas or charcoal grill, set it up for medium high heat.
2. Make the burgers: in a large bowl, mix together the ground beef and Hickory Bacon seasoning until the seasoning is well incorporated. Use the Burger Press to make burger patties. Repeat until all the ground beef is gone.
3. In a small bowl, toss the sliced raw jalapenos with the olive oil and place them in the vegetable grill basket. Grill the jalapenos, stirring occasionally, until soft and charred in some spots. Remove from the grill and set aside.
4. Place the bacon on the vegetable grill basket and grill for 5-7 minutes, or until the bacon is crispy and brown. Remove from the grill and set aside.
5. Grill the burgers: place the burger patties on the grill and, if desired, sprinkle more Hickory Bacon seasoning on the patties. Grill the burgers for 5 minutes on one side, then flip and top with a slice of pepper jack cheese and grill for another 5-7 minutes, or until the internal temperature of the burgers is 135-140°F.
6. Remove the burgers from the grill and place on an onion bun. Top with the bacon, grilled jalapenos, crisped onions, and a spoonful of barbecue sauce.

Grilled Bacon-wrapped Hot Dogs

Servings: 8
Cooking Time: 20 Minutes

Ingredients:
- 12 Whole hot dogs
- 8 Ounce Cheese, Colby/Cheddar
- 12 Bacon, sliced
- 12 hot dog buns

Directions:
1. Slice the cheese into 8 long strips. Slice the hot dogs lengthwise, leaving a "hinge" on one side, and tuck a piece of cheese into each.

2. Wrap a slice of bacon in a spiral fashion around each hot dog and secure with toothpicks.
3. Supply your smoker with wood pellets and follow the start-up procedure. Preheat the grill, with the lid closed, to 350° F.
4. Arrange the bacon-wrapped hot dogs on the grill grate and cook for 20 to 30 minutes, or until the cheese is melted and the bacon has crisped up. Grill: 350 °F
5. Transfer to the buns and serve immediately with your favorite condiments. Enjoy!

Slow Smoked Rib-eye Roast

Servings: 6
Cooking Time: 240 Minutes

Ingredients:
- 1 (4-6 lb) rib-eye roast
- 4 Tablespoon yellow mustard
- 1 Tablespoon Worcestershire sauce
- 1 Clove garlic, minced
- Prime Rib Rub
- 4 Sprig fresh thyme

Directions:
1. Supply your smoker with wood pellets and follow the start-up procedure. Preheat the grill, with the lid closed, to 250° F.
2. While the Traeger is warming up, prepare roast. Trim excess fat from the top of the roast down to 1/4 inch thick.
3. In a small bowl, combine the mustard, Worcestershire sauce and garlic. Cover entire roast with the mustard mixture and season liberally with Traeger Prime Rib rub.
4. Lay the sprigs of fresh thyme on the top of the roast.
5. Place the roast directly on the grill grate and smoke until the internal temperature of the roast reaches 135°F for rare or 145°F for medium, about 3 to 4 hours. Grill: 250 °F Probe: 135 °F
6. Remove roast from grill. Tent with foil and rest for 20 minutes before carving. Enjoy!

Italian Meatballs

Servings: 6
Cooking Time: 90 Minutes

Ingredients:
- 1lb (450g) ground beef (85/15), well chilled
- ½lb (225g) Italian sausage, well chilled
- 1 large egg, beaten
- ½ cup finely grated Parmesan, Asiago, or Romano cheese
- ½ cup panko or other breadcrumbs
- 1 tsp Italian seasoning
- 1 tsp coarse salt
- ½ tsp freshly ground black pepper
- 1lb (450g) thin-sliced bacon, halved crosswise
- low-carb barbecue sauce, (optional)

Directions:
1. Supply your smoker with wood pellets and follow the start-up procedure. Preheat the grill, with the lid closed, to 250° F.
2. Place the ground beef, Italian sausage, egg, cheese, breadcrumbs, Italian seasoning, and salt and pepper in a large bowl. Wet your hands with cold water. Form your hands into claw shapes and combine the ingredients using a light touch.
3. Form the mixture into 24 equal-sized balls. Wrap each with a half strip of bacon and secure the ends with a toothpick.
4. Place the meatballs on the grate and smoke until the bacon has rendered its fat and the internal temperature reaches 160°F (71°C), about 1 to 1½ hours. Brush the meatballs with barbecue sauce (if using) during the last 10 minutes of smoking.
5. Transfer the meatballs to a platter. Let rest for 5 minutes before serving.

Grilled Double Burgers With Texas Spicy Bbq Sauce

Servings: 4
Cooking Time: 30 Minutes

Ingredients:
- 3 Pound ground beef
- 4 Tablespoon Beef Rub
- 1/2 Pound bacon
- 8 Slices cheddar cheese

- 4 Whole burger buns, for serving
- 1 Cup Texas Spicy BBQ Sauce
- sliced pickles, for serving

Directions:
1. Form ground beef into eight 1/3 pound patties. Season each patty on both sides with Traeger Beef Rub.
2. Supply your smoker with wood pellets and follow the start-up procedure. Preheat the grill, with the lid closed, to 350° F.
3. For the Bacon: Place bacon slices directly on grill grate and cook for 15 to 20 minutes, or until crispy. Grill: 350 °F
4. Increase the Traeger temperature to 450°F and preheat. Grill: 450 °F
5. Place burger patties directly on grill grate and cook for 4 minutes on each side, or to desired doneness. Grill: 450 °F
6. Top each patty with a slice of cheddar cheese and cook, lid closed, until cheese melts.
7. To serve, spread the Traeger Texas Spicy BBQ Sauce onto each bottom bun and top with the pickles and patty, then repeat with BBQ sauce, pickles, patty, BBQ sauce, and finally the bacon. Top with top bun. Enjoy!

Roasted Mustard Crusted Prime Rib

Servings: 6
Cooking Time: 180 Minutes

Ingredients:
- 1 3-bone prime rib roast
- 1 Tablespoon black pepper
- 2 Tablespoon kosher salt
- 2 Tablespoon garlic, minced to a paste
- 1 Cup whole grain mustard

Directions:
1. Combine salt, black pepper, whole grain mustard and garlic in a small bowl and mix well. Rub mixture all over the exterior of the roast making sure each section is evenly coated.
2. Supply your smoker with wood pellets and follow the start-up procedure. Preheat the grill, with the lid closed, to 450° F.
3. Place the roast directly on the grill grate with the ribs facing the back of the grill. Close the lid and cook for 45 minutes or until the exterior of the roast has an even layer of browning. Grill: 450 °F
4. Reduce the temperature to 325 degrees F and continue to cook for 2.5 hours or until the internal temperature reaches 125 degrees F. Grill: 325 °F Probe: 125 °F
5. Remove roast from grill and allow to rest 15 minutes before slicing. After roast has rested, remove trussing and bones and slice into 1" inch sections. Enjoy!

Wagyu Corned Beef Hash

Servings: 8
Cooking Time: 360 Minutes

Ingredients:
- 2 1/2 Pound Wagyu Corned Beef Roast
- 2 red bell pepper, diced
- 1 green bell pepper, diced
- 2 Pound Southern Hash Brown
- 3 Cup shredded cheddar cheese
- 2 Tablespoon kosher salt
- 2 Tablespoon black pepper
- 7 eggs
- 1/2 Cup whole milk

Directions:
1. Corned Beef: Corned beef needs to be cooked at least one day prior to making the hash.
2. Supply your smoker with wood pellets and follow the start-up procedure. Preheat the grill, with the lid closed, to 275° F.
3. Rinse the corned beef and place on grill. Cook for 4 to 4.5 hours. Wrap in a double layer of heavy duty tin foil and put back on the grill. Grill: 275 °F
4. Cook meat until it reaches an internal temperature of 204 degrees F. This should take 2-3 more hours. Let vent for 2 hours and place in fridge. Refrigerate overnight. Grill: 275 °F Probe: 204 °F
5. Corned Beef Hash: Chop and cook the peppers in cast iron for 20 minutes.

6. When ready to cook, start the Traeger and set the temperature to 350 degrees F and preheat, lid closed, for 10 minutes. Grill: 350 °F
7. Cut the corned beef into bite-sized pieces. Combine the hash browns, corned beef, bell peppers, cheese, salt and pepper. Mix well and place in a 9x13 baking dish.
8. Mix eggs and milk in a separate bowl. Pour over the top of the hash brown mixture.
9. Cover with foil and set on the grill for a 1.5 hours. The internal temperature should reach 165 degrees F. Serve and enjoy! Grill: 350 °F Probe: 165 °F

Beer Chili Bratwurst

Servings: 4
Cooking Time: 45 Minutes

Ingredients:
- 1 Chopped Chipotle In Adobo
- 3 - 4 Cans Of Beer, Any Brand
- 4 Bratwursts, Raw
- 4 Bratwurst Buns
- ½ Cup Prepared Nacho Cheese Sauce
- 1 Cup Chili, Prepared
- Caramelized Onions
- Sweet Rib Rub

Directions:
1. Supply your smoker with wood pellets and follow the start-up procedure. Preheat the grill, with the lid closed, to 350° F. If you're using charcoal or gas, set the temperature to medium high.
2. Place a pot filled with beer, Sweet Rib Rub, caramelized onions and raw brats. Place on grill and par-boil for 20 minutes.
3. Grill the brats for 7-10 minutes, or until internal temperature of the brats is 160°F. Remove the brats from the grill and allow them to rest for 5 minutes.
4. While the brats rest, place the chili in a sauce pan, and place the sauce pan on the grill. Heat the chili all the way through.
5. In a separate sauce pan, add the nacho cheese to the pan, add adobo chili peppers and a shake of Sweet Rib Rub. Place the saucepan on the grill and heat until warm all the way through.
6. Assemble the brats: place a brat in a bun, then top with a spoonful of chili and a spoonful of nacho cheese. Serve immediately.

Standing Venison Rib Roast

Servings: 6
Cooking Time: 30 Minutes

Ingredients:
- 1 (2 To 2-1/2 Lb) 8-Bone Venison Roast
- 1 Tablespoon extra-virgin olive oil
- Prime Rib Rub
- Blackened Saskatchewan Rub
- Coffee Rub

Directions:
1. Supply your smoker with wood pellets and follow the start-up procedure. Preheat the grill, with the lid closed, to 375° F.
2. Rub the olive oil over the roast coating evenly. Then season with Traeger Prime Rib Rub liberally.
3. Place the roast directly on the grill grate bone side down.
4. Cook for 20-25 minutes or until the internal temperature reaches 125°F when an instant read thermometer is inserted into the thickest part of the roast. Grill: 375 °F Probe: 125 °F
5. Remove from the grill and let rest 5-10 minutes before carving. Enjoy!

Hot Coffee-rubbed Brisket

Servings: 8
Cooking Time: 240 Minutes

Ingredients:
- aluminum foil
- 12 lbs beef brisket, packer cut
- java chop house rub

Directions:
1. Inject the brisket with 1 cup of beef broth, being sure to inject with the grain, spacing 1 inch apart.
2. Season the whole brisket with Java Chophouse, then set aside.
3. Supply your smoker with wood pellets and follow the start-up procedure. Preheat the grill, with the lid

closed, to 350° F. If using a gas or charcoal grill, set it up for medium heat.

4. Place the brisket, directly on the grill grate, fat side down, and cook for 1 hour. Begin spraying with broth (1 cup total) every 15 minutes until the internal temperature reaches 160 to 165° F (about 30 to 60 min).

5. Remove brisket from the grill and set on a foil-lined tray. Bring up the sides of the foil, then slowly pour the remaining cup of broth over the top of the brisket, giving time to allow broth to seep into the brisket. Wrap with foil, then set on a sheet tray and return to the grill.

6. Reduce temperature to 275°F and cook for an additional 1 ½ to 2 1/2 hours.

7. Begin checking the brisket for tenderness after 1 hour. Punch thermometer probe or skewer into brisket. Desired tenderness is achieved when the probe or skewer easily slides into the brisket, like butter. If the brisket is slightly tough, repeat this test every 30 minutes. The target temperature is between 206 and 210° F.

8. Remove the brisket from the grill, and cut foil to vent. Allow the brisket to rest for 30 to 45 minutes before slicing. Separate the point from the flat. Slice the flat against the grain, then cube the brisket point for burnt ends. Serve warm.

Spiced Smoked Kielbasa Dogs

Servings: 12
Cooking Time: 300 Minutes

Ingredients:
- 1 tsp all spice, ground
- 2 tsp black peppercorns, ground
- 3 tbsp brown sugar
- 1 cup distilled ice water, divided
- 1 1/2 tsp garlic powder
- 1 1/2 lbs ground beef
- 5 lbs ground pork
- 32 - 35 hog casings
- 2 tbsp kosher salt
- 2 tsp marjoram, dried
- 1 1/2 tsp paprika
- 1 1/4 tsp speed cure, pink salt curing

Directions:

1. In a glass bowl or measuring cup, cover hog casings in warm water and let soak for 1 hour.

2. In a small bowl, whisk together brown sugar, salt, black pepper, marjoram, garlic powder, paprika, allspice, and speed cure.

3. In a large tub, combine ground pork and ground beef. Mix together by hand, then add seasoning and distilled ice water. Mix mixture by hand for 1 minute, until seasoning is incorporated throughout.

4. Prepare the sausage stuffer, and fit one hog casing over a 1 to 1 ¼ inch horn. Place a sheet tray, with a bit of water on it, underneath the nozzle of the stuffer and start filling the casings.

5. Once the casings are filled, twist off into desired lengths, and refrigerate overnight.

6. Hang the links with S-hooks from the top rack of your Grill or Smoker. Smoke on SMOKE mode for 3 hours. Supply your smoker with wood pellets and follow the start-up procedure. Preheat the grill, with the lid closed, to 300° F, which will raise the temperature of the smoking cabinet to 170°F. If using a vertical smoker, keep smoking on SMOKE mode. Continue smoking the sausage for another 1 to 2 hours, until the internal temperature of the sausage reaches 155° F.

7. Remove sausage from the smoking cabinet and either enjoy hot with your favorite toppings, or place in an ice water bath for 15 minutes, dry at room temperature and refrigerate or freeze for future use.

Irish Pasties

Servings: 4
Cooking Time: 20 Minutes

Ingredients:
- 1 Pound Roast Beef, cubed & browned
- 4 Whole Potatoes, cooked & cut into 1/2" cubes
- salt and pepper
- 1 Piecrust
- milk
- 2 Cup Beef Gravy

Directions:

1. Supply your smoker with wood pellets and follow the start-up procedure. Preheat the grill, with the lid closed, to 425° F.
2. Mix the beef, potatoes, salt, and pepper in a large mixing bowl. Unroll the piecrust, and cut in half. Put a good amount of filling in each half, fold over, and seal shut. Brush with a little milk.
3. Place on a greased basking sheet, and poke a few holes in the top of each pasty. Bake for 16-20 minutes, or until the crust is golden brown. Grill: 425 °F
4. Remove from the Traeger, brush with butter, and serve with gravy. Enjoy!

Flavour Smoked Tri Tip

Servings: 4
Cooking Time: 90 Minutes

Ingredients:
- 3 Tbsp Olive Oil
- 2 Tbsp Java Chophouse Seasoning
- 1 - 3 Pound Fat Cap And Silver Skin Removed Tri-Tip Roast

Directions:
1. Supply your smoker with wood pellets and follow the start-up procedure. Preheat the grill, with the lid closed, to 225° F.
2. Rub the tri-tip with olive oil and generously season on all sides with Java Chop House.
3. Place the tri-tip on the smoker rack and smoke until the internal temperature reads 140°F, or about 1 ½ hours.
4. Remove the tri-tip from the smoker and allow to rest for 10 minutes. Slice the tri-tip against the grain and serve.

Bison Tomahawk Steak

Servings: 2
Cooking Time: 15 Minutes

Ingredients:
- 2 1/2 Whole Thick Bone-in Buffalo Rib-eye Steak
- 2 Teaspoon Jacobsen Salt Co. Cherrywood Smoked Salt
- 1 1/2 Tablespoon black pepper

Directions:

1. Supply your smoker with wood pellets and follow the start-up procedure. Preheat the grill, with the lid closed, to 450° F.
2. Combine salt and pepper and evenly coat steak with seasoning. Place steak directly on grill grate.
3. Grill for 6 minutes on one side, then flip steak and continue cooking until the internal temperature reaches 140 degrees for medium rare, 145 for medium. Enjoy!

Smoked Beer Corned Beef

Servings: 6
Cooking Time: 240 Minutes

Ingredients:
- 6 lb corned beef brisket raw
- 2 tbsp black pepper
- 8 oz light beer

Directions:
1. Supply your smoker with wood pellets and follow the start-up procedure. Preheat the grill, with the lid closed, to 275 °F.
2. Cut open packaging of corned beef and drain off liquid. Be sure to grab the spice packet included with the brisket. Gently rinse off corned beef and then pat dry with a paper towel.
3. Open the spice packet included with your corned beef and sprinkle contents over the brisket, then sprinkle a light dusting of black pepper according to your preference.
4. Once pellet grill has reached temperature, insert probes into corned beef brisket pieces. If you only have a single probe, insert that probe in the center of the smallest piece because it will cook the fastest.
5. Smoke for 3 to 4 hours until corned beef reaches an internal temperature of 175 degrees F. Next transfer briskets to an aluminum pan and pour just enough beer in to cover the bottom of the pan. Cover with foil leaving one corner open to let out steam.
6. Continue cooking for another 2-3 hours until internal temperature reaches about 205 degrees F. Use an instant read thermometer and poke different parts of the brisket checking for tenderness. If probe goes into the

meat with very little tension than it is done. If not, continue cooking until it becomes tender.

7. Once meat is tender and fully cooked, remove pan from pellet grill and let the corned beef rest for about 30 minutes still covered with one corner open to prevent overcooking.

8. Slice corned beef into 1/8 inch slices cutting against the grains of the brisket. If brisket crumbles make slices a little thicker.

Smoked Spiced Pulled Beef Chuck Roast

Servings: 6-8
Cooking Time: 360 Minutes

Ingredients:
- 1 chuck roast (3-4 pounds)
- 1 yellow or white onion (sliced)
- 3 cups beef stock (divided use)
- SIMPLE BEEF RUB
- 2 Tablespoons kosher salt
- 2 Tablespoons coarse black pepper
- 2 Tablespoons garlic powder

Directions:
1. Supply your smoker with wood pellets and follow the start-up procedure. Preheat the grill, with the lid closed, to 225 °F.

2. Combine all of the ingredients for the rub in a small bowl and rub liberally onto your beef roast, using your hands to press the rub into every surface of the meat.

3. Put the roast directly on your grill grate, fat-side up, and cook for 3 hours. Spray with 1 cup of the beef stock every hour (reserve the other 2 cups of stock).

4. Turn up the heat after 3 hours. Place the sliced onions in the bottom of a large disposable aluminum foil pan and pour the remaining 2 cups of stock in the bottom of the pan. Transfer the roast into the pan on top of the onions and place the pan into the grill.

5. Increase your grill temperature to 250 degrees F, and cook until the internal temperature reaches 165 degrees F (about 3 more hours).

6. Cover the pan tightly with aluminum foil once your roast hits 165 degrees F, and continue cooking until thermometer inserted in the thickest part of the meat reads 200 to 202 degrees F (this step can take another 3 hours). Every roast will be done at a slightly different temperature, so look for your probe to slide into the meat like it is sliding into softened butter.

7. Remove the pan from the smoker and let rest for a few minutes. Separate the roast from the cooking liquid. Shred the roast and separate the fat from the cooking liquid. Moisten the roast with the remaining cooking liquid, or make it into jus for dipping, or turn it into gravy.

Blackened Saskatchewan Tomahawk Steaks

Servings: 4
Cooking Time: 45 Minutes

Ingredients:
- 2 Whole tomahawk steaks
- 4 Tablespoon Blackened Saskatchewan Rub
- 2 Tablespoon butter

Directions:
1. Supply your smoker with wood pellets and follow the start-up procedure. Preheat the grill, with the lid closed, to 225° F.

2. Cover cold steaks in the Blackened Saskatchewan Rub. Let rest 10 minutes for the seasoning to adhere.

3. Place steaks directly on grill grates and smoke for about 40 minutes, or until an internal temp reaches 119°F. Remove from grill and wrap tightly in foil to rest.

4. Turn up temperature on the grill to 400°F - with a cast iron pan or griddle inside. When the pan is hot, add 2 Tbsp of butter and sear the first steak, about 2-4 minutes per side, or until the internal temperature reads 125°F - 130°F. Repeat with the other Tomahawk. Rest, slice, serve. Enjoy!

Whiskey Bourbon Bbq Cheeseburger

Servings: 4
Cooking Time: 45 Minutes

Ingredients:
- 3 Pound ground beef
- Rub
- 1/2 Cup brown sugar
- 1 To Taste hot sauce
- 1/2 Cup bourbon whiskey
- 1 Pound bacon
- 4 Slices cheddar cheese

Directions:
1. In a medium bowl, combine ground beef and Traeger Rub and mix well using caution not to overwork or allow the beef to get too warm.
2. Divide the ground beef in quarters and put each quarter in a 6" cake ring. Press down and form the beef into a patty.
3. With a skewer, poke about 40 holes about ¾" of the way through each patty. Spread brown sugar all over the top of the patties then drizzle with hot sauce. Pour whiskey over each burger, transfer to the fridge and let sit for about a half hour.
4. Supply your smoker with wood pellets and follow the start-up procedure. Preheat the grill, with the lid closed, to 225° F.
5. Remove burgers from the cake rings. When the grill is to temp, place bacon and burgers directly on the grill grate and cook until burgers internal temperature reaches 165 °F. In the last ten minutes of cooking, top with cheddar cheese to melt. Grill: 225 °F Probe: 165 °F
6. Remove burgers and bacon from the grill and build your burger to your liking. Enjoy!

Rosemary-smoked Lamb Chops

Servings: 4
Cooking Time: 125 Minutes

Ingredients:
- 4½ pounds bone-in lamb chops
- 2 tablespoons olive oil
- Salt
- Freshly ground black pepper
- 1 bunch fresh rosemary

Directions:
1. Supply your smoker with wood pellets and follow the start-up procedure. Preheat the grill, with the lid closed, to 180°F.
2. Rub the lamb chops all over with olive oil and season on both sides with salt and pepper.
3. Spread the rosemary directly on the grill grate, creating a surface area large enough for all the chops to rest on. Place the chops on the rosemary and smoke until they reach an internal temperature of 135°F.
4. Increase the grill's temperature to 450°F, remove the rosemary, and continue to cook the chops until their internal temperature reaches 145°F.
5. Remove the chops from the grill and let them rest for 5 minutes before serving.

Smoked Beef Ribs

Servings: 4-8
Cooking Time: 360 Minutes

Ingredients:
- 2 (2- or 3-pound) racks beef ribs
- 2 tablespoons yellow mustard
- 1 batch Sweet and Spicy Cinnamon Rub

Directions:
1. Supply your smoker with wood pellets and follow the start-up procedure. Preheat the grill, with the lid closed, to 225°F.
2. Remove the membrane from the backside of the ribs. This can be done by cutting just through the membrane in an X pattern and working a paper towel between the membrane and the ribs to pull it off.
3. Coat the ribs all over with mustard and season them with the rub. Using your hands, work the rub into the meat.
4. Place the ribs directly on the grill grate and smoke until their internal temperature reaches between 190°F and 200°F.
5. Remove the racks from the grill and cut them into individual ribs. Serve immediately.

Savory Leftover Brisket Tostadas

Servings: 4
Cooking Time: 30 Minutes

Ingredients:
- 2 Cups Leftover Chopped Brisket
- Lime, Wedges
- Pickled Jalapeno
- 1 Cup Refried Beans
- ½ Cup Salsa
- 8 Tostada Shells
- ½ Cup Shredded Cheddar Cheese

Directions:
1. Supply your smoker with wood pellets and follow the start-up procedure. Preheat the grill, with the lid closed, to 300° F.
2. Assemble the tostadas: smear a tostada shell with refried beans and top with cheese and brisket. Repeat with a second shell and place on top of the first.
3. Grill the tostadas for 5-10 minutes, or until everything is warmed through and the cheese is melty. Remove from the grill.
4. Top the tostadas with tomatoes, cilantro, pickled jalapenos, etc and serve immediately!

Smoked Corned Beef Brisket

Servings: 4
Cooking Time: 300 Minutes

Ingredients:
- 1 (3 lb) flat cut corned beef brisket, fat cap at least 1/4 inch thick
- 1 Bottle Apricot BBQ Sauce
- 1/4 Cup Dijon mustard

Directions:
1. Remove the corned beef brisket from its packaging and discard the spice packet, if any. Soak the corned beef in water for at least 8 hours changing the water every 2 hours.
2. Supply your smoker with wood pellets and follow the start-up procedure. Preheat the grill, with the lid closed, to 275° F.
3. Put the brisket directly on the grill grate, fat side up and cook for 2 hours. Grill: 275 °F
4. Meanwhile, combine the Traeger Apricot BBQ Sauce and the Dijon mustard in a medium bowl, whisking to mix.
5. Pour half of the BBQ sauce-mustard mixture in the bottom of a disposable aluminum foil pan. With tongs, transfer the brisket to the pan, fat-side up. Pour the remainder of the BBQ sauce-mustard mixture over the top of the brisket, using a spatula to spread the sauce evenly. Cover the pan tightly with aluminum foil.
6. Return the brisket to the grill and continue to cook for 2 to 3 hours, or until the brisket is tender. The internal temperature should be 203°F on an instant-read meat thermometer. Probe: 203 °F
7. Remove from the grill and allow the meat to rest for 15 to 20 minutes at room temperature. Slice across the grain into 1/4 inch slices with a sharp knife and serve immediately. Enjoy!

Savory Cheese Steak Rolls With Puff Pastry

Servings: 4
Cooking Time: 25 Minutes

Ingredients:
- 4 oz american or jack cheese, shredded, divided
- 2 tbsp butter
- to taste, chop house steak rub
- to taste, chop house steak rub (for sauce)
- 3 oz cream cheese
- 1 egg, beaten
- 1 tbsp flour
- 1 tbsp flour (for sauce)
- 1 puff pastry sheet, thawed
- 1 lb sandwich steak, shaved/sliced thin
- 1 tbsp vegetable oil
- 1 cup yellow onion, sliced thin
- 2/3 cup milk

Directions:
1. Supply your smoker with wood pellets and follow the start-up procedure. Preheat the grill, with the lid closed, to 400° F. If using a gas or charcoal grill, set it up

for medium-high heat. Preheat the griddle to medium flame.
2. Add oil to the griddle, then cook steak for 2 to 3 minutes, turning with a spatula. Add onions, season with Chop House and cook another minute to soften. Transfer steak and onions to a bowl, then set aside to cool.
3. Meanwhile, melt butter in a sauté pan on the griddle. Stir in flour, then cook for 1 minute. Whisk in milk, then add cream cheese, and 2 ounces of shredded cheese. Whisk until smooth, then remove from the griddle to cool slightly. Use half of the sauce in the pastry, and the other half for serving/dipping once baked.
4. Flour your rolling surface, then set the pastry sheet on top of the flour. Roll the pastry sheet into a 10 to 12 inch square, then cut into 4 squares.
5. Spoon cheese sauce on each pastry square, then divide the steak and onion mixture among the pastries. Top each with remaining shredded cheese, brush sides with beaten egg, then fold pastries over, corner to corner. Secure the seams by pressing down with a fork. Brush the top with beaten egg, then place on a sheet tray.
6. Place the sheet tray on the grill and bake for 18 to 20 minutes, until golden. Remove from the grill, cool for 5 minutes, then cut in half and serve warm with cheese sauce.

Smoked Garlic Meatloaf

Servings: 8
Cooking Time: 180 Minutes

Ingredients:
- 2 Tsp Apple Cider Vinegar
- 2 Lbs Beef, Ground
- 1/2 Tsp Chipotle Pepper Flakes
- 3 Cups Crushed Chips Corn Tortillas
- 2 Grated Garlic, Cloves
- 2/3 Cup Ketchup
- 1 Small Grated Onion, Chopped
- 4 Oz Into Sticks Pepper Jack Cheese, Sliced
- 2 Tbsp Competition Smoked Rub
- 1 Lbs Pork, Ground
- 1/4 Cup Tomato Paste
- 1 Tsp Worcestershire Sauce

Directions:
1. Supply your smoker with wood pellets and follow the start-up procedure. Preheat the grill, with the lid closed, to 250° F.
2. First make the glaze: in a bowl, combine the ketchup, tomato paste, vinegar, Worcestershire, chipotle flakes and Competition Smoked Seasoning. Whisk well to combine and set aside.
3. In a large bowl, mix together the crushed corn chips, eggs, onion and garlic. Add 2/3rds of the glaze to this mixture, reserving the rest for glazing the meatloaf. Mix well to combine and allow to sit until the corn chips have hydrated.
4. Add the ground beef and pork to the corn chip mixture and mix until everything is well distributed.
5. Form the meatloaf into a log and push the sticks of pepper jack cheese into the center of the meatloaf and cover with the meat mixture. Loosely wrap in tin foil and poke holes in the foil with a knife to allow smoke to penetrate.
6. Grill for 1 ½ hours covered, then remove the top half of the tin foil, glaze with reserved glaze, and grill for another 1 ½ hours or until the internal temperature is 165F.

Savory Teriyaki Smoked Steak Bites

Servings: 2
Cooking Time: 90 Minutes

Ingredients:
- Sirloin steak
- Teriyaki sauce
- Light brown sugar
- Garlic powder
- Garlic salt
- Soy sauce
- Apple cider vinegar
- Pepper

Directions:
1. Mix all ingredients for the marinade.
2. Trim steak and cut into 2 inches pieces.

3. Place in a zip lock bag and pour marinade over the steak. Squeeze as much air out as possible and tightly seal the bag.
4. Freeze the steak for at least 8 hours or overnight.
5. Supply your smoker with wood pellets and follow the start-up procedure. Preheat the grill, with the lid closed, to 225 °F.
6. Place the steak bites directly on the rack. Discard remaining marinade.
7. Smoke for 1 hour and 30 minutes or until the internal temp is 135-140 degrees F.

Cheese Onion Steak Sandwiches

Servings: 4
Cooking Time: 10 Minutes

Ingredients:
- 2 tbsp, divided butter
- 4 hoagie rolls, sliced lengthwise
- 2 tbsp olive oil
- 1-2 tbsp chop house steak rub
- 8 slices provolone cheese, sliced
- 2 lbs, sliced thinly rib-eye steaks
- 1 yellow onion, sliced

Directions:
1. Supply your smoker with wood pellets and follow the start-up procedure. Preheat the grill, with the lid closed, to 375° F. If using a gas or charcoal grill, set heat to medium heat. For all other grills, preheat cast iron skillet on grill grates.
2. Melt 1 tablespoon of butter and 1 tablespoon of olive oil on griddle. With a serrated knife, slice rolls 3/4 of the way through, then place facedown onto griddle and cook until toasted. Set aside.
3. Melt remaining tablespoon of butter and olive oil on the griddle. Add sliced onions and cook for 2 minutes, or until lightly caramelized. Move to the lower-right corner of griddle to keep warm.
4. Season steak generously with Chop House Steak Rub, then place on griddle and cook for 3 minutes, stirring to brown all sides. Mix in caramelized onions.
5. Divide steak and onions into 4 portions on the griddle, then top each with 2 slices of provolone cheese. Let cheese melt slightly and transfer to a toasted hoagie roll using a bench scraper or metal spatula. Serve hot and enjoy!

Smoked Black Pepper Beef Cheeks

Servings: 6
Cooking Time: 240 Minutes

Ingredients:
- 4 beef cheeks, trimmed and with silver skin removed
- Beef Rub:
- 2 parts ground black pepper
- 1 part kosher salt
- 1 part brown sugar (optional)

Directions:
1. Supply your smoker with wood pellets and follow the start-up procedure. Preheat the grill, with the lid closed, to 275 °F.
2. Trim silver skin and excess fat from the beef cheeks.
3. In a bowl combine beef rub ingredients and apply generously to all sides of the beef, including crevices.
4. Transfer to grill grates. Leave to smoke for 4 hours, lid closed.
5. Remove from smoker and wrap in aluminum foil, or place in an aluminum tray and cover with foil.
6. Transfer back to the smoker and leave to smoke for one more hour.
7. Allow to cook until the internal temperature has reached 210 °F.
8. Remove from smoker and leave wrapped in foil. Let it rest for about 10 minutes.
9. Slice and serve, or pulled for beef cheek tacos or sandwiches.

Smoked Teriyaki Jerky

Servings: 6
Cooking Time: 240 Minutes

Ingredients:
- 1/2 Cup soy sauce
- 1/4 Cup mirin or sweet cooking wine
- 2 Tablespoon sugar
- 3 coins fresh ginger, each ¼ inch thick
- 1 Clove garlic, crushed

- 1/2 Teaspoon onion powder
- 1/2 Teaspoon black pepper
- 2 Pound trimmed beef top or bottom round, sirloin tip, flank steak or wild game

Directions:

1. In a mixing bowl, combine soy sauce, mirin, sugar, ginger, garlic, onion powder and black pepper.
2. With a sharp knife, slice the beef into 1/4 inch thick slices with the grain. This is much easier to do if the meat is partially frozen. Trim off any fat or connective tissue.
3. Put the beef slices in a large resealable plastic bag and pour the marinade over the beef. Massage the bag so all the slices get coated with the marinade. Seal the bag and refrigerate for several hours or overnight.
4. Supply your smoker with wood pellets and follow the start-up procedure. Preheat the grill, with the lid closed, to 180° F.
5. Remove the beef from the marinade and discard the marinade.
6. Dry the beef slices between paper towels and arrange the meat in a single layer on the grill grate.
7. Smoke on the Traeger for 4 to 5 hours or until the jerky is dry but still pliant when bent. Grill: 180 °F
8. Immediately transfer the jerky to a resealable plastic bag and let it rest for an hour at room temperature.
9. Squeeze the air out of the bag and keep the jerky in the refrigerator. Enjoy!

Smoked Red Wine Beef Roast

Servings: 8
Cooking Time: 180 Minutes

Ingredients:

- 12 oz beef broth
- 6 lbs eye of round beef roast
- 2 tbsp black pepper
- ½ tbsp celery salt
- ½ tbsp garlic powder
- 2 tbsp kosher salt
- ½ tbsp onion powder
- 2 cups red wine
- 1/3 cup Worcestershire sauce

Directions:

1. Supply your smoker with wood pellets and follow the start-up procedure. Preheat the grill, with the lid closed, to 225 °F.
2. Mix the beef broth, red wine, and Worcestershire sauce in a mixing bowl. Fill your meat injector with the mixture.
3. Mix the seasonings in a spice bottle and apply the rub all over the roast, making sure to coat the whole roast evenly.
4. Place the beef roast in the foil pan, fat side up. Using the meat injector, inject the liquid into all areas of the beef roast. Fill the bottom of the pan with the remaining liquid.
5. Place the pan in the smoker and let it cook for 3 hours, basting with the juices in the pan every hour or so.
6. After 3 hours, start checking the roast for the desired internal temperature (Rare: 135 °F, Medium Rare: 145 °F, Medium: 155 °F, Well Done: 170 °F).
7. Remove from the grill and the pan, and let the roast rest for 20 to 30 minutes before slicing.
8. Slice against the grain and enjoy!

Bbq Beef Short Ribs

Servings: 8
Cooking Time: 600 Minutes

Ingredients:

- 4 (4 bone) beef short rib racks
- 1/2 Cup Beef Rub
- 1 Cup apple juice

Directions:

1. If your butcher has not already done so, remove the thin papery membrane from the bone-side of the ribs by working the tip of a butter knife underneath the membrane over a middle bone. Use paper towels to get a firm grip, then tear the membrane off.
2. Season both sides of ribs with Traeger Beef Rub.
3. Supply your smoker with wood pellets and follow the start-up procedure. Preheat the grill, with the lid closed, to 225° F.
4. Arrange the ribs on the grill grate, bone-side down. Grill: 225 °F

5. Cook for 8 to 10 hours, spritzing or mopping with apple juice every 60 minutes until internal temperature reaches 205°F. Grill: 225 °F Probe: 205 °F
6. Slice between ribs and serve immediately. Enjoy!

Green Bell Pepper Cheese Steak Burger

Servings: 4
Cooking Time: 30 Minutes

Ingredients:
- 4 Burger Buns
- 1 Green Bell Pepper, Sliced
- 1 Pound Ground Beef
- 1 Tablespoon Olive Oil
- 1 Tablespoon Chop House Steak Seasoning
- 4 Provolone Cheese, Sliced

Directions:
1. In a large bowl, mix the ground beef and Chop House Steal seasoning together until well combined. Form into patties. Supply your smoker with wood pellets and follow the start-up procedure. Preheat the grill, with the lid closed, to 350° F and grill for 5-7 minutes, flipping halfway through. Once you flip the burgers, top with a slice of provolone cheese.
2. Once the burgers have cooked to your desired degree of doneness, remove from the grill and set aside.
3. For the pepper and onion: in a sauté pan over medium heat, heat the olive oil until it shimmers, then add the onion and pepper. Cook until the pepper and onion are soft and start to caramelize and develop a little char, about 15 minutes.

Garlic Cheese Bacon Burger

Servings: 7
Cooking Time: 16 Minutes

Ingredients:
- 14 Bacon, Strip
- 3 Lbs Chuck Beef, Ground
- 7 Burger Buns
- 4 Cloves Garlic, Minced
- 1 Onion, Chopped
- 1 Tsp Pepper
- 8 Oz Pepper Jack Cheese, Sliced
- 2 Tomato, Sliced

Directions:
1. Supply your smoker with wood pellets and follow the start-up procedure. Preheat the grill, with the lid closed, to 400° F.
2. In a bowl, mix together the ground chuck, garlic, onion, and pepper. Separate the beef mixtures into about 7 equal bundles and form hamburger patties.
3. Brush the grate with oil, then add the patties and grill them on about 5-8 minutes on each side, or until desired doneness.
4. Remove the burgers from the grill. On the bottom half of the burger bun, add two tomato slices, top with a slice of pepper jack cheese, add the patty,
5. Place another slice of cheese on top, add two slices of bacon and top it off with the other half of the burger bun and serve.

Smoked Texas Bbq Brisket

Servings: 8
Cooking Time: 600 Minutes

Ingredients:
- 1 (14-18 lb) whole packer brisket
- Meat Church Holy Cow BBQ Rub
- Meat Church Holy Gospel BBQ Rub

Directions:
1. Trim any hard fat from all sides of the brisket, being careful not to dig too deep into the meat. Trim the sides of any excess or loose fat. Trim the fat side of the brisket to 1/4 inch thick.
2. Season all sides evenly with Meat Church Holy Cow Rub. Optionally add a light layer of Meat Church Holy Gospel Rub. Let the brisket sit in the seasoning at room temp for 20 to 30 minutes.
3. Supply your smoker with wood pellets and follow the start-up procedure. Preheat the grill, with the lid closed, to 275° F.
4. Place the brisket fat side up on the grill grate. Cook until it reaches an internal temperature of 165°F, about 5 to 6 hours

5. Remove brisket and wrap tightly in Traeger Butcher Paper.
6. Place the wrapped brisket back on the grill and cook until it reaches an internal temperature of 204°F, about 3-4 hours. Grill: 275 °F Probe: 204 °F
7. When the brisket reaches 204°F, remove from grill and let rest for 30 minutes. When ready to eat, unwrap brisket and slice against the grain. Enjoy!

New York Strip Steaks With Blue Cheese Butter

Servings: 4
Cooking Time: 8 Minutes

Ingredients:

- 4 boneless New York strip steaks, each about 12oz (340g) and 1 inch (2.5cm) thick
- coarse salt
- freshly ground black pepper
- for the butter
- 8 tbsp unsalted butter, at room temperature
- 1 garlic clove, peeled and finely minced
- ⅓ cup crumbled blue cheese, mashed with a fork
- 1 tbsp minced chives
- 1 tsp Worcestershire sauce
- ½ tsp fresh coarsely ground black pepper

Directions:

1. Approximately 45 minutes before you're ready to cook, lightly season the steaks on both sides with salt and pepper. Place the steaks on a wire rack on a rimmed sheet pan.
2. Supply your smoker with wood pellets and follow the start-up procedure. Preheat the grill, with the lid closed, to 450° F.
3. In a small bowl, make the blue cheese butter by combining the ingredients. Mix thoroughly. Set aside.
4. Place the steaks on the grate at an angle to the bars. Sear until the internal temperature reaches 130°F (54°C), about 3 to 4 minutes per side, turning once.
5. Transfer the steaks to a platter and immediately top with a spoonful of room temperature blue cheese butter. Tent the steaks with aluminum foil for 2 to 3 minutes to encourage the butter to melt before serving.

Flavour Bbq Brisket Burnt Ends

Servings: 6-8
Cooking Time: 420 Minutes

Ingredients:

- 1 Brisket Point
- Georgia Style BBQ Sauce (Mustard Base)
- As Needed Chop House Steak Rub

Directions:

1. Supply your smoker with wood pellets and follow the start-up procedure. Preheat the grill, with the lid closed, to 250° F.
2. Place your brisket on the grates, cook for 6 to 7 hours or until the internal temperature reaches 190°F
3. Remove from the grill and cut into 1-inch cubes. Toss brisket cubes with seasoning and your favorite BBQ sauce into a pan.
4. Place the pan in the grill for 2 hours, stirring halfway through.

Roasted Prime Rib With Mustard And Herbs De Provence

Servings: 8
Cooking Time: 180 Minutes

Ingredients:

- 1 Whole 7-bone prime rib roast
- extra-virgin olive oil
- kosher salt
- coarse ground black pepper
- 2 Cup Dijon mustard
- 2 Cup herbs de Provence

Directions:

1. Note: this recipe requires an overnight marinade, plan ahead. A day before you are ready to cook, prep your prime rib. Trim any excess fat.
2. Coat the prime rib evenly with olive oil to allow the seasoning to adhere. Season all sides of the roast generously with salt and pepper. Next, coat all sides evenly with a layer of Dijon mustard, and season liberally with the herbs de Provence. Let sit in the refrigerator for up to 24 hours, uncovered.

3. Supply your smoker with wood pellets and follow the start-up procedure. Preheat the grill, with the lid closed, to 325° F.
4. Place the prime rib fat side up, directly on the grill grate or on a sheet tray, and roast for 3 to 3 ½ hours, or until the internal temperature reaches 110°F.
5. Pull the prime rib off the grill and allow to rest for one hour. The internal temperature will continue to rise as it rests, you are looking for a finished temp of 130°F for medium rare.
6. Carve the roast. First stand the prime rib upright, and using a sharp, thin-bladed carving knife, carve along the bones, following the curvature of the bones as closely as you can until you cut through the base. Next, slice the roast into even slices, about 1" thick. To carve the bones, stand it upright again and slice along the bones. Enjoy!

Delicious Grilled Steak

Servings: 2-4
Cooking Time: 25 Minutes

Ingredients:
- Steak Seasoning
- 2 (1 1/4 Thick) Steak, Bone-In Ribeye

Directions:
1. Make some perfectly grilled steaks and add some Chop House Steak Rub seasoning too!
2. No more than an hour before grilling, let steaks come to room temperature.
3. Generously sprinkle Chop House Steak Rub to both sides of each steak, allowing time for the rub to melt into the meat.
4. Supply your smoker with wood pellets and follow the start-up procedure. Preheat the grill, with the lid closed, to 400° F.
5. Once the grill reaches temperature, Place steaks directly on the grill. For a medium done steak, sear each side for 5-7 minutes, flipping the steaks only one. Adjust time to your desired doneness.
6. Remove steaks from the grill, cover with tin foil, and let it sit 10 minutes before slicing and serving. Note: Use tongs to flip steaks. Do not flip steaks with a fork or cut into the meat until ready to serve. Any cuts or punctures in the meat will cause juices to escape and dry out your steak.

Texas Shoulder Clod

Servings: 16-20
Cooking Time: 960 Minutes

Ingredients:
- ½ cup sea salt
- ½ cup freshly ground black pepper
- 1 tablespoon red pepper flakes
- 1 tablespoon minced garlic
- 1 tablespoon cayenne pepper
- 1 tablespoon smoked paprika
- 1 (13- to 15-pound) beef shoulder clod

Directions:
1. In a small bowl, combine the salt, pepper, red pepper flakes, minced garlic, cayenne pepper, and smoked paprika to create a rub. Generously apply it to the beef shoulder.
2. Supply your smoker with wood pellets and follow the start-up procedure. Preheat, with the lid closed, to 250°F.
3. Put the meat on the grill grate, close the lid, and smoke for 12 to 16 hours, or until a meat thermometer inserted deeply into the beef reads 195°F. You may need to cover the clod with aluminum foil toward the end of smoking to prevent over-browning.
4. Let the meat rest for about 15 minutes before slicing against the grain and serving.

Savory Smoked Brisket

Servings: 10
Cooking Time: 600 Minutes

Ingredients:
- 4 Tbsp Apple Cider Vinegar
- 10Lb Trimmed Brisket
- 2 Cups Broth, Beef
- Sweet Heat Rub
- 2 Tbsp Worcestershire Sauce

Directions:
1. Trim the fat cap from your brisket, leaving enough fat to baste the meat during the smoke process.

2. Generously coat the brisket with Sweet Heat rub, and massage into the brisket.
3. In a bowl, whisk together the apple cider vinegar, Worcestershire sauce and beef broth, then pour into a clean spray bottle.
4. Supply your smoker with wood pellets and follow the start-up procedure. Preheat the grill, with the lid closed, to 225° F. Once the smoker is up to temperature, place the brisket inside and insert the temperature probe. Smoke for 10 to 12 hours, or until the internal temperature of the brisket reaches 200°F at the thickest part. Once an hour, spray the brisket with the mop sauce to baste it.
5. Once the brisket is done, remove from the smoker, allow to rest for 30 minutes under tin foil, then slice and enjoy!

Lime Carne Asada Tacos

Servings: 4
Cooking Time: 10 Minutes

Ingredients:
- 1/2 Tsp Black Pepper
- 1 Tsp Garlic Powder
- 2 Lime, Juiced
- 1 Tsp Salt
- 1 1/2 Lbs Steak, Skirt
- 8 Tortilla

Directions:
1. Supply your smoker with wood pellets and follow the start-up procedure. Preheat the grill, with the lid closed, to 400° F. Place the steaks on the grill, and grill them for 4-8 minutes, then flip the steaks and grill for an additional 4-8 minutes.
2. Remove steaks from the grill, loosely cover them with foil, and let them sit for 5-10 minutes. Next chop the steaks into pieces and serve with tortillas and any desired toppings.

Beef Caldereta Stew

Servings: 12
Cooking Time: 240 Minutes

Ingredients:
- 1/2 cup cheddar cheese, grated
- 2 lbs, cut into 1 1/2" cubes chuck roast
- 4 garlic cloves, chopped
- 1 tsp kosher salt
- 2 tbsp olive oil
- 2 large yukon gold potatoes
- 5 chopped serrano peppers
- 2 tbsp tomato paste
- 2 cups tomato sauce
- 2 cups water

Directions:
1. Place beef in a cast iron skillet, then transfer to smoking cabinet. Make sure that the sear slide and side dampers are open, then supply your smoker with wood pellets and follow the start-up procedure. Preheat the grill to 375° F, to ensure the cabinet maintains temperature between 225°F and 250°F (If you're cooking on a different Pellet Grill, set the temperature to 225°F).
2. Smoke beef for 1½ hours, then turn cubed beef, and smoke an additional 1½ hours.
3. Place cast iron Dutch oven on the grill, over flame. Add olive oil, potatoes, and carrots. Cook for 3 to 5 minutes, stirring occasionally. Then add leeks and garlic and cook for 2 minutes, until fragrant.
4. Remove skillet from smoking cabinet and add beef pieces to potato mixture.
5. Add tomato sauce, tomato paste, water, and serrano peppers. Bring to a boil, then cover with lid. Set temperature to 275°F, and allow stew to simmer for 1 hour, until beef and potatoes are tender.
6. Add liver and cheese, and gently stir to combine, until the sauce thickens and cheese has melted.
7. Add bell peppers and olives. Stir, cover and cook an additional 2 minutes. Season with salt, and serve hot.

Spicy Beer Beef Jerky

Servings: 4-6
Cooking Time: 240 Minutes

Ingredients:
- 1 12 Oz Bottle Dark Beer
- 1/4 Cup Brown Sugar
- 2 Tbsp Coarse Black Pepper

- 4 Tbsp Garlic Salt
- 2 Tbsp Hot Sauce
- 2 Tablespoons, Divided   Sweet Heat Rub
- 1 Tablespoon Quick Curing Salt
- 1 Cup Soy Sauce
- 2 Pounds Trimmed Flank Steak
- ¼ Worcestershire Sauce

Directions:
1. When you are ready to smoke your jerky, remove the beef from the marinade and discard the marinade.
2. Supply your smoker with wood pellets and follow the start-up procedure. Preheat the grill, with the lid closed, to 200° F. If using a sawdust or charcoal smoker, set it up for medium low heat.
3. Arrange the meat in a single layer directly on the smoker grate. Smoke the beef for 4-5 hours, or until the jerky is dry but still chewy and still bends somewhat.
4. Remove the jerky from the grill with tongs and transfer to a resealable plastic bag while still warm. Let the jerky rest for 1 hour at room temperature.
5. Squeeze any air out of the resealable plastic bag and refrigerate the jerky. It will keep for several weeks. Enjoy!

Grilled Balsamic & Blue Steak

Servings: 2
Cooking Time: 12 Minutes

Ingredients:
- 3 Tablespoon olive oil
- 6 Tablespoon balsamic vinegar
- 1 Tablespoon Prime Rib Rub
- 4 Clove garlic, minced
- 1 1/2 Pound top round London broil steak
- 1/4 Cup butter
- 1/4 Cup crumbled blue cheese
- 2 Whole red onion
- 2 Whole Tomatoes, sliced

Directions:
1. Add the olive oil, balsamic vinegar, Prime Rib Rub, thyme, rosemary, and 3 cloves of garlic to a large bowl, whisking to combine. Place the steak in a large, plastic zipper bag. Pour the mixture over the steak, seal the bag, and marinate in the refrigerator for a minimum of 4 hours, or overnight.
2. Remove the steak from the refrigerator 45 minutes before grilling to bring it to room temperature.
3. Combine the butter, blue cheese, and 1 clove of garlic in a small bowl. Mix well. Refrigerate until ready to serve.
4. Supply your smoker with wood pellets and follow the start-up procedure. Preheat the grill, with the lid closed, to 450° F.
5. Place the steak towards the front of the grill grate for 6 minutes on each side to give it a sear, for medium rare (Place in the middle of the grill grate for a few more minutes if you prefer your steak medium or well). Remove from heat and rest for 10-15 minutes.
6. Brush the onion and tomato slices with olive oil, sprinkle with salt and pepper, place towards the front of the grill until they develop slight grill marks, then move them to the middle for 4 more minutes.
7. Slice the steak against the grain, with the grilled onions and tomatoes, a sprinkling of additional rosemary, and a dollop of blue cheese butter. Enjoy!

Delicious Reverse Seared Picanha Steak

Servings: 4
Cooking Time: 120 Minutes

Ingredients:
- olive oil
- 3 lbs picanha steak, top sirloin cap, fat cap removed
- chop house steak rub

Directions:
1. Supply your smoker with wood pellets and follow the start-up procedure. Preheat the grill, with the lid closed, to 225° F. If using a gas or charcoal grill, set it up for low, indirect heat.
2. Generously season both sides of steak with Chop House, insert temperature probe, and place steak directly on the grill grate.
3. Cover grill and cook 1 ½ to 2 hours, or until internal temperature reads 125°F to 130°F.

4. Remove steak from grill, then preheat KC Combo griddle to medium-high flame. Heat olive oil on the griddle, then sear steak 2 minutes per side on all sides.
5. Remove steak from the griddle, and allow to rest on a cutting board for 10 minutes. Slice steak, against the grain, and serve warm.

Flavour Texas Twinkies

Servings: 7-14
Cooking Time: 40 Minutes

Ingredients:
- 14, slices bacon
- ½ cup BBQ sauce
- 1 lb. brisket
- 8 oz. cream cheese
- 1 tsp cumin
- 14 large jalapeños
- ½ tsp pepper
- 1 cup pepper jack cheese, grated
- 2 tsp hickory bacon rub
- ½ tsp salt

Directions:
1. Supply your smoker with wood pellets and follow the start-up procedure. Preheat the grill, with the lid closed, to 400° F. If using a gas or charcoal grill, set it for medium-high heat.
2. In a food processor, combine the brisket, Hickory Bacon, cumin, salt, pepper, pepper jack and cream cheese. Pulse several times until well combined. Transfer to a bowl and place into refrigerator to chill while preparing jalapeños.
3. Place jalapeños on a sheet tray. Cut each in half lengthwise and remove the seeds and rib with a spoon or by hand, then discard. Note: we recommend using gloves when handling jalapenos, as the seeds can be very hot.
4. Fill each jalapeño half with cream cheese mixture until full, then place other jalapeño half on top. Wrap each jalapeño with a slice of bacon, then skewer crosswise with toothpicks.
5. Place a mesh, metal pan on grill grate and transfer jalapeños to pan. Cover grill and cook for 35 minutes.
6. Open grill and baste jalapeños generously with BBQ sauce, close grill and continue to cook another 5 minutes.
7. Remove from grill and serve hot.

Grilled Beef Shawarma

Servings: 4
Cooking Time: 10 Minutes

Ingredients:
- arugula
- 1/2 tsp cayenne pepper
- 1/2 tsp cinnamon, ground
- 1/2 tsp cloves, ground
- 1 1/2 tsp coriander, ground
- 1 1/2 lbs flank steak
- 2 garlic cloves, minced
- 2 tsp olive oil
- 1 tsp paprika
- 4 pita
- red onion
- tt salt and pepper
- tahini
- tomatoes
- 1/2 tsp turmeric, powder

Directions:
1. Use a meat mallet to tenderize the steak, then transfer to a glass baking dish and season with salt and pepper. Drizzle with olive oil, then rub minced garlic on steak. Season with spice rub. Cover with plastic wrap and refrigerate overnight.
2. Remove steak from the refrigerator, 1 hour prior to grilling. Supply your smoker with wood pellets and follow the start-up procedure. Preheat the grill, with the lid closed, to 450° F. If using a gas or charcoal grill, set it up for medium-high heat.
3. Grill steak 3 to 5 minutes per side, then remove from grill and rest for 10 minutes. While steak is grilling, place pitas in the upper smoke cabinet of the Lockhart to warm. Slice steak thinly, against the grain and wrap in flatbread or pita with arugula, tomatoes, onion, and tahini.

Flank Steak Breakfast Potato Burrito

Servings: 4
Cooking Time: 30 Minutes

Ingredients:
- 2 avocado
- 1 cup bacon slices, diced
- 2 tbsp butter
- 1 cup cheddar cheese, shredded
- 2 lbs flank steak
- 4 large flour tortillas
- tt hot sauce
- 2 tsp olive oil
- 1/2 cup onion, chopped
- chop house steak rub
- 2 cups potatoes, diced

Directions:
1. Supply your smoker with wood pellets and follow the start-up procedure. Preheat the grill, with the lid closed, to 425° F. If using a gas or charcoal grill, set it up for medium-high heat. Preheat griddle to medium-low flame.
2. Drizzle olive oil over steak, then generously season steak with the Chop House Steak Rub. Grill steak 3 minutes [depending on thickness of steak] per side for medium-rare. Remove steak from grill and allow the steak to rest for 10 minutes, then thinly slice against the grain. Set aside.
3. Turn off the grill, then place tortillas inside to warm.
4. Add bacon to the griddle and cook for 2 minutes, then add potatoes to bacon and cook for 2 minutes. Add onions, then cook mixture until bacon is crisp, potatoes have browned, and onions are translucent. Set mixture aside.
5. Melt butter on griddle and then cook scrambled eggs. Set aside.
6. To assemble breakfast burritos, sprinkle cheddar cheese on tortillas. Add scrambled egg, sliced steak, potatoes, and sprinkle with more cheese. Wrap tortillas, by folding sides in, then rolling from the bottom up.
7. Serve hot with fresh avocado and hot sauce.

Smoked New York Steaks

Servings: 4
Cooking Time: 120 Minutes

Ingredients:
- 4 (1-inch-thick) New York steaks
- 2 tablespoons olive oil
- Salt
- Freshly ground black pepper

Directions:
1. Supply your smoker with wood pellets and follow the start-up procedure. Preheat the grill, with the lid closed, to 180°F.
2. Rub the steaks all over with olive oil and season both sides with salt and pepper.
3. Place the steaks directly on the grill grate and smoke for 1 hour.
4. Increase the grill's temperature to 375°F and continue to cook until the steaks' internal temperature reaches 145°F for medium-rare.
5. Remove the steaks and let them rest 5 minutes, before slicing and serving.

Sweetheart Steak With Lobster Ceviche

Servings: 2
Cooking Time: 15 Minutes

Ingredients:
- 1 (20 Oz) Boneless Strip Steak Or Rib Steak, Butterflied Into Heart Shape
- 2 Teaspoon Jacobsen Salt Co. Pure Kosher Sea Salt
- 2 Teaspoon black pepper
- 2 Tablespoon Raw Dark Chocolate, finely chopped
- 1/2 Tablespoon olive oil
- 1 1/2 Pound Lobster Tail
- 1 Cup lemon juice
- 1/3 Cup lime juice
- 1/2 jalapeño, diced

Directions:
1. For the Sweetheart Steak, draw a large heart on a piece of cardboard, shape to size of meat selected. Cut

out cardboard heart shape, then trim meat into heart shape.

2. Combine Jacobsen Salt, pepper, chocolate, and olive oil in a small bowl. Place on top of cut steak.

3. Cut raw lobster tail, remove meat, and chop. In a separate medium bowl, combine the lemon juice, lime juice, and jalapeno.

4. Toss in the lobster meat; ensure it is completely submerged in the liquid. Let lobster soak for 30 minutes. The citric acid actually cooks the lobster meat. If you prefer to have fully-cooked meat, grill lobster in shell for 3-5 minutes at 350 degrees F. Grill: 350 °F

5. Remove from grill, then toss with lemon juice, lime juice, and jalapeno.

6. Supply your smoker with wood pellets and follow the start-up procedure. Preheat the grill, with the lid closed, to 450° F.

7. Place the steak directly on the grill grate and cook for 5 to 7 minutes per side, or until you've reached desired doneness. Remove from grill. Let rest for 5 minutes. Grill: 450 °F

8. Serve lobster ceviche over steak. Enjoy!

Garlic Pigs In A Blanket

Servings: 10
Cooking Time: 15 Minutes

Ingredients:
- 1 Crescent Dough, Can
- 1 Egg
- 1 Tsp Garlic, Minced
- 20 Hot Dog, Mini
- 1/4 Cup Mustard, Dijon
- 1 Tbsp Onion, Diced
- 2 Tbsp Poppy Seeds
- 1 Tsp Salt, Coarse

Directions:
1. Supply your smoker with wood pellets and follow the start-up procedure. Preheat the grill, with the lid closed, to 350° F. Combine the poppy seeds, dried minced onion, minced garlic, and salt in a bowl.

2. Unroll the crescent roll dough, pull apart the triangles and slice each segment into three little triangle pieces. Try to get 3 strips for each roll for the mini hot dogs.

3. After the strips are cut, spread some Dijon mustard on each piece of dough. Roll the dough around mini hot dogs. Lay the pigs in a blanket on a greased cookie sheet. Brush with egg wash and sprinkle with the prepared seasoning.

4. Bake for 15 minutes, serve hot and enjoy!

Spicy Chopped Brisket Sandwich

Servings: 4
Cooking Time: 10 Minutes

Ingredients:
- 3 Cups Cooked And Chopped Brisket
- Dill Pickle, Slice
- Pickled Jalapeno, Sliced
- 4 Sandwich Buns
- 1 Cup Spicy Barbecue Sauce
- White Onion, Sliced

Directions:
1. Supply your smoker with wood pellets and follow the start-up procedure. Preheat the grill, with the lid closed, to 350° F. If you're using gas or charcoal, prep your grill to cook with medium indirect heat.

2. Add the chopped brisket and spicy barbecue sauce to the aluminum pan and mix well. The brisket should be fully coated with sauce. If 1 cup is not enough, feel free to more sauce ¼ cup at a time.

3. Cover the aluminum pan tightly with foil and place it in the center of the grill. Close the lid and cook the brisket for about 10 minutes or until it's heated all the way through.

4. Remove the brisket from the grill and pile the meat on top of the sandwich buns. Top the brisket sandwich with pickle slices, jalapeno slices, and sliced onions. Serve immediately.

Carrot Elk Burgers

Servings: 4
Cooking Time: 15 Minutes

Ingredients:
- To Taste, Blackened Sriracha Rub Seasoning
- 1/2 Tbsp Butter
- To Taste, Cilantro Mayonnaise
- 4 Pieces Green Leaf Lettuce
- 2 Lbs Ground Elk
- 4 Hamburger Buns
- 1 Jalepeno, Sliced
- 4 Pickled Carrots

Directions:
1. Place ground elk in a mixing bowl and season with Blackened Sriracha. Divide into 4 portions, then form into large patties.
2. Supply your smoker with wood pellets and follow the start-up procedure. Preheat the grill, with the lid open, to medium heat. If using a gas or charcoal grill, set it up for medium heat and use a cast iron skillet.
3. Place butter on the left side of the griddle and let melt. Place buns on the left side (on melted butter), and burger patties on the right side.
4. Toast the buns, then turn off the burner, keeping the buns in place to keep warm. Cook the burgers 2 to 3 minutes per side, then remove from the griddle and allow to rest for 5 minutes.
5. Assemble burger: bottom bun, cilantro mayonnaise, lettuce, burger, pickled carrots, sliced jalapeño, cilantro mayonnaise on top bun.

Reuben Sandwich

Servings: 4
Cooking Time: 10 Minutes

Ingredients:
- 2 Cup mayonnaise
- 1/2 Cup ketchup
- 1/4 Cup pickle relish
- 2 Tablespoon Chicken Rub
- 4 Pound leftover corned beef, thinly sliced
- 2 1/2 Cup sauerkraut
- 10 Slices Swiss cheese
- 10 Slices marble rye bread
- 6 Tablespoon butter, room temperature

Directions:
1. See Traeger Smoked Corned Beef Brisket recipe for corned beef instructions.
2. Supply your smoker with wood pellets and follow the start-up procedure. Preheat the grill, with the lid closed, to 350° F.
3. Place a large griddle directly on the grill grate to heat up while the sandwiches are being assembled.
4. Combine the mayonnaise, ketchup, relish and Traeger Chicken Rub in a bowl and stir until well mixed.
5. Butter the outsides of the bread (the side that goes on the grill). Place a layer of sauce on the other side of the bread and top with the corned beef, sauerkraut and 2 Swiss cheese slices. Top with another slice of sauced bread.
6. Place sandwiches on the hot griddle in the Traeger and cook for 5 minutes. Using a spatula, flip the sandwiches and cook for an additional 5 minutes, or until toasted with melty cheese and warm meat. Grill: 350 °F
7. Remove sandwiches from the Traeger. Enjoy!

Smoked Chuck Roast Tater Tot Casserole

Servings: 6
Cooking Time: 635 Minutes

Ingredients:
- 2 cups beef stock, divided
- 1 cup cheddar cheese, shredded
- 2 lbs chuck roast
- 1 tbsp cilantro, chopped
- 1 tsp cumin, ground
- 2 jalapeños, chopped
- to taste, lone star brisket rub
- 14 oz tater tots, miniature
- 1 lb white American cheese, cubed
- 1 yellow onion
- 1 cup milk

Directions:

1. Supply your smoker with wood pellets and follow the start-up procedure. Preheat the grill, with the lid closed, to 225° F. If using a gas or charcoal grill, set it up for low, indirect heat.
2. Set the chuck roast on a sheet tray, then season with Lonestar Brisket.
3. Place the chuck roast directly on the grill grate. Close the lid and smoke for 3 hours, spraying with ½ cup of beef stock after the 1st and 2nd hours.
4. Slice the onion and place in a cast iron skillet/Dutch oven with a lid, or aluminum pan. Pour the remaining 1 ½ cups of stock over the onions and set roast on top of onions.
5. Increase the temperature to 275° F and cook an additional 2 ½ to 3 hours, or until internal temperature reaches 165° F.
6. Once 165 F internal temperature is reached, cover the roast with a lid or aluminum foil, and cook another 2 ½ to 3 hours, or until the internal temperature reaches 200° F.
7. Remove the lid then pull the chuck roast apart with tongs. Remove from the grill and set aside.
8. Heat another cast iron skillet on the grill. Open the sear slide, then to the skillet add the cubed cheese, milk, jalapeño, milk, cumin, and cilantro. Stir occasionally, for 5 minutes, until the cheese melts. Close the lid and allow the cheese to smoke for 30 to 45 minutes, then remove from the grill and set aside for casserole assembly.
9. Assemble the casserole: In a deep cast iron skillet, layer the smoked chuck roast, smoked queso, and tater tots.
10. Increase the temperature of the grill to 375° F. If using a gas or charcoal grill, set it to medium heat.
11. Place the skillet on the grill, over indirect heat. Bake for 25 to 30 min, until tater tots begin to brown. Add shredded cheese, then continue baking on the grill for 5 minutes, until the cheese has melted.
12. Remove the casserole from the grill, rest for 10 minutes, then serve warm with additional cilantro, if desired.

Garlic Standing Rib Roast

Servings: 4
Cooking Time: 240 Minutes

Ingredients:
- 1 tbsp cracked black pepper
- 1/2 tbsp granulated garlic
- 1/2 tbsp granulated onion
- 2 tbsp kosher salt
- 1 tbsp olive oil
- 2 tsp oregano, dried
- 1/2 tbsp parsley, dried
- 5 1/2 lbs prime rib roast, bone-in
- 2 tsp smoked paprika

Directions:
1. Place the roast in a glass baking dish. In a small mixing bowl, combine the salt, pepper, granulated garlic, granulated onion, parsley, oregano and smoked paprika. Season the entire roast with the spice blend, then cover and refrigerate overnight.
2. One hour prior to cooking, remove roast from the refrigerator, uncover, and let it sit out at room temperature.
3. Supply your smoker with wood pellets and follow the start-up procedure. Preheat the grill, with the lid closed, to 225° F. If using a gas or charcoal grill, set it up for low, indirect heat.
4. Place seasoned roast on a cast iron skillet, drizzle with olive oil, and transfer to the grill. Smoke the roast for 1 hour 45 minutes, or until internal temperature reaches 120° F. Remove from the grill and allow roast to rest for 15 minutes.
5. Increase the grill temperature to 450 F, then return roast to grill for an additional 10 to 15 minutes. Allow roast to rest for 15 minutes, slice and serve warm.

Grilled Dill Pickle Tri Tip Steak

Servings: 4
Cooking Time: 300 Minutes

Ingredients:
- BBQ sauce
- dill pickles
- jalapeño
- to taste, java chophouse seasoning
- 2 tbsp mustard

- onion, sliced & minced
- 2 lbs tri tip steak

Directions:
1. Supply your smoker with wood pellets and follow the start-up procedure. Preheat the grill, with the lid closed, to 225° F. If using a gas or charcoal grill, set it up for low, indirect heat.
2. Rub the mustard all over the tri tip, then season with Java Chophouse.
3. Place the tri tip directly on the grill grates and smoke until the internal temperature reaches 165° F (about 2 1/2 hours).
4. Remove the tri tip from the grill and wrap it in butcher paper. Return the tri tip to the grill and continue to smoke until the internal temperature reaches 200° F (an additional 2 ½ to 3 hours).
5. Remove the tri tip from the grill, and rest for 30 minutes. Slice thin and serve with pickles, jalapeño, onion, and BBQ sauce, if desired.

Mustard Garlic Crusted Prime Rib

Servings: 8
Cooking Time: 195 Minutes

Ingredients:
- 1 (3 Rib) Beef, Prime Rib Roast
- 1 Tbsp Black Pepper
- 2 Tbsp Garlic, Crushed
- 1 Cup Mustard, Whole Grain
- 2 Tbsp Salt, Kosher

Directions:
1. Supply your smoker with wood pellets and follow the start-up procedure. Preheat the grill, with the lid closed, to 450° F.
2. Combine salt, black pepper, mustard and garlic in a bowl. Evenly rub the seasoning all over coating the entire surface of the roast.
3. Once your grill is preheated, place the roast on the grates, ensuring the ribs are facing the back end of the grill. Once the roast is placed on the grill, shut the lid to the grill.
4. After 45 minutes, lower the temperature of the grill to 325°F. Cook for an additional 2.5 hours or until the internal temperature reaches 125°F. Remove the roast, letting it rest for about 15 minutes. Slice and enjoy!

Smoked Longhorn Brisket

Servings: 8
Cooking Time: 420 Minutes

Ingredients:
- 1 (12-14 lb) whole packer brisket, trimmed
- 1/4 Cup Prime Rib Rub
- 2 Tablespoon coffee grounds

Directions:
1. Supply your smoker with wood pellets and follow the start-up procedure. Preheat the grill, with the lid closed, to 250° F.
2. Rub brisket with Traeger Prime Rib Rub and coffee grounds.
3. Place brisket on the grill grate fat-side down and smoke until it reaches an internal temperature of 160°F, this should take about 4 to 5 hours. Grill: 250 °F Probe: 160 °F
4. Remove brisket from grill and double wrap in foil. Return wrapped brisket to grill and cook until brisket reaches an internal temperature of 204°F, about 2-1/2 to 3 hours. Grill: 250 °F Probe: 204 °F
5. Once finished, remove from grill, unwrap and let rest for 15 minutes. Slice against the grain and serve. Enjoy!

Smoked Tri-tip

Servings: 4
Cooking Time: 300 Minutes

Ingredients:
- 1½ pounds tri-tip roast
- Salt
- Freshly ground black pepper
- 2 teaspoons garlic powder
- 2 teaspoons lemon pepper
- ½ cup apple juice

Directions:
1. Supply your smoker with wood pellets and follow the start-up procedure. Preheat the grill, with the lid closed, to 180°F.

2. Season the tri-tip roast with salt, pepper, garlic powder, and lemon pepper. Using your hands, work the seasoning into the meat.
3. Place the roast directly on the grill grate and smoke for 4 hours.
4. Pull the tri-tip from the grill and place it on enough aluminum foil to wrap it completely.
5. Increase the grill's temperature to 375°F.
6. Fold in three sides of the foil around the roast and add the apple juice. Fold in the last side, completely enclosing the tri-tip and liquid. Return the wrapped tri-tip to the grill and cook for 45 minutes more.
7. Remove the tri-tip roast from the grill and let it rest for 10 to 15 minutes, before unwrapping, slicing, and serving.

Grilled Rib Eyes With Hasselback Sweet Potatoes

Servings: 4
Cooking Time: 60 Minutes

Ingredients:
- 2 (1-1/2 to 2 lb) bone-in rib-eye steaks
- 4 sweet potatoes
- extra-virgin olive oil
- salt and pepper

Directions:
1. One hour before preparing, remove the steaks from the refrigerator to allow them to come to room temperature.
2. Supply your smoker with wood pellets and follow the start-up procedure. Preheat the grill, with the lid closed, to 400° F.
3. Place the cut potatoes on a sheet pan. Drizzle with oil and season generously with salt and pepper. Place the pan on the grill. Roast until the potatoes are browned on the outside and tender in the center, 50 to 60 minutes.
4. While the sweet potatoes are roasting, prep the steaks. Rub each steak with oil, and sprinkle salt and pepper generously over each side.
5. When the sweet potatoes are almost done, place the steaks on the grill and cook, allowing each side to sear, until the internal temperature reaches 130°F for medium-rare, 4 to 5 minutes per side. Grill: 400 °F Probe: 130 °F

6. Remove the steaks from the grill, and let rest for 10 minutes.

Smoked Burgers

Servings: 8
Cooking Time: 120 Minutes

Ingredients:
- 2 Pound ground beef
- 1 Tablespoon Worcestershire sauce
- 2 Tablespoon Beef Rub

Directions:
1. Mix ground beef with Worcestershire sauce and Traeger Beef rub.
2. Form beef mixture into 8 hamburger patties.
3. Supply your smoker with wood pellets and follow the start-up procedure. Preheat the grill, with the lid closed, to 180° F.
4. Place patties directly on the grill grate and smoke for 2 hours. Grill: 180 °F
5. After 2 hours, remove from grill and serve with your favorite toppings. Enjoy!

Flavour Texas Smoke Beef

Servings: 8
Cooking Time: 315 Minutes

Ingredients:
- 1 Cup Strong Brewed Coffee or Espresso, Cold
- 1 Cup Cola
- 1/2 Cup Soy Sauce
- 1/4 Cup Worcestershire Sauce
- 1/4 Cup Brown Sugar
- 1 Tablespoon Morton Tender Quick Home Meat Cure
- 1 1/2 Teaspoon Freshly Ground Black Pepper
- 1 Tablespoon Hot Sauce
- 2 Pound Trimmed Beef Top Or Bottom Round

Directions:
1. Plan ahead! This recipe requires marinating time overnight. In a mixing bowl, combine the coffee, cola, soy sauce, Worcestershire sauce, brown sugar, curing salt (if using), pepper, and hot sauce.
2. With a sharp knife, slice the beef into 1/4" thick slices against the grain. (This is easier if the meat is partially frozen.)

3. Trim any fat or connective tissue.
4. Put the beef slices in a large resealable plastic bag.
5. Pour the marinade mixture over the beef, and massage the bag so that all the slices get coated with the marinade.
6. Seal the bag and refrigerate for several hours, or overnight.
7. Supply your smoker with wood pellets and follow the start-up procedure. Preheat the grill, with the lid closed, to 180 °F.
8. Remove the beef from the marinade and discard the marinade.
9. Dry the beef slices between paper towels. Arrange the meat in a single layer directly on the grill grate.
10. Smoke for 4 to 5 hours, or until the jerky is dry but still chewy and somewhat pliant when you bend a piece.

Grilled Skirt Steak Quesadillas

Servings: 4
Cooking Time: 15 Minutes

Ingredients:
- 2 Tablespoon chili powder
- 2 Teaspoon kosher salt
- 1 Teaspoon ground cumin
- 1/2 Teaspoon Chipotle Chili Powder
- 1/2 Teaspoon cayenne pepper
- 1 Teaspoon lime zest
- 1 1/2 Pound skirt steak
- 12 Whole Corn Tortillas, 6 inch
- 1 vegetable oil
- 1/2 Cup shredded pepper jack cheese

Directions:
1. For the skirt steak, combine the chili powder, salt, cumin, chipotle powder, cayenne and lime zest in a small bowl.
2. Rub the spice mixture over entire skirt steak and let marinate in a zip-top bag at least 20 to 25 minutes.
3. Supply your smoker with wood pellets and follow the start-up procedure. Preheat the grill, with the lid closed, to 400° F.
4. Place skirt steak on grill 3-4 minutes per side. Let rest for 20 minutes before cutting into bite sized pieces. Grill: 400 °F
5. For the quesadillas, take the tortillas and fill with cheese and grilled skirt steak. Cook on a grill pan or in a sauté pan with extra oil to prevent burning.
6. Serve with guacamole, sour cream or salsa. Enjoy!

Smoked Beer Brisket

Servings: 16
Cooking Time: 420 Minutes

Ingredients:
- 1 15 lb brisket
- Brisket Baste:
- 1 cup beer
- 1/4 cup apple cider vinegar
- 1/4 cup beef stock
- 5 tbsp butter, melted
- Brisket Rub:
- 2 tbsp garlic powder
- 2 tbsp onion powder
- 2 tbsp paprika
- 2 tbsp chili powder
- 2 tbsp kosher salt
- 2 tbsp coarse ground black pepper
- 1 tbsp brown sugar

Directions:
1. Supply your smoker with wood pellets and follow the start-up procedure. Preheat the grill, with the lid closed, to 225 °F.
2. In a small bowl, mix together garlic powder, onion powder, paprika, chili pepper, kosher salt, and pepper.
3. Rub the seasonings on all sides of the brisket.
4. Place the brisket on the grill grate, fat side down.
5. Cook the brisket until it reaches an internal temperature of 160 °F(about 3 to 4 hours).
6. When brisket reaches an internal temperature of 160 °F, remove it from the grill.
7. Double wrap the meat in aluminum foil and add the beef broth to the foil packet.
8. Return brisket to the grill grate and cook until it reaches an internal temperature of 204 °F(about 3 hours more).
9. Once finished, remove the brisket from the grill, unwrap from foil and let it rest for 15 minutes.
10. Cut against the grain and serve. Enjoy!

COCKTAILS RECIPES

Smoked Berry Cocktail

Servings: 2
Cooking Time: 15 Minutes

Ingredients:
- 1/2 Cup strawberries, stemmed
- 1/2 Cup blackberries
- 1/2 Cup blueberries
- 8 Ounce bourbon or iced tea
- 2 Ounce lime juice
- 3 Ounce simple syrup
- soda water
- fresh mint, for garnish

Directions:
1. Supply your smoker with wood pellets and follow the start-up procedure. Preheat the grill, with the lid closed, to 180° F.
2. Wash berries well, spread them on a clean cookie sheet and place on the grill. Smoke berries for 15 minutes. Grill: 180 °F
3. Remove berries from grill and transfer to a blender. Puree berries until smooth then pass through a fine mesh strainer to remove seeds.
4. To create a layered cocktail, pour 2 ounces of berry puree in the bottom of a glass. Next, pour 2 ounces of bourbon or iced tea over the back of a spoon into the glass, then 1/2 ounce lime juice and 1/2 ounce simple syrup, top with soda water and ice. Finish with mint or extra berries for garnish.
5. Repeat the same process for 3 more servings. Enjoy!

Smoking Gun Cocktail

Servings: 2
Cooking Time: 45 Minutes

Ingredients:
- 2 Jar vermouth soaked cocktail onions
- 3 Ounce vodka
- 1 Ounce dry vermouth

Directions:
1. Supply your smoker with wood pellets and follow the start-up procedure. Preheat the grill, with the lid closed, to 180° F.
2. To make the smoked onion vermouth: Pour jar of vermouth soaked cocktail onions onto a shallow sheet pan. Smoke for 45 minutes. Remove from grill and set aside to chill. Grill: 180 °F
3. To make the cocktail: Add vodka, 1 teaspoon liquid from the smoked onions and dry vermouth to a mixing glass. Shake and strain into a chilled martini glass.
4. Garnish with smoked cocktail onions on a skewer. Enjoy!

Traeger Smoked Daiquiri

Servings: 2
Cooking Time: 25 Minutes

Ingredients:
- 2 limes, sliced
- 2 Tablespoon granulated sugar
- 3 Ounce Rum
- 1 Ounce Smoked Simple Syrup
- 1 1/2 Ounce lime juice

Directions:
1. Supply your smoker with wood pellets and follow the start-up procedure. Preheat the grill, with the lid closed, to 350° F.
2. Toss the lime slices with granulated sugar and place directly on the grill grate. Cook 20-25 minutes or until grill marks form. Remove from grill and cool. Grill: 350 °F
3. In a mixing glass add rum, Traeger Simple Syrup, and fresh lime juice. Add ice to the mixing glass and shake. Strain contents into a chilled glass.
4. Garnish with a grilled lime wheel. Enjoy!

In Traeger Fashion Cocktail

Servings: 2
Cooking Time: 20 Minutes

Ingredients:
- 2 Whole orange peel
- 2 Whole lemon peel
- 3 Ounce bourbon
- 1 Ounce Smoked Simple Syrup
- 6 Dash Bitters Lab Charred Cedar & Currant Bitters

Directions:
1. Supply your smoker with wood pellets and follow the start-up procedure. Preheat the grill, with the lid closed, to 350° F.
2. Place the lemon and orange peel directly on the grill grate and cook 20 to 25 minutes or until lightly browned. Grill: 350 °F
3. Add bourbon, Traeger Smoked Simple Syrup and bitters to a mixing glass and stir over ice. Stir until glass is chilled and contents are well diluted.
4. Strain into a new glass over fresh ice and garnish with grilled lemon and orange peel. Enjoy!

Smoked Apple Cider

Servings: 2
Cooking Time: 30 Minutes

Ingredients:
- 32 Ounce apple cider
- 2 cinnamon sticks
- 4 whole cloves
- 3 star anise
- 2 Pieces orange peel
- 2 Pieces lemon peel

Directions:
1. Supply your smoker with wood pellets and follow the start-up procedure. Preheat the grill, with the lid closed, to 225° F.
2. Combine the cider, cinnamon stick, star anise, clove, lemon and orange peel in a shallow baking dish.
3. Place directly on the grill grate and smoke for 30 minutes. Remove from grill, strain and transfer to four mugs. Grill: 225 °F
4. Finish with a slice of apple and a cinnamon stick to serve. Enjoy!

Grilled Blood Orange Mimosa

Servings: 4
Cooking Time: 15 Minutes

Ingredients:
- 3 blood orange, halved
- 2 Tablespoon granulated sugar
- 1 Bottle sparkling wine
- thyme sprigs, for garnish

Directions:
1. Supply your smoker with wood pellets and follow the start-up procedure. Preheat the grill, with the lid closed, to 375° F.
2. When the grill is hot, dip the cut side of the orange halves in sugar and place cut side down directly on the grill grate. Grill: 375 °F
3. Grill the oranges for 10-15 minutes or until grill marks develop. Grill: 375 °F
4. Remove from the grill and let cool at room temperature.
5. When cool enough to handle, juice the oranges and strain through a fine strainer removing any pulp.
6. Pour 5 oz of sparkling wine into each glass and top with 1 oz blood orange juice.
7. Garnish with a sprig of thyme. Enjoy!

Sunset Margarita

Servings: 2
Cooking Time: 55 Minutes

Ingredients:
- 4 oranges
- 2 Cup plus 1 teaspoon agave
- 1/2 Cup water
- 1 Ounce burnt orange agave
- 3 Ounce reposado tequila
- 1 1/2 Ounce fresh squeezed lime juice
- Jacobsen Salt Co. Cherrywood Smoked Salt

Directions:
1. Supply your smoker with wood pellets and follow the start-up procedure. Preheat the grill, with the lid closed, to 350° F.
2. For the Burnt Orange Agave Syrup: Cut one orange in half and brush cut side with agave. Place cut side down directly on the grill grate and grill for 15 minutes or until grill marks develop. Grill: 350 °F
3. While the orange halves are grilling, slice the other orange and brush both sides of the slices with agave. Place slices directly on the grill grate next to the halves and cook for 15 minutes or until grill marks develop. Grill: 350 °F
4. Remove orange halves from grill grate and let cool. After they have cooled, juice halves and strain. Set aside.
5. Combine 1/4 cup water and agave in a shallow dish and mix well. Remove orange slices from the grill and place in the agave mixture, reserving a few for garnish.
6. Reduce the grill temperature to 180 degrees F and place the shallow dish with agave and oranges directly on the grill grate. Smoke for 40 minutes. Remove from heat and strain. Set aside. Grill: 180 °F
7. To Mix Drink: Rim glass with Jacobsen Smoked Salt. Combine tequila, fresh lime juice, grilled orange juice and burnt orange agave syrup in a glass. Add ice and shake well.
8. Strain into a rimmed glass over clean ice. Garnish with a grilled orange slice. Enjoy!

Ryes And Shine Cocktail

Servings: 2
Cooking Time: 30 Minutes

Ingredients:
- 2 lemon, cut into wheels for garnish
- 6 Tablespoon granulated sugar
- 2 Ounce rye
- 1 Ounce bourbon
- 3 Ounce lemon juice
- 1 Ounce Smoked Simple Syrup
- 6 Dash Fernet-Branca

Directions:
1. Supply your smoker with wood pellets and follow the start-up procedure. Preheat the grill, with the lid closed, to 325° F.
2. Toss lemon wheels with granulated sugar to coat on both sides. Place wheels directly on the grill grate and cook for 15 minutes on each side or until grill marks form. Grill: 325 °F
3. Add rye, bourbon, lemon juice, Traeger Smoked Simple Syrup and Fernet-Branca to a shaker and shake until slightly diluted (about 10 to 15 seconds).
4. Pour into a fresh glass, serve neat and garnish with a grilled lemon wheel. Enjoy!

Grilled Peach Sour Cocktail

Servings: 2
Cooking Time: 15 Minutes

Ingredients:
- 2 peach, sliced
- 2 Tablespoon sugar
- 1 1/2 Ounce Smoked Simple Syrup
- 4 Ounce bourbon
- 6 Dash Bitters Lab Apricot Vanilla Bitters
- 2 Sprig fresh thyme, for garnish

Directions:
1. Supply your smoker with wood pellets and follow the start-up procedure. Preheat the grill, with the lid closed, to 325° F.
2. Toss peach slices with granulated sugar and place directly on grill grate. Cook for 20 minutes or until grill marks form. Remove from grill and let cool. Grill: 325 °F
3. Place peaches and Traeger Smoked Simple Syrup into tin and muddle. Peaches should form about an ounce of juice during the muddling. Once completed, add remaining ingredients and shake.
4. Pour contents into glass over fresh ice and garnish with fresh thyme. Enjoy!

Zombie Cocktail Recipe

Servings: 2
Cooking Time: 45 Minutes

Ingredients:
- fresh squeezed orange juice
- pineapple juice
- 2 Ounce light rum
- 2 Ounce dark rum
- 2 Ounce lime juice
- 1 Ounce Smoked Simple Syrup
- 6 Ounce smoked orange and pineapple juice
- 2 grilled orange peel, for garnish
- 2 grilled pineapple chunks, for garnish

Directions:
1. Supply your smoker with wood pellets and follow the start-up procedure. Preheat the grill, with the lid closed, to 180° F.
2. Smoked Orange and Pineapple Juice: Pour equal parts fresh squeezed orange juice and pineapple juice into a shallow sheet pan and smoke for 45 minutes. Remove and let cool. Measure out 3 ounces of juice and reserve any remaining juice in the refrigerator for future use. Grill: 180 °F
3. Add dark and light rums, 3 ounces smoked orange and pineapple juice, lime juice and Traeger Smoked Simple Syrup to a mixing glass.
4. Add ice, shake and strain over clean ice into a Tiki glass.
5. Garnish with a grilled orange peel and grilled pineapple. Enjoy!

Smoked Hot Buttered Rum

Servings: 4
Cooking Time: 30 Minutes

Ingredients:
- 2 Cup water
- 1/4 Cup brown sugar
- 1/2 Stick butter, melted
- 1 Teaspoon ground cinnamon
- 1/4 Teaspoon ground nutmeg
- ground cloves
- salt
- 6 Ounce Rum

Directions:
1. Supply your smoker with wood pellets and follow the start-up procedure. Preheat the grill, with the lid closed, to 180° F.
2. In a shallow baking dish, combine 2 cups water with all ingredients except for the rum and place directly on the grill grate. Smoke for 30 minutes. Grill: 180 °F
3. Remove from the grill and pour into the pitcher of a blender. Process until somewhat frothy.
4. Pour 1.5 ounces of rum each into 4 glasses. Split hot butter mixture evenly between the four glasses.
5. Garnish with a cinnamon stick and freshly grated nutmeg. Enjoy!

Strawberry Mule Cocktail

Servings: 2
Cooking Time: 15 Minutes

Ingredients:
- 8 grilled strawberries, plus more for serving
- 3 Ounce vodka
- 1 Ounce Smoked Simple Syrup
- 1 Ounce lemon juice
- 6 Ounce ginger beer
- fresh mint leaves

Directions:
1. Supply your smoker with wood pellets and follow the start-up procedure. Preheat the grill, with the lid closed, to 400° F.
2. Place strawberries directly on the grill grate and cook 15 minutes or until grill marks appear. Grill: 400 °F
3. For the cocktail: Add vodka, grilled strawberries, Traeger Smoked Simple Syrup and lemon juice to a shaker. Shake vigorously.
4. Double strain into a fresh glass or copper mug with crushed ice.
5. Top with ginger beer and garnish with extra grilled strawberries and fresh mint. Enjoy!

Garden Gimlet Cocktail

Servings: 2
Cooking Time: 45 Minutes

Ingredients:

- 2 Cup honey
- 4 lemons, zested
- 4 Sprig rosemary, plus more for garnish
- 1/2 Cup water
- 4 Slices cucumber
- 1 1/2 Ounce lime juice
- 3 Ounce vodka

Directions:

1. Supply your smoker with wood pellets and follow the start-up procedure. Preheat the grill, with the lid closed, to 180° F.
2. To make smoked lemon and rosemary honey syrup, thin 1 cup honey by adding 1/4 cup water to a shallow pan. Add lemon zest and 2 sprigs rosemary.
3. Place the pan directly on the grill grate and smoke 45 minutes to an hour. Remove from heat, strain and cool. Grill: 180 °F
4. In a cocktail shaker, muddle the cucumbers and 1oz of the smoked lemon and rosemary honey syrup.
5. After muddling, add lime juice, vodka, and ice. Shake and double strain into a coup glass.
6. Garnish with a sprig of rosemary. Enjoy!

Grilled Hawaiian Sour

Servings: 2
Cooking Time: 15 Minutes

Ingredients:

- 2 Whole pineapple, trimmed and sliced
- 1/2 Cup palm sugar
- 3 Ounce bourbon
- 2 Ounce grilled pineapple juice
- 2 Ounce Smoked Simple Syrup
- 10 Ounce lemon juice
- 2 grilled pineapple chunk, for garnish
- 2 pineapple leaf, for garnish

Directions:

1. Supply your smoker with wood pellets and follow the start-up procedure. Preheat the grill, with the lid closed, to 350° F.
2. For the Grilled Pineapple Juice: Dust pineapple slices with palm sugar. Place directly on the grill grate and cook for 8 minutes per side. Grill: 350 °F
3. Remove from grill and let cool. Reserve a few pieces for garnish. Run remaining pineapple pieces through centrifugal juicer to extract juice.
4. To Make the Drink: Add bourbon, grilled pineapple juice, simple syrup and lemon juice to a cocktail strainer with ice. Shake vigorously. Double strain into a chilled coupe glass. Garnish with grilled pineapple chunk and pineapple leaf. Enjoy!

Smoked Pomegranate Lemonade Cocktail

Servings: 2
Cooking Time: 45 Minutes

Ingredients:

- 32 Ounce POM Juice
- 2 Cup pomegranate seeds
- 3 Ounce vodka
- 8 Ounce lemonade
- lemon wheel, for garnish
- fresh mint, for garnish

Directions:

1. Supply your smoker with wood pellets and follow the start-up procedure. Preheat the grill, with the lid closed, to 225° F.
2. For the Smoked Pomegranate Ice Cubes: Pour one small container of POM juice and 1 cup of pomegranate seeds into a shallow sheet pan. Smoke on the Traeger for 45 minutes. Pull off grill and let sit until cooled. Grill: 180 °F
3. Pour smoked POM juice into ice molds of your choice and put into freezer.
4. When ready to serve, place the frozen pomegranate cubes into a mason jar. Pour vodka and lemonade over the ice cubes.
5. Garnish with a lemon wheel and fresh mint. Enjoy!

Smoked Mulled Wine

Servings: 10
Cooking Time: 60 Minutes

Ingredients:
- 2 Bottle red wine
- 1/2 Cup whiskey
- 1/2 Cup white rum
- 1/2 Cup honey
- 1 cinnamon stick
- 2 pods star anise
- 4 whole cloves
- 1 (3 in) orange peel

Directions:
1. Supply your smoker with wood pellets and follow the start-up procedure. Preheat the grill, with the lid closed, to 180° F.
2. In a shallow baking dish, combine wine, whiskey, rum, honey, cinnamon stick, star anise, cloves and orange peel. Stir well until combined.
3. Place the dish directly on the grill grate and smoke for one hour until the mixture is warm. Grill: 180 °F
4. Remove from grill and ladle into mugs leaving the mulling spices behind. Garnish with fresh cinnamon sticks, anise, orange zest or a combination. Enjoy!

Batter Up Cocktail

Servings: 2
Cooking Time: 60 Minutes

Ingredients:
- 2 whole nutmeg
- 4 Ounce Michter's Bourbon
- 3 Teaspoon pumpkin puree
- 1 Ounce Smoked Simple Syrup
- 2 Large egg

Directions:
1. Supply your smoker with wood pellets and follow the start-up procedure. Preheat the grill, with the lid closed, to 180° F.
2. Place whole nutmeg on a sheet tray and place in the grill. Smoke 1 hour. Remove from grill and let cool. Grill: 180 °F

3. Add everything to a shaker and shake without ice. Add ice, then shake and strain into a chilled highball glass.
4. Garnish with grated, smoked nutmeg. Enjoy!

Smoked Ice Mojito Slurpee

Servings: 2
Cooking Time: 30 Minutes

Ingredients:
- water
- 1 Cup white rum
- 1/2 Cup lime juice
- 1/4 Cup Smoked Simple Syrup
- 12 Whole fresh mint leaves
- 4 Sprig mint
- 4 Whole lime wedge, for garnish

Directions:
1. Supply your smoker with wood pellets and follow the start-up procedure. Preheat the grill, with the lid closed, to 180° F.
2. For optimal flavor, use Super Smoke if available. Grill: 180 °F
3. Remove water from grill and pour smoked water into ice cube trays. Place in freezer until frozen.
4. Add rum, lime juice, Traeger Smoked Simple Syrup, mint and smoked ice to a blender.
5. Blend until a slushy consistency and pour into glasses.
6. Garnish with a mint sprig and lime wedge. Enjoy!

Grilled Frozen Strawberry Lemonade

Servings: 4
Cooking Time: 15 Minutes

Ingredients:
- 1 Pound fresh strawberries
- 1/2 Cup turbinado sugar
- 8 lemon, halved
- 1/4 Cup Cointreau
- 1/4 Cup simple syrup
- 2 Cup ice
- 1 Cup Titos Vodka

Directions:

1. Supply your smoker with wood pellets and follow the start-up procedure. Preheat the grill, with the lid closed, to High heat.
2. Dip the lemon halves in turbinado sugar and place directly on the grill grate. Toss the strawberries with remaining sugar and place next to the lemons.
3. Cook until grill marks develop on both, about 15 min for lemons and 10 min for strawberries.
4. Remove from heat and let cool.
5. Juice grilled lemons straining out any seeds or pulp. Pour into a blender pitcher.
6. Remove stems from grilled strawberries and place in blender pitcher with lemon juice. Add simple syrup, vodka, cointreau, and 2 cups of ice.
7. Puree until smooth and transfer to 4-6 glasses. Garnish with grilled strawberries and grilled lemon slices if desired. Enjoy!

Smoked Sangria

Servings: 6
Cooking Time: 45 Minutes

Ingredients:
- 1 (750 ml) medium-bodied red wine
- 1/4 Cup Grand Marnier
- 1/4 Cup Smoked Simple Syrup
- 1 Cup fresh cranberries
- 1 Whole apple, sliced
- 2 Whole limes, sliced
- 4 cinnamon stick
- soda water

Directions:
1. Supply your smoker with wood pellets and follow the start-up procedure. Preheat the grill, with the lid closed, to 180° F.
2. In a shallow dish, combine red wine, Grand Marnier, Traeger Smoked Simple Syrup and cranberries, and place directly on the grill grate.
3. Smoke for 30 to 45 minutes or until the liquid picks up desired amount of smoke. Remove from grill and place in the fridge to cool. Grill: 180 °F
4. When the mixture has cooled, place in a large pitcher. Add sliced apples, limes, cinnamon sticks and ice to pitcher.
5. Top with soda water, if desired. Enjoy!

Smoked Pumpkin Spice Latte

Servings: 4
Cooking Time: 45 Minutes

Ingredients:
- 1 Small sugar pumpkin
- olive oil
- 1 Can sweetened condensed milk
- 1 Cup whole milk
- 2 Tablespoon Smoked Simple Syrup
- 1 Teaspoon pumpkin pie spice
- pinch of salt
- cinnamon
- whipped cream
- shaved nutmeg
- 8 Ounce smoked cold brew coffee

Directions:
1. Supply your smoker with wood pellets and follow the start-up procedure. Preheat the grill, with the lid closed, to 325° F.
2. Cut the sugar pumpkin in half, scoop out the seeds and discard. Place the pumpkin halves cut side up on a baking sheet and brush lightly with olive oil.
3. Place the sheet tray directly on the grill grate and cook 45 minutes or until the flesh is tender. Remove from heat and place on the counter to cool. Grill: 325 °F
4. When the pumpkin is cool enough to handle, scoop out the flesh and mash until smooth.
5. Place 3 Tbsp of the pumpkin puree in a separate bowl and reserve the remaining for another use.
6. Add the sweetened condensed milk, whole milk, Traeger Smoked Simple Syrup, pumpkin pie seasoning and salt to the pumpkin puree. Whisk to combine.
7. Pour the cold brew over ice, add desired amount of pumpkin spice creamer and top with whipped cream, cinnamon, and shaved nutmeg if desired. Enjoy!

Fig Slider Cocktail

Servings: 2
Cooking Time: 15 Minutes

Ingredients:
- 2 peach, halved
- 4 oranges
- honey
- sugar
- 2 Teaspoon orange fig spread
- 1 Ounce fresh lemon juice
- 4 Ounce bourbon
- 3 Ounce honey glazed grilled orange juice

Directions:
1. Supply your smoker with wood pellets and follow the start-up procedure. Preheat the grill, with the lid closed, to 325° F.
2. Pit the peach and cut in half. Cut one of the oranges in half. Glaze the peach and orange cut sides with honey and set directly on the grill grate until the honey caramelizes and fruit has grill marks. Grill: 325 °F
3. Cut the second orange into wheels and coat with granulated sugar on both sides. Place directly on the grill grate and cook 15 minutes each side or until grill marks form. Grill: 325 °F
4. In a mixing tin, add grilled peaches, bourbon, orange fig spread, fresh lemon juice and honey glazed orange juice.
5. Shake vigorously to blend the juices and fig spread. Strain over clean ice. Garnish with grilled orange wheel. Enjoy!

Bacon Old-fashioned Cocktail

Servings: 2
Cooking Time: 20 Minutes

Ingredients:
- 16 Slices bacon
- 1/2 Cup warm water (110°F to 115°F)
- 1500 mL bourbon
- 1/2 Fluid Ounce maple syrup
- 4 Dash Angostura bitters
- 2 fresh orange peel

Directions:
1. Smoke bacon prior to making Old Fashioned using this recipe for Applewood Smoked Bacon.
2. To Make Bacon: Supply your smoker with wood pellets and follow the start-up procedure. Preheat the grill, with the lid closed, to 325° F.
3. Place bacon in a single layer on a cooling rack that fits inside a baking sheet pan. Cook in Traeger for 15-20 minutes or until bacon is browned and crispy. Reserve bacon for later. Let the fat cool slightly; you'll use the fat to infuse the bourbon. Grill: 325 °F
4. Combine 1/4 cup of warm (not hot) liquid bacon fat with the entire contents of a 750ml bottle of bourbon in a glass or heavy plastic container.
5. Use a fork to stir well. Let it sit on the counter for a few hours, stirring every so often.
6. After about four hours, put bourbon fat mixture into the freezer. After about an hour, the fat will congeal and you can simply scoop it out with a spoon. You can fine-strain the mixture through a sieve to remove all fat if desired.
7. Combine ingredients with ice and stir until cold. Strain over fresh ice in an Old Fashioned glass and garnish with reserved bacon and orange peel. Enjoy!

Smoked Salted Caramel White Russian

Servings: 4
Cooking Time: 20 Minutes

Ingredients:
- 16 Ounce half-and-half
- salted caramel sauce
- 6 Ounce vodka
- 6 Ounce Kahlúa

Directions:
1. Supply your smoker with wood pellets and follow the start-up procedure. Preheat the grill, with the lid closed, to 180° F.
2. Pour the half-and-half in a shallow baking dish and place directly on the grill grate. In another shallow baking dish, pour 2 to 3 cups of water and place on the grill next to the half-and-half.

3. Smoke both the half-and-half and water for 20 minutes. Remove from the grill and let cool. Grill: 180 °F
4. Place the half-and-half in the fridge until ready to use. Pour the smoked water into ice cube trays and transfer to the freezer until completely frozen.
5. Separate the smoked ice cubes into four glasses. Drizzle the salted caramel sauce around the inside of the glass.
6. Pour 1-1/2 ounce vodka and 1-1/2 ounce Kahlúa into each of the glasses and top with the smoked half-and-half. Enjoy!

Smoky Scotch & Ginger Cocktail

Servings: 2
Cooking Time: 60 Minutes

Ingredients:
- 1 Ounce ginger syrup
- 1/2 Ounce brandied cherry juice
- 1/2 Ounce agave nectar
- 4 Ounce scotch
- 1 1/2 Ounce lemon juice
- 2 Slices grilled lemon, for garnish
- 2 cherry, for garnish

Directions:
1. Supply your smoker with wood pellets and follow the start-up procedure. Preheat the grill, with the lid closed, to 180° F.
2. For the smoked ginger cherry syrup: Place ginger syrup, cherry juice and agave nectar in a shallow dish and place the dish directly on the grill grate.
3. Smoke for 60 minutes, or until the mixture has picked up the smoke flavor. Remove from grill and allow to cool for 30 minutes. Grill: 180 °F
4. Place smoked ginger cherry syrup, scotch and lemon juice into a shaker tin and shake with ice. Strain into a glass over fresh ice and garnish with a grilled lemon wheel and cherry. Enjoy!

A Smoking Classic Cocktail

Servings: 2
Cooking Time: 60 Minutes

Ingredients:
- 2 Bottle Angostura orange bitters
- 10 sugar cubes
- 8 Ounce Champagne
- lemon twist

Directions:
1. Supply your smoker with wood pellets and follow the start-up procedure. Preheat the grill, with the lid closed, to 180° F.
2. For the Smoked Orange Bitters: In a small skillet, combine 1 bottle of Angostura orange bitters with a splash of water and 4 sugar cubes.
3. Place skillet on the grill grate and smoke for 60 minutes. Cool the smoked bitters and put back into the bottle. Grill: 180 °F
4. Add a sugar cube to each Champagne flute and soak the sugar cubes with the smoked bitters.
5. Add champagne and a lemon twist in a flute glass. Enjoy!

Cran-apple Tequila Punch With Smoked Oranges

Servings: 2
Cooking Time: 15 Minutes

Ingredients:
- 6 Cup apple juice, chilled
- 6 Cup light cranberry cocktail
- 1 Cup cranberries, fresh or thawed
- 3 Large oranges, halved
- 1 Cup sugar, for rimming glasses
- 2 Tablespoon lemon juice
- 2 Cup reposado tequila
- 1 Cup orange-flavored liqueur, such as Grand Marnier or Cointreau
- 2 Bottle sparkling wine (such as prosecco) or sparkling water

Directions:
1. Combine 1 cup each of the apple and cranberry juices, then pour into ice cube trays. If the cube molds are big enough, place a few cranberries into each cube. Freeze for 6 hours to overnight.

2. Supply your smoker with wood pellets and follow the start-up procedure. Preheat the grill, with the lid closed, to 180° F.

3. Place the orange halves cut-side down on the grill and smoke for 15 minutes. Remove from the grill and juice oranges. Reserve smoked orange juice. Grill: 180 °F

4. When ready to serve, place the sugar on a flat plate. Pour the lemon juice into a bowl that will fit the rim of each glass.

5. Carefully dip the rim of each glass in the lemon juice, then dip in the sugar to create a 1/8" sugar rim. Turn the glass right-side up and allow to dry for a few minutes before using.

6. Just before serving, mix the remaining apple juice, cranberry cocktail and smoked orange juice with the tequila, orange liqueur, and sparkling wine in a large bowl or pitcher. Taste, adding more of any ingredient to meet your preference.

7. When ready to serve, place a few ice cubes in each glass, then pour a cup of the punch over the top. Alternatively, place all of the ice cubes in the punch bowl and allow guests to help themselves. Enjoy!

Smoked Cold Brew Coffee

Servings: 8
Cooking Time: 120 Minutes

Ingredients:
- 12 Ounce coarse ground coffee
- heavy cream or milk
- sugar

Directions:
1. Place half the coffee grounds in a plastic container and slowly pour 3-1/2 cups water over the top of the grounds. Add remaining grounds and pour another 3-1/2 cups water over the top in a circular motion.

2. Press the grounds down into the water using the back of a spoon. Cover and transfer to the refrigerator and let sit for 18 to 24 hours.

3. Remove from refrigerator and strain into a clean container through a fine mesh strainer or double layer of cheese cloth.

4. Supply your smoker with wood pellets and follow the start-up procedure. Preheat the grill, with the lid closed, to 180° F.

5. Pour cold brew into a shallow baking dish and place directly on the grill grate. Smoke for 1 to 2 hours depending on desired level of smoke. Grill: 180 °F

6. Remove from grill and place over an ice bath to cool. Drink as is over ice, with cream or sugar or use in your favorite coffee recipes. Enjoy!

Smoked Hibiscus Sparkler

Servings: 4
Cooking Time: 30 Minutes

Ingredients:
- 1/2 Cup sugar
- 2 Tablespoon dried hibiscus flowers
- 1 Bottle sparkling wine
- crystallized ginger, for garnish

Directions:
1. Supply your smoker with wood pellets and follow the start-up procedure. Preheat the grill, with the lid closed, to 180° F.

2. Place water in a shallow baking dish and place directly on the grill grate. Smoke the water for 30 minutes or until desired smoke flavor is achieved. Grill: 180 °F

3. Pour water into a small saucepan and add sugar and hibiscus flowers. Bring to a simmer over medium heat and cook until sugar is dissolved.

4. Strain out the hibiscus flowers and transfer your simple syrup to a small container and refrigerate until chilled.

5. Pour 1/2 ounce smoked hibiscus simple syrup in the bottom of a champagne glass and top with sparkling wine.

6. Drop in a few pieces of crystallized ginger to garnish. Enjoy!

Smoked Jacobsen Salt Margarita

Servings: 2
Cooking Time: 1 Day

Ingredients:
- kosher sea salt
- 3 Cup Jacobsen Co. Honey
- 6 Ounce tequila
- 4 Ounce fresh squeezed lime juice
- 1/2 Cup Jacobsen Salt Co. Cherrywood Smoked Salt or smoked kosher salt
- 2 Ounce simple syrup
- 2 Teaspoon orange liqueur

Directions:
1. If making your own smoked salt, take kosher sea salt (however much you want to smoke) and spread it out on a tray.
2. Supply your smoker with wood pellets and follow the start-up procedure. Preheat the grill, with the lid closed, to 165° F.
3. Place tray of salt directly on the grill grate and smoke for about 24 hours, stirring the salt every 8 hours. Once it has smoked for 24 hours, take off grill and use in all your favorite dishes. Note: If you want to skip the long smoke session, use Jacobsen Salt Co. Cherrywood Smoked Salt. Grill: 165 °F
4. Simple Syrup: Put the honey and 1 cup water in a small saucepan. Cook over low heat, stirring, for about 20 min.
5. Fill a cocktail shaker with ice. Add tequila, lime juice, simple syrup and orange liqueur. Cover and shake until mixed and chilled, about 30 seconds.
6. Place smoked salt on a plate. Press the rim of a chilled rocks glass into the salt to rim the edge. Strain margarita into the glass. Enjoy!

Smoked Barnburner Cocktail

Servings: 2
Cooking Time: 45 Minutes

Ingredients:
- 16 Ounce fresh raspberries
- 1/2 Cup Smoked Simple Syrup
- 1 1/2 Ounce smoked raspberry syrup
- 3 Ounce reposado tequila
- 1 Ounce lime juice
- 1 Ounce lemon juice
- 2 grilled lime wheel, for garnish

Directions:
1. Supply your smoker with wood pellets and follow the start-up procedure. Preheat the grill, with the lid closed, to 180° F.
2. For Smoked Raspberry Syrup: Place fresh raspberries on a grill mat and smoke for 30 minutes. After the raspberries have been smoked, reserve a few for garnish and place the remainder into a shallow sheet pan with Traeger Smoked Simple Syrup. Grill: 180 °F
3. Place sheet pan on the grill grate and smoke for 45 minutes. Remove from grill and let cool. Strain through a fine mesh sieve discarding solids. Transfer the syrup to the refrigerator until ready to use. Makes about 1/2 cup of smoked raspberry syrup. Grill: 180 °F
4. For cocktail: Add 3/4 ounce smoked raspberry syrup, tequila, lime juice and lemon juice with ice into a mixing glass. Shake and pour over clean ice. Garnish with smoked raspberries and a grilled lime wheel. Enjoy!

Smoked Pineapple Hotel Nacional Cocktail

Servings: 2
Cooking Time: 20 Minutes

Ingredients:
- 2 pineapple
- 1/2 Cup water
- 1/2 Cup sugar
- 3 Fluid Ounce white rum
- 1 1/2 Fluid Ounce lime juice
- 1 1/2 Fluid Ounce Pineapple Syrup
- 1 Fluid Ounce apricot brandy
- 2 Dash Angostura bitters

Directions:
1. For the Syrup: Supply your smoker with wood pellets and follow the start-up procedure. Preheat the grill, with the lid closed, to 180° F.
2. Trim both ends of the pineapple, discard the ends. Cut the pineapple into slices about 3/4" thick. Don't

worry about the skin, it doesn't hurt to leave it on. Place the pineapple slices on the grill and smoke for about 15 minutes on each sideTrim both ends of the pineapple and discard the ends. Cut the pineapple into slices about 3/4 inch thick. Don't worry about the skin, it doesn't hurt to leave it on. Place the pineapple slices on the grill and smoke for about 15 minutes per side. Grill: 180 °F
3. While the pineapple is smoking, combine 1/4 cup water and sugar in a saucepan over low heat, stirring constantly, until sugar is dissolved. Pour syrup into a large bowl and set aside.
4. When the pineapple is done cooking, cut each slice into eight or so wedges and add the wedges to the bowl with the simple syrup, tossing to coat and cover.
5. Leave the mixture to macerate for at least 4 hours (or up to 24) in the refrigerator, stirring from time to time.
6. Strain the syrup into a clean bowl through a fine-mesh strainer and press on the pineapple with a ladle to extract as much liquid as possible. You can bottle and refrigerate the syrup for up to 4 days.
7. To make the cocktail: Combine the rum, lime juice, pineapple syrup, apricot brandy, and bitters in a cocktail shaker or mixing glass. Fill with ice cubes and shake until cold.
8. Strain into a chilled cocktail glass. Garnish with a lime wheel and serve. Enjoy!

Dublin Delight Cocktail

Servings: 2
Cooking Time: 20 Minutes
Ingredients:
- 2 orange, sliced
- 3 Fluid Ounce Teeling Whiskey
- 1 1/2 Fluid Ounce Smoked Simple Syrup
- 6 Dash aromatic bitters
- 6 Fluid Ounce Guinness beer
- 2 Amarena cherry, for garnish

Directions:
1. Supply your smoker with wood pellets and follow the start-up procedure. Preheat the grill, with the lid closed, to 450° F.
2. Place orange slices directly on the grill grate and cook 20 to 25 minutes. Remove from grill and let cool. Grill: 450 °F
3. In a mixing glass, add whiskey, Traeger Smoked Simple Syrup and bitters. Add ice and shake. Pour over a beer glass filled with ice and top off with cold Guinness.
4. Garnish with a grilled orange slice and Amarena cherry. Enjoy!

Grilled Peach Mint Julep

Servings: 2
Cooking Time: 45 Minutes
Ingredients:
- 2 Whole peach
- 4 Ounce whiskey
- 2 Cup sugar
- 4 Tablespoon pink peppercorns
- 20 Whole fresh mint leaves, plus more for garnish
- 2 lime wedge, for garnish
- 4 Ounce bourbon

Directions:
1. For the Grilled Whiskey Peaches: cut peach into slices, then soak peach slices in whiskey in the refrigerator for 4 to 6 hours.
2. For the Pink Peppercorn Simple Syrup: In a shallow pan, combine sugar, 1 cup water and pink peppercorns.
3. Supply your smoker with wood pellets and follow the start-up procedure. Preheat the grill, with the lid closed, to 180° F.
4. Cook syrup down on the grill for 30 minutes, or until desired smoke flavor has been reached. Remove from the grill. Grill: 180 °F
5. Increase Traeger temperature to 350°F and preheat. Place the whiskey peach slices directly on the grill grate and cook 10 to 12 minutes or until peaches soften and get grill marks. Grill: 350 °F
6. To make the Julep: Muddle 1/2 ounce Pink Peppercorn Simple Syrup with 10 fresh mint leaves and 4 slices of grilled whiskey peaches.
7. Add crushed ice over the rim of the glass. Pour bourbon over the crushed ice and stir. Garnish with 1 large sprig of mint and fresh lime. Enjoy!

Smoked Irish Coffee

Servings: 2
Cooking Time: 15 Minutes

Ingredients:
- 10 Ounce hot coffee
- 1/2 Cup heavy cream
- 1 Tablespoon sugar
- 2 Ounce Irish whiskey
- freshly grated nutmeg, for garnish (optional)

Directions:
1. Supply your smoker with wood pellets and follow the start-up procedure. Preheat the grill, with the lid closed, to 180° F.
2. Place the coffee and cream in separate shallow baking dishes and place both directly on the grill grate. Smoke for 10 to 15 minutes until the liquids pick up a slight smoke flavor. Grill: 180 °F
3. Remove from the grill and cool the cream. When the cream is cool, add sugar and whip in a stand mixer or by hand to soft peaks.
4. Pour the hot coffee into two mugs then add 2 ounces of whiskey to each.
5. Top with smoked whipped cream and finish with freshly grated nutmeg, if desired. Enjoy!

Smoked Texas Ranch Water

Servings: 4
Cooking Time: 60 Minutes

Ingredients:
- 3 Whole limes
- 1 Tablespoon Blackened Saskatchewan Rub
- 12 Ounce blanco tequila
- 24 Ounce Topo Chico or other sparkling mineral water
- 8 Slices jalapeño, optional

Directions:
1. Supply your smoker with wood pellets and follow the start-up procedure. Preheat the grill, with the lid closed, to 225° F.
2. Cut two of the limes in half and sprinkle with Traeger Blackened Saskatchewan Rub. Place the four lime halves on the edge of the grill grate and smoke for 1 hour. Remove from grill and set aside to cool. Grill: 225 °F
3. Pour some of the rub onto a small plate. Cut the third lime into 1/4 wedges and use the lime to rub the rim of 4 cocktail glasses, turn the glasses upside down, and into the rub to salt the rim.
4. Place several ice cubes into your rimmed glasses and pour 3 ounces tequila, 6 ounces Topo Chico, squeeze the juice of one smoked lime (discard after squeezing), and add one fresh lime wedge to each. If using the jalapeño, add one or two slices to each glass (muddle if desired).
5. Stir to combine and enjoy!

Traeger Old Fashioned

Servings: 2
Cooking Time: 60 Minutes

Ingredients:
- 2 orange
- 2 Cup cherries
- 3 Ounce bourbon
- 1 Ounce Smoked Simple Syrup
- 8 Dash Bitters Lab Apricot Vanilla Bitters

Directions:
1. Supply your smoker with wood pellets and follow the start-up procedure. Preheat the grill, with the lid closed, to 180° F.
2. While Traeger preheats, slice whole orange into wheels.
3. Place cherries on a small sheet pan and place in the Traeger. Place orange slices directly on the grill grate.
4. Smoke cherries for 1 hour and oranges for 25 minutes, depending on taste, before removing from the grill. Let oranges and cherries cool. Grill: 180 °F
5. Pour bourbon into glass, followed by Traeger Smoked Simple Syrup and bitters. Add ice and stir for 45 seconds or until drink is well-diluted.
6. Strain contents into new glass over fresh ice. Skewer orange wheel and add cherry for garnish. Enjoy!

Traeger Boulevardier Cocktail

Servings: 2
Cooking Time: 60 Minutes

Ingredients:
- 4 oranges
- 1/2 Cup honey
- 1500 mL rye whiskey
- 1 1/2 Ounce Campari
- 1 1/2 Ounce sweet vermouth
- 2 Tablespoon granulated sugar
- 3 Ounce grilled orange infused rye

Directions:
1. Supply your smoker with wood pellets and follow the start-up procedure. Preheat the grill, with the lid closed, to 350° F.
2. Slice 2 oranges in half and coat cut side with honey. Peel remaining orange and place peels on the grill. Cook 20 to 25 minutes. Grill: 350 °F
3. Remove from grill and let cool. Place orange halves cut side down directly on the grill grate and cook 20 to 30 minutes or until dark grill marks appear. Remove orange halves and allow to cool. Grill: 350 °F
4. Place orange halves into a bottle of rye whiskey and let steep for 10 to 12 hours. The longer they steep, the sweeter and more pronounced the orange flavor will be.
5. Add all ingredients into a mixing glass and stir until diluted. Strain into a fresh coupe glass and serve neat.
6. Garnish with grilled orange peel. Enjoy!

Grilled Rabbit Tail Cocktail

Servings: 2
Cooking Time: 25 Minutes

Ingredients:
- 1 1/2 Ounce lemon juice
- 4 Ounce Apple Brandy
- 1 Ounce orange juice
- 1 Ounce Smoked Simple Syrup

Directions:
1. Supply your smoker with wood pellets and follow the start-up procedure. Preheat the grill, with the lid closed, to 350° F.
2. Place lemon halves directly on the grill grate and cook for 20-25 minutes or until grill marks appear. Remove from grill and let cool. Once cool enough to handle, juice the lemons then chill and reserve the juice. Grill: 350 °F
3. Using the proportions listed above and considering the size and consumption rate of your tailgate crew or party, mix all the above ingredients in a large thermos and top with a bit of ice.
4. Using 6-8 oz glasses or cups, guests can serve themselves from the thermos and garnish each drink with a grilled apple slice. Enjoy!

Traeger Paloma Cocktail

Servings: 2
Cooking Time: 25 Minutes

Ingredients:
- 4 grapefruit, halved
- Smoked Simple Syrup
- 10 Stick cinnamon
- 3 Ounce reposado tequila
- 1 Ounce lime juice
- 1 Ounce Smoked Simple Syrup
- grilled lime, for garnish
- cinnamon stick, for garnish

Directions:
1. Supply your smoker with wood pellets and follow the start-up procedure. Preheat the grill, with the lid closed, to 350° F.
2. Grilled Grapefruit Juice: Cut 2 grapefruits in half. Place a cinnamon stick in each grapefruit half and glaze with Traeger Smoked Simple Syrup. Place on grill grate and cook for 20 minutes or until edges start to burn and it acquires grill marks. Remove from heat and let cool. Grill: 350 °F
3. After grapefruits have cooled, squeeze and strain juice. It should yield 10 to 12 ounces of juice.
4. In a mixing glass, add tequila, lime juice, Traeger Smoked Simple Syrup and 2 ounces of the grilled grapefruit juice.
5. Add ice and shake. Strain over ice in an old fashioned glass.
6. Add a grilled lime slice and cinnamon stick to garnish. Enjoy!

Smoked Grape Lime Rickey

Servings: 4
Cooking Time: 45 Minutes

Ingredients:
- 1/2 Pound red grapes
- 1/2 Cup plus 1 tablespoon sugar
- 1/2 Cup water
- 1 limes, sliced
- 2 limes, halved
- 1 Tablespoon sugar
- 1 L lemon lime soda

Directions:
1. Supply your smoker with wood pellets and follow the start-up procedure. Preheat the grill, with the lid closed, to 180° F.
2. Rinse grapes well and place in a shallow baking dish. Combine 1/2 cup sugar and water and stir until sugar dissolves. Pour over grapes.
3. Place the baking dish directly on the grill grate and smoke for 30 to 40 minutes until grapes are tender. Grill: 180 °F
4. Remove from the grill and pour entire contents of the baking dish in a blender. Puree on high until smooth then pass the mixture through a fine mesh strainer.
5. Increase Traeger temperature to 350°F. Grill: 350 °F
6. Toss the lime slices and lime halves with 1 tablespoon sugar and place directly on the grill grate. Cook for 15 to 20 minutes or until grill marks develop. Remove from grill and set slices aside. When cool enough to handle, juice grilled lime halves. Grill: 350 °F
7. To build the drink, fill a pint glass with ice. Pour in 1-1/2 ounce grilled lime juice, 1-1/2 ounce smoked grape syrup and top off with soda. Garnish with grilled lime slice. Enjoy!

Honey Glazed Grapefruit Shandy Cocktail

Servings: 2
Cooking Time: 20 Minutes

Ingredients:
- 4 grapefruits
- 4 Tablespoon honey
- granulated sugar
- 2 Ounce bourbon
- 1 Ounce Smoked Simple Syrup
- 4 Ounce honey glazed grilled grapefruit, juiced
- 2 Bottle Ballast Point Grapefruit Sculpin

Directions:
1. Supply your smoker with wood pellets and follow the start-up procedure. Preheat the grill, with the lid closed, to 375° F.
2. For the honey glazed grapefruit: Slice one grapefruit in half and coat with 2 tablespoons honey.
3. Take the other grapefruit and slice into wheels. Toss the wheels in granulated sugar until well coated.
4. Place the grapefruit halves and wheels directly on the grill grate, cut side down, and cook for 20 to 30 minutes. Remove from grill and set the wheels aside. Grill: 375 °F
5. Squeeze the grapefruit halves into a measuring cup. It should yield about 2 oz juice.
6. Pour the grapefruit juice into a shaker and add bourbon and Traeger Smoked Simple Syrup then top with ice. Shake for 10-15 seconds.
7. Strain into glass, add ice and fill with beer. Garnish with the grilled grapefruit wheel. Enjoy!

Smoked Plum And Thyme Fizz Cocktail

Servings: 2
Cooking Time: 60 Minutes

Ingredients:
- 6 fresh plums
- 4 Fluid Ounce vodka
- 1 1/2 Fluid Ounce fresh lemon juice
- 2 Ounce smoked plum and thyme simple syrup
- 4 Fluid Ounce club soda
- 2 Slices smoked plum, for garnish
- 2 Sprig fresh thyme, for garnish
- 8 Sprig thyme
- 2 Cup Smoked Simple Syrup

Directions:

1. Supply your smoker with wood pellets and follow the start-up procedure. Preheat the grill, with the lid closed, to 180° F.
2. Cut plums in half and remove the pit. Place the plum halves directly on the grill grate and smoke for 25 minutes. Grill: 180 °F
3. For the Plum and Thyme Simple Syrup: After 25 minutes, remove plums from the grill and cut into quarters. Add plums and thyme sprigs to 1 cup of Traeger Smoked Simple Syrup. Smoke the mixture for 45 minutes. Remove from grill, strain and let cool. Grill: 180 °F
4. Add vodka, fresh lemon juice and smoked plum and thyme simple syrup to a mixing glass.
5. Add ice and shake. Strain over clean ice, top off with club soda and garnish with a piece of thyme and slice of smoked plum. Enjoy!

Grilled Peach Smash Cocktail

Servings: 2
Cooking Time: 10 Minutes

Ingredients:
- 2 peach, sliced and grilled
- 10 fresh mint leaves
- 1 1/2 Ounce Smoked Simple Syrup
- 4 Ounce bourbon
- 2 mint sprig, for garnish

Directions:
1. Supply your smoker with wood pellets and follow the start-up procedure. Preheat the grill, with the lid closed, to 375° F.
2. Cut the peach into 6 slices and brush with Traeger Smoked Simple Syrup. Place directly on the grill grate and cook 10 to 12 minutes or until peaches soften and get grill marks. Grill: 375 °F
3. In a mixing glass, add 3 slices of grilled peaches, 5 mint leaves and Traeger Smoked Simple Syrup.
4. Muddle ingredients to release oils of the mint and juices from the grilled peaches. Add bourbon and crushed ice.
5. Shake and pour into a stemless wine glass. Top off with more crushed ice. Garnish with a grilled peach and mint sprig. Enjoy!

Smoked Eggnog

Servings: 4
Cooking Time: 60 Minutes

Ingredients:
- 2 Cup whole milk
- 1 Cup heavy cream
- 4 egg yolk
- Cup sugar
- 3 Ounce bourbon
- 1 Teaspoon vanilla extract
- 1 Teaspoon nutmeg
- 4 egg white
- whipped cream

Directions:
1. Plan ahead, this recipe requires chill time.
2. Supply your smoker with wood pellets and follow the start-up procedure. Preheat the grill, with the lid closed, to 180° F.
3. Pour the milk and the cream into a baking pan and smoke on the Traeger for 60 minutes. Grill: 180 °F
4. Meanwhile, in the bowl of a stand mixer, beat the egg yolks until they lighten in color. Gradually add 1/3 cup sugar and continue to beat until sugar completely dissolves.
5. After the milk and cream have smoked, add them along with the bourbon, vanilla and nutmeg into the egg mixture and stir to combine.
6. Place the egg whites in the bowl of a stand mixer and beat to soft peaks. When you lift the beaters the whites will make a peak that slightly curls down.
7. With the mixer still running, gradually add 1 tablespoon of sugar and beat until stiff peaks form.
8. Gently fold the egg whites into the cream mixture and then whisk to thoroughly combine.
9. Chill eggnog for a couple hours to let the flavors meld. Garnish with a dash of nutmeg and whipped cream on top. Enjoy!

Traeger Gin & Tonic

Servings: 2
Cooking Time: 45 Minutes

Ingredients:
- 1/2 Cup berries
- 2 orange, sliced
- 4 Tablespoon granulated sugar
- 3 Ounce gin
- 1 Cup tonic water
- 2 Sprig fresh mint, for garnish

Directions:
1. Supply your smoker with wood pellets and follow the start-up procedure. Preheat the grill, with the lid closed, to 180° F.
2. For the Smoked Berries: Spread mixed fresh berries on a sheet pan and place directly on the grill grate. Smoke for 30 minutes then remove from grill. Grill: 180 °F
3. For the Orange Slices: Increase the grill temperature to 450°F and preheat, lid closed for 15 minutes. Grill: 450 °F
4. Toss the orange slices with granulated sugar and place directly on grill grate. Cook for about 5 minutes, turning once or until the slices have developed grill marks. Grill: 450 °F
5. Pour gin into a glass, add ice and berries, then top with tonic water. Garnish with a fresh mint sprig and grilled orange wheel. Enjoy!

Smoke And Bubz Cocktail

Servings: 2
Cooking Time: 45 Minutes

Ingredients:
- 16 Ounce POM Juice
- 2 Cup pomegranate seeds
- 6 Ounce sparkling white wine
- 2 lemon twist, for garnish
- 2 Teaspoon pomegranate seeds

Directions:
1. Supply your smoker with wood pellets and follow the start-up procedure. Preheat the grill, with the lid closed, to 180° F.
2. For the Smoked Pomegranate Juice: Pour POM juice and a cup of pomegranate seeds into a shallow sheet pan. Smoke on the Traeger for 45 minutes. Pull off grill, strain, discard seeds and let sit until chilled. Grill: 180 °F
3. Add 1-1/2 ounces of the smoked pomegranate juice to the bottom of a champagne flute.
4. Add sparkling white wine, a few fresh pomegranate seeds and a lemon twist to garnish. Enjoy!

Smoked Raspberry Bubbler Cocktail

Servings: 2
Cooking Time: 45 Minutes

Ingredients:
- 2 Cup fresh raspberries
- Smoked Simple Syrup
- 8 Ounce sparkling wine

Directions:
1. Supply your smoker with wood pellets and follow the start-up procedure. Preheat the grill, with the lid closed, to 180° F.
2. Smoked Raspberry Syrup: Place 1 cup fresh raspberries on a grill mat and smoke for 30 minutes. Grill: 180 °F
3. After the raspberries have been smoked, set a few aside for garnish. Place the remainder into a shallow sheet pan with Traeger Smoked Simple Syrup. Place back on the grill grate and let smoke for 45 minutes. Remove from heat and allow to cool. Strain and refrigerate until ready to use. Grill: 180 °F
4. Place 1 ounce of the smoked raspberry syrup in the bottom of a champagne flute and top off with sparkling white wine or champagne.
5. Garnish with smoked raspberries. Enjoy!

Smoky Mountain Bramble Cocktail

Servings: 2
Cooking Time: 15 Minutes

Ingredients:
- 16 Ounce blackberries
- 2 Cup sugar
- 10 smoked blackberries
- 3 Ounce vodka
- 1 1/2 Ounce Alpine Distilling Preserve Liqueur
- 1 1/2 Ounce lemon juice
- 1 Ounce smoked blackberry syrup

Directions:

1. Supply your smoker with wood pellets and follow the start-up procedure. Preheat the grill, with the lid closed, to 180° F.

2. To make Smoked Blackberry Simple Syrup: Place blackberries on a grill mat and smoke for 15 to 20 minutes. Grill: 180 °F

3. Combine 1 cup water and sugar in a small sauce pan and warm over medium heat until sugar dissolves. Remove from heat and place 2/3 of blackberries in the simple syrup and macerate.

4. Strain through a fine mesh strainer and store for up to 14 days.

5. To make the cocktail: Muddle 4 to 5 smoked blackberries in a cocktail shaker. Add vodka, Preserve Liqueur, lemon and smoked blackberry syrup. Add ice and shake vigorously. Double strain into an old fashioned glass.

6. Garnish with a smoked blackberry and lemon twist. Enjoy!

PORK RECIPES

Southern Sugar-glazed Ham

Servings: 12-15
Cooking Time: 300 Minutes

Ingredients:
- 1 (12- to 15-pound) whole bone-in ham, fully cooked
- ¼ cup yellow mustard
- 1 cup pineapple juice
- ½ cup packed light brown sugar
- 1 teaspoon ground cinnamon
- ½ teaspoon ground cloves

Directions:
1. Supply your smoker with wood pellets and follow the start-up procedure. Preheat, with the lid closed, to 275°F.
2. Trim off the excess fat and skin from the ham, leaving a ¼-inch layer of fat. Put the ham in an aluminum foil–lined roasting pan.
3. On your kitchen stove top, in a medium saucepan over low heat, combine the mustard, pineapple juice, brown sugar, cinnamon, and cloves and simmer for 15 minutes, or until thick and reduced by about half.
4. Baste the ham with half of the pineapple–brown sugar syrup, reserving the rest for basting later in the cook.
5. Place the roasting pan on the grill, close the lid, and smoke for 4 hours.
6. Baste the ham with the remaining pineapple–brown sugar syrup and continue smoking with the lid closed for another hour, or until a meat thermometer inserted in the thickest part of the ham reads 140°F.
7. Remove the ham from the grill, tent with foil, and let rest for 20 minutes before carving.

Pulled Pork Sliders Hawaiian Rolls

Servings: 6 - 8
Cooking Time: 5 Minutes

Ingredients:
- ½ Cup Apple Cider Vinegar
- 1 Package Of Cabbage
- 2 Tbsp Minced Cilantro
- 1/3 Cup Green Onions, Diced
- 1 Tbsp Mango Magic
- 1 ½ Cup Mayonnaise
- 1 Cup Pineapple, Diced
- 1 Lbs Pulled Pork
- 8 Hawaiian Rolls

Directions:
1. In a large bowl mix together all of the coleslaw ingredients and let set in refrigerator for at least 2 hours.
2. Reheat the pulled pork in a microwave or grill.
3. Serve over the pulled pork on the Hawaiian rolls.

Smoked Baby Back Ribs

Servings: 4
Cooking Time: 180 Minutes

Ingredients:
- 3 Rack baby back ribs
- kosher salt
- cracked black pepper

Directions:
1. Peel membrane from back side of the ribs and season both sides with salt and pepper.
2. Supply your smoker with wood pellets and follow the start-up procedure. Preheat the grill, with the lid closed, to 225° F.
3. Cook meat side up for two hours. Flip ribs so the meat side is down and cook for an additional hour. Enjoy! Grill: 225 °F

Lynchburg Bacon

Servings: 4
Cooking Time: 20 Minutes

Ingredients:
- 1 Pound country-style bacon
- 1 Cup Tennessee whiskey, such as Jack Daniel's or apple juice
- 1 Tablespoon Pork & Poultry Rub
- 3/4 Cup all-purpose flour

- 1/3 Cup brown sugar
- 1 Teaspoon freshly ground black pepper

Directions:

1. Separate the bacon slices and place them into a large resealable bag.
2. Stir the Traeger Pork & Poultry Rub into the whiskey (or apple juice). Pour the whiskey over the bacon, massaging the bag to coat all the slices.
3. Set aside for at least 30 minutes.
4. On a piece of wax paper, sift together the flour, brown sugar and black pepper. Transfer to a second resealable bag.
5. Drain the bacon and add to the flour mixture a few slices at a time.
6. Shake the bag to coat each piece evenly, then arrange in a single layer on a baking pan.
7. Supply your smoker with wood pellets and follow the start-up procedure. Preheat the grill, with the lid closed, to 375° F.
8. Bake the bacon until it is golden brown and crisp, about 20 to 25 minutes. Enjoy! Grill: 375 °F

Bbq Baby Back Ribs With Bacon Pineapple Glaze By Scott Thomas

Servings: 4
Cooking Time: 180 Minutes

Ingredients:

- 2 Rack baby back ribs
- 1 As Needed salt and pepper
- 1 As Needed Your Favorite Spicy Rub
- 6 Slices bacon
- 6 Fluid Ounce pineapple juice
- 1 Teaspoon garlic, minced
- 2 Tablespoon honey

Directions:

1. Remove the membrane from the bone side of the ribs and apply the salt, pepper and rub to that side. Flip the ribs over and season the meat side.
2. Supply your smoker with wood pellets and follow the start-up procedure. Preheat the grill, with the lid closed, to 350° F.
3. While the grill heats up, cook the bacon in a frying pan. As the bacon is cooking, pour the pineapple juice, garlic and honey into an oven safe pot.
4. Remove the bacon from the grease and let the pan and bacon fat cool down. After the pan has cooled for a while, pour the bacon grease in with the pineapple juice, garlic and honey and stir to combine.
5. Place the ribs and the pot on the grill and close the lid. After an hour, the slurry will have reduced down a bit and can be applied to the ribs. Slather the ribs with the reduction every 15 minutes. When the bones peek out about a quarter to a third of an inch, the ribs are done which is about 2 hours and 15 minutes. Grill: 350 °F
6. For fall off the bone ribs, go another 30-45 minutes, continuing to glaze every 15 minutes. Grill: 350 °F
7. The sweet and savory of the reduction will temper the heat of the spicy rub forming an outstanding and complex blend of flavors. Enjoy!

Bbq Sweet & Smoky Ribs

Servings: 6
Cooking Time: 300 Minutes

Ingredients:

- 2 Rack Pork, Spare Ribs Trimmed
- 6 Cup apple juice
- 2 Tablespoon Big Game Rub
- 2 Cup 'Que BBQ Sauce
- 1/4 Cup brown sugar

Directions:

1. If your butcher has not already done so, remove the thin papery membrane from the bone-side of the ribs by working the tip of a butter knife underneath the membrane over a middle bone. Use paper towels to get a firm grip, then tear the membrane off.
2. Lay the ribs in a baking dish. Pour the apple juice over ribs, using as much apple juice as needed to submerge the meaty side of the ribs. Turn to coat.
3. Cover and refrigerate ribs for 4 to 6 hours or overnight. Remove the ribs from the apple juice; reserve juice.

4. Sprinkle ribs on all sides with Traeger Big Game Rub.
5. Supply your smoker with wood pellets and follow the start-up procedure. Preheat the grill, with the lid closed, to 225° F.
6. Transfer the apple juice to a saucepan and place in a corner of the grill, the juice will keep the cooking environment moist.
7. Arrange the ribs bone side down, directly on the grill grate. Cook for 4 to 5 hours, or until a skewer or paring knife inserted between the bones goes in easily.
8. Check the internal temperature of the ribs, the desired temperature is 202°F. If not at temperature, cook for an additional 30 minutes or until temperature is reached.
9. Meanwhile, combine the BBQ sauce and brown sugar in a small saucepan. Generously brush the ribs on all sides with the BBQ sauce the last hour of cooking
10. Using a sharp knife, cut the slabs into individual ribs. Serve. Enjoy!

Pork Belly Burnt Ends

Servings: 8-10
Cooking Time: 360 Minutes

Ingredients:
- 1 (3-pound) skinless pork belly (if not already skinned, use a sharp boning knife to remove the skin from the belly), cut into 1½- to 2-inch cubes
- 1 batch Sweet Brown Sugar Rub
- ½ cup honey
- 1 cup The Ultimate BBQ Sauce
- 2 tablespoons light brown sugar

Directions:
1. Supply your smoker with wood pellets and follow the start-up procedure. Preheat the grill, with the lid closed, to 250°F.
2. Generously season the pork belly cubes with the rub. Using your hands, work the rub into the meat.
3. Place the pork cubes directly on the grill grate and smoke until their internal temperature reaches 195°F.
4. Transfer the cubes from the grill to an aluminum pan. Add the honey, barbecue sauce, and brown sugar. Stir to combine and coat the pork.
5. Place the pan in the grill and smoke the pork for 1 hour, uncovered. Remove the pork from the grill and serve immediately.

Dry Rub Grilled Ribs

Servings: 4
Cooking Time: 300 Minutes

Ingredients:
- 1 Rack Baby Back Rib
- 1 Tablespoon Olive Oil
- Sweet Heat Rub

Directions:
1. Supply your smoker with wood pellets and follow the start-up procedure. Preheat the grill, with the lid open, to 225° F.
2. Remove the membrane from the back of the ribs. Rub the ribs down with olive oil, then generously coat both sides with Sweet Heat Rub. For deeper flavor penetration, gently pat the spices into the meat and let sit in the refrigerator for at least an hour.
3. Smoke the ribs for about 5 hours or until the temperature is between 180°F and 195°F, and the meat is dark, glossy and easily tears apart.
4. When the ribs are finished, remove from the grill and let them rest for 5 minutes before serving.

Bbq Pork Shoulder Steaks

Servings: 4
Cooking Time: 120 Minutes

Ingredients:
- 4 (1 to 1-1/4 inch thick) pork shoulder steaks
- 1/2 Cup mustard
- Pork & Poultry Rub
- 1/2 Cup apple juice
- 1 Cup 'Que BBQ Sauce

Directions:
1. Slather the pork steaks on all sides with the mustard and season with the Traeger Pork & Poultry Rub. (The

mustard will help keep the pork moist, but the taste will be unnoticeable in the final product.)

2. Supply your smoker with wood pellets and follow the start-up procedure. Preheat the grill, with the lid closed, to 180° F.

3. Arrange the steaks on the grill grate. Smoke for 1-1/2 hours. Grill: 180 °F

4. Remove the pork steaks to a plate and increase temperature to 225°F. Preheat 5 to 10 minutes. Grill: 225 °F

5. Meanwhile, wrap each steak with aluminum foil, adding in a couple tablespoons of apple juice.

6. Cook the steaks for another hour or so or until they are tender (about 160°F on an instant-read meat thermometer). Grill: 225 °F Probe: 160 °F

7. The last 15 minutes, take the pork steaks out of the foil and put them directly on the grill.

8. Brush each steak on both sides with the Traeger 'Que BBQ Sauce or your favorite barbecue sauce.

9. Let the steaks rest for 3 minutes before serving. Enjoy!

Spiced Coffee-rubbed Ribs

Servings: 6 - 8
Cooking Time: 360 Minutes

Ingredients:
- 1 Tbsp Ancho Chili Powder
- Ground Black Pepper
- ½ Tsp Cocoa Powder
- 2 Tbsp Coffee
- ½ Tsp Coriander, Ground
- 1 Tbsp Dark Brown Sugar
- 1 Tsp Garlic Powder
- 2 Tbsp Kosher Salt
- 1 Tsp Onion Powder
- 1 Tsp Oregano
- 2 Tbsp Paprika
- 8 Lbs. Pork Spareribs

Directions:
1. Begin by preparing the dry rub. In a mixing bowl, whisk together the coffee, salt, paprika, brown sugar, oregano, garlic powder, onion powder, black pepper, cocoa powder and coriander. Set aside.

2. Remove the membrane from the back of your ribs: Take a butter knife and wedge it just underneath the membrane to loosen it. Using your hands or a paper towel to grip, pull the membrane up and off the bone. Place the ribs on a sheet tray, then rub each rack generously with dry rub. Wrap ribs in foil, then refrigerate overnight.

3. When ready to cook, remove ribs from the refrigerator and let come to room temp. Supply your smoker with wood pellets and follow the start-up procedure. Preheat the grill, with the lid open, to 225° F. If using a gas or charcoal grill, set it up for low indirect heat.

4. Place foil-wrapped ribs on the grill and close lid. Cook for 4 hours then remove foil from ribs and pour accumulated juices into a glass measuring cup. Pour the sauce over the ribs, then continue to cook for an additional 1 ½ - 2 hours or until tender. Remove from grill, slice and serve.

Grilled Pork Loin

Servings: 4
Cooking Time: 30 Minutes

Ingredients:
- 2 Tablespoons Balsamic Vinegar
- 2 Cups Fresh Washed And Dried Blackberries
- ¼ Cup Seedless Blackberry Preserve
- ½ Teaspoon Dijon Mustard
- Pinch Of Kosher Salt
- 1 Tablespoon Olive Oil
- 1 Pound Silver Skin And Extra Fat Removed Pork Loin
- 2 Tablespoons Sweet Rib Rub
- 1 Tablespoon Worcestershire Sauce

Directions:
1. Place your pork loin on a flat work surface. Trim the pork loin if necessary. Rub the tenderloin all over with olive oil until it is fully coated. Once the pork loin is completely coated, generously season all over with Sweet Rib Rub until every part of the pork loin is coated. Allow

the pork tenderloin to rest at room temperature for 30 minutes.

2. While the pork loin rests, make the blackberry sauce. In a small bowl, place a metal strainer on top combine the fresh blackberries, seedless blackberry preserves, balsamic vinegar, Worcestershire sauce, Dijon mustard, and Sweet Rib Rub. Mix well and set aside.

3. Supply your smoker with wood pellets and follow the start-up procedure. Preheat the grill, with the lid open, to 350° F. If you're using a gas or charcoal grill, set it up for medium heat. Insert a temperature probe into the thickest part of the pork loin and smoke at 225°F for 4-5 hours, flipping once, until the pork loin is golden brown and charred in some spots, and reaches an internal temperature of 145°-165°F. Remove the pork loin from the grill and allow it to rest for 5 minutes.

4. Slice the pork loin thinly and serve with the blackberry sauce.

Grilled Pork Belly

Servings: 15
Cooking Time: 370 Minutes

Ingredients:
- Peanut Oil
- Mandarin Habanero Spice
- 13 Lbs Pork, Belly (Skin And Fat)
- Salt
- Sweet Barbecue Sauce

Directions:
1. Supply your smoker with wood pellets and follow the start-up procedure. Preheat the grill, with the lid open, to 250° F.

2. Place the pork belly on the grates of your preheated, meat side down. Smoke until the internal temperature reaches 195°F (this normally takes about 6 hours).

3. Open the flame broiler and flip the pork belly so that the meat side is up. Brush on the BBQ Sauce (on meat side). Sear the fat side for about 5 minutes, or until crispy.

4. Using your grill gloves, remove the pork belly from the grill and wrap in aluminum foil for 15 minutes or until it's cool enough to pull apart with your Meat Claws. Or dice into cubes with a knife. Serve hot.

Grilled Bbq Pork Chops

Servings: 6
Cooking Time: 12 Minutes

Ingredients:
- 6 Thick-Cut Pork Chops
- Generous amounts BBQ rub

Directions:
1. Supply your smoker with wood pellets and follow the start-up procedure. Preheat the grill, with the lid closed, to 450° F. Place seasoned pork chops on grill. Cook 6 minutes per side, or until internal temps reach 145 °F.

2. Remove from heat and let sit for 5-10 minutes before serving.

3-2-1 Spare Ribs

Servings: 4
Cooking Time: 180 Minutes

Ingredients:
- 2 racks of St. Louis–cut pork spare ribs, each about 3lb (1.4kg)
- all-purpose barbecue rub
- 3 tbsp unsalted butter, cut into cubes
- 1 cup apple juice or apple cider
- low-carb barbecue sauce

Directions:
1. Supply your smoker with wood pellets and follow the start-up procedure. Preheat the grill, with the lid closed, to 225° F.

2. Place the ribs on a rimmed sheet pan and dust with the rub. Place the ribs bone side down on the grate and smoke for 3 hours.

3. Tear off 2 large sheets of heavy-duty aluminum foil. Place one rack of ribs bone side down on the foil and top with half the butter cubes. Place the second rack of ribs bone side down on the butter cubes and top with the remaining butter cubes.

4. Bring up all 4 sides of the foil and pour in the apple juice. Crimp the edges of the foil so the ribs are tightly

enclosed. Place the foil package on the grate and smoke for 2 hours more.

5. Transfer the ribs to a workspace and carefully open the foil package. (Be careful of escaping steam.) Discard the foil and any accumulated juices. Brush the ribs on both sides with barbecue sauce. Place the ribs on the grate and smoke for 1 hour more to set the sauce and firm up the bark.

6. Transfer the ribs to a cutting board. Use a sharp knife to cut the slabs in half or into individual ribs. Serve immediately.

Maple Syrup Bacon Wrapped Tenderloin

Servings: 5
Cooking Time: 30 Minutes

Ingredients:
- 1 Package Bacon, Thick Cut
- 1/4 Cup Maple Syrup
- 2 Tbsp Olive Oil
- 3 Tbsp Competition Smoked Rub
- 1 Trimmed With Silver Skin Removed Pork, Tenderloin

Directions:
1. Lay the strips of bacon out flat, with each strip slightly overlapping the other.
2. Sprinkle the pork tenderloin with 1 tablespoon of the Competition Smoked Rub and lay in the center.
3. Wrap with bacon over the tenderloin and tuck in the ends.
4. In a small bowl, mix the olive oil, maple syrup and remaining seasoning together and brush onto the wrapped tenderloin.
5. Supply your smoker with wood pellets and follow the start-up procedure. Preheat the grill, with the lid open, to 350° F.
6. When the grill is ready, place your tenderloin on the grill and cook, turning, for 15 minutes.
7. Increase the grill temperature to 400°F and grill for another 15 minutes or until the internal temperature is 145°F. Serve and enjoy!

Pulled Pork Taquitos With Sour Cream

Servings: 4
Cooking Time: 300 Minutes

Ingredients:
- ⅓ Cup Apple Cider Vinegar
- ½ Cup, Plus Extra For Dipping Bbq Sauce
- 4 Cups Chicken Broth
- 1 Teaspoon Chili Powder
- ⅓ Cup Mustard
- 2 Tbsp Olive Oil
- 6 Tbsp Pulled Pork Rub
- 4 Lb. Pork Shoulder, Bone In
- 1 ½ Cup Sharp Cheddar Cheese, Shredded
- ¼ Cup Sour Cream
- 10 Flour Tortillas

Directions:
1. Supply your smoker with wood pellets and follow the start-up procedure. Preheat the grill, with the lid open, to 400° F. If using a gas or charcoal grill, set the temp to medium heat. In a bowl, combine the chicken broth, mustard, apple cider vinegar, and 1 tablespoon of Pulled Pork Seasoning. Whisk well to combine and set aside.
2. Generously season the pork shoulder with the remaining 3 tablespoons of Pulled Pork Seasoning on all sides of the pork shoulder, then place on the grill and sear on all sides until golden brown, about 10 minutes.
3. Remove the pork shoulder from the grill and place in the disposable aluminum pan. Pour the chicken broth mixture over the pork shoulder. It should come about 1/3 to ½ way up the side of the pork shoulder. Cover the top of the pan tightly with aluminum foil.
4. Reduce the temperature of your grill to 250°F. Place the foil pan on the grill and grill for four to five hours, or until the pork is tender and falling off the bone.
5. Remove the pork from the grill and allow to cool slightly. Place on a cutting board and shred with meat claws, reserving about 2.5 cups. Fire up grill to 425°F.
6. In a mixing bowl, combine sour cream, BBQ sauce, and chili powder. Stir in cheddar cheese and pork until well combined.

7. Lay each tortilla flat on your work surface and scoop about ¼ cup of pork mixture in the center, lengthwise. Roll up tightly and place seam side down on baking sheet. Repeat with all tortillas, then brush tops lightly with olive oil.

8. Transfer baking sheet to grill and cook for 15-20 minutes at 400°F, or until cheese has melted and tortilla edges have turned a golden brown. Serve with extra BBQ sauce for dipping and enjoy!

Asian-style Pork Tenderloin

Servings: 6
Cooking Time: 15 Minutes

Ingredients:
- 2 Whole Pork Tenderloin, 8-10 oz each
- 2 Tablespoon canola oil
- 2 Tablespoon Sambai Oelek
- 1 Teaspoon sesame oil
- 1 Teaspoon garlic, minced
- 1 Teaspoon fresh ginger
- 1 Teaspoon fish sauce
- 1 Teaspoon soy sauce
- 1/4 Cup brown sugar

Directions:
1. Use a sharp paring knife to remove the silver skin of the pork tenderloin.
2. Combine all the ingredients together. Cover the tenderloins in the mixture and allow them to marinate in the refrigerator for 30 minutes.
3. Supply your smoker with wood pellets and follow the start-up procedure. Preheat the grill, with the lid closed, to 450° F.
4. Place the loins towards the very front of the grill; turn periodically until there are dark grill marks all around. Transfer them to the middle of the grill to finish cooking. Cook for an addition 7-10 minutes for a medium rare tenderloin. When they are done cooking, remove them from the grill and let them rest for 10 minutes before slicing. Enjoy!

Baked Candied Bacon Cinnamon Rolls

Servings: 6
Cooking Time: 35 Minutes

Ingredients:
- 12 Slices Bacon, sliced
- 1/3 Cup brown sugar
- pre-made cinnamon rolls
- 2 Ounce cream cheese

Directions:
1. Supply your smoker with wood pellets and follow the start-up procedure. Preheat the grill, with the lid closed, to 350° F.
2. Dredge 8 of the slices of bacon in brown sugar, making sure to cover both sides of the bacon.
3. Place the brown sugared bacon slices along with the other slices of bacon on a cooling rack placed on top of a large baking sheet.
4. Cook the bacon on the Traeger for 15-20 minutes or until the fat renders but bacon is still pliable. Turn the Traeger down to 325°F.
5. Open and unroll the cinnamon rolls. While bacon is still warm, place 1 slice of the brown sugared bacon on top of 1 of the unrolled rolls and roll back up. Repeat for all the rolls.
6. Place cinnamon rolls in an 8" x 8" baking dish or cake pan that has been sprayed with nonstick cooking spray. Cook the cinnamon rolls at 325°F for 10 to 15 minutes or until golden. Rotate the pan a half turn halfway through cooking time. Grill: 325 °F
7. Meanwhile, take the provided cream cheese frosting and mix in the softened cream cheese. Crumble the cooked bacon and add into the cream cheese frosting.
8. Spread frosting over warm cinnamon rolls. Serve warm, enjoy!

Chinese Alcoholic Bbq Pork Tenderloin

Servings: 4
Cooking Time: 30 Minutes

Ingredients:
- 14 Cup Bbq Sauce
- 2 Garlic Cloves, Minced
- 14 Cup Hoisin Sauce

- 2 Lbs Pork Tenderloin, Trimmed With Silver Skins Removed
- 1 Tbsp Sugar, Granulated
- 1 Tsp Sweet Rib Rub Seasoning
- 14 Cup Tamari
- 14 Cup White Wine

Directions:

1. In a glass measuring cup, whisk together the hoisin sauce, tamari, wine, garlic, sugar, and Sweet Rib Rub.

2. Place pork tenderloin in a resealable bag, then pour the marinade over the pork and allow to marinate in the refrigerator for 4 to 6 hours.

3. Supply your smoker with wood pellets and follow the start-up procedure. Preheat the grill, with the lid open, to 400° F. If using a gas or charcoal grill, preheat to medium-high heat.

4. Remove the pork from the marinade, then pour the marinade into a grill-safe pan.

5. Place the marinade on the grill and bring to a boil for 3 minutes. Add the BBQ sauce and simmer for 2 minutes. Remove from the grill, and set aside.

6. Place the pork on the grill and cook for 18 to 20 minutes, until an internal temperature of 145° F. Flip and baste the pork with the sauce every 3 to 5 minutes.

7. Remove the pork from the grill and allow it to rest on a cutting board for 10 minutes, prior to serving warm with additional sauce.

Bbq Bacon-wrapped Water Chestnuts

Servings: 6
Cooking Time: 35 Minutes

Ingredients:

- 1 Pound bacon
- 2 Can Water Chestnuts
- 1/3 Cup brown sugar
- 1/3 Cup mayonnaise
- 1/3 Cup Texas Spicy BBQ Sauce

Directions:

1. Supply your smoker with wood pellets and follow the start-up procedure. Preheat the grill, with the lid closed, to 350° F.

2. Line a rimmed baking sheet with aluminum foil. Cut each piece of bacon into thirds or halves. Wrap each water chestnut with a piece of bacon large enough to encircle it and secure the bacon with a toothpick.

3. Arrange the bacon-wrapped chestnuts in a single layer on the prepared baking sheet. Bake for 20 minutes. Leave the grill on. Grill: 350 °F

4. Meanwhile, whisk the mayonnaise, brown sugar, and Traeger Spicy Barbecue Sauce in a mixing bowl. Pour the sauce over the chestnuts and return to the grill to bake for 10 to 15 minutes more. Transfer to a platter for serving. Enjoy!

Smoked Pork Loin With Sauerkraut And Apples

Servings: 4
Cooking Time: 120 Minutes

Ingredients:

- 1 (2 to 2-1/2 lb) pork loin roast
- Pork & Poultry Rub
- 1 Pound sauerkraut
- 2 Large cooking apples, peeled, cored and sliced
- 1 Large sweet onion, thinly sliced
- 1/3 Cup brown sugar
- 1 Cup dark beer
- 2 Tablespoon butter
- 2 Whole bay leaves

Directions:

1. Supply your smoker with wood pellets and follow the start-up procedure. Preheat the grill, with the lid closed, to 180° F.

2. Season the pork loin on all sides with Traeger Pork & Poultry Rub or salt and pepper. Place the roast directly on the grill grate, close the lid, and smoke for 1 hour. Grill: 180 °F

3. In a large Dutch oven or glass baking dish, layer the sauerkraut, apples, onions, brown sugar, beer, butter and bay leaves. Lay the smoked pork loin directly on top of the sauerkraut mixture. Top the pan with a lid or a layer of foil.

4. Increase Traeger temperature to 350°F, and return the pan to the grill. Close the lid and roast the pork for

an additional hour, or until the internal temperature on an instant-read meat thermometer reads 160°F. Grill: 350°F Probe: 160°F

5. Transfer the roast to a cutting board and let it rest. Meanwhile, gently stir the sauerkraut mixture and arrange on a serving platter. Slice the pork roast and layer on the sauerkraut and apples. Enjoy!

Bbq Breakfast Grits

Servings: 12-15
Cooking Time: 40 Minutes

Ingredients:
- 2 cups chicken stock
- 1 cup water
- 1 cup quick-cooking grits
- 3 tablespoons unsalted butter
- 2 tablespoons minced garlic
- 1 medium onion, chopped
- 1 jalapeño pepper, stemmed, seeded, and chopped
- 1 teaspoon cayenne pepper
- 2 teaspoons red pepper flakes
- 1 tablespoon hot sauce
- 1 cup shredded Monterey Jack cheese
- 1 cup sour cream
- Salt
- Freshly ground black pepper
- 2 eggs, beaten
- ⅓ cup half-and-half
- 3 cups leftover pulled pork (preferably smoked)

Directions:
1. Supply your smoker with wood pellets and follow the start-up procedure. Preheat, with the lid closed, to 350°F.
2. On your kitchen stove top, in a large saucepan over high heat, bring the chicken stock and water to a boil.
3. Add the grits and reduce the heat to low, then stir in the butter, garlic, onion, jalapeño, cayenne, red pepper flakes, hot sauce, cheese, and sour cream. Season with salt and pepper, then cook for about 5 minutes.
4. Temper the beaten eggs (see Tip below) and incorporate into the grits. Remove the saucepan from the heat and stir in the half-and-half and pulled pork.
5. Pour the grits into a greased grill-safe 9-by-13-inch casserole dish or aluminum pan.
6. Transfer to the grill, close the lid, and bake for 30 to 40 minutes, covering with aluminum foil toward the end of cooking if the grits start to get too brown on top.

Whiskey- & Cider-brined Pork Shoulder

Servings: 8
Cooking Time: 540 Minutes

Ingredients:
- 1 bone-in pork shoulder, about 5 to 7lb (2.3 to 3.2kg)
- fresh coarsely ground black pepper
- granulated garlic
- 1 cup apple juice or apple cider
- low-carb barbecue sauce, warmed
- hamburger buns (optional)
- for the brine
- 1 gallon (3.8 liters) cold distilled water
- 1 cup coarse salt
- 1¼ cup whiskey, divided
- ½ cup light brown sugar or low-carb substitute

Directions:
1. In a large saucepot on the stovetop over medium-high heat, make the brine by bringing the water, salt, 1 cup of whiskey, and brown sugar to a boil. Stir with a long-handled wooden spoon until the salt and sugar dissolve. Let the brine cool to room temperature. Cover and cool completely in the refrigerator.
2. Submerge the pork in the brine. If it floats, place a resealable bag of ice on top. Refrigerate for 24 hours.
3. Supply your smoker with wood pellets and follow the start-up procedure. Preheat the grill, with the lid closed, to 250° F.
4. Remove the pork shoulder from the brine and pat dry with paper towels. (Discard the brine.) Season the pork with pepper and granulated garlic. Place the pork on the grate and smoke until the internal temperature reaches 165°F (74°C), about 5 hours.
5. Transfer the pork to an aluminum foil roasting pan and add the apple juice and the remaining ¼ cup of whiskey. Cover tightly with aluminum foil. Place the pan

on the grate and cook the pork until the bone releases easily from the meat and the internal temperature reaches 200°F (93°C), about 3 hours more. (Be careful when lifting a corner of the foil to check on the roast because steam will escape.)

6. Remove the pan from the grill and let the pork rest for 20 minutes. Reserve the juices.

7. Wearing heatproof gloves, pull the pork into chunks. Discard the bone or any large lumps of fat. Pull the meat into shreds and transfer to a clean aluminum foil roasting pan. Moisten with the barbecue sauce or serve the sauce on the side. Stir in some of the drippings—not too much because you don't want the pork to be swimming in its juices. Serve on buns (if using).

Pig On A Stick With Buffalo Glaze

Servings: 12
Cooking Time: 75 Minutes

Ingredients:

- 4lb (1.8kg) pork shanks, each about 4 to 6oz (110 to 170g), trimmed and thawed if frozen
- 1½ cups sugar-free dark-colored soda, sugar-free root beer, or no-sugar-added apple juice
- for the brine (optional)
- 1 gallon (3.8 liters) distilled water
- ¾ cup kosher salt
- 5 tsp pink curing salt #1
- for the glaze (optional)
- ½ cup unsalted butter
- 1 cup hot sauce
- 2 tsp granulated garlic
- 1 tsp Worcestershire sauce

Directions:

1. In a stockpot on the stovetop over medium-high heat, make the brine by combining the ingredients and bringing the mixture to a boil. Stir until the salts dissolve. Remove the pot from the stovetop and let the brine cool to room temperature.

2. Add the pork shanks to the brine. Cover and refrigerate for 2 days.

3. Supply your smoker with wood pellets and follow the start-up procedure. Preheat the grill, with the lid closed, to 180° F.

4. Drain the pork shanks and discard the brine. (If you didn't brine the pork shanks, season them on all sides with your favorite barbecue rub.) Place the pork on the grate and smoke for 3 hours. Transfer the shanks to an aluminum roasting pan.

5. Raise the temperature to 275°F (135°C).

6. Add the soda to the pan and cover tightly with aluminum foil. Place the pan on the grate and braise the meat until it's tender but still attached to the bone, about 2 to 3 hours. Be careful when removing the foil because steam will escape. Remove the pan from the grill and set aside.

7. Raise the temperature to 325°F (163°C).

8. In a saucepan on the stovetop over medium heat, make the buffalo glaze by melting the butter. Stir in the remaining ingredients. Let the sauce simmer for 5 minutes to allow the flavors to blend.

9. Dip the pork shanks into the glaze and then transfer them to an aluminum foil roasting pan. Cover tightly with aluminum foil. Place the pan on the grate and cook the shanks until hot, about 30 minutes.

10. Remove the pan from the grill. Serve the pork with plenty of napkins.

Traeger Roasted Easter Ham

Servings: 8
Cooking Time: 60 Minutes

Ingredients:

- 1 (6-7 lb) bone-in ham
- 1 Cup Sweet & Heat BBQ Sauce
- 2 Cup brown sugar
- 1/2 Cup pineapple juice

Directions:

1. Supply your smoker with wood pellets and follow the start-up procedure. Preheat the grill, with the lid closed, to 225° F.

2. Place ham in grill and cook for 60 minutes. Grill: 225 °F

3. While the ham is cooking, mix together the Traeger Sweet & Heat BBQ Sauce, brown sugar and pineapple juice.
4. Glaze ham with the sauce every 10 minutes during the last 30 minutes. Remove ham from grill and serve. Enjoy!

Simple Smoked Ribs

Servings: 6
Cooking Time: 240 Minutes

Ingredients:
- 3 Rack baby back ribs
- 3/4 Cup Pork & Poultry Rub
- 3/4 Cup 'Que BBQ Sauce

Directions:
1. Peel membrane from the back side of ribs and trim any excess fat.
2. Season both sides of ribs with Traeger Pork & Poultry Rub, about 1/4 cup per rack.
3. Supply your smoker with wood pellets and follow the start-up procedure. Preheat the grill, with the lid closed, to 180° F.
4. Place ribs on the grill and smoke for 3 to 4 hours. Grill: 180 °F Probe: 160 °F
5. When the internal temperature registers between 160°F to 165°F, remove ribs from the grill and increase Traeger temperature to 350°F. Grill: 350 °F
6. Place about 1/4 cup of Traeger 'Que BBQ Sauce on a large sheet of heavy-duty aluminum foil, then place a rack of ribs meat-side down on top and wrap tightly. Repeat with each rack.
7. Place the wrapped ribs back on the grill and cook for 45 minutes, or until internal temperature registers 204°F. Grill: 350 °F Probe: 204 °F
8. Remove from grill and let rest 20 minutes before slicing. Enjoy!

Grilled Mac And Cheese Quesadillas

Servings: 4
Cooking Time: 75 Minutes

Ingredients:
- 1/2 Lb Bacon, Sliced And Halved
- 3 Tbsp Butter
- 1 Cup Cheddar Cheese, Shredded
- 1 Cup Cheddar Jack Cheese, Shredded
- 4 Oz Cream Cheese
- 2 Tbsp Flour
- 4 Flour Tortillas
- 1 1/2 Tsp Hickory Bacon Seasoning
- 8 Oz Macaroni, Cooked Al Dente
- 1 Tsp Mustard Powder
- 1/2 Cup Parmesan Cheese, Grated
- 1 2/3 Cups Whole Milk

Directions:
1. Fire up your Platinum Series KC Combo and with the lid open, set your temperature to SMOKE mode.
2. Supply your smoker with wood pellets and follow the start-up procedure. Preheat the grill, with the lid open, to 225° F. If using a gas or charcoal grill, set it up for low, indirect heat.
3. Set a cast iron skillet on the grill. Melt the butter then whisk in flour until smooth. Cook for 1 minute, then whisk in Hickory Bacon and mustard powder.
4. Pour in milk and bring to a boil, whisking constantly. When sauce begins to thicken, whisk in the cream cheese until smooth, then add cheddar and parmesan and stir until melted
5. Add the pasta to the cheese sauce. Close the lid, and smoke for 1 hour.
6. Fire up your griddle to medium-low flame, and cook bacon, turning occasionally, until desired crispness is reached, about 3 to 5 minutes.
7. Set bacon aside, then place 4 tortillas on the griddle. Sprinkle cheddar jack cheese on top of the tortilla, a heaping scoop of smoked mac 'n cheese on one side, topped with bacon.
8. Fold over the tortilla and press down gently with a spatula. Remove from the griddle, rest for 2 minutes, then cut into wedges, and serve warm with an extra side of smoked mac 'n cheese.

Grilled Prosciutto Wrapped Asparagus

Servings: 6
Cooking Time: 15 Minutes

Ingredients:
- 2 Bunch asparagus
- 4 Ounce prosciutto
- olive oil
- salt and pepper
- 1 Medium lemon, zested
- 2 Tablespoon balsamic vinegar, divided
- 3 Tablespoon toasted pine nuts, for serving

Directions:
1. Supply your smoker with wood pellets and follow the start-up procedure. Preheat the grill, with the lid closed, to 400° F.
2. Rinse the asparagus and pat dry with a paper towel. Cut the bottom third off of the asparagus stalks and discard.
3. Wrap a piece of prosciutto around 4 to 5 stalks, and place on a baking sheet. Drizzle the asparagus with olive oil, then sprinkle with salt, pepper and lemon zest.
4. Place the baking sheet on the grill and cook. After 5 minutes, shake the pan to turn the asparagus once, then drizzle with 1 tablespoon balsamic vinegar. Grill: 400 °F
5. Place back on the grill and cook until the prosciutto is crispy and the asparagus is cooked through, about 5 to 8 minutes. Grill: 400 °F
6. Place the asparagus on the serving tray and sprinkle with the pine nuts and drizzle with remaining balsamic. Enjoy!

Smoked Sausage & Potatoes

Servings: 4
Cooking Time: 50 Minutes

Ingredients:
- 2 Pound Hot Sausage Links
- 2 Pound fingerling potatoes
- 1 Tablespoon fresh thyme
- 4 Tablespoon butter

Directions:
1. Supply your smoker with wood pellets and follow the start-up procedure. Preheat the grill, with the lid closed, to 375° F.
2. Put your sausage links on the grill to get some color. This should take about 3 minutes on each side. Grill: 375 °F
3. While sausage is cooking, cut the potatoes into bite size pieces all about the same size so they cook evenly. Chop the thyme and butter, then combine all the ingredients into a Traeger cast iron skillet.
4. Pull your sausage off the grill, slice into bite size pieces and add to your cast iron.
5. Turn grill down to 275°F and put the cast iron in the grill for 45 minutes to an hour or until the potatoes are fully cooked. Grill: 275 °F
6. After 45 minutes, use a butter knife to test your potatoes by cutting into one to see if its done. To speed up cook time you can cover cast iron will a lid or foil. Serve. Enjoy!

Mini Sausage Rolls

Servings: 4
Cooking Time: 25 Minutes

Ingredients:
- 3/4 Cup dry mustard
- 3/4 Cup distilled white vinegar
- 1/2 Cup honey
- 4 egg yolk, beaten
- 2 Pound Sausage, Uncooked
- ground sage
- 1 Small onion, diced small
- 17 1/2 Ounce frozen puff pastry

Directions:
1. Make the mustard: Combine the mustard and vinegar in a small mixing bowl. Cover with plastic wrap and let sit overnight at room temperature to develop the flavors. Transfer the mustard mixture to a small heavy saucepan and add the honey and egg yolks. Cook over low heat, whisking constantly, until thickened, about 7 minutes. Cool, then refrigerate until serving time.
2. In a medium mixing bowl, thoroughly combine the sausage and onion. On a lightly floured work surface, roll

each sheet of thawed puff pastry - there are two to a package - into an 11 by 10-1/2 inch rectangle.

3. Using a pizza cutter or knife, cut each rectangle widthwise into three strips, each 3-1/2 inches wide. Wet your hands and mold some of the sausage into a tube-like shape. Lay it down the center of one of the puff pastry strips.

4. Wrap the pastry around the sausage and seal the seams with a bit of beaten egg. Repeat with the remaining sausage and puff pastry. Put all the rolls seam side down on your work surface and brush the tops lightly with the egg.

5. Cut the rolls into pieces about 1-1/2 inches long and transfer to a rimmed baking sheet lined with parchment paper. Leave about an inch between each roll. Supply your smoker with wood pellets and follow the start-up procedure. Preheat the grill, with the lid closed, to 350° F.

6. Bake the sausage rolls for about 25 minutes, or until the sausage is cooked through and the pastry is golden brown. Serve hot with the honey mustard. Grill: 350 °F

Bbq Pork Shoulder Roast With Sugar Lips Glaze

Servings: 8
Cooking Time: 540 Minutes

Ingredients:
- 1 (8-10 lb) bone-in pork butt
- 1/4 Cup Pork & Poultry Rub, divided
- 1 1/2 Cup apple juice, divided
- 4 Tablespoon brown sugar
- 1 Tablespoon salt
- 1/2 Cup apple juice
- Sugar Lips Glaze

Directions:
1. Trim pork butt of all excess fat leaving 1/4 inch of the fat cap attached.
2. Combine 2 tablespoons Traeger Pork & Poultry Rub, 1 cup apple juice, brown sugar and salt in a small bowl stirring until most of the sugar and salt are dissolved. Inject the pork butt every square inch or so with the apple juice mixture.
3. Season the exterior of the pork butt with remaining Traeger Pork & Poultry Rub.
4. Supply your smoker with wood pellets and follow the start-up procedure. Preheat the grill, with the lid closed, to 250° F.
5. Place pork butt directly on the grill grate and cook for about 6 hours or until the internal temperature reaches 160°F. Grill: 250 °F Probe: 160 °F
6. Wrap the pork butt in two layers of foil and pour in 1/2 cup of apple juice. Secure tin foil tightly to contain the apple juice.
7. Increase Traeger temperature to 275°F and return wrapped pork butt to grill in a pan large enough to hold the pork butt in case it leaks. Cook an additional 3 hours or until internal temperature reaches 195°F. Grill: 275 °F Probe: 195 °F
8. Remove from the grill and allow to rest 10 to 15 minutes. Slice the pork butt around the bone and top with Traeger Sugar Lips BBQ Sauce. Serve with your favorite sides. Enjoy!

Smoked Chorizo & Arugula Pesto

Servings: 4
Cooking Time: 20 Minutes

Ingredients:
- 4 Cup Arugula, fresh
- 1 Clove garlic
- 1/2 Cup Parmesan cheese, grated
- 1/2 Cup pine nuts
- 1/4 Cup extra-virgin olive oil
- 1/4 Cup grapeseed oil
- sea salt
- freshly ground black pepper
- water

Directions:
1. To make the pesto, add arugula, garlic, cheese, and nuts to the bowl of a food processor or blender, and puree. As the processor is running, drizzle in the oil. Season the mixture with salt and pepper, to taste. If the pesto is too thick, thin it out with water.

2. Supply your smoker with wood pellets and follow the start-up procedure. Preheat the grill, with the lid closed, to 375° F.

3. Smoke the sausages whole for 20 minutes, or until it reaches an internal temperature of 170°F. Grill: 375 °F Probe: 170 °F

4. Let rest for 10 minutes, then cut the sausage links into large 1-1/2" chunks. Transfer the sausage to a platter and serve with dollops of the arugula pesto. Enjoy!

Wet-rubbed St. Louis Ribs

Servings: 2
Cooking Time: 240 Minutes

Ingredients:
- 1/2 Cup brown sugar
- 1 Tablespoon ground cumin
- 1 Tablespoon ancho chile powder
- 1 Tablespoon smoked paprika
- 1 Tablespoon garlic salt
- 3 Tablespoon balsamic vinegar
- 1 Rack St. Louis-style ribs
- 2 Cup apple juice

Directions:
1. In a bowl, combine all ingredients except ribs. Place wet rub on both sides of ribs; let sit for at least 10 minutes.

2. Supply your smoker with wood pellets and follow the start-up procedure. Preheat the grill, with the lid closed, to 180° F.

3. Turn temperature to 250°F; transfer the ribs into a foil pan, or wrap in tinfoil. Pour apple juice in the foil. Place foiled ribs back on grill. Cook for 2 hours. Remove from grill and let rest 10 minutes. Enjoy! Grill: 250 °F

Savory Pork Belly Banh Mi

Servings: 4
Cooking Time: 420 Minutes

Ingredients:
- 2 Carrots, Sliced
- 1 Tbsp Cilantro, Minced
- 1 Tbsp Honey
- 2 Kirby Cucumbers, Sliced Thin
- 1 Lime, Zest & Juice
- 2 Tbsp Pickling Spice
- 1 Tbsp Ponzu
- 2 Lbs Pork Belly
- 1 Cup Rice Wine Vinegar
- 2 Tbsp Salt
- 4 Sandwich Buns
- 1 Small Daikon Radish, Sliced Thin
- To Taste, Smoky Salt & Cracked Pepper Rub
- 2 Tbsp Soy Sauce
- 1/2 Cup Sriracha Hot Sauce
- 4 Cloves Star Anise
- 1/2 Cup Sugar
- 1 Cup Water

Directions:
1. 30 minutes before you plan to put the belly on the smoker season liberally with the Smoky Salt and Cracked Pepper rub.

2. Supply your smoker with wood pellets and follow the start-up procedure. Preheat the grill, with the lid open, to 240° F. If using a gas or charcoal grill, set it up for low, indirect heat.

3. Place the belly on the smoker with a tin pan underneath the meat to catch the drippings. Smoke for 7 hours or until you reach an internal temp of 195 degrees. Remove the pork and let rest for 30 minutes.

4. Make the homemade pickles: Place pickling spice and star anise in a small sauce pan and toast. Once fragrant add vinegar and bring to a boil, cook for 3 minutes. Add the water, sugar, and salt and return to a boil, cook for 5 minutes. Strain the liquid and immediately pour over the vegetables, making sure the vegetables are submerged. Set in the fridge once cool.

5. Make the Sriracha Lime Sauce: Combine the sriracha, lime, soy sauce, honey, cilantro and ponzu in a mixing bowl and whisk until combined.

6. Assemble the sandwiches, placing sliced pork belly and homemade pickles on a roll before topping it with the sriracha lime sauce.

Double-decker Pulled Pork Nachos With Smoked Cheese

Servings: 4
Cooking Time: 55 Minutes

Ingredients:
- 8 Ounce pepper jack cheese
- 8 Ounce Cheese, sharp cheddar
- tortilla chips
- 2 Cup leftover pulled pork
- black olives
- jalapeño, diced
- cilantro

Directions:
1. Supply your smoker with wood pellets and follow the start-up procedure. Preheat the grill, with the lid closed, to 165° F.
2. Place the cheese (frozen) on a rack on top of a tray filled with ice. You may want to cut the cheese into smaller portions, maybe 2 or 3 chunks per block, to help it smoke more quickly.
3. Smoke the cheeses for 45 to 60 minutes; allow to cool. Shred the cheeses (about 1 cup of each), and set aside. Grill: 165 °F
4. Turn the heat on the Traeger up to 350 degrees and preheat, lid closed, for 10 to 15 minutes. Grill: 350 °F
5. Lay out your tortilla chips on large baking sheet and top evenly with the shredded, smoked cheeses. Place the baking sheet on the Traeger grill grate and cook for about 10 minutes, or until the cheese is melted and bubbly. Grill: 350 °F
6. Remove the pan from the Traeger and start to assemble the double-decker nachos. Assemble the nachos with a layer of cheesy chips on the bottom, some pulled pork, and more cheesy chips on top. Finish it off with your favorite nacho toppings. Serve warm.

Bacon Stuffed Onion Rings

Servings: 6
Cooking Time: 120 Minutes

Ingredients:
- 1 Pack Bacon
- 2 White Onions

Directions:
1. Supply your smoker with wood pellets and follow the start-up procedure. Preheat the grill, with the lid open, to 250° F.
2. Peel each onion and cut into thirds, separating the onion slices into rings. Using two slices of bacon, wrap around the onion ring until the ring is fully covered, securing in place with a toothpick. Continue until all the bacon is used up.
3. Place the onion rings on the and smoke until the bacon is cooked, about 120 minutes.

Baked German Pork Schnitzel With Grilled Lemons

Servings: 2
Cooking Time: 20 Minutes

Ingredients:
- 16 Ounce pork chops
- salt
- black pepper
- 1 Teaspoon garlic powder
- 1 Teaspoon paprika
- 2 eggs
- 1 Cup panko breadcrumbs
- 1/2 Cup flour
- 2 Whole lemon, halved

Directions:
1. Supply your smoker with wood pellets and follow the start-up procedure. Preheat the grill, with the lid closed, to High heat.
2. Place pork chops individually between 2 pieces of plastic wrap. Pound with a meat mallet until they are around 1/4 to 1/8" thick. Season both sides generously with salt and black pepper.
3. Mix the garlic powder and paprika in a bowl. In another bowl whisk the eggs. In a third bowl add the breadcrumbs.
4. Dip pork cutlets one by one into flour shaking off any excess, then into eggs and then into the breadcrumbs. Place breaded pork cutlets onto a lightly oiled wire rack over a baking sheet.

5. Cook for 15 minutes then flip and bake for another 5 minutes. When you open the grill to flip pork, place sliced lemons directly on grill grate flesh side down. Grill: 500 °F

6. Remove from grill and serve immediately with grilled lemons. Enjoy!

Smoked Bacon Roses

Servings: 2
Cooking Time: 60 Minutes

Ingredients:
- 1 Pack Bacon, Thick Cut
- 1 Dozen Roses, Fake

Directions:

1. Supply your smoker with wood pellets and follow the start-up procedure. Preheat the grill, with the lid open, to 225° F.

2. Roll each piece of bacon tightly, starting on the thicker side of the strip. Take a toothpick and skewer the middle of the bottom of the bacon roll to keep the bacon from unraveling. With a second toothpick, skewer the bacon roll so that the two toothpicks form an "X" at the bottom of the roll of bacon. Do this to every piece of bacon.

3. Place the bacon rolls directly on the grates of your preheated Grill and smoke for an hour, checking on them every 20 minutes.

4. While the bacon is smoking, rip the petals of the fake roses off of the steams.

5. Once the bacon is fully cooked, remove the toothpicks and pierce the bacon in the head of the steam (where the fake flowers once were). If the bacon isn't staying, you can break a toothpick in half and stick it in the tip of the steam, press firmly and try piercing the bacon again.

6. Place in a nice vase with some babies breath and gift to your Valentine.

Bbq Pork Short Ribs

Servings: 4
Cooking Time: 360 Minutes

Ingredients:
- 2 Pork Short Rib Racks With At Least 1 1/2-2" of Meat On Bone
- Pork & Poultry Rub

Directions:

1. Clean and trim short ribs. Season generously on all sides with Traeger Pork and Poultry rub.

2. Supply your smoker with wood pellets and follow the start-up procedure. Preheat the grill, with the lid closed, to 250° F.

3. Place ribs directly on the grill grate and cook for 4-6 hours or until the internal temperature reaches 202-204°F when an instant read thermometer is inserted in the thickest part of meat. Spritz with apple juice every hour if desired. Grill: 250 °F Probe: 202 °F

4. Remove from grill and allow to rest 10 minutes before slicing. Cut into individual ribs and serve with your favorite sides. Enjoy!

Pork Loin Porchetta

Servings: 8
Cooking Time: 120 Minutes

Ingredients:
- 1 center-cut pork loin roast, about 2½ to 3lb (1.2 to 1.4kg)
- Mustard Caviar
- for the paste
- 4 garlic cloves, peeled and coarsely chopped
- zest and juice of 1 lemon
- ½ cup coarsely chopped fresh curly or flat-leaf parsley
- 2 tbsp coarsely chopped fresh rosemary
- 2 tbsp coarsely chopped fresh sage
- 2 tsp fennel seeds
- 1 tsp coarse salt, plus more
- 1 tsp freshly ground black pepper, plus more
- 1 tsp crushed red pepper flakes
- ¼ cup extra virgin olive oil, plus more

Directions:

1. Supply your smoker with wood pellets and follow the start-up procedure. Preheat the grill, with the lid closed, to 450° F.

2. Use a sharp, slender knife to slice the pork almost in half lengthwise, leaving a 1-inch (5cm) hinge. (This is called "butterflying.") Open like a book and make a similar lengthwise cut on either side of the first cut—stopping when you reach the last 1 inch (2.5cm) of meat.
3. In a food processor, make the seasoning paste by combining the garlic, lemon zest and juice, parsley, rosemary, sage, fennel seeds, salt and pepper, and red pepper flakes. With the machine running, add the olive oil in a thin stream. Thinly spread the paste on the interior surfaces of the pork loin, leaving a 1-inch (2.5cm) border. Starting on a long side, reform the pork loin and tie at 2-inch (5cm) intervals with butcher's twine. Brush the outside surface with olive oil and then season with salt and pepper.
4. Place the pork on the grate and roast for 30 minutes. Lower the temperature to 325°F (163°C) and continue to roast the pork until the internal temperature reaches 145°F (63°C), about 60 to 90 minutes more.
5. Transfer the porchetta to a cutting board and let rest for 10 minutes. Remove the butcher's twine and carve the meat into finger-thick slices. Serve with the mustard caviar or a good-quality aged balsamic vinegar.

Prosciutto Wrapped Dates With Marcona Almonds

Servings: 8
Cooking Time: 5 Minutes

Ingredients:
- 24 Whole medjool dates
- 1 Small container Marcona salted almonds
- 8 Ounce prosciutto
- 2 Tablespoon olive oil
- 2 limes, washed and dried for zesting
- honey, for serving
- flake salt, for serving

Directions:
1. Supply your smoker with wood pellets and follow the start-up procedure. Preheat the grill, with the lid closed, to 400° F.
2. Place a large cast iron pan into the grill to preheat. Using a small paring knife, cut a slit lengthwise across the top of each date. Remove the pit. Replace pits with 1 to 2 Marcona almonds, then press the dates back together with your fingers to seal.
3. Cut the prosciutto into 24 pieces lengthwise. To wrap each date, place one at the bottom of a strip of prosciutto, then roll the prosciutto around the date to cover, leaving a little bit of the date showing on each end.
4. Add 2 Tablespoons olive oil to the preheated cast iron pan. Place the dates in the pan and cook, searing the prosciutto on all sides, turning as needed, about 3 to 5 minutes total. When the prosciutto is crispy, carefully remove the pan from the grill.
5. Zest the limes over the pan so the citrus zest is absorbed into the olive oil and onto the dates. Place the dates on a serving platter. Sprinkle with flake salt, an additional drizzle of olive oil, honey and serve. Enjoy!

Jamaican Jerk Pork Chops

Servings: 4
Cooking Time: 720 Minutes

Ingredients:
- 4 thick pork rib or loin chops, each about 12oz (340g) and 1 inch (2.5cm) thick
- for the marinade
- ½ to 1 Scotch bonnet or habanero pepper, destemmed, deseeded, and coarsely chopped, plus more
- 2 scallions, trimmed, white and green parts coarsely chopped
- 1 garlic clove, peeled and coarsely chopped
- juice of 1 lime
- 2 tbsp vegetable oil
- 2 tbsp distilled water
- 1 tbsp light soy sauce
- 2 tsp coarsely chopped fresh thyme leaves
- 2 tsp peeled and minced fresh ginger
- 2 tsp dark brown sugar or low-carb substitute, plus more
- 1 tsp coarse salt, plus more
- ½ tsp freshly ground black pepper
- ½ tsp ground allspice
- ½ tsp ground nutmeg
- ½ tsp ground cinnamon

Directions:

1. In a blender, make the jerk marinade by combining the ingredients. Blend until fairly smooth. Taste for seasoning, adding more Scotch bonnet, brown sugar, or salt. Place the pork chops in a resealable plastic bag and pour the marinade over them, turning and massaging the bag to thoroughly coat the meat. Refrigerate for 2 to 4 hours.
2. Supply your smoker with wood pellets and follow the start-up procedure. Preheat the grill, with the lid closed, to 425° F.
3. Remove the pork from the marinade and scrape off the excess. (Discard the marinade.) Grill the chops until the internal temperature reaches 145°F (63°C), about 6 to 8 minutes per side.
4. Transfer the chops to a platter. Let rest for 2 minutes before serving.

Spiced Grilled Pork Chops

Servings: 4
Cooking Time: 30 Minutes

Ingredients:

- 3 Tbsp Black Peppercorns, Ground
- 1 Tbsp Coriander, Seed
- 1/4 Cup Cumin
- 1 - 2 Tsp Dry Rub
- 1 Tsp Olive Oil
- 4 Pork, Chop Bone-In
- 1 1/2 Tsp Salt
- 2 Tbsp Sugar

Directions:

1. Supply your smoker with wood pellets and follow the start-up procedure. Preheat the grill, with the lid open, to 450° F.
2. Combine the cumin seeds, whole black peppercorns, and coriander seeds in a cast iron skillet. Stir over medium heat for about 8 minutes until toasted. Let them cool slightly. Finely grind toasted spices in a blender and transfer to a small bowl, then mix in sugar and salt.
3. Rub the spices into the pork chops on both sides. Place cast iron skillet inside the grill. Once hot, add the olive oil to the skillet and coat the bottom. Sprinkle the pork chops with salt, and then add to the skillet. Make sure that each pork chop has enough space in between one another. Cook the chops for about 30 minutes. Once pork chops are fully cooked, turn off the grill, remove skillet, plate and enjoy!

Maple-smoked Pork Chops

Servings: 4
Cooking Time: 55 Minutes

Ingredients:

- 1 (12-pound) full packer brisket
- 2 tablespoons yellow mustard
- 1 batch Espresso Brisket Rub
- Worcestershire Mop and Spritz, for spritzing

Directions:

1. Supply your smoker with wood pellets and follow the start-up procedure. Preheat the grill, with the lid closed, to 180°F.
2. Season the pork chops on both sides with salt and pepper.
3. Place the chops directly on the grill grate and smoke for 30 minutes.
4. Increase the grill's temperature to 350°F. Continue to cook the chops until their internal temperature reaches 145°F.
5. Remove the pork chops from the grill and let them rest for 5 minutes before serving.

Beer Pork Belly Chili Con Carne

Servings: 4
Cooking Time: 120 Minutes

Ingredients:

- Avocado, Diced
- 2 Bay Leaves
- 1 Lbs Beef Stew Meat
- 12 Oz Beef Stock
- 12 Oz Beer, Bottle
- 15 Oz Black Beans, Rinsed And Drained
- 3 Tbsp Chili Powder
- Cilantro, Chopped
- 1 Tsp Coriander, Ground
- 2 Tsp Cumin, Ground

- 1 Tbsp Flour
- 4 Garlic Cloves, Minced
- 2 Tsp Mexican Oregano, Dried
- 2 Tbsp Olive Oil
- 2 Oz Pancetta, Diced
- Pork Belly, Cut Into 1 Inch Chunks
- 2 Red Onion, Chopped
- Rice, Cooked
- To Taste, Salt & Pepper
- Scallion, Sliced Thin
- 1/4 Cup Tomato Purée

Directions:
1. Supply your smoker with wood pellets and follow the start-up procedure. Preheat the grill, with the lid open, to 425° F. If using a gas or charcoal grill, set it up for medium-high heat. Place Dutch oven on grill and allow to preheat.
2. Heat the olive oil in the Dutch oven, then sauté the pancetta until crisp. Add the onions and sauté for 3 minutes, then add the garlic and sauté 1 minute, until fragrant. Remove mixture with a slotted spoon and set aside.
3. Add the pork belly and beef to the pot to brown, then add the chili powder, cumin, oregano, and coriander. Add the flour and cook for 2 minutes, stirring constantly.
4. Add the beer, beef stock, and tomato purée. Stir well, then return the pancetta mixture to the pot. Add the black beans and bay leaves, then season with salt and pepper.
5. Bring chili to a simmer, then reduce temperature to 325°F and simmer, uncovered, for 2 hours, stirring occasionally, until meat is tender, and sauce has thickened.
6. Remove the chili from the grill, then serve warm with cooked rice, avocado, fresh cilantro, and scallions.

Competition Style Bbq Pulled Pork

Servings: 8
Cooking Time: 600 Minutes

Ingredients:
- 1 (8-10 lb) bone-in pork butt
- 1 Cup Pork & Poultry Rub, divided
- 2 3/4 Cup apple juice, divided
- 1/4 Cup Butcher BBQ Pork Injection
- meat injector

Directions:
1. Supply your smoker with wood pellets and follow the start-up procedure. Preheat the grill, with the lid closed, to 225° F.
2. While the grill heats up, trim excess fat from pork.
3. In a small bowl, mix together half the Traeger Pork & Poultry Rub, 2 cups apple juice and butchers pork injection. Thoroughly inject pork butt throughout using an injector.
4. Season the pork with a layer of Traeger Pork & Poultry Rub. Let pork rest for 20 minutes.
5. Place pork on the grill and cook for 4-1/2 to 5-1/2 hours. After 4-1/2 hours, check the internal temperature of the pork. It should be between 155-165°F. If not, check again in 30 minutes. Grill: 225 °F Probe: 155 °F
6. When the temperature reaches 155-165°F, wrap the pork in a double layer of heavy duty aluminum foil. Pour 3/4 cup reserved apple juice in a foil packet with the pork and place back on the grill.
7. Turn the grill temperature up to 250°F and cook for another 3 to 4 hours. Check the internal temperature after 3 hours. The desired temperature is between 204°F and 206°F in the thickest part of the pork. If the pork is not to temperature, check back every 30 minutes until it reaches 204-206°F. The entire cook time should be between 8-10 hours depending on the size of the pork. Grill: 250 °F Probe: 204 °F
8. Remove pork from grill and open the foil packet to vent for 10 minutes. Seal back up and let rest for 45 minutes to one hour.
9. After resting, pour the liquid out of the foil and separate the fat from the broth using a fat separator. Remove the bone and pull the meat. Add 2 cups of the broth to the pulled meat. Add extra broth, if necessary, to achieve desired moisture level. Enjoy!

Roasted Ham With Apricot Sauce

Servings: 8
Cooking Time: 120 Minutes

Ingredients:
- 1 (8-10 lb) Snake River Farms Kurobuta Whole Bone-In Ham
- 1 Bottle Apricot BBQ Sauce
- 1/4 Cup horseradish
- 2 Tablespoon Dijon mustard

Directions:
1. Supply your smoker with wood pellets and follow the start-up procedure. Preheat the grill, with the lid closed, to 325° F.
2. Place ham in a large roasting pan lined with aluminum foil. Place pan on grill and cook for 90 minutes. Grill: 325 °F
3. For the Glaze: In a saucepan over medium heat, combine the Traeger Apricot BBQ Sauce, horseradish and mustard. Set aside and keep warm.
4. After 90 minutes, brush the ham with the glaze. Continue to cook for another 30 minutes or until a thermometer inserted into the thickest part of the ham reaches an internal temperatures of 135°F. Grill: 325 °F Probe: 135 °F
5. Remove ham from grill and rest for 20 minutes before slicing.
6. Serve with remaining glaze if desired. Enjoy!

Pulled Pork Corn Tortillas

Servings: 4
Cooking Time: 15 Minutes

Ingredients:
- Cilantro
- Cilantro, Chopped
- 8 Corn Tortillas
- Jalepeno, Sliced
- 1 Lime, Wedges
- 2 Cups Pulled Pork
- Radishes, Sliced
- White Onion, Diced

Directions:
1. Supply your smoker with wood pellets and follow the start-up procedure. Preheat the grill, with the lid open, to 350° F. Grill the corn tortillas until they are softened and have charred spots, about 30 seconds.
2. To assemble the carnitas, add the pulled pork to the tortillas, and top with radishes, diced onion, cilantro, jalapeno and a squeeze of lime juice, if desired. Serve and enjoy!

Texas Grilled Ribs

Servings: 4
Cooking Time: 240 Minutes

Ingredients:
- 1 Cup Apple Cider Vinegar
- 1 Rack Baby Back Rib
- 2 Tablespoons Whole Grain Mustard
- 2 Tablespoons Olive Oil
- 1 Bottle Sweet Heat Rub
- 1 Tablespoons Worcestershire Sauce

Directions:
1. Remove the ribs from their packaging and pat dry.
2. Flip to back of ribs and score the membrane with a knife, then peel off the membrane.
3. Rub the ribs with the olive oil, followed by a generous amount of Sweet Heat Rub & Grill, on both sides.
4. In a small bowl, mix together the mustard, apple cider vinegar, and Worcestershire. Set aside.
5. Supply your smoker with wood pellets and follow the start-up procedure. Preheat the grill, with the lid open, to 225° F. Add the ribs and smoke for 3 hours.
6. Transfer the ribs onto a foil lined sheet pan and brush both sides with the apple cider vinegar mixture. Wrap the ribs tightly in foil and place back on the smoker for 2 more hours.
7. Carefully remove the ribs from the foil and brush with more of the apple cider vinegar mixture. Place the ribs back on the smoker grates and smoke for 1 additional hour.
8. Remove from the smoker and let rest for 5 minutes before serving.

Hot & Fast Smoked Baby Back Ribs

Servings: 6
Cooking Time: 180 Minutes

Ingredients:
- 3 Rack baby back ribs
- Pork & Poultry Rub
- 2 Cup apple juice

Directions:
1. Supply your smoker with wood pellets and follow the start-up procedure. Preheat the grill, with the lid closed, to 300° F.
2. Pull membrane from back of the ribs and trim any excess fat.
3. Season front and back of ribs with the Traeger Pork & Poultry Rub. Let rest on counter for 10 minutes. Grill: 300 °F
4. Place ribs directly on the grill and cook for 30 minutes. Grill: 300 °F
5. While ribs cook, put apple juice in a spray bottle. Spray ribs with apple juice after the first 30 minutes of cooking and every 30 minutes after, about 2-1/2 hours. Grill: 300 °F Probe: 202 °F
6. Check the internal temperature of the ribs. The desired temperature is 202°F. If the desired temperature has not been reached, check every 20 minutes until it comes to temperature. Grill: 300 °F Probe: 202 °F
7. Remove ribs from grill and let rest 10 minutes before slicing and serving. Enjoy!

Bourbon Chile Glazed Ham

Servings: 8 – 10
Cooking Time: 90 Minutes

Ingredients:
- ¼ Cup Apple Cider Vinegar
- 2 Cups Bourbon
- 1 Cup Brown Sugar
- 2 Canned Chipotle Chiles In Adobo Sauce
- 2 Cups Chicken Stock
- 2 Dried Ancho Chiles
- 1 Dried Arbol Chile
- 2 Dried Guajillo Chiles
- 2 Tbsp Extra Virgin Olive Oil
- 4 Fresh Garlic, Roughly Chopped
- 4 Cloves Roasted Garlic
- Salt
- 2 Shallots, Roughly Chopped
- 1 Spiral Cut Ham

Directions:
1. Supply your smoker with wood pellets and follow the start-up procedure. Preheat the grill, with the lid open, to 450° F.
2. In a large, heavy-bottomed skillet, heat the oil over medium-high heat. Add the shallots and cook for 5 minutes, or until softened.
3. Add the roasted and fresh garlic and cook, stirring occasionally, for 3 to 4 minutes, until the garlic is browned.
4. Remove the skillet from the heat and add the bourbon.
5. Return the skillet to medium-high heat, add the vinegar, and cook until the liquid is reduced by one third, about 10 minutes.
6. Add the ancho, guajillo, árbol, and chipotle chiles and the brown sugar, then add the chicken stock and continue to cook until the mixture reduces by two thirds, about 15 minutes.
7. Strain the reduction through a fine-mesh strainer into a bowl, then pour it into a small saucepan.
8. Return to the heat over medium and reduce until the glaze coats the back off a spoon. Taste and add salt if needed.

Grilled Pork Tacos Al Pastor

Servings: 8
Cooking Time: 15 Minutes

Ingredients:
- 2 Tsp Annatto Powder
- Cilantro, Chopped
- Corn Tortillas
- 2 Tsp Cumin
- 1 Tsp Granulated Garlic
- 2 Tbsp Guajillo Chili Powder
- Jalapeno Pepper, Minced
- Lime, Wedges

- 1 Tsp Oregano, Dried
- 1/2 Tsp Pepper
- 1/2 Cup Pineapple, Juice
- 1/2 Pineapple, Skinned & Cored
- 2 Lbs Pork Shoulder, Boneless, Sliced Thin
- 1 1/2 Tsp Salt
- 2 Tbsp Tomato Paste
- 2 Tbsp Vegetable Oil
- 1/4 Cup White Vinegar
- Yellow Onion, Chopped

Directions:

1. Prepare marinade: In a mixing bowl, whisk together pineapple juice, vinegar, oil, tomato paste, chili powder, annatto, cumin, granulated garlic, oregano, salt, and pepper. Set aside.
2. Slice pork shoulder into thin slices (around ¼" thick), then place in a resealable plastic bag. Pour marinade over pork, seal bag, and turn to coat. Refrigerate overnight.
3. Supply your smoker with wood pellets and follow the start-up procedure. Preheat the grill, with the lid open, to 450° F. If using a gas or charcoal grill, set it up for high heat.
4. Remove the pork from the marinade and set on the grill. Grill over high heat for 3 to 5 minutes, turning frequently. Transfer to a cutting board to rest for 10 minutes, then slice thin.
5. Grill pineapple for 3 minutes, turning once. Set aside on a cutting board, and chop once cooled.
6. Assemble tacos: tortillas, pork, pineapple, jalapeño, onion, and cilantro. Serve warm with fresh lime wedges.

Egg Bacon French Toast Panini

Servings: 2
Cooking Time: 10 Minutes

Ingredients:

- 6 Bacon Slices
- 1 Tbsp Black Pepper
- 4 Brioche Sandwich Slices, Day Old
- 2 Tbsp Butter
- 1 Tbsp Cinnamon-Sugar
- 6 Eggs
- 1 Tbsp Heavy Cream
- 1 Tbsp Maple Syrup
- 1 Tbsp Salt

Directions:

1. Supply your smoker with wood pellets and follow the start-up procedure. Preheat the grill, with the lid open, to 375° F. If using a gas or charcoal grill, set heat to medium heat. For all other grills, preheat cast iron skillet on grill grates.
2. Place butter on griddle and spread to coat surface.
3. In a pie plate, whisk together 2 eggs, heavy cream, and maple syrup.
4. Soak both sides of bread slices in egg mixture and transfer to griddle. Cook for 2 minutes, flipping halfway until egg mixture is cooked and golden. Set aside.
5. Lay bacon on the griddle, and cook 3 minutes per side, until golden.
6. Transfer to lower right-hand corner of griddle to keep warm.
7. Crack 4 eggs on top of rendered bacon fat. Season with salt and pepper. Cook 1 minute per side, or to desired doneness.
8. Lay eggs on top of French toast, add bacon, then place the other slice of French Toast on top.
9. Transfer back to griddle for another minute to warm, sprinkle with extra cinnamon-sugar, then slice in half and serve hot.

Smoked Rendezvous Ribs

Servings: 4
Cooking Time: 120 Minutes

Ingredients:

- 1/2 Cup apple cider vinegar
- 1/2 Cup water
- 1/2 Cup BBQ Sauce
- 2 Tablespoon Pork & Poultry Rub
- 3 Rack baby back pork ribs, membrane removed
- 1 As Needed Pork & Poultry Rub

Directions:

1. In a mixing bowl, combine vinegar, water, barbecue sauce, and Traeger Pork and Poultry rub. Set the sauce and a barbecue mop or basting brush grill-side.

2. Supply your smoker with wood pellets and follow the start-up procedure. Preheat the grill, with the lid closed, to 325° F.
3. Arrange the ribs on the grill grate, meat-side up.
4. Grill for 30 minutes, then start mopping. Mop every 15 minutes. After 2 hours, check the ribs for doneness. Grill: 325 °F
5. Insert a toothpick between the bones in the center of a rack. If there is little or no resistance, the ribs are done (or close to it). If the ribs are not to your liking, continue to grill them in 30-minute increments, mopping every 15 minutes. Grill: 325 °F
6. When the ribs are done, transfer them to a cutting board and give them a final dose of the mop sauce. Sprinkle lightly with Traeger Pork and Poultry Rub.
7. Let the ribs rest for a few minutes before cutting into half slabs or individual ribs. Enjoy!

Bbq 3-2-1 St. Louis Ribs

Servings: 6
Cooking Time: 360 Minutes

Ingredients:
- 2 Rack St. Louis-style ribs
- Pork & Poultry Rub
- 1/2 Cup brown sugar, divided
- 1/3 Cup honey, divided
- 1 Cup BBQ Sauce
- BBQ Sauce

Directions:
1. If your butcher has not done so already, remove the thin silverskin membrane from the bone-side of the ribs by working the tip of a butter knife underneath the membrane over a middle bone. Use paper towels to get a firm grip, then tear the membrane off.
2. Season both sides of the ribs generously with Traeger Pork & Poultry Rub.
3. Supply your smoker with wood pellets and follow the start-up procedure. Preheat the grill, with the lid closed, to 180° F.
4. Smoke the ribs, meat-side up for 3 hours. Transfer the ribs to a rimmed baking sheet and increase the grill temperature to 225°F. Preheat the grill with the lid closed. Grill: 225 °F
5. Tear off four long sheets of heavy-duty aluminum foil. Top with a rack of ribs. Sprinkle half the brown sugar on the rack then top with half the honey. Tightly wrap the ribs with the foil to create a leak-proof pouch. Repeat with remaining rack of ribs. Grill: 225 °F
6. Return the foiled ribs to the grill, meat side down and cook for an additional two hours. Grill: 225 °F
7. Carefully remove the foil from the ribs – watch out for hot steam – and brush the ribs on both sides with your favorite Traeger BBQ sauce. Discard the foil. Arrange the ribs directly on the grill grate, bone side down and continue to grill until the sauce tightens, about 30 minutes to 60 minutes more. Let the ribs rest for a few minutes before serving. Enjoy! Grill: 225 °F

Baked Pig Candy

Servings: 4
Cooking Time: 60 Minutes

Ingredients:
- 1 Pound thin sliced bacon
- 1/2 Cup maple syrup or corn syrup
- 2 Cup light brown sugar, packed
- 3 Tablespoon chipotle chile powder

Directions:
1. Supply your smoker with wood pellets and follow the start-up procedure. Preheat the grill, with the lid closed, to 250° F.
2. Place the bacon slices in a single layer on a large disposable, perforated aluminum pan. Brush each bacon slice with maple syrup. Sprinkle generously with brown sugar, then chipotle powder.
3. Place the pan on the grill and cook until the bacon has absorbed the brown sugar and is crispy, about 1 hour. Remove the bacon from the pan and place in a single layer on a wire rack set over a rimmed baking sheet. Grill: 250 °F
4. Set aside at room temperature until the surface of the bacon is dry. Refrigerate in an airtight container with parchment paper between the layers and use within 1 week. Enjoy!

Sweet Bacon

Servings: 4
Cooking Time: 60 Minutes

Ingredients:
- 1 Pack Bacon, Thick Cut
- 1/2 Cup Brown Sugar
- 1/2 Cup Maple Syrup
- Mandarin Habanero Seasoning

Directions:
1. Place the bacon in a deep dish. Add the maple syrup, cover and refrigerate 2 - 3 hours or overnight.
2. Supply your smoker with wood pellets and follow the start-up procedure. Preheat the grill, with the lid open, to 225° F.
3. When the grill has preheated, place the bacon directly on the cooking grids and sprinkle with brown sugar and Mandarin Habanero. Check every 15-20. After 30 minutes, flip and rotate bacon and baste with syrup. Allow to hot smoke for another 20 to 30 minutes or until the bacon is done to your desired liking.
4. Allow to cool on a rack and serve.
5. Can be refrigerated in an airtight container.

Roasted Bacon Weave Holiday Ham

Servings: 6
Cooking Time: 180 Minutes

Ingredients:
- 1 1/2 Pound Bacon, sliced
- 1 Large Ham, Bone-In
- whole cloves
- 1 1/2 Cup pineapple juice
- 2 Cup ginger beer
- 1/4 Cup brown sugar
- 2 Tablespoon mustard

Directions:
1. Create a bacon weave on parchment paper.
2. Put the ham in a disposable roasting pan. Gently transfer the bacon weave to the top of the ham and stud the bacon with the cloves (if desired).
3. Pour 1 cup of pineapple juice and 1 cup of ginger beer/ale into the bottom of the roasting pan.
4. Supply your smoker with wood pellets and follow the start-up procedure. Preheat the grill, with the lid closed, to 300° F.
5. Cover the roasting pan with foil and put on the Traeger. Cook the ham until it reaches 145°F (somewhere between 2 to 3 hours). Grill: 300 °F Probe: 145 °F
6. Meanwhile mix together the glaze. Combine the remaining 1/2 cup of pineapple juice, 1 cup ginger beer/ale, brown sugar and mustard in a saucepan on the stovetop. Cook until it thickens slightly, then brush on the ham.
7. Put the uncovered ham back on Traeger and cook until the temperature reaches 160°F. Grill: 300 °F Probe: 160 °F
8. Let the ham rest 5 minutes before slicing and serving. Reserve the juices to pour over the ham. Enjoy!

Raspberry Spiral Ham With Glaze

Servings: 12
Cooking Time: 120 Minutes

Ingredients:
- 1 Ham, Spiral (Precooked)
- Raspberry Chipotle Spice Rub
- 1/2 Jar Raspberry Jam
- 1 Quart Raspberry, Fresh
- 1/4 Cup Sugar
- 1/3 Cup Water, Warm

Directions:
1. Supply your smoker with wood pellets and follow the start-up procedure. Preheat the grill, with the lid open, to 225° F.
2. Season the ham with Raspberry Chipotle Spice, taking care to season in between each slice. Place in your Grill and smoke for about 2 hours.
3. Just before you pull the ham, combine glaze ingredients in a saucepan over medium heat until raspberries are no longer whole and the glaze is runny. If you want a smoother glaze, remove the raspberry seeds by draining the glaze through cheesecloth.
4. Pour glaze over the ham just before serving. Slice and serve hot. Enjoy!

Pork & Pepperoni Burgers

Servings: 4
Cooking Time: 60 Minutes

Ingredients:
- 1lb (450g) bulk pork sausage, preferably Italian
- 1lb (450g) ground pork, well chilled
- 8 slices of bacon, preferably thick-cut
- 8oz (225g) grated mozzarella cheese, plus more
- 1 tsp Italian seasoning
- ½ cup pizza sauce
- 1½oz (40g) pepperoni, roughly chopped

Directions:
1. Wet your hands with cold water. In a large bowl, combine the sausage and ground pork until well mixed. Line a rimmed sheet pan with aluminum foil. Divide the meat into 4 equal-sized balls and place on the sheet pan. Spray the lower third of a soda can (including the bottom) with cooking spray. Firmly press the can into one of the meatballs to create a meat bowl with uniform sides. Gently twist or rock the can to remove. Use your hands to repair any cracks in the bowl.
2. Wrap 2 slices of bacon around the circumference of the bowl and secure with toothpicks. Repeat with the remaining meatballs, respraying the can with cooking spray as necessary. Chill for 1 hour.
3. Supply your smoker with wood pellets and follow the start-up procedure. Preheat the grill, with the lid closed, to 300° F.
4. Place the patties cup side up on the grate and grill for 30 minutes. Use paper towels to blot any grease that pools at the bottom of the cups.
5. Sprinkle 2 tablespoons of cheese into each cup. Top each patty with equal amounts of Italian seasoning, pizza sauce, and pepperoni. Generously sprinkle more cheese over the top. Continue to grill until the bacon crisps, the cheese melts, and the internal temperature reaches 160°F (71°C), about 20 to 30 minutes more.
6. Remove the burgers from the grill and rest for 3 minutes. Remove the toothpicks and serve immediately.

Bbq Brown Sugar Pork Belly

Servings: 8
Cooking Time: 180 Minutes

Ingredients:
- 1 (3-4 lb) pork belly
- 4 Tablespoon brown sugar
- 4 Tablespoon salt

Directions:
1. The night before you plan to cook, take your pork belly out of the fridge and pat dry with paper towels. Score fat with a very sharp knife in a diamond pattern making sure not to cut into the meat.
2. Combine salt and brown sugar and rub pork belly on all sides. Place on a drying rack on a pan and refrigerate uncovered overnight.
3. Thirty minutes before cooking, remove pork belly from fridge. Rinse under cold water and pat very dry with paper towels.
4. Supply your smoker with wood pellets and follow the start-up procedure. Preheat the grill, with the lid closed, to 450° F.
5. Place the pork belly directly on grill grate, fat side up, for 30 minutes. Grill: 500 °F
6. After 30 minutes, reduce the grill temperature to 325°F and cook for 3 hours or until pork is tender and fat is crisp. Grill: 325 °F
7. Remove from grill and allow to rest for 30 minutes before slicing.
8. Serve with baked beans, potato salad, coleslaw, white bread, BBQ sauce, or your favorite BBQ sides. Enjoy!

Classic Pulled Pork

Servings: 8-12
Cooking Time: 1200 Minutes

Ingredients:
- 1 (6- to 8-pound) bone-in pork shoulder
- 2 tablespoons yellow mustard
- 1 batch Pork Rub

Directions:
1. Supply your smoker with wood pellets and follow the start-up procedure. Preheat the grill, with the lid closed, to 225°F.

2. Coat the pork shoulder all over with mustard and season it with the rub. Using your hands, work the rub into the meat.
3. Place the shoulder on the grill grate and smoke until its internal temperature reaches 195°F.
4. Pull the shoulder from the grill and wrap it completely in aluminum foil or butcher paper. Place it in a cooler, cover the cooler, and let it rest for 1 or 2 hours.
5. Remove the pork shoulder from the cooler and unwrap it. Remove the shoulder bone and pull the pork apart using just your fingers. Serve immediately as desired. Leftovers are encouraged.

Everything Pigs In A Blanket

Servings: 4
Cooking Time: 15 Minutes

Ingredients:
- 2 Tablespoon poppy seeds
- 1 Tablespoon dried minced onion
- 2 Teaspoon garlic, minced
- 2 Tablespoon sesame seeds
- 1 Teaspoon salt
- 8 Ounce (8 oz) Can Pillsbury Original Crescent Rolls
- 1/4 Cup Dijon mustard
- 1 Large egg, beaten

Directions:
1. Supply your smoker with wood pellets and follow the start-up procedure. Preheat the grill, with the lid closed, to 350° F.
2. Mix together poppy seeds, dried minced onion, dried minced garlic, salt and sesame seeds. Set aside.
3. Cut each triangle of crescent roll dough into thirds lengthwise, making 3 small strips from each roll.
4. Brush the dough strips lightly with Dijon mustard. Put the mini hot dogs on 1 end of the dough and roll up.
5. Arrange them, seam side down, on a greased baking pan. Brush with egg wash and sprinkle with seasoning mixture.
6. Bake in Traeger until golden brown, about 12 to 15 minutes.
7. Serve with mustard or dipping sauce of your choice. Enjoy!

St. Louis–style Pork Steaks

Servings: 4
Cooking Time: 120 Minutes

Ingredients:
- 1 cup low-carb barbecue sauce
- ¼ cup low-carb beer or sugar-free dark-colored soda or sugar-free root beer
- 4 bone-in pork shoulder steaks, each about 1lb (450g) and at least 1 inch (2.5cm) thick
- for the rub
- 1 tbsp coarse salt
- 1 tbsp freshly ground black pepper
- 1 tbsp granulated light brown sugar or low-carb substitute
- 1 tbsp sweet or smoked paprika
- 1 tsp granulated garlic or garlic powder
- 1 tsp celery salt

Directions:
1. Supply your smoker with wood pellets and follow the start-up procedure. Preheat the grill, with the lid closed, to 250° F.
2. In a small bowl, combine the barbecue sauce and beer. Set aside.
3. In a small bowl, make the rub by combining the ingredients. Mix well. Season the steaks on both sides with some of the rub.
4. Place the steaks on the grate at an angle to the bars and smoke for 30 minutes. Transfer the steaks to an aluminum foil roasting pan. Pour the barbecue mixture over them. Use tongs to turn the steaks, making sure each is coated well with the sauce.
5. Tightly wrap aluminum foil over the top of the pan and place it on the grate. Braise the steaks until they're fork tender, about 1½ hours. (Protect your hands when lifting a corner of the foil because steam will escape.)
6. Remove the pan from the grill and serve the steaks immediately.

Apple & Bourbon Glazed Ham

Servings: 6
Cooking Time: 60 Minutes

Ingredients:
- 1 Large ham
- 1 Cup apple jelly
- 2 Tablespoon Dijon mustard
- 2 Tablespoon bourbon
- 2 Teaspoon fresh lemon juice
- 1/2 Teaspoon ground cloves
- 2 Cup apple juice or cider

Directions:
1. Supply your smoker with wood pellets and follow the start-up procedure. Preheat the grill, with the lid closed, to 325° F.
2. When the grill is hot, place ham directly on the grill grate. Cook for 30 minutes. Grill: 325 °F
3. Meanwhile, in a small saucepan over medium-low heat, melt the apple jelly. Whisk in the apple juice, mustard, bourbon, lemon juice and ground cloves, then remove from the heat and set aside.
4. After 30 minutes, glaze ham with the apple bourbon mixture. Continue cooking for another 30 minutes or until a thermometer that is inserted into the thickest part of the meat reaches an internal temperature of 135°F. Grill: 325 °F Probe: 135 °F
5. Remove ham from grill and allow to rest for 20 minutes before serving. Warm remaining sauce and serve with ham if desired. Enjoy!

Spicy Ribs

Servings: 4
Cooking Time: 300 Minutes

Ingredients:
- 2 Finely Minced Chipotle In Adobo
- 1 Cup (Any Kind) Barbecue Sauce
- 1/2 Cup Brown Sugar
- 1/4 Cup Honey
- 1/4 Cup Olive Oil
- 1 Rack St. Louis-Style Rib(S)
- 3 Tablespoons Sweet Heat Rub

Directions:
1. Remove the ribs from their packaging, drain, and pat dry. Using a paper towel, grip the membrane on the back of the ribs and pull off. Discard the membrane and paper towel.
2. In a small mixing bowl, combine the brown sugar, olive oil, honey, BBQ sauce, and chiles in adobo. Using a basting brush, brush the front and back of the ribs generously with the BBQ mixture. Save the basting brush for later along with half of the sauce.
3. Generously season the ribs with Sweet Heat rub, making sure to focus especially on the front of the ribs.
4. Supply your smoker with wood pellets and follow the start-up procedure. Preheat the grill, with the lid open, to 225° F. If you're using a gas or charcoal grill, set it up for low heat. Place the ribs on the grill and smoke at 225°F for 4-6 hours making sure to baste in the sauce every 2 hours.
5. Remove from the grill and serve with additional barbecue sauce.

Pineapple-pepper Pork Kebabs

Servings: 12-15
Cooking Time: 240 Minutes

Ingredients:
- 1 (20-ounce) bottle hoisin sauce
- ½ cup Sriracha
- ¼ cup honey
- ¼ cup apple cider vinegar
- 2 tablespoons canola oil
- 2 teaspoons minced garlic
- 2 teaspoons onion powder
- 1 teaspoon ground ginger
- 1 teaspoon salt
- 1 teaspoon freshly ground black pepper
- 2 pounds thick-cut pork chops or pork loin, cut into 2-inch cubes
- 10 ounces fresh pineapple, cut into chunks
- 1 red onion, cut into wedges
- 1 bag mini sweet peppers, tops removed and seeded
- 12 metal or wooden skewers (soaked in water for 30 minutes if wooden)

Directions:

1. In a small bowl, stir together the hoisin, Sriracha, honey, vinegar, oil, minced garlic, onion powder, ginger, salt, and black pepper to create the marinade. Reserve ¼ cup for basting.
2. Toss the pork cubes, pineapple chunks, onion wedges, and mini peppers in the remaining marinade. Cover and refrigerate for at least 1 hour or up to 4 hours.
3. Supply your smoker with wood pellets and follow the start-up procedure. Preheat, with the lid closed, to 450°F.
4. Remove the pork, pineapple, and veggies from the marinade; do not rinse. Discard the marinade.
5. Use the double-skewer technique to assemble the kebabs (see Tip below). Thread each of 6 skewers with a piece of pork, a piece of pineapple, a piece of onion, and a sweet mini pepper, making sure that the skewer goes through the left side of the ingredients. Repeat the threading on each skewer two more times. Double-skewer the kebabs by sticking another 6 skewers through the right side of the ingredients.
6. Place the kebabs directly on the grill, close the lid, and smoke for 10 to 12 minutes, turning once. They are done when a meat thermometer inserted in the pork reads 160°F.

Delicious Smoked Bone-in Pork Chops

Servings: 4
Cooking Time: 90 Minutes

Ingredients:

- 1/2 Cup Apple Cider Vinegar
- 4 Pork Butt Roast, Bone-In
- 2 Tbsp Salt
- 1 Tbsp Sugar
- 4 Tablespoons Tennessee Apple Butter Seasoning
- 1/4 Cup Vinegar, Red Wine
- 1/4 Cup Water

Directions:

1. Supply your smoker with wood pellets and follow the start-up procedure. Preheat the grill, with the lid closed, to 250° F.
2. In a large mixing bowl, combine the sugar, red wine vinegar, salt, 2 tablespoons of Tennessee Apple Butter and water to create a brine for the pork chops. Whisk the brine well until the sugar, salt and Tennessee Apple Butter have dissolved.
3. Generously rub the pork chops on all sides with olive oil and season on all sides with the Tennessee Apple Butter. Make sure the meat is coated on all sides.
4. Place the pork chops in the smoker, insert a temperature probe into the thickest part of one of the pork chops, and smoke until the internal temperature reaches 145°F, or about 1 hour 30 minutes. The pork chops should have developed a good color and be juicy, but no longer be pink in the center.
5. Remove the pork chops from the smoker and allow them to rest for 5-10 minutes under tented aluminum foil, then slice along the grain and serve.

3-2-1 Bbq Baby Back Ribs

Servings: 6
Cooking Time: 360 Minutes

Ingredients:

- 2 Rack baby back pork ribs
- 1/3 Cup yellow mustard
- 1/2 Cup apple juice, divided
- 1 Tablespoon Worcestershire sauce
- Pork & Poultry Rub
- 1/2 Cup dark brown sugar
- 1/3 Cup honey, warmed
- 1 Cup 'Que BBQ Sauce

Directions:

1. If your butcher has not already done so, remove the thin silverskin membrane from the bone-side of the ribs by working the tip of a butter knife or a screwdriver underneath the membrane over a middle bone. Use paper towels to get a firm grip, then tear the membrane off.
2. In a small bowl, combine the mustard, 1/4 cup of apple juice (reserve the rest) and the Worcestershire sauce. Spread the mixture thinly on both sides of the ribs and season with Traeger Pork & Poultry Rub.

3. Supply your smoker with wood pellets and follow the start-up procedure. Preheat the grill, with the lid closed, to 180° F. Smoke the ribs, meat-side up for 3 hours.

4. After the ribs have smoked for 3 hours, transfer them to a rimmed baking sheet and increase the grill temperature to 225°F.

5. Tear off four long sheets of heavy-duty aluminum foil. Top with a rack of ribs and pull up the sides to keep the liquid enclosed. Sprinkle half the brown sugar on the rack, then top with half the honey and half the remaining apple juice. Use a bit more apple juice if you want more tender ribs. Lay another piece of foil on top and tightly crimp the edges so there is no leakage. Repeat with the remaining rack of ribs.

6. Return the foiled ribs to the grill and cook for an additional 2 hours.

7. Carefully remove the foil from the ribs and brush the ribs on both sides with Traeger 'Que Sauce. Discard the foil. Arrange the ribs directly on the grill grate and continue to grill until the sauce tightens, 30 to 60 minutes more.

8. Let the ribs rest for a few minutes before serving. Enjoy!

Old-fashioned Roasted Glazed Ham

Servings: 8
Cooking Time: 60 Minutes

Ingredients:
- 1 (10 lb) fully cooked bone-in spiral cut ham
- 1 Cup pineapple juice
- 1/2 Cup brown sugar
- 1 cinnamon stick
- 14 whole cloves
- 1 Whole Pineapple, fresh
- 10 Cherries, fresh, sweet

Directions:
1. Supply your smoker with wood pellets and follow the start-up procedure. Preheat the grill, with the lid closed, to 325° F.

2. Rinse ham under cold water and pat dry with paper towel.

3. In a saucepan combine pineapple juice, brown sugar, cinnamon stick and four cloves. Bring to a boil. Reduce heat to medium low and simmer for about 15 minutes or until pineapple juice is reduced by half, thick and syrupy.

4. Brush half of the glaze onto the ham and into the folds of the cut slices. Reserve the other half of the glaze for later.

5. Cut pineapple in desired sized pieces, about 2 inch squares, then place on ham with a cherry and a clove to pin in place, repeating all over ham.

6. Put ham in a deep baking dish with fat side up. Place on the Traeger and cook for about 1-¼ hours. Grill: 325 °F

7. Carefully remove from Traeger and brush remaining glaze onto ham.

8. Return ham to Traeger and continue cooking for another 15 to 20 minutes, until internal temperature of ham reaches 160°F. Grill: 325 °F Probe: 160 °F

9. Allow ham to rest for 15 – 20 minutes before serving. Enjoy!

Smoked Pork Spare Ribs

Servings: 8
Cooking Time: 240 Minutes

Ingredients:
- 2 Rack (6 lb) pork spare ribs, trimmed
- 3 Tablespoon Pork & Poultry Rub
- 1 Cup apple juice, cider or beer
- 9 Ounce BBQ Sauce

Directions:
1. Supply your smoker with wood pellets and follow the start-up procedure. Preheat the grill, with the lid closed, to 250° F.

2. If your butcher hasn't done so already, remove the silver-skin on the back of the ribs and trim off any excess fat.

3. Season the ribs on all sides with Traeger Pork & Poultry rub.

4. Arrange the racks of spare ribs on the grill grate, bone-side down and cook for 3 to 4 hours. After the first hour, spray the ribs with apple juice. Continue spraying every hour after that with apple juice. Grill: 250 °F

5. Start checking the temp after 2 hours. The finished internal temperature should be 203°F, about 3 to 4 hours. Grill: 250 °F Probe: 203 °F

6. When the internal temperature registers 203°F, brush the ribs on all sides with Traeger BBQ sauce of your choice. Return ribs to the grill and cook for an additional 30 to 60 minutes to tighten the sauce.

7. To serve, cut each slab in half or into individual ribs and serve with additional BBQ sauce on the side. Enjoy!

Baked Maple And Brown Sugar Bacon

Servings: 4
Cooking Time: 60 Minutes

Ingredients:
- 1 Pound cold bacon
- 1/2 Cup pure maple syrup, warmed
- 1/2 Cup brown sugar, plus more as needed

Directions:
1. Supply your smoker with wood pellets and follow the start-up procedure. Preheat the grill, with the lid closed, to 300° F.
2. Line a rimmed baking sheet with foil and place a wire rack on top. Lay bacon strips in a single layer on the wire rack.
3. Using a pastry brush, brush each strip of bacon on both sides with the warmed maple syrup, then sprinkle brown sugar evenly on both sides.
4. Put the baking sheet in the grill and cook bacon for 60-75 minutes, or until bacon browns and appears to be crisping. Grill: 300 °F
5. Allow the bacon to cool slightly before eating. Enjoy!

Bbq Brown Sugar Bacon Bites

Servings: 2
Cooking Time: 25 Minutes

Ingredients:
- 1/2 Cup brown sugar
- 1 Tablespoon Fennel, ground
- 2 Teaspoon kosher salt
- 1 Teaspoon ground black pepper
- 1 Pound Pork Belly, diced

Directions:

1. Fold a 12" x 36" piece of aluminum foil in half and crimp the edges so there is a rim. Using a fork, poke holes in the bottom of the foil. This way some of the bacon fat will be rendered out and the bacon bites will crisp.
2. Supply your smoker with wood pellets and follow the start-up procedure. Preheat the grill, with the lid closed, to 350° F.
3. In a large bowl, combine the brown sugar, ground fennel, salt, and black pepper. Stir to combine.
4. Place the diced pork belly into the mixture and toss until well-coated. Transfer the pork pieces to the foil.
5. Place on the grill and bake until the pieces are crispy, glazed, and bubbly, about 20-30 minutes. Enjoy!

Apple-smoked Bacon

Servings: 4-6
Cooking Time: 30 Minutes

Ingredients:
- 1 (1-pound) package thick-sliced bacon

Directions:
1. Supply your smoker with wood pellets and follow the start-up procedure. Preheat the grill, with the lid closed, to 275°F.
2. Supply your smoker with wood pellets and follow the start-up procedure. Preheat the grill, with the lid closed, to 275°F.

Smoky Bratwurst

Servings: 8 – 12
Cooking Time: 120 Minutes

Ingredients:
- 12 Fresh Bratwurst, Linked

Directions:
1. Supply your smoker with wood pellets and follow the start-up procedure. Preheat the grill, with the lid open, to 225° F. If using gas or charcoal grill, set it up for low indirect heat.
2. Place metal hooks on shelves about 6" apart. Cut bratwurst links into pairs and string on metal hooks. If you don't have metal hooks, you can place bratwurst directly on grill grate, but we recommend brushing the

casing lightly in oil to ensure it doesn't stick during smoking.
3. Smoke bratwurst for one hour, then increase temperature to 300°F. Cook for one additional hour, or until bratwurst skin is golden brown and they've wrinkled slightly. If using a temperature probe, the brats are finished when internal temp reaches 160°F.
4. Remove from smoker and serve immediately. We recommend with buns and/or caramelized onions and sauerkraut.

Holiday Smoked Cheese Log

Servings: 8
Cooking Time: 60 Minutes

Ingredients:
- 16 Ounce cream cheese
- 3 Cup shredded cheddar cheese
- 1 Tablespoon Worcestershire sauce
- 1 Teaspoon hot sauce
- 8 Slices bacon
- 2 green onion
- 1 Cup coarsely chopped pecans

Directions:
1. In a mixing bowl, using an electric mixer or large spoon, combine the cream cheese (room temperature) and the cheddar cheese.
2. Add in the Worcestershire sauce and hot sauce. Mix again.
3. Add in the cooked and crumbled bacon and chopped green onions. Mix until combined.
4. Cover the bowl with plastic wrap and refrigerate for 4 hours or until the cheese mixture is firm enough to mold. Shape it into a log and layer the outside with the toasted pecans.
5. Cover with plastic wrap. Freeze the cheese log overnight to make sure it doesn't get too soft while it's smoking.
6. The next day supply your smoker with wood pellets and follow the start-up procedure. Preheat the grill, with the lid closed, to 180° F.
7. Take the cheese log out of the freezer and unwrap. Place on a cooking sheet and smoke for 1 hour. Keep an eye on it to make sure it doesn't get too soft. Grill: 180 °F
8. Move the cheese log to a serving tray and serve with your favorite crackers. (If the cheese is too soft, throw it in the fridge for an hour or two.)

Stuffed Pork Crown Roast

Servings: 2-4
Cooking Time: 180 Minutes

Ingredients:
- 10 Pound Crown Roast of Pork, 12-14 ribs
- 1 Cup apple juice or cider
- 2 Tablespoon apple cider vinegar
- 2 Tablespoon Dijon mustard
- 1 Tablespoon brown sugar
- 2 Clove garlic, minced
- 2 Tablespoon Thyme or Rosemary, fresh
- 1 Teaspoon salt
- 1 Teaspoon coarse ground black pepper, divided
- 1/2 Cup olive oil
- 8 Cup Your Favorite Stuffing, Prepared According to the Package Directions, or Homemade

Directions:
1. Set the pork on a flat rack in a shallow roasting pan. Cover the end of each bone with a small piece of foil.
2. Make the marinade: Bring the apple cider to a boil over high heat and reduce by half. Remove from the heat, and whisk in the vinegar, mustard, brown sugar, garlic, thyme, and salt and pepper. Slowly whisk in the oil.
3. Using a pastry brush, apply the marinade to the roast, coating all surfaces. Cover it with plastic wrap and allow it to sit until the meat comes to room temperature, about 1 hour.
4. When ready to cook, set grill temperature to High and preheat, lid closed for 15 minutes.
5. Arrange the roasting pan with the pork on the grill grate. Roast for 30 minutes.
6. Reduce the heat to 325°F. Loosely fill the crown with the stuffing, mounding it at the top. Cover the stuffing with foil. (Alternatively, you can bake the stuffing in a separate pan alongside the roast.)

7. Roast the pork for another 1-1/2 hours. Remove the foil from the stuffing and continue to roast until the internal temperature of the meat is 150°F, about 30 minutes to an hour. Make sure the temperature probe doesn't touch bone or you will get a false reading.

8. Remove roast from grill and allow to rest for 15 minutes. Remove the foil covering the bones, but leave the butcher's string on the roast until ready to carve. Transfer to a warm platter.

9. To serve, carve between the bones. Enjoy!

Smoked Sugar Pork Steaks

Servings: 4
Cooking Time: 300 Minutes

Ingredients:
- 3 1.5" Thick Pork Steaks, Cut from a Bone-in Pork Shoulder
- 3 tbsp Yellow Mustard
- 1/4 cup BBQ Rub
- 3 tbsp Unsalted Butter
- 3 tbsp Brown Sugar OR Sugar in the raw
- 1/2 cup BBQ Sauce
- 3 tbsp Honey or Agave Syrup

Directions:
1. Supply your smoker with wood pellets and follow the start-up procedure. Preheat the grill, with the lid closed, to 250° F.
2. Apply a thin coat of yellow mustard to each pork steak and season both sides with the BBQ rub.
3. Place the seasoned pork steaks on the smoker and cook for 2 hours.
4. Remove the pork steaks from the grill and place them in a foil pan.
5. Add the butter, honey, BBQ sauce, sugar to the foil pan and mix them with the pork steaks.
6. Cover the foil pan tightly with foil and return to the smoker.
7. Cook for an additional 2-3 hours until the pork is fork tender.
8. Remove the pan from the grill. Cover the steaks with the juices from the pan and enjoy!

Competition Style Bbq Pork Ribs

Servings: 6
Cooking Time: 300 Minutes

Ingredients:
- 2 Rack St. Louis-style ribs
- 1 Cup Pork & Poultry Rub
- 1/8 Cup brown sugar
- 4 Tablespoon butter
- 4 Tablespoon agave
- 1 Bottle Sweet & Heat BBQ Sauce

Directions:
1. Supply your smoker with wood pellets and follow the start-up procedure. Preheat the grill, with the lid closed, to 225° F.
2. Remove membrane from back of ribs. Season with Traeger Pork & Poultry Rub on all sides. Let ribs rest for 15 to 20 minutes.
3. Place ribs on the grill, bone-side down and cook for 3 hours. While ribs are cooking, prepare the brown sugar wrap. Spread (approximately the same size as the rack of ribs) half the brown sugar, half the butter and half the agave on top of a double layer of aluminum foil. Repeat for second rack. Grill: 225 °F
4. After 3 hours, place one rack of ribs meat side down in the brown sugar, butter and agave, and wrap. Repeat with second rack. Turn grill up to 250°F and place wrapped ribs, meat side down in grill. Grill: 250 °F
5. Cook for another 1-1/2 hours and check the internal temperature. Desired temperature is 204°F to 205°F. If not at temperature, cook for an additional 30 minutes until temperature is reached. Grill: 250 °F Probe: 204 °F
6. Remove ribs from the grill and foil packet. Place unwrapped ribs back in the grill for an additional 10 minutes. Remove from grill and sauce the meat and bone side with Traeger Sweet & Heat BBQ Sauce and cook for another 10 minutes. Slice ribs and serve. Enjoy!

Grilled Ham & Egg Cups

Servings: 6
Cooking Time: 25 Minutes

Ingredients:
- 12 Pieces ham
- 12 eggs
- Cup Cream, whipping
- salt and pepper
- 1 Cup shredded cheddar cheese
- chives, chopped

Directions:
1. Supply your smoker with wood pellets and follow the start-up procedure. Preheat the grill, with the lid closed, to 350° F.
2. Spray the wells of a muffin tin with cooking spray. Cut the ham to be sized just a little bigger than each muffin well.
3. Arrange the ham slices directly on the grill grate and cook for 5 to 10 minutes per side, or until nice grill marks appear. Leave the grill on.
4. Whisk together eggs and heavy whipping cream. Season mixture with salt and pepper.
5. Bake for 12 to 15 minutes, or until the eggs are cooked to your liking. Top with cheese the last few minutes of cooking, if desired.
6. Carefully remove the ham and egg cups and serve immediately with some fresh chopped chives or cilantro. Enjoy!

Baked Beans

Servings: 12
Cooking Time: 180 Minutes

Ingredients:
- 1 Pack Bacon
- 1/2 Cup Brown Sugar
- 1 Coca Cola, Can
- 2 Cans Mixed Beans
- 1/3 Cup Molasses
- 4 Cans Pork And Beans
- 1 Red Onion, Chopped
- 1/3 Cup Yellow Mustard

Directions:
1. Supply your smoker with wood pellets and follow the start-up procedure. Preheat the grill, with the lid closed, to 275° F.
2. Combine all the ingredients and stir until combined.
3. Smoked for 2.5 hours covered. For the last 30 minutes, smoke uncovered.
4. Serve hot. Enjoy!

APPETIZERS AND SNACKS

Chicken Wings With Teriyaki Glaze

Servings: 4
Cooking Time: 50 Minutes

Ingredients:
- 16 large chicken wings, about 3lb (1.4kg) total
- 1 to 1½ tbsp toasted sesame oil
- for the glaze
- ½ cup light soy sauce or tamari
- ¼ cup sake or sugar-free dark-colored soda
- ¼ cup light brown sugar or low-carb substitute
- 2 tbsp mirin or 1 tbsp honey
- 1 garlic clove, peeled, minced or grated
- 2 tsp minced fresh ginger
- 1 tsp cornstarch mixed with 1 tbsp distilled water (optional)
- for serving
- 1 tbsp toasted sesame seeds
- 2 scallions, trimmed, white and green parts sliced sharply diagonally

Directions:
1. Supply your smoker with wood pellets and follow the start-up procedure. Preheat the grill, with the lid closed, to 350° F.
2. Place the chicken wings in a large bowl, add the sesame oil, and turn the wings to coat thoroughly.
3. Place the wings on the grate at an angle to the bars. Grill for 20 minutes and then turn. Continue to cook until the wings are nicely browned and the meat is no longer pink at the bone, about 20 minutes more.
4. To make the glaze, in a saucepan on the stovetop over medium-high heat, combine the ingredients and bring the mixture to a boil. Reduce the glaze by 1/3, about 6 to 8 minutes. If you prefer your glaze to be glossy and thick, add the cornstarch and water mixture to the glaze and cook until it coats the back of a spoon, about 1 to 2 minutes more.
5. Transfer the wings to an aluminum foil roasting pan. Pour the glaze over them, turning to coat thoroughly. Place the pan on the grate and cook the wings until the glaze sets, about 5 to 10 minutes.
6. Transfer the wings to a platter. Scatter the sesame seeds and scallions over the top. Serve with plenty of napkins.

Bacon-wrapped Jalapeño Poppers

Servings: 12
Cooking Time: 30 Minutes

Ingredients:
- 8 ounces cream cheese, softened
- ½ cup shredded Cheddar cheese
- ¼ cup chopped scallions
- 1 teaspoon chipotle chile powder or regular chili powder
- 1 teaspoon garlic powder
- 1 teaspoon salt
- 18 large jalapeño peppers, stemmed, seeded, and halved lengthwise
- 1 pound bacon (precooked works well)

Directions:
1. Supply your smoker with wood pellets and follow the start-up procedure. Preheat, with the lid closed, to 350°F. Line a baking sheet with aluminum foil.
2. In a small bowl, combine the cream cheese, Cheddar cheese, scallions, chipotle powder, garlic powder, and salt.
3. Stuff the jalapeño halves with the cheese mixture.
4. Cut the bacon into pieces big enough to wrap around the stuffed pepper halves.
5. Wrap the bacon around the peppers and place on the prepared baking sheet.
6. Put the baking sheet on the grill grate, close the lid, and smoke the peppers for 30 minutes, or until the cheese is melted and the bacon is cooked through and crisp.
7. Let the jalapeño poppers cool for 3 to 5 minutes. Serve warm.

Bacon Pork Pinwheels (kansas Lollipops)

Servings: 4-6
Cooking Time: 20 Minutes

Ingredients:
- 1 Whole Pork Loin, boneless
- To Taste salt and pepper
- To Taste Greek Seasoning
- 4 Slices bacon
- To Taste The Ultimate BBQ Sauce

Directions:
1. When ready to cook, start the smoker and set temperature to 500F. Preheat, lid closed, for 10 to 15 minutes.
2. Trim pork loin of any unwanted silver skin or fat. Using a sharp knife, cut pork loin length wise, into 4 long strips.
3. Lay pork flat, then season with salt, pepper and Cavender's Greek Seasoning.
4. Flip the pork strips over and layer bacon on unseasoned side. Begin tightly rolling the pork strips, with bacon being rolled up on the inside.
5. Secure a skewer all the way through each pork roll to secure it in place. Set the pork rolls down on grill and cook for 15 minutes.
6. Brush BBQ Sauce over the pork. Turn each skewer over, then coat the other side. Let pork cook for another 5-10 minutes, depending on thickness of your pork. Enjoy!

Bayou Wings With Cajun Rémoulade

Servings: 8
Cooking Time: 40 Minutes

Ingredients:
- 16 large whole chicken wings or 32 drumettes and flats, about 3lb (1.4kg) total
- for the rub
- 1 tbsp kosher salt
- 1 tsp freshly ground black pepper
- 1 tsp paprika
- ½ tsp ground cayenne, plus more
- ½ tsp garlic powder
- ½ tsp celery salt
- ½ tsp dried thyme
- 2 tbsp vegetable oil
- for the rémoulade
- 1¼ cups reduced-fat mayo
- ¼ cup Creole-style or whole grain mustard
- 2 tbsp horseradish
- 2 tbsp pickle relish
- 1 tbsp freshly squeezed lemon juice
- 1 tsp paprika, plus more
- 1 tsp hot sauce, plus more
- 1 tsp Worcestershire sauce
- coarse salt
- for serving
- lemon wedges
- pickled okra (optional)

Directions:
1. Supply your smoker with wood pellets and follow the start-up procedure. Preheat the grill, with the lid closed, to 350° F.
2. If using whole wings, cut through the two joints, separating them into drumettes, flats, and wing tips. (Discard the wing tips or save them for chicken stock.) Alternatively, leave the wings whole. Place the chicken in a resealable plastic bag.
3. In a small bowl, make the rub by combining the ingredients. Mix well. Pour the rub over the wings and toss them to thoroughly coat. Refrigerate for 2 hours.
4. In a small bowl, make the Cajun rémoulade by whisking together the mayo, mustard, horseradish, pickle relish, lemon juice, paprika, hot sauce, and Worcestershire. Season with salt to taste. The mixture should be highly seasoned. Transfer to a serving bowl and lightly dust with paprika. Cover and refrigerate until ready to serve.
5. Remove the wings from the refrigerator and allow the excess marinade to drip off. Place the wings on the grate at an angle to the bars. Grill for 20 minutes and then turn. (They'll brown more evenly but will also have less of a tendency to stick.) Continue to cook until the wings are nicely browned and the meat is no longer pink at the bone, about 20 minutes more.
6. Remove the wings from the grill and pile them on a platter. Serve with the Cajun rémoulade, lemon wedges, and pickled okra (if using).

Pulled Pork Loaded Nachos

Servings: 4
Cooking Time: 10 Minutes

Ingredients:
- 2 cups leftover smoked pulled pork
- 1 small sweet onion, diced
- 1 medium tomato, diced
- 1 jalapeño pepper, seeded and diced
- 1 garlic clove, minced
- 1 teaspoon salt
- 1 teaspoon freshly ground black pepper
- 1 bag tortilla chips
- 1 cup shredded Cheddar cheese
- ½ cup The Ultimate BBQ Sauce, divided
- ½ cup shredded jalapeño Monterey Jack cheese
- Juice of ½ lime
- 1 avocado, halved, pitted, and sliced
- 2 tablespoons sour cream
- 1 tablespoon chopped fresh cilantro

Directions:
1. Supply your smoker with wood pellets and follow the start-up procedure. Preheat, with the lid closed, to 375°F.
2. Heat the pulled pork in the microwave.
3. In a medium bowl, combine the onion, tomato, jalapeño, garlic, salt, and pepper, and set aside.
4. Arrange half of the tortilla chips in a large cast iron skillet. Spread half of the warmed pork on top and cover with the Cheddar cheese. Top with half of the onion-jalapeño mixture, then drizzle with ¼ cup of barbecue sauce.
5. Layer on the remaining tortilla chips, then the remaining pork and the Monterey Jack cheese. Top with the remaining onion-jalapeño mixture and drizzle with the remaining ¼ cup of barbecue sauce.
6. Place the skillet on the grill, close the lid, and smoke for about 10 minutes, or until the cheese is melted and bubbly. (Watch to make sure your chips don't burn!)
7. Squeeze the lime juice over the nachos, top with the avocado slices and sour cream, and garnish with the cilantro before serving hot.

Citrus-infused Marinated Olives

Servings: 6
Cooking Time: 30 Minutes

Ingredients:
- 1½ cups mixed brined olives, with pits
- ½ cup extra virgin olive oil
- 1 tbsp freshly squeezed lemon juice
- 1 garlic clove, peeled and thinly sliced
- 1 tsp smoked Spanish paprika
- 2 sprigs of fresh rosemary
- 2 sprigs of fresh thyme
- 2 bay leaves, fresh or dried
- 1 small dried red chili pepper, deseeded and flesh crumbled, or ¼ tsp crushed red pepper flakes
- 3 strips of orange zest
- 3 strips of lemon zest

Directions:
1. Supply your smoker with wood pellets and follow the start-up procedure. Preheat the grill, with the lid closed, to 180° F.
2. Drain the olives, reserving 1 tablespoon of brine. Spread the olives in a single layer in an aluminum foil roasting pan. Place the pan on the grate and cook the olives for 30 minutes, stirring the olives or shaking the pan once or twice.
3. In a small saucepan on the stovetop over low heat, warm the olive oil. Whisk in the lemon juice and the reserved 1 tablespoon of brine. Stir in the garlic and paprika. Add the rosemary, thyme, bay leaves, chili pepper, and orange and lemon zests. Warm over low heat for 10 minutes. Remove the saucepan from the heat.
4. Transfer the olives and olive oil mixture to a pint jar. Tuck the aromatics around the sides of the jar. Let cool and then cover and refrigerate for up to 5 days. Let the olives come to room temperature before serving.

Chorizo Queso Fundido

Servings: 4-6
Cooking Time: 20 Minutes

Ingredients:
- 1 poblano chile
- 1 cup chopped queso quesadilla or queso Oaxaca

- 1 cup shredded Monterey Jack cheese
- ¼ cup milk
- 1 tablespoon all-purpose flour
- 2 (4-ounce) links Mexican chorizo sausage, casings removed
- ⅓ cup beer
- 1 tablespoon unsalted butter
- 1 small red onion, chopped
- ½ cup whole kernel corn
- 2 serrano chiles or jalapeño peppers, stemmed, seeded, and coarsely chopped
- 1 tablespoon minced garlic
- 1 tablespoon freshly squeezed lime juice
- 1 teaspoon ground cumin
- 1 teaspoon salt
- 1 teaspoon freshly ground black pepper
- 1 tablespoon chopped fresh cilantro
- 1 tablespoon chopped scallions
- Tortilla chips, for serving

Directions:

1. Supply your smoker with wood pellets and follow the start-up procedure. Preheat, with the lid closed, to 350°F.
2. On the smoker or over medium-high heat on the stove top, place the poblano directly on the grate (or burner) to char for 1 to 2 minutes, turning as needed. Remove from heat and place in a closed-up lunch-size paper bag for 2 minutes to sweat and further loosen the skin.
3. Remove the skin and coarsely chop the poblano, removing the seeds; set aside.
4. In a bowl, combine the queso quesadilla, Monterey Jack, milk, and flour; set aside.
5. On the stove top, in a cast iron skillet over medium heat, cook and crumble the chorizo for about 2 minutes.
6. Transfer the cooked chorizo to a small, grill-safe pan and place over indirect heat on the smoker.
7. Place the cast iron skillet on the preheated grill grate. Pour in the beer and simmer for a few minutes, loosening and stirring in any remaining sausage bits from the pan.
8. Add the butter to the pan, then add the cheese mixture a little at a time, stirring constantly.
9. When the cheese is smooth, stir in the onion, corn, serrano chiles, garlic, lime juice, cuvmin, salt, and pepper. Stir in the reserved chopped charred poblano.
10. Close the lid and smoke for 15 to 20 minutes to infuse the queso with smoke flavor and further cook the vegetables.
11. When the cheese is bubbly, top with the chorizo mixture and garnish with the cilantro and scallions.
12. Serve the chorizo queso fundido hot with tortilla chips.

Grilled Guacamole

Servings: 6
Cooking Time: 30 Minutes

Ingredients:

- 3 large avocados, halved and pitted
- 1 lime, halved
- ½ jalapeño, deseeded and deveined
- ½ small white or red onion, peeled
- 2 garlic cloves, peeled and skewered on a toothpick
- 1 tsp coarse salt, plus more
- 1½ tbsp reduced-fat mayo
- 2 tbsp chopped fresh cilantro
- 2 tbsp crumbled queso fresco (optional)
- tortilla chips

Directions:

1. Supply your smoker with wood pellets and follow the start-up procedure. Preheat the grill, with the lid closed, to 225° F.
2. Place the avocados, lime, jalapeño, and onion cut sides down on the grate. Use the toothpicks to balance the garlic cloves between the bars. Smoke for 30 minutes. (You want the vegetables to retain most of their rawness.)
3. Transfer everything to a cutting board. Remove the garlic cloves from the toothpick and roughly chop. Sprinkle with the salt and continue to mince the garlic until it begins to form a paste. Scrape the garlic and salt into a large bowl.
4. Scoop the avocado flesh from the peels into the bowl. Squeeze the juice of ½ lime over the avocado. Mash the avocados but leave them somewhat chunky. Finely dice the jalapeño. Dice 2 tablespoons of onion. (Reserve the

remaining onion for another use.) Add the jalapeño, onion, mayo, and cilantro to the bowl. Stir gently to combine. Taste for seasoning, adding more salt, lime juice, and jalapeño as desired.
5. Transfer the guacamole to a serving bowl. Top with the queso fresco (if using). Serve with tortilla chips.

Pigs In A Blanket

Servings: 4-6
Cooking Time: 15 Minutes

Ingredients:
- 2 Tablespoon Poppy Seeds
- 1 Tablespoon Dried Minced Onion
- 2 Teaspoon garlic, minced
- 2 Tablespoon Sesame Seeds
- 1 Teaspoon salt
- 8 Ounce Original Crescent Dough
- 1/4 Cup Dijon mustard
- 1 Large egg, beaten

Directions:
1. When ready to cook, start your smoker at 350 degrees F, and preheat with lid closed, 10 to 15 minutes.
2. Mix together poppy seeds, dried minced onion, dried minced garlic, salt and sesame seeds. Set aside.
3. Cut each triangle of crescent roll dough into thirds lengthwise, making 3 small strips from each roll.
4. Brush the dough strips lightly with Dijon mustard. Put the mini hot dogs on 1 end of the dough and roll up.
5. Arrange them, seam side down, on a greased baking pan. Brush with egg wash and sprinkle with seasoning mixture.
6. Bake in smoker until golden brown, about 12 to 15 minutes.
7. Serve with mustard or dipping sauce of your choice. Enjoy!

Simple Cream Cheese Sausage Balls

Servings: 5
Cooking Time: 30 Minutes

Ingredients:
- 1 pound ground hot sausage, uncooked
- 8 ounces cream cheese, softened
- 1 package mini filo dough shells

Directions:
1. Supply your smoker with wood pellets and follow the start-up procedure. Preheat, with the lid closed, to 350°F.
2. In a large bowl, using your hands, thoroughly mix together the sausage and cream cheese until well blended.
3. Place the filo dough shells on a rimmed perforated pizza pan or into a mini muffin tin.
4. Roll the sausage and cheese mixture into 1-inch balls and place into the filo shells.
5. Place the pizza pan or mini muffin tin on the grill, close the lid, and smoke the sausage balls for 30 minutes, or until cooked through and the sausage is no longer pink.
6. Plate and serve warm.

Deviled Eggs With Smoked Paprika

Servings: 6
Cooking Time: 30 Minutes

Ingredients:
- 6 large eggs
- 3 tbsp reduced-fat mayo, plus more
- 1 tsp Dijon or yellow mustard
- ½ tsp Spanish smoked paprika or regular paprika, plus more
- dash of hot sauce
- coarse salt
- freshly ground black pepper
- for garnishing
- small sprigs of fresh parsley, dill, tarragon, or cilantro
- chopped chives
- minced scallions
- Mustard Caviar
- sliced green or black olives
- celery leaves
- sliced radishes
- diced bell peppers
- sliced cherry tomatoes
- fresh or pickled jalapeños
- sliced or diced pickles

- slivers of sun-dried tomatoes
- bacon crumbles
- smoked salmon
- Hawaiian black salt
- Caviar

Directions:
1. Supply your smoker with wood pellets and follow the start-up procedure. Preheat the grill, with the lid closed, to 180° F.
2. On the stovetop over medium-high heat, bring a saucepan of water to a boil. (Make sure there's enough water in the saucepan to cover the eggs by 1 inch [5cm].) Use a slotted spoon to gently lower the eggs into the water. Lower the heat to maintain a simmer. Set a timer for 13 minutes.
3. Prepare an ice bath by combining ice and cold water in a large bowl. Carefully transfer the eggs to the ice bath when the timer goes off.
4. When the eggs are cool enough to handle, gently tap them all over to crack the shell. Carefully peel the eggs. Rinse under cold running water to remove any clinging bits of shell, but don't dry the eggs. (A damp surface will help the smoke adhere to the egg whites.)
5. Place the eggs on the grate and smoke until the eggs take on a light brown patina from the smoke, about 25 minutes. Transfer the eggs to a cutting board, handling them as little as possible.
6. Slice each egg in half lengthwise with a sharp knife. Wipe any yolk off the blade before slicing the next egg. Gently remove the yolks and place them in a food processor. Pulse to break up the yolks. Add the mayo, mustard, paprika, and hot sauce. Season with salt and pepper to taste. Pulse until the filling is smooth. Add additional mayo 1 teaspoon at a time if the mixture is a little dry. (It shouldn't be too loose either.)
7. Spoon the filling into each egg half or pipe it in using a small resealable plastic bag. You can also use a pastry bag fitted with a fluted tip.
8. Place the eggs on a platter and lightly dust with paprika. Accompany with one or more of the suggested garnishes.

Smoked Cashews

Servings: 6
Cooking Time: 60 Minutes

Ingredients:
- 1 pound roasted, salted cashews

Directions:
1. Supply your smoker with wood pellets and follow the start-up procedure. Preheat the grill, with the lid closed, to 120°F.
2. Pour the cashews onto a rimmed baking sheet and smoke for 1 hour, stirring once about halfway through the smoking time.
3. Remove the cashews from the grill, let cool, and store in an airtight container for as long as you can resist.

Pig Pops (sweet-hot Bacon On A Stick)

Servings: 24
Cooking Time: 30 Minutes

Ingredients:
- Nonstick cooking spray, oil, or butter, for greasing
- 2 pounds thick-cut bacon (24 slices)
- 24 metal skewers
- 1 cup packed light brown sugar
- 2 to 3 teaspoons cayenne pepper
- ½ cup maple syrup, divided

Directions:
1. Supply your smoker with wood pellets and follow the start-up procedure. Preheat, with the lid closed, to 350°F.
2. Coat a disposable aluminum foil baking sheet with cooking spray, oil, or butter.
3. Thread each bacon slice onto a metal skewer and place on the prepared baking sheet.
4. In a medium bowl, stir together the brown sugar and cayenne.
5. Baste the top sides of the bacon with ¼ cup of maple syrup.
6. Sprinkle half of the brown sugar mixture over the bacon.
7. Place the baking sheet on the grill, close the lid, and smoke for 15 to 30 minutes.

8. Using tongs, flip the bacon skewers. Baste with the remaining ¼ cup of maple syrup and top with the remaining brown sugar mixture.

9. Continue smoking with the lid closed for 10 to 15 minutes, or until crispy. You can eyeball the bacon and smoke to your desired doneness, but the actual ideal internal temperature for bacon is 155°F

10. Using tongs, carefully remove the bacon skewers from the grill. Let cool completely before handling.

Chuckwagon Beef Jerky

Servings: 6
Cooking Time: 300 Minutes

Ingredients:
- 2½lb (1.2kg) boneless top or bottom round steak, sirloin tip, flank steak, or venison
- 1 cup sugar-free dark-colored soda
- 1 cup cold brewed coffee
- ½ cup light soy sauce
- ¼ cup Worcestershire sauce
- 2 tbsp whiskey (optional)
- 2 tsp chili powder
- 1½ tsp garlic salt
- 1 tsp onion powder
- 1 tsp pink curing salt

Directions:

1. Slice the meat into ¼-inch-thick (.5cm) strips, trimming off any visible fat or gristle. (Slice against the grain for more tender jerky and with the grain for chewier jerky.) Place the meat in a large resealable plastic bag.

2. In a small bowl, whisk together the soda, coffee, soy sauce, Worcestershire sauce, whiskey (if using), chili powder, garlic salt, onion powder, and curing salt (if using). Whisk until the salt dissolves. Pour the mixture over the meat and reseal the bag. Refrigerate for 24 to 48 hours, turning the bag several times to redistribute the brine.

3. Supply your smoker with wood pellets and follow the start-up procedure. Preheat the grill, with the lid closed, to 150° F.

4. Drain the meat and discard the brine. Place the strips of meat in a single layer on paper towels and blot any excess moisture.

5. Place the meat in a single layer on the grate and smoke for 4 to 5 hours, turning once or twice. (If you're aware of hot spots on your grate, rotate the strips so they smoke evenly.) To test for doneness, bend one or two pieces in the middle. They should be dry but still somewhat pliant. Or simply eat a piece to see if it's done to your liking.

6. For the best texture, when you remove the meat from the grill, place the still-warm jerky in a resealable plastic bag and let rest for 30 minutes. (You might see condensation form on the inside of the bag, but the moisture will be reabsorbed by the meat.) Or let the meat cool completely and then store in a resealable plastic bag or covered container. The jerky will last a few days at room temperature but will last longer (up to 2 weeks) if refrigerated.

Smoked Cheese

Servings: 4
Cooking Time: 150 Minutes

Ingredients:
- 1 (2-pound) block medium Cheddar cheese, or your favorite cheese, quartered lengthwise

Directions:

1. Supply your smoker with wood pellets and follow the start-up procedure. Preheat the grill, with the lid closed, to 90°F.

2. Place the cheese directly on the grill grate and smoke for 2 hours, 30 minutes, checking frequently to be sure it's not melting. If the cheese begins to melt, try flipping it. If that doesn't help, remove it from the grill and refrigerate for about 1 hour and then return it to the cold smoker.

3. Remove the cheese, place it in a zip-top bag, and refrigerate overnight.

4. Slice the cheese and serve with crackers, or grate it and use for making a smoked mac and cheese.

Roasted Red Pepper Dip

Servings: 8
Cooking Time: 45 Minutes

Ingredients:

- 4 red bell peppers, halved, destemmed, and deseeded
- 1 cup English walnuts, divided
- 1 small white onion, peeled and coarsely chopped
- 2 garlic cloves, peeled and smashed with a chef's knife
- ¼ cup extra virgin olive oil, plus more
- 1 tbsp balsamic vinegar or balsamic glaze
- 1 tsp honey (eliminate if using balsamic glaze)
- 1 tsp coarse salt, plus more
- 1 tsp ground cumin
- 1 tsp smoked paprika
- ½ to 1 tsp Aleppo red pepper flakes, plus more
- ¼ cup fresh white breadcrumbs (optional)
- distilled water (optional)
- assorted crudités or wedges of pita bread

Directions:

1. Supply your smoker with wood pellets and follow the start-up procedure. Preheat the grill, with the lid closed, to 400° F.

2. Place the peppers skin side down on the grate and grill until the skins blister and the flesh softens, about 30 minutes. Transfer the peppers to a bowl and cover with plastic wrap. Let cool to room temperature. Remove the skins with a paring knife or your fingers. Coarsely chop or tear the peppers.

3. Place ¾ cup of walnuts in an aluminum foil roasting pan. Place the pan on the grate and toast for 10 to 15 minutes, stirring twice. Remove the pan from the grill and let the walnuts cool.

4. Place the peppers, onion, garlic, and walnuts in a food processor fitted with the chopping blade. Pulse several times. Add the olive oil, balsamic vinegar, honey, salt, cumin, paprika, and red pepper flakes. Process until the mixture is fairly smooth. Taste for seasoning, adding more salt or red pepper flakes (if desired). (If the mixture is too loose, add breadcrumbs until the texture is to your liking. If it's too thick, add olive oil or water 1 tablespoon at a time.)

5. Transfer the dip to a serving bowl. Use the back of a spoon to make a shallow depression in the center. Top with the remaining ¼ cup of walnuts and drizzle olive oil in the depression. Serve with crudités or pita bread.

RECIPE INDEX

3-2-1 Bbq Baby Back Ribs 222
3-2-1 Spare Ribs 199

A
A Smoking Classic Cocktail 185
Alder Smoked Scallops With Citrus & Garlic Butter Sauce 87
Anzac Coconut Biscuits 54
Apple & Bourbon Glazed Ham 221
Apple-smoked Bacon 224
Applewood-smoked Whole Turkey 35
Asian Bbq Chicken 36
Asian-style Pork Tenderloin 201

B
Bacon Chocolate Chip Cookies 61
Bacon Old-fashioned Cocktail 184
Bacon Pork Pinwheels (kansas Lollipops) 229
Bacon Stuffed Onion Rings 209
Bacon Weaved Stuffed Turkey Breast 37
Bacon Wrapped Chicken Wings 25
Bacon Wrapped Corn On The Cob 116
Bacon Wrapped Shrimp 84
Bacon Wrapped Turkey Legs 44
Bacon-wrapped Chicken Breasts 45
Bacon-wrapped Jalapeño Poppers 228
Baked Artichoke Parmesan Mushrooms 128
Baked Bacon Green Bean Casserole 121
Baked Beans 227
Baked Bourbon Maple Pumpkin Pie 53
Baked Breakfast Mini Quiches 124
Baked Candied Bacon Cinnamon Rolls 201
Baked Cast Iron Berry Cobbler 51
Baked Cheesy Parmesan Grits 81
Baked Chocolate Brownie Cookies With Egg Nog 78
Baked Chocolate Coconut Brownies 69
Baked Garlic Duchess Potatoes 119
Baked German Pork Schnitzel With Grilled Lemons 209
Baked Heirloom Tomato Tart 130
Baked Irish Creme Cake 51
Baked Kale Chips 127
Baked Loaded Tater Tots 139
Baked Maple And Brown Sugar Bacon 224

Baked Parker House Rolls 67
Baked Peach Cobbler Cupcakes 75
Baked Pear Tarte Tatin 63
Baked Pig Candy 217
Baked Potatoes & Celery Root Au Gratin 79
Baked Prosciutto-wrapped Chicken Breast With Spinach And Boursin 24
Baked Pumpkin Pie 57
Baked Steelhead 113
Baked Stuffed Avocados 131
Baked Sweet And Savory Yams By Bennie Kendrick 119
Baked Sweet Potato Casserole With Marshmallow Fluff 123
Baked Sweet Potatoes 132
Baked Venison Tater Tot Casserole 147
Baked Whole Fish In Sea Salt 98
Bananas Rum Foster 78
Barbecued Scallops 89
Barbecued Shrimp 100
Basil Margherita Pizza 62
Batter Up Cocktail 182
Bayou Wings With Cajun Rémoulade 229
Bbq 3-2-1 St. Louis Ribs 217
Bbq Baby Back Ribs With Bacon Pineapple Glaze By Scott Thomas 196
Bbq Bacon-wrapped Water Chestnuts 202
Bbq Beef Ribs 148
Bbq Beef Short Ribs 163
Bbq Breakfast Grits 203
Bbq Brown Sugar Bacon Bites 224
Bbq Brown Sugar Pork Belly 219
Bbq Chicken Drumsticks 22
Bbq Chicken Legs 45
Bbq Chicken Thighs 43
Bbq Chicken Tostada 34
Bbq Oysters 108
Bbq Pork Short Ribs 210
Bbq Pork Shoulder Roast With Sugar Lips Glaze 207
Bbq Pork Shoulder Steaks 197
Bbq Roasted Salmon 108
Bbq Spatchcocked Chicken 28
Bbq Sweet & Smoky Ribs 196
Bbq Turkey Drumsticks 20

Beef Caldereta Stew 167
Beer Bread 59
Beer Chicken 46
Beer Chili Bratwurst 155
Beer Pork Belly Chili Con Carne 212
Bison Tomahawk Steak 157
Blackened Saskatchewan Tomahawk Steaks 158
Blueberry Bread Pudding 58
Blueberry Pancakes 49
Blueberry Sour Cream Muffins 83
Bourbon Chicken Waffles 25
Bourbon Chile Glazed Ham 215
Braised Creamed Green Beans 115
Broccoli-cauliflower Salad 125
Burnt Beer Beef Brisket 146
Butter Braised Green Beans 126
Butternut Squash 125

C
Cajun Brined Maple Smoked Turkey Breast 15
Cajun Catfish 104
Cajun-blackened Shrimp 94
Cake With Smoked Berry Sauce 66
Carolina Baked Beans 118
Carrot Celery Chicken Drumsticks 41
Carrot Elk Burgers 172
Cast Iron Pineapple Upside Down Cake 82
Cast Iron Potatoes 117
Cedar Smoked Garlic Salmon 103
Cheddar Bacon Beef Burgers 145
Cheese Mac 56
Cheese Onion Steak Sandwiches 162
Chef Curtis' Famous Chimichurri Sauce 132
Cherry Ice Cream Cobbler 54
Chicken Cordon Bleu Rollups 36
Chicken Egg Rolls With Buffalo Sauce 35
Chicken Lollipops 22
Chicken On A Throne 18
Chicken Parmesan Sliders With Pesto Mayonnaise 26
Chicken Pizza On The Grill 58
Chicken Pot Pie 55
Chicken Wings With Teriyaki Glaze 228
Chile Chicken Thighs 26
Chile Cilantro Lime Chicken Wings 19
Chili Cheese Fries 49
Chinese Alcoholic Bbq Pork Tenderloin 201

Chocolate Lava Cake With Smoked Whipped Cream 81
Chocolate Peanut Cookies 50
Chorizo Queso Fundido 230
Christmas Brussel Sprouts 121
Chuckwagon Beef Jerky 234
Cider Hot-smoked Salmon 90
Cinnamon Pull-aparts 80
Citrus-infused Marinated Olives 230
Citrus-smoked Trout 90
Classic Pulled Pork 219
Competition Style Bbq Pork Ribs 226
Competition Style Bbq Pulled Pork 213
Cornbread Chicken Stuffing 48
Cornish Game Hen 37
Cornish Game Hens 38
County Fair Turkey Legs 40
Cran-apple Tequila Punch With Smoked Oranges 185
Crème Brûlée 48
Crescent Rolls 54

D
Dark Chocolate Brownies With Bacon-salted Caramel 71
Delicious Grilled Steak 166
Delicious Reverse Seared Picanha Steak 168
Delicious Smoked Bone-in Pork Chops 222
Delicious Smoked Trout 104
Delicious Sweet And Sour Chicken Drumsticks 34
Deviled Eggs With Smoked Paprika 232
Donut Bread Pudding 65
Double Chocolate Chip Brownie Pie 73
Double Vanilla Chocolate Cake 76
Double-decker Pulled Pork Nachos With Smoked Cheese 209
Double-smoked Cheese Potatoes 141
Dry Brine Traeger Turkey 42
Dry Rub Grilled Ribs 197
Dublin Delight Cocktail 188

E
Easy Bbq Chicken Wings 17
Easy Smoked Cornbread 80
Egg Bacon French Toast Panini 216
Eggs Ham Benedict 72
Everything Pigs In A Blanket 220
Eyeball Cookies 68

F
Fig Glazed Chicken Stuffed Cornbread 16
Fig Slider Cocktail 184
Flank Steak Breakfast Potato Burrito 170
Flavour Bbq Brisket Burnt Ends 165
Flavour Fire Spiced Shrimp 94
Flavour Smoked Tri Tip 157
Flavour Texas Smoke Beef 175
Flavour Texas Twinkies 169
Flavour Tri Tip Burnt Ends 151
Florentine Shrimp Al Cartoccio 96
Fried Chicken Sliders 39

G
Garden Gimlet Cocktail 181
Garlic Beef Meatballs 150
Garlic Blackened Catfish 106
Garlic Blackened Salmon 101
Garlic Cheese Bacon Burger 164
Garlic Cheese Pull Apart Bread 69
Garlic Grilled Shrimp Skewers 109
Garlic Lemon Pepper Chicken Wings 82
Garlic Pepper Shrimp Pesto Bruschetta 107
Garlic Pigs In A Blanket 171
Garlic Standing Rib Roast 173
Grass-fed Beef Burgers 152
Green Bean Casserole 132
Green Bean Casserole Circa 1955 64
Green Bell Pepper Cheese Steak Burger 164
Green Chile Chicken Enchiladas 27
Grilled Apple Pie 60
Grilled Artichoke Cheese Salmon 100
Grilled Asparagus & Honey-glazed Carrots 121
Grilled Asparagus And Hollandaise Sauce 140
Grilled Asparagus And Spinach Salad 141
Grilled Bacon-wrapped Hot Dogs 152
Grilled Balsamic & Blue Steak 168
Grilled Bbq Pork Chops 199
Grilled Beef Shawarma 169
Grilled Beer Cabbage 115
Grilled Beer Cheese Dip 60
Grilled Blackened Saskatchewan Salmon 107
Grilled Blood Orange Mimosa 178
Grilled Broccoli Rabe 120
Grilled Cabbage Steaks With Warm Bacon Vinaigrette 144
Grilled Chicken Wings 46
Grilled Chili-lime Corn 118
Grilled Chipotle Chicken Skewers 27
Grilled Corn On The Cob With Parmesan And Garlic 137
Grilled Dill Pickle Tri Tip Steak 173
Grilled Double Burgers With Texas Spicy Bbq Sauce 153
Grilled Fingerling Potato Salad 120
Grilled Fresh Fish 103
Grilled Frozen Strawberry Lemonade 182
Grilled Garlic Chicken Kabobs 29
Grilled Garlic Lobster Tails 92
Grilled Garlic Tri Tip 147
Grilled Guacamole 231
Grilled Ham & Egg Cups 227
Grilled Hand Pulled Chicken 36
Grilled Hawaiian Sour 181
Grilled Honey Chicken Kabobs 38
Grilled Honey Chicken Wings 17
Grilled Honey Garlic Wings 42
Grilled Lemon Lobster Tails 112
Grilled Lemon Shrimp Scampi 103
Grilled Lobster Tails With Smoked Paprika Butter 89
Grilled Mac And Cheese Quesadillas 205
Grilled Maple Syrup Salmon 86
Grilled Mussels With Lemon Butter 107
Grilled Oysters With Mignonette 95
Grilled Parmesan Chicken Wings 30
Grilled Peach Mint Julep 188
Grilled Peach Smash Cocktail 192
Grilled Peach Sour Cocktail 179
Grilled Pepper Lobster Tails 85
Grilled Pork Belly 199
Grilled Pork Loin 198
Grilled Pork Tacos Al Pastor 215
Grilled Prosciutto Wrapped Asparagus 206
Grilled Rabbit Tail Cocktail 190
Grilled Rib Eyes With Hasselback Sweet Potatoes 175
Grilled Salmon Gravlax 101
Grilled Salmon Steaks With Dill Sauce 99
Grilled Shrimp Brochette 93
Grilled Skirt Steak Quesadillas 176
Grilled Street Corn 124
Grilled Tomahawk Steak 147
Grilled Whole Steelhead Fillet 111

Grilled Zucchini Squash Spears 140

H
Herb Chipotle Lamb 149
Holiday Smoked Cheese Log 225
Honey Glazed Grapefruit Shandy Cocktail 191
Hot & Fast Smoked Baby Back Ribs 215
Hot Coffee-rubbed Brisket 155
Hot Turkey Sandwich With Gravy 29
Hot-smoked Salmon 85

I
In Traeger Fashion Cocktail 178
Irish Pasties 156
Irish Soda Bread 75
Italian Grilled Barbecue Chicken Wings 16
Italian Meatballs 153

J
Jalapeno Chicken Sliders 20
Jalapeno Pepper Jack Cheese Bacon Burgers 152
Jamaican Jerk Pork Chops 211
Juicy Jerk Chicken Kebabs 23

K
Kimi's Simple Grilled Fresh Fish 96

L
Lemon Chicken, Broccoli, String Beans Foil Packs 79
Lemon Herb Grilled Salmon 97
Lemon Lobster Rolls 96
Lemon Parmesan Chicken Wings 31
Lemon Scallops Wrapped In Bacon 110
Lemon Shrimp Scampi 87
Lemon Tomahawk Steak 149
Lime Carne Asada Tacos 167
Lime Mahi Mahi Fillets 91
Lobster Tail 89
Lynchburg Bacon 195

M
Maple Syrup Bacon Wrapped Tenderloin 200
Maple Syrup Pancake Casserole 69
Maple-smoked Pork Chops 212
Mashed Red Potatoes 118
Mexican Black Bean Cornbread Casserole 71
Mini Sausage Rolls 206
Mint Butter Chocolate Chip Cookies 72
Moules Marinières With Garlic Butter Sauce 108

Mustard Garlic Crusted Prime Rib 174

N
Nashville Spiced Smoked Chicken 46
New York Strip Steaks With Blue Cheese Butter 165

O
Old-fashioned Roasted Glazed Ham 223
Onion Cheese Nachos 63
Oysters In The Shell 106
Oysters Margarita 102

P
Pacific Northwest Salmon 112
Parmesan Roasted Cauliflower 141
Peanut Butter Chicken Wings 17
Peper Fish Tacos 86
Pig On A Stick With Buffalo Glaze 204
Pig Pops (sweet-hot Bacon On A Stick) 233
Pigs In A Blanket 232
Pineapple Cake 74
Pineapple-pepper Pork Kebabs 221
Pizza Bites 74
Planked Trout With Fennel, Bacon & Orange 109
Pork & Pepperoni Burgers 219
Pork Belly Burnt Ends 197
Pork Loin Porchetta 210
Portobello Marinated Mushroom 124
Potluck Salad With Smoked Cornbread 143
Pound Cake 72
Pretzel Rolls 52
Prosciutto Wrapped Dates With Marcona Almonds 211
Prosciutto-wrapped Scallops 88
Pull-apart Dinner Rolls 76
Pulled Pork Corn Tortillas 214
Pulled Pork Loaded Nachos 230
Pulled Pork Sliders Hawaiian Rolls 195
Pulled Pork Taquitos With Sour Cream 200
Pumpkin Bread 50

Q
Quick Baked Dinner Rolls 51

R
Raspberry Spiral Ham With Glaze 218
Red Potato Grilled Lollipops 129
Reuben Sandwich 172
Roasted Artichokes With Garlic Butter 125
Roasted Asparagus 140

Roasted Bacon Weave Holiday Ham 218
Roasted Beet & Bacon Salad 137
Roasted Do-ahead Mashed Potatoes 135
Roasted Duck 145
Roasted Fall Vegetables 129
Roasted Garlic Herb Fries 131
Roasted Halibut With Spring Vegetables 84
Roasted Ham With Apricot Sauce 214
Roasted Hasselback Potatoes By Doug Scheiding 127
Roasted Honey Bourbon Glazed Turkey 39
Roasted Jalapeño Poppers 133
Roasted Mashed Potatoes 135
Roasted Mustard Crusted Prime Rib 154
Roasted New Potatoes 130
Roasted New Potatoes With Compound Butter 136
Roasted Olives 132
Roasted Pickled Beets 116
Roasted Potato Poutine 117
Roasted Prime Rib With Mustard And Herbs De Provence 165
Roasted Prosciutto Stuffed Chicken 31
Roasted Pumpkin Seeds 119
Roasted Red Pepper Dip 235
Roasted Red Pepper White Bean Dip 138
Roasted Sheet Pan Vegetables 135
Roasted Stuffed Turkey Breast 40
Roasted Sweet Potato Steak Fries 133
Roasted Tomatoes 122
Roasted Tomatoes With Hot Pepper Sauce 134
Roasted Vegetable Napoleon 139
Roasted Whole Chicken 28
Rosemary Cranberry Apple Sage Stuffing 70
Rosemary-smoked Lamb Chops 159
Ryes And Shine Cocktail 179

S
S'mores Dip Skillet 55
Salmon Cakes With Homemade Tartar Sauce 114
Salt Crusted Baked Potatoes 127
Savory Beaver Tails 57
Savory Cajun Bbq Chicken 41
Savory Cheese Steak Rolls With Puff Pastry 160
Savory Cheesecake With Bourbon Pecan Topping 77
Savory Grilled Chicken Burrito Bowls 44
Savory Leftover Brisket Tostadas 160
Savory Pork Belly Banh Mi 208
Savory Smoked Brisket 166
Savory Smoked Turkey Legs 28
Savory Teriyaki Smoked Steak Bites 161
Seared Ahi Tuna Steak With Soy Sauce 110
Shrimp Cabbage Tacos With Lime Cream 105
Sicilian Stuffed Mushrooms 122
Simple Cream Cheese Sausage Balls 232
Simple Glazed Salmon Fillets 95
Simple Smoked Ribs 205
Skillet Buttermilk Cornbread 49
Skillet Potato Cake 139
Slow Smoked Rib-eye Roast 153
Smoke And Bubz Cocktail 193
Smoke Roasted Chicken With Herb Butter 31
Smoked & Loaded Baked Potato 130
Smoked Apple Cider 178
Smoked Asparagus Soup 134
Smoked Avocado Turkey Tamale Pie 32
Smoked Baby Back Ribs 195
Smoked Bacon Brisket Flat 145
Smoked Bacon Roses 210
Smoked Barnburner Cocktail 187
Smoked Bbq Onion Brussels Sprout 126
Smoked Beef Ribs 159
Smoked Beer Brisket 176
Smoked Beer Corned Beef 157
Smoked Beet-pickled Eggs 140
Smoked Berry Cocktail 177
Smoked Black Pepper Beef Cheeks 162
Smoked Boneless Chicken Thighs 15
Smoked Brisket With Traeger Coffee Rub 148
Smoked Burgers 175
Smoked Cashews 233
Smoked Cedar Plank Salmon 112
Smoked Cheese 234
Smoked Cheesy Alfredo Sauce 65
Smoked Chicken Leg & Thigh Quarters 23
Smoked Chicken Vermicelli Noodles 18
Smoked Chicken With Apricot Bbq Glaze 21
Smoked Chorizo & Arugula Pesto 207
Smoked Chuck Roast Tater Tot Casserole 172
Smoked Cold Brew Coffee 186
Smoked Corned Beef Brisket 160
Smoked Crab Legs 94
Smoked Eggnog 192
Smoked Fish Chowder 114

Smoked Garlic Meatloaf 161
Smoked Grape Lime Rickey 191
Smoked Hibiscus Sparkler 186
Smoked Honey Salmon 91
Smoked Hot Buttered Rum 180
Smoked Ice Mojito Slurpee 182
Smoked Irish Coffee 189
Smoked Jacobsen Salt Margarita 187
Smoked Jalapeño Poppers 125
Smoked Lemon Cheesecake 73
Smoked Lemon Tea 64
Smoked Lobster Scampi 97
Smoked Longhorn Brisket 174
Smoked Mango Shrimp 88
Smoked Maple Syrup Thanksgiving Turkey 43
Smoked Mashed Potatoes 122
Smoked Mulled Wine 182
Smoked New York Steaks 170
Smoked Parmesan Herb Popcorn 134
Smoked Pickled Green Beans 115
Smoked Pico De Gallo 136
Smoked Pineapple Hotel Nacional Cocktail 187
Smoked Plum And Thyme Fizz Cocktail 191
Smoked Pomegranate Lemonade Cocktail 181
Smoked Pork Loin With Sauerkraut And Apples 202
Smoked Pork Spare Ribs 223
Smoked Pumpkin Spice Latte 183
Smoked Raspberry Bubbler Cocktail 193
Smoked Red Wine Beef Roast 163
Smoked Rendezvous Ribs 216
Smoked Salmon Candy 112
Smoked Salt Cured Lox 105
Smoked Salted Caramel White Russian 184
Smoked Sangria 183
Smoked Sausage & Potatoes 206
Smoked Spiced Pulled Beef Chuck Roast 158
Smoked Sugar Halibut 96
Smoked Sugar Pork Steaks 226
Smoked Teriyaki Jerky 162
Smoked Texas Bbq Brisket 164
Smoked Texas Ranch Water 189
Smoked Tri-tip 174
Smoked Turkey Breast 15
Smoked Turkey Wings 27
Smoked Vanilla Apple Pie 77
Smoked Whiskey Peach Pulled Chicken 37
Smoked Whole Chicken 43
Smoked Wings 26
Smoked, Salted Caramel Apple Pie 66
Smoker Wheat Bread 82
Smokin' Lemon Bars 70
Smoking Gun Cocktail 177
Smoky Apple Crepes 64
Smoky Bratwurst 224
Smoky Crab Dip 93
Smoky Mountain Bramble Cocktail 194
Smoky Pimento Cheese Cornbread 80
Smoky Scotch & Ginger Cocktail 185
Sopapilla Cheesecake By Doug Scheiding 56
Sourdough Pizza 58
Southern Sugar-glazed Ham 195
Spatchcocked Chicken With Toasted Fennel & Garlic 20
Spatchcocked Turkey 33
Spiced Carrot Cake 62
Spiced Coffee-rubbed Ribs 198
Spiced Cornish Hens With Cilantro Chutney 33
Spiced Cowboy Steak 150
Spiced Grilled Pork Chops 212
Spiced Lemon Cherry Pie 67
Spiced Smoked Chicken Quarters 21
Spiced Smoked Kielbasa Dogs 156
Spiced Smoked Swordfish 99
Spicy Asian Brussels Sprouts 142
Spicy Beer Beef Jerky 167
Spicy Chopped Brisket Sandwich 171
Spicy Crab Poppers 85
Spicy Lime Shrimp 100
Spicy Ribs 221
St. Louis–style Pork Steaks 220
Standing Venison Rib Roast 155
Steak Fries With Horseradish Creme 129
Strawberry Basil Daiquiri 55
Strawberry Mule Cocktail 180
Stuffed Jalapenos 143
Stuffed Pork Crown Roast 225
Sunset Margarita 178
Sweet Bacon 218
Sweet Cajun Wings 43
Sweet Potato Marshmallow Casserole 120
Sweet Smoked Salmon Jerky 98
Sweetheart Steak With Lobster Ceviche 170

Swordfish With Sicilian Olive Oil Sauce 90

T

Tandoori Chicken Leg Quarters 47
Tater Tot Bake 123
Tequila & Lime Shrimp With Smoked Tomato Sauce 111
Teriyaki Smoked Honey Tilapia 106
Texas Grilled Ribs 214
Texas Hill Country Brisket With Mustard Barbecue Sauce 150
Texas Shoulder Clod 166
Texas Style Black Pepper Turkey 40
Thai Chicken Satays 19
Thai-style Swordfish Steaks With Peanut Sauce 104
The Dan Patrick Show Pull-apart Pesto Bread 60
The Grilled Chicken Challenge 34
The Perfect T-bones 146
Traeger Baked Focaccia 52
Traeger Baked Potato Torte 137
Traeger Baked Protein Bars 63
Traeger Baked Rainbow Trout 102
Traeger Boulevardier Cocktail 190
Traeger Crab Legs 113
Traeger Gin & Tonic 193
Traeger Grilled Whole Corn 128
Traeger Jerk Shrimp 88
Traeger Mandarin Wings 24
Traeger Old Fashioned 189
Traeger Paloma Cocktail 190
Traeger Roasted Easter Ham 204
Traeger Smoked Coleslaw 116
Traeger Smoked Daiquiri 177
Traeger Smoked Salmon 92
Turkey & Bacon Kebabs With Ranch-style Dressing 30
Twice-smoked Potatoes 138

U

Ultimate Baked Garlic Bread 59

V

Vanilla Chocolate Chip Cookies 61
Vodka Brined Smoked Wild Salmon 93

W

Wagyu Corned Beef Hash 154
Wet-rubbed St. Louis Ribs 208
Whiskey- & Cider-brined Pork Shoulder 203
Whiskey Bourbon Bbq Cheeseburger 159
Whole Roasted Cauliflower With Garlic Parmesan Butter 128
Whole Smoked Chicken 21
Whole Smoked Honey Chicken 41
Whole Vermillion Red Snapper 98
Wild West Wings 24
Wood-fired Halibut 106

Z

Zombie Cocktail Recipe 180

www.ingramcontent.com/pod-product-compliance
Lightning Source LLC
Chambersburg PA
CBHW081408080526
44589CB00016B/2499